Get Your Knee Off Our Necks!

Essays on Race in America

ISAAC MADISON

ISBN: 978-1-968397-19-7
First Edition
Published by Viral Book Nation
Artesia, California, USA

TABLE OF CONTENTS

Introduction

"Every white person isn't guilty for every bad thing that's been done to every black person." "But if we benefit from cooperating with white supremacy, then we are responsible for changing it. To tolerate racism in our social system is to be complicit."
-The Rev. Jim Wallis

I want to make it understood from the start that not all whites are responsible for racism or the damages caused by it. There have been many great white men and women who have helped me in my life. Men and women who were there for me in times of need. People who visited me when I was sick, fed me when I had nothing to eat and gave me a couch when I had nowhere to stay. I should not have to write this disclaimer. Still, because of a particular part of our citizenry that has been able to flood society with false grievances, anyone of color speaking out on continuing white racism must provide this disclaimer so as not to offend the people who want to make excuses for what has been done. If you don't offer such a disclaimer, you get unprecedented whining, and to some who are extremely fragile or purposefully ignorant of history, you become a hate-filled black racist.

To borrow a line from the late great Richard Pryor, "There is an attack of lunacy going on here." How do some people believe that white "is the new black"? What makes some of them feel like this is spoken gospel from the good lord himself? I have heard of cultural appropriation, but this is taking it to the extreme. Blacks and other people of color are called racists for pointing out the racism that has continued to impact our lives. Women are called sexists for talking about the wrong men have done to them. We endured the presidency of an idiot who knew nothing about public policy, the constitution, and governing just because we were tired of "political correctness."

Police are murdering citizens, it's seen on video, but few go to prison. The same police complain about people holding them accountable for their killing like it's wrong to do so. Blacks protesting murders of innocent blacks are considered the same as white supremacists; a particular section of the white community digs up anything to try making black discontent into the same thing as systemic white racism. Whites ignore the high crime in their communities to lecture us on how terrible crime is in black ones. We have blacks telling other blacks that racism does not exist anymore. Then we have the *"we cannot hold people from the past by the same standards as today"* folks who hold us to standards written over two centuries ago on parchment. The whole world where whites live, they complain about how they are losing their "culture and identity." Some of them seem to have forgotten how whites have dismantled cultures all over this planet.

In America, some whites seem to have forgotten over 400 years of racial oppression and today want everybody affected by it to forget that it happened. While blacks and other people of color have been in America longer than many whites, even though our ancestors have fought in every war, some whites believe this is their country only.

I keep getting told how much better things are for blacks today, yet I saw the same things happening to blacks 50 years ago. "When does it end?"

I have asked myself that question for a long time. As a younger man, I fooled myself into believing things had dramatically changed after watching the civil rights battles as a child growing up in the 1960s. While we have seen improvements, we have not seen complete equality. I am not a famous person. I am no academic hero. I am not employed by a think tank or have written multiple bestselling books. I don't have my name attached to any groundbreaking peer-reviewed studies. I am just an average guy who struggles day to day.

I have written this book after decades of discussions with whites on the issue of race in almost every social setting where people interact. There will be few long-winded explanations, yet racism is complex and snappy answers are not the solution. If you are white and looking for comfortable words, return this book and get your money back. If you are black and subscribe to the belief of racial accommodation, you might want to do the same. While all whites have not practiced racism, the American system was created based on white racial preference. While all whites are not racists, there is a subculture in the white community that is. That subculture exists right now in the third decade of the 21st century, still making comments like this:

"I have innumerable faults, but ignoring reality isn't one of them. Poor white trash that vote for Trump, hey, they aren't burning down cities and, what's the thing about black rapers and dominance and homophobia and killing cops. We all know poor black culture is toxic. Deep down in your dark heart, poor black culture is anti-human

and toxic to everyone and you know it."
-White internet forum poster, 2021

It is this subculture that I will be referring to when I make references to whites. Racism is ignorance. It allows people to speak about others without knowing the facts. You will be shown examples from writings, books, studies, statistics, and legal decisions in this book. Documented evidence provides the basis for what I have written, and for some, the truth about the complete story of America is hard to accept. There has NEVER BEEN a United States of America. There has been America, there have been states, but at no time has there been unity.

Rev. Sharpton expressed the feelings of many of us in the black community when he spoke the words that I use for the title of this book during the funeral of George Floyd. "Get your knee off our necks!" American society still has a long way to go. In this century, we need to begin making a more significant effort to change people among us who display racist attitudes. Continuing the teaching of a lie will only keep us divided. One definition of insanity is doing the same thing repeatedly while expecting a different result. It is time to do something else. So here we go. Enjoy.

"We need someone who will stand up and speak up and speak out for the people who need help, for people who are being discriminated against. And it doesn't matter whether they are black or white, Latino, Asian or Native American, whether they are straight or gay, Muslim, Christian, or Jews."
-John Lewis

The Root Cause of the Problems Blacks Face is White Racism

"It would neither be true or honest to say that the Negros problem is what it is because he is innately inferior or because he is basically lazy and listless or because he has not lifted himself by his own bootstraps. To find the origins of the Negro problem we must turn to the white man's problem."
-Rev. Martin Luther King Jr.

For years black religious leaders, intellectuals, businesspeople, politicians, and activists have tried in the kindest way possible to explain to whites what the problem is and where it starts. There have been whites who have actively studied racism who have also spoken in the hopes that if the racists refuse to listen to blacks, they will at least listen to them. Instead, the same idiots who get to talk the loudest among a specific part of society refuse to listen and have pushed the same old, stump stupid, bird-brained racist garbage.

In the movie *"The Shawshank Redemption,"* Andy Dufresne went to the warden after listening to a story from a prisoner who got transferred into Shawshank and had been a cellmate with the man who committed the murders that got Dufresne sent to prison. Dufresne repeated the story to the Warden. After listening, Warden Norton knew that Dufresne was telling the truth. Instead of letting Dufresne get a new trial, the Warden started making excuses for why he could not do it. The denials were because Warden Norton was being paid under the table as he ran a contracting scam that included laundering money using Dufresne as an accountant. After listening to the many excuses from Norton, Dufresne asked the question, "How can you be so obtuse?"

This is a perfect analogy to describe the relationship between many in the white community and us as black people. History is documented. There really can be no denial of what has gone on. Despite the facts, some whites believe these things have no relationship to how and why things are as they are now. Like Norton, they have lived in a system that has afforded them wealth and do not want it changed. There are some whites, regardless of party or ideology, who refuse to take a realistic look at the issue of race. It seems people want to solve race-based problems without looking at race to solve them. As mentioned earlier, I do not attest to being the most brilliant or most intellectual man. Still, common sense says that if a system is built on denying specific races access to opportunity, racism will be at least part of the reason for the problems that exist due to that exclusion.

> **ALL** *of us has their cross to bear. Maybe the blacks ought to look back into history and realize the mistakes they've made*
> ### - white internet forum poster 2018

We've heard all the so-called "politically incorrect" comments telling us that the problems plaguing black communities are self-inflicted and include: unmarried births, fatherless homes, refusal to take education seriously, rap music, worship of thug culture, genetic inferiority, low IQ, making up racism to get paid, the victim mentality, waiting for a handout, government dependence, special rights and whatever else. All of this is incorrect. Let us genuinely step out of the box. It is time to get honest about leaving the so-called plantation. Other blacks have tried to be polite and politically correct about this. I won't be. The root cause of the problems blacks face today is white racism. Don't conflate what you just read. I said white racism, not white people. Every white person is NOT a racist.

Yes, that's what I said. I am not waiting for whites to give me anything free. I do not have some so-called victim mentality whereby I blame whites for my failings. If I have failed at things, I failed on my own. It is time some whites stopped the juvenile name-calling and tightened up. The reality of racism is not about failing. It is about denial—the denial of opportunity. The failure lies in those who have chosen to fall for what white race pimps have told them. White racism IS the root cause; it is the fundamental reason for the occurrence of problems in the black community.

So why do I say such a thing? Am I a black racist for saying this? No. To start with, America was founded upon racist principles. We can recite the Bill of Rights, Declaration of Independence, The Constitution of the United States, The Federalist Papers, or any other writings from the so-called founders all we want, yet they saw blacks and members of the First Nations as less than human and inferior to whites.

*"White supremacy in its most benign form is a **belief**, not fact, that the white race is superior to all other races and that being born into the white race means one is a superior individual to any other individual not of the white race.*

In its most pernicious form, it is a system of laws, government policies, practices, social mores,

3

*court rulings, etc. which enforce this **belief** resulting in the subjugation of and discrimination against non-whites, specifically in the United States those designated to be of "African descent". This system of **institutional racism** which **legally** rationalized justified, and allowed crimes to be committed against black people which currently are forbidden and in fact where forbidden to be committed against white people is what allow white racists to plunder the lives and resources however meager initially, of an entire race of people. This is what they're referring to as "superiority" and denigrating black people for not having been able to prevent it. It is more than telling that these laws that were passed to basically "contain" the black race included some of the first gun control laws in the country. The white racists were adamant that black could not be able to take up arms even in their defense against the Klan or any other white person meaning them harm to the extent that they were prohibited from owning dogs, who could be used for protection.*

This is not superiority, this a brutal dominion enforced by white laws specifically against black people and enforced at the end of a gun under the threat of loss of life, loss of freedom, and/or a life of hard labor which is little more than a return to slavery. This is American Apartheid. And the term "White Privilege" stems from the obvious benefit of being born into the white race with all of its societal, and legal benefits that are built-in that one inherits by mere membership."
-black internet forum poster, 2019

The same people who fought a war over taxation without representation refused to let women, blacks, and Native Americans have representation in the deliberations that created the founding documents of this nation. It was because of racism and sexism. We were enslaved due to racism. Enslaved people were not taught to read or write due to laws that made it a crime. If blacks were illiterate at that time, it was not because they were stupid, it was because of racism. Blacks were denied the right to bear arms for most of American history. The U.S. Supreme Court made it plain that blacks and all other people of color did not have equal protection under the law.

According to every definition, personal or individual responsibility is the idea that human beings create their own life experiences by their choices. I say this because it is apparent that today, some whites do not seem to understand what it means. The racist subculture is part of a 400-year pattern of behavior that has been consistent, and it is based on a belief in superiority. Our problems are primarily due to choices whites in power have made. Whites chose to deny blacks equal rights by various American laws for nearly 200 years, and some still choose to reject complete equality today. Those who like to preach to people about taking personal responsibility should consider these inconvenient truths.

The root cause of the problems blacks face today is white racism. Again, you will ask, "Why?" Because there is proven or observable evidence that shows this to be true. We know blacks were denied constitutional rights such as citizenship, habeas corpus, unreasonable search or seizure, and freedom itself, which deprived blacks of every opportunity we were supposed to be granted by law. The suburbs were built with guaranteed government loans given primarily to whites. We know that black communities were redlined, making loans for blacks trying to buy homes in those neighborhoods risks banks refused to take. We know that federal housing policy created the slums and ghettos. City zoning policy created black communities divided by freeways and close to industries spewing poisonous waste. We know that government policy consistently underfunds schools in the black community. In the 21st century, we know that a process called retail redlining exists whereby retail businesses refuse to go into black communities. Today, political donors from outside the black community have undue influence relative to city policies, and that influence has negatively impacted black communities.

>*"You think the root cause is racism. Yes?*
>
>*Blacks were doing better in nearly all societal categories when racism was much more apparent. This fact would seem to dispute your opinion.*
>
>*I do not dispute that racism still exists. I dispute that it is the primary cause of all the dysfunction in the black community. When humans must endure drugs, gangs, violence, abortion, teenage childbirth, lack of fathers, poor schools, filthy run-down neighborhoods, lack of good jobs, lack of effective policing, etc, on a daily basis, succeeding life is nearly impossible.*
>
>*So, I suspect all this dysfunction has a much greater impact than white racism."*
>
>**-white internet forum poster, 2020**

To repeat a phrase from Funkadelic, *"You can't know what's going on if you seek."* We are now into the third decade of the 21st century, therefore it has become time for some whites to understand they are not experts on the problems in the black community, the causes of those problems, or the solutions. Anybody can have an opinion, and if blacks were doing so much better when racism was more apparent, there would have been no need for the Civil Rights Movement. Before I go any further, let us review some definitions from Merriam Webster.

Definition of fact:

1.)   a: something that has actual existence.
       b: an actual occurrence.

2.)   a piece of information presented as having objective reality.

3.)   the quality of being actual.

4.)   a: thing done.
        b: archaic: action.
        c; obsolete: feat

Definition of opinion:

1.)   a view, judgment, or appraisal formed in the mind about a particular matter.

2.)   a: belief stronger than impression and less strong than positive knowledge.
        b: a generally held view.

3.)   a: a formal expression of judgment or advice by an expert.
        b: the formal expression (as by a judge, court, or referee) of the legal reasons and principles upon which a legal decision is based.

Definition of delusion:

1.)   a: something that is falsely or delusively believed or propagated.
        b: psychology: a persistent false psychotic belief regarding the self or persons or objects outside the self that is maintained despite indisputable evidence to the contrary; also: the abnormal state marked by such beliefs.

2.)   the act of tricking or deceiving someone; the state of being deluded.

Definition of empirical:

1.)   originating in or based on observation or experience.

2.)   relying on experience or observation alone often without due regard for system and theory.

3.)   capable of being verified or disproved by observation or experiment.

4.)   of or relating to empiricism.

I present these definitions because so much of racism is fiction, yet people will believe something is valid if it is repeated often enough and not challenged. Fiction is the foundation on which racist beliefs have been built. I have stated that the root cause of the problems blacks face is white racism. Throughout this book, you will be shown examples based on something that has actual existence, originating in or based on observation or experience, relying on experience or observation alone, often without due regard for system and theory, and capable of being verified or disproved by observation or experience.

More like 99% of white people don't think about negro's or their self-inflicted problems. They have been free to do and chose their life's path for over 150 years. So it's about time they take responsibility for their lives and quit playing the victim card and blaming everybody else for their lack of goals and ambition. ...

-white internet forum poster, 2018

Ozzy Osbourne wrote a song called "Crazy Train," apparently this person was a passenger. However, the quotes I have used exemplify an attitude that creates stumbling blocks to racial progress. Blacks have not had 150 years to do anything, but to some, once slavery ended magically the attitudes that decided slavery was legal suddenly just went away. After President Johnson signed the Civil Rights Act, some believe that Jim Crow magically disappeared even as we are today looking at lawmakers who were born and raised during Jim Crow. Throughout the remainder of this book, the goal is to render comments like this to their true lunacy.

Books such as *"Color of Law" "White Rage" "American Apartheid" "The New Jim Crow" "A Colony In A Nation,"* or *"Racism without Racists,"* provide examples of the great pains the American government took to establish and maintain a system based on white racial supremacy. They detail the toll such policies have inflicted upon blacks and all other people of color in America. Countless studies document the adverse effects of purposefully designed racially exclusionary American public policy on black communities. Despite the findings, anyone concluding the cause is white racism will get a person ridiculed by some members of the white community. In addition, one must battle people of color who have been shamed into adopting right-wing opinions about some kind of imaginary victim mentality.

The United States has a history of implementing half measures to address conditions created by white racism. We will now look at two commissions designed to address the needs that arose due to individual and systemic white racism resulting in riots: the McCone Commission and The Kerner Commission.

On August 25, 1965, California Governor Edmund

Brown established the McCone Commission to study the Watts Riots.[1] The objective: Make sure that an event like Watts never happens again in Los Angeles. During the next 100 days, the members of this commission held meetings to find out the cause for the discontent that created an uprising resulting in 34 deaths, over 1,000 injuries, and nearly 40 million dollars' worth of damage. Governor Brown wanted a holistic account of what caused the violence. In short, the committee tried to find out the cause and propose a solution to a 100-year-old problem in 100 days.

On December 2, 1965, the commission submitted the report to Governor Brown. The first nine pages of the information were an overview of the riots and conditions the commission felt created the unrest. The commission cited three areas of primary importance: "Negro idleness" from unemployment, lack of education or undereducation, and crime prevention.[2] Not until page 46 is racial discrimination mentioned. It seems the commission tried to downplay the existing racism in Los Angeles. Somebody claimed in the report that Los Angeles was the number 1 ranked American city for blacks in 1965. That ranking had to be based on a low bar, given the amount of violence initiated against blacks moving into homes in Lost Angeles during its history.

> *Mary Johnson, an African-American woman, bought a house on an all-white street in 1914. She returned home to find her possessions strewn across the lawn, and a threatening sign on her nailed-up door. She called the Eagle. Bass "responded in grand style...mobilizing 100 women to go to the house." They camped out on the lawn and stood guard over her possessions until the sheriff came. "With his help," Gibbons writes, "the house was opened, the belongings moved inside, and Mrs. Johnson remained in her home."[3]*

The McCone Commission chose to deny years of racial

problems caused by the police department under Police Chief William Parker. Community citizens testified to the commission about police brutality in the LAPD under Parker and Parker's racist attitude. It fell upon deaf ears as Parker played the commission with a fake show of racial fairness with black officers while the commission watched him on the job. Parker's acting job fooled the commission enough to conclude that the complaints were unwarranted.[4]

In the history of the LAPD, there have only been 3 Chiefs who were not white men. Chief Willie L. Williams, Chief Bernard C. Parks and Chief Dominic Choi. The department has a history of racism; most infamously in my lifetime was the reign of the racist Daryl Gates, who reportedly made comments about blacks and monkeys. Gates ran the department from 1978 until 1992. He was chief when Rodney King was beaten on camera. But let me get back on the subject because if the LAPD was that wrong in 1992, consider what it was like from 1950 until 1966, which was the reign of William Parker.

> *"Who was William H. Parker? Yes, he did "transform" LAPD. From an urban, western, up-south "Mayberry" police force, to a para-military organization based on his own military. William H. Parker was an urban segregationist, no different from Bull Connor or Jim Clark down in Alabama. Parker enforced racial protocols and Los Angeles' race caste system that held until the early 1970s (some say the mid-80s, as far as the Valley areas go)."[5]*

The McCone Commission consisted of 6 whites and two blacks. The meeting results were a report filled with proposed solutions such as preschool programs, more low-income housing, and job training, to name 3 of the proposed solutions.[6] *"While some of the recommendations were adopted and sustained, bringing with them a handful of substantive changes in Watts, most were not. Some were enacted and then, for a variety of reasons, were scaled back or allowed to die out altogether. Others were simply ignored."* [7] In writing this book, I have read the report and two evaluations of the McCone Commission, one by the Los Angeles County Commission on Human Relations in 1985, the other an article in the Los Angeles Times in 1990. Both these evaluations tell the same story; that conditions in South Central Los Angeles had not improved.

Nothing more illustrates this than the 1992 riots due to the LAPD beating of Rodney King. The aftermath was virtually a carbon copy of 1965 created by practically the same conditions. Then in 2020, Los Angeles again was home to a massive protest after the police murder of George Floyd. The goal of the McCone Commission was to address problems that resulted in a riot of historic proportions. In the final analysis, the city of Los Angeles or the state of California was not prepared to provide the resources necessary to address the problems mainly because they severely underestimated the size and scope of the problem. California was not by itself in this regard.

On July 28, 1967, President Lyndon Johnson established the National Advisory Commission on Civil Disorders. The more common name for this is The Kerner Commission. This commission was tasked to answer three basic questions about the racial unrest in American cities: *"What happened" "Why did it happen" "What can be done to prevent it from happening again?"* [8] It is common knowledge that this commission deemed that two separate Americas existed, one for whites and the other for blacks. The commission also made this statement:

"What white Americans have never fully understood but what the Negro can never forget--is that white society is deeply implicated in the ghetto. White institutions created it, white institutions maintain it,

and white society condones it. It is time now to turn with all the purpose at our command to the major unfinished business of this nation. It is time to adopt strategies for action that will produce quick and visible progress. It is time to make good the promises of American democracy to all citizens-urban and rural, white and black, Spanish-surname, American Indian, and every minority group." [9]

On February 26, 2018, 50 years after the Kerner Commission findings, the Economic Policy Institute published a report evaluating the progress of the black community since the Kerner Report was released. The study compared the improvement in black communities in 2018 with the black community at the time of the Kerner Commission. Titled *"50 Years After the Kerner Commission,"* the study concluded that there had been some improvements in the situation blacks faced, but blacks still faced disadvantages based on race. These are some of the findings:

• *African Americans today are much better educated than they were in 1968 but still lag behind whites in overall educational attainment. More than 90 percent of younger African Americans (ages 25 to 29) have graduated from high school, compared with just over half in 1968—which means they've nearly closed the gap with white high school graduation rates. They are also more than twice as likely to have a college degree as in 1968 but are still half as likely as young whites to have a college degree.*

• *The substantial progress in educational attainment of African Americans has been accompanied by significant absolute improvements in wages, incomes, wealth, and health since 1968. But black workers still make only 82.5 cents on every dollar earned by white workers, African Americans are 2.5 times as likely to be in poverty as whites, and the median white family has almost 10 times as much wealth as the median black family.*

- *With respect to homeownership, unemployment, and incarceration, America has failed to deliver any progress for African Americans over the last five decades. In these areas, their situation has either failed to improve relative to whites or has worsened. In 2017 the black unemployment rate was 7.5 percent, up from 6.7 percent in 1968, and is still roughly twice the white unemployment rate. In 2015, the black homeownership rate was just over 40 percent, virtually unchanged since 1968, and trailing a full 30 points behind the white homeownership rate, which saw modest gains over the same period. And the share of African Americans in prison or jail almost tripled between 1968 and 2016 and is currently more than six times the white incarceration rate.[10]*

Following up on this, Richard Rothstein of the Economic Policy Institute wrote an op-ed published in the February 28 edition of the New York Daily News titled, *"50 years after the Kerner Commission, minimal racial progress."* After studying the Kerner Report, Rothstein stated: *"So little has changed since 1968 that the report remains worth reading as a near-contemporary description of racial inequality."* [11] There is a reason little has changed.

The Kerner Commission recommended solutions based on the following three principles: *1. "To mount programs on a scale equal to the dimension of the problems." 2. "To aim these programs for high impact in the immediate future in order to close the gap between promise and performance." 3. "To undertake new initiatives and experiments that can change the system of failure and frustration that now dominates the ghetto and weakens our society."* [12]

I do not believe the commission members truly understood the actual size of the problem. For a problem to be solved, society must be willing to solve that problem by any means necessary. Problems do not get solved by a half measure here and a half measure there. Principle number 1 was to create programs equal to the dimension of the problem. That's a laudable goal, but the dimension of the problem in 1968 was a minimum of 192 years of denied education, housing, and wages. What programs could be proposed to a nation when millions of people believed that "extremism in the defense of liberty is no vice?"

> *"These programs will require unprecedented levels of funding and performance, but they neither probe deeper nor demand more than the problems which called them forth. There can be no higher priority for national action and no higher claim on the nation's conscience."* [13]

So in 1968, a nation that refused equal funding, facilities, housing, or income for blacks even as the supreme court in 1897 determined it was acceptable to be separate if everything else was equal; a nation still fighting integration by using state laws; a nation that had just decided to allow blacks to vote and to not be denied access to public accommodations was going to give up billions of dollars to fix an almost 200-year-old problem that would help black people. It has yet to be done.

As a result of this study, the commission identified 12 grievances in all the communities they visited: "1. Police practices. 2. Unemployment and underemployment. 3. Inadequate housing. 4. Inadequate education. 5. Poor recreation facilities and programs. 6. Ineffectiveness of the political structure and grievance mechanisms. 7. Disrespectful white attitudes. 8. Discriminatory administration of justice. 9. Inadequacy of federal programs. 10. Inadequacy of municipal services. 11. Discriminatory consumer and credit practices. 12.

Inadequate welfare programs."[14]

> *"Social and economic conditions in the riot cities constituted a clear pattern of severe disadvantage for Negroes compared with whites, whether the Negroes lived in the area where the riot took place or outside it. Negroes had completed fewer years of education and fewer had attended high school. Negroes were twice as likely to be unemployed and three times as likely to be in unskilled and service jobs. Negroes averaged 70 percent of the income earned by whites and were more than twice as likely to be living in poverty. Although housing cost Negroes relatively more, they had worse housing-three times as likely to be overcrowded and substandard. When compared to white suburbs, the relative disadvantage is even more pronounced."[15]*

The Kerner Commission was created to find out why the racial unrest happened. Instead of blaming blacks for being angry about how they were treated and inventing terms like victim mentality, the commission took a long hard look at American societal issues. The bottom line is that the Kerner Commission determined in 1968 what blacks already knew and what whites refused to hear. This quote from Nathaniel Jones, Assistant General Counsel for the Commission says it all, *"One of the conclusions of the Kerner Report was that white racism was at work, was the cause of the upsets and the uprisings that we had. In fact, the report stated that white society created it, perpetuates it, and sustains it."*[16][17]

In other words, "The root cause of the problems blacks face is white racism." That conclusion made it possible for much of white America to ignore the findings. Once whites felt as if they were to blame for the conditions of black people in America, they resisted the conclusions of this study. President Johnson called for the research but never implemented the suggested actions. He wasted government money by increasing spending on the Vietnam war and claimed he did not have the funds to implement the types of programs proposed in the report.

Americans would be hard-pressed to say the grievances presented by the commission do not still exist. Martin Luther King called it over 50 years ago; *"A nation that continues year after year to spend more money on military defense than on programs of social uplift is approaching spiritual doom."* The Kerner Commission report was perhaps the most definitive government study done on race in the history of this nation. As I wrote earlier, there is a reason why Rothstein came to his conclusion. We are now more than 50 years past the Kerner Commission findings. There has been little progress because at no level of government or society has America met even the first principle of the Kerner Commission. That is, "To mount programs on a scale equal to the dimension of the problems."

"All insane nonsense used to keep black racists mad at white people, instead of taking personal responsibility to fix the destructive thug ghetto culture that you, yourselves have created."
-white internet forum poster, 2019

People want to lecture us on taking personal responsibility for our situation. Since our problem is caused by white racism, we are personally responsible for pointing it out and then demanding that it stop. As this book continues, you will read an unashamed criticism of people who hijacked conservatism. Many conservatives, real ones, are not racists. I have friends and people who have helped me in life who are conservatives. I may disagree with their politics because I believe there is a place for responsible government, but that does not change their fundamental goodness as people. Real conservatives are about smaller government and fiscal responsibility. I am all for not wasting tax dollars. But these fakes who have hijacked the term are about white power and cutting anything they perceive gives nonwhites equal opportunity. That is not conservatism; it is racism.

> *"When the Kerner Commission told white America what black America has always known, that prejudice and hatred built the nation's slums, maintains them and profits by them, white America could not believe it. But it is true. Unless we start to fight and defeat the enemies in our own country, poverty and racism, and make our talk of equality and opportunity ring true, we are exposed in the eyes of the world as hypocrites when we talk about making people free."*

> **-Shirley Chisholm**

Racism is Abuse

"Bryant-Davis and Ocampo (2005) noted similar courses of psychopathology between rape victims and victims of racism. Both events are an assault on the personhood and integrity of the victim. Similar to rape victims, race-related trauma victims may respond with disbelief, shock, or dissociation, which can prevent them from responding to the incident in a healthy manner. The victim may then feel shame and self-blame because they were unable to respond or defend themselves, which may lead to low self-concept and self-destructive behaviors. In the same study, a parallel was drawn between race-related trauma victims and victims of domestic violence. Both survivors are made to feel shame over allowing themselves to be victimized. For instnce, someone who may have experienced a racist incident may be told that if they are polite, work hard, and/or dress in a certain way, they will not encounter racism. When these rules are followed yet racism persists, powerlessness, hyper vigilance, and other symptoms associated with PTSD may develop or worsen." [1]

Studies and testimonies from survivors show that abuse can cause different types of behaviors, both positive and negative. The psychological impact of racism must be taken seriously if there is going to be a genuine reduction in the behavior. There has been a refusal to accept that certain

19

behaviors by nonwhites are caused by white racism. Like many other blacks, I have discussed racism with whites at work, on sports teams, in social gatherings, online forums, message walls, chat rooms, social media, and other personal relationships. I have tried to inform on the impact of racism from the perspective of being black. What I discovered is that many whites do not have to understand what racism can do to a person and because they don't, they dismiss the lived experiences of blacks and anyone else of color. So many who have not experienced the feelings that hit a black person or any person of color when they experience a racist incident are willing to speak as experts on what they believe cannot happen. Yet if you talk to this same person about child abuse, sexual abuse, or other types of abuse, they are more than able to talk about the behaviors that can result. But racism, well, that's just something you can quickly get beyond. Meanwhile, every other type of abuse is a lifelong struggle for those who must deal with it.

I presented the idea that racism was abuse in an internet forum, and a white individual who had experienced different maltreatment while growing up exploded like an atomic bomb. She was offended that I could compare racism to such a significant thing as abuse. She threatened physical violence against me. I don't know how she would do that through a computer, but let's go on. This exemplifies how ignorant some people continue to be to the reality of what racism is. Racism includes Emotional, Psychological, Financial, Physical, Sexual, Verbal, and Spiritual abuse.[2] Many individual victims of racism have experienced multiple cases of these abuses simultaneously.

Physical and psychological damage has been wrought upon nonwhites because of racist policies and individual actions in America. But some whites seem to think that racism carries no psychological consequences to those who are victims. They do so because they see nonwhites coping the best we can. Secondly, they tend to look at things based on their perspective, meaning that when they see blacks acting in various ways, they look at it from their experience, never factoring in the damage at every level caused by past and continuing white racism.

> *"On occasion, the emotional weight of racism can lead African Americans to engage in maladaptive coping, such as remaining in denial, engaging in substance use, aggression, self-blame – even in extreme cases suicide (i.e., Black Lives Matter activist Marshawn McCarrel) and terrorism (i.e., Dallas shooter Micah Xavier Johnson). These responses are harmful and lead to negative, long-term consequences."* [3]

It is essential to understand these realities. If not, we will eventually end up with a chain of black and other nonwhite mass killers because people ignore the psychological damage created by racism. I remember being asked to speak to a class of students in the university located in my hometown on racial stereotypes in the media. It was shortly after the mass shooting at Virginia Tech. I began my talk by trying to provide an example of how white racism could have been a factor in the shooting. After all, the shooter was an Asian student that lived in a predominantly white dorm. No one knows how many times white Virginia descendants of the confederacy taunted him. Cho Seung-Hui was deemed mentally ill,[4] and I was almost fired from my job because my comment offended my boss at the time who was also speaking to the same class. This person was in no manner a racist; in fact, she was a warrior for human equality. The reality of this example is that no matter how much a white person is nonracist, they do not personally experience the racism nonwhites face and therefore should probably listen to those of us who have. There is no telling how much racism Cho endured during his life and eventually that racism contributed to his mental decline.

Not only do some whites want to deny the extent of what racism can cause, but some whites tell us that what we see does not exist. Some tell us how these are just a small number of random cases that mean nothing and are not serious. I have been asked to provide the percentage of whites that I think are racists as if there is an acceptable percentage for racism. This cannot end well for anyone. We do not see this being done with any other form of abuse. No one tells the victim of child abuse that what they experienced are random occurrences that are not serious. I did not see any senators asking those heroic U.S. gymnasts to tell them what percentage of people are child molesters during their testimony. Individuals who advocate for an end to other types of abuse are rightfully hailed as heroes for surviving. Not so much for racism. Survivors of racism who fight to end it are called names and told to be quiet. This must end. Racism is more than a word used as a slur, and it causes damage that is not temporary.

Many outside of the African American or other non-white communities do not seem to understand the extent racism can drive a person to unhealthy and societally harmful behaviors. Reality dictates that emotions are involved in this matter, and there is a vast spectrum of emotions people express in such situations. To understand the dual standards in such thinking, white people have used drugs and became addicted to them to escape a bad situation; but when it comes to blacks or other minorities and drug use, there is no excuse for "you people" to get strung out. Blacks or other nonwhites can't say how they have endured racism and are addicted because of the pain that it causes. Instead, our "inferior culture" is a failure, and we have to get over it.

"I would agree with some of this in Obama's first term. It was in his 2nd term when it went south once he got involved with Trayvon Martin shooting. From then on he tried to create racial divide every chance

he would get. He set us so far back with the white people I didn't think we would ever recover into unity again. Thankfully, President Trump has tried to bring prosperity and unity back from day one of his election and he's doing a damn good job!"
-black internet forum user,-2019

"*The Boondocks*" is an animated show about a black grandfather who took care of his two grandchildren. One of the characters in the show is a blue-collar black man named Uncle Ruckus. Uncle Ruckus held white supremacist views and despised everything about being black. He disliked being black so much that he claimed to have a skin disease that made him dark called "revitiligo." Uncle Ruckus is an example of a person with internalized racism. Dr. Karen Pyke defines internalized racism as the "*internalization of racial oppression by the racially subordinated.*"[5] Blacks who suffer from internalized racism believe and promote negative stereotypes of black people. They will adopt white racist beliefs and thinking. This is the literal meaning of acting white, and it has nothing to do with getting good grades or going to college.

"The dominant group [whites] control the construction of reality through the production of ideologies or "knowledge" that circulate throughout society where they inform social norms, organizational practices, bureaucratic procedures, and common-sense knowledge. In this way, the interests of the oppressors are presented as reflecting everyone's best interests, thereby getting oppressed groups to accept the dominant group's interests as their own and minimize conflict."[6]
-Dr. Karen Pyke

This acceptance of white supremacy as the norm leads to conclusions that racism is not a problem or does not exist. Internalized racism creates a justification for racism. As this happens, people in racially oppressed groups internalize the validity of their oppression. Because they have done so, they find no reason to question or fight the system. These types will argue how racism would be no problem by pathologizing blacks while reciting the same anti-black memes as the racist subculture. They refuse to debate the implications of racist policies and the damage they have created because that will not be acceptable in the social circles where they desire acceptance. Internalized racism is a behavior exhibited in right wing blacks who have been allowed into the national discourse on race. These people have achieved great success and can make fundamental changes relative to erasing the stain of white racism from this system. But they do not.

On March 7, 2018, one week after the Economic Policy Institute presented the study that detailed how little blacks had progressed since the Kerner Commission report, a black journalist named Jason Riley wrote an op-ed that was printed in The Wall Street Journal titled, *"50 Years of Blaming Everything on Racism."* No greater example of internalized racism exists than what Riley wrote in this article. He claimed that the findings of the Kerner Commission absolved blacks of personal responsibility because they cited white racism as the problem for blacks in 1968 while ignoring the progress that had taken place.

> *"The Kerner report's most famous assertion was that the U.S. was "moving toward two societies, one black, one white—separate and unequal," even though the decades leading up to the riots had suggested the opposite. The Truman administration's desegregation of the armed forces in the 1940s was followed by Martin Luther King Jr.'s successful civil-rights movement of the 1950s and the passage of landmark civil-rights and voting-rights legislation in the 1960s. The educational and economic strides blacks made during this period were also unprecedented, and*

racial disparities were narrowing."[7]

    Jason Riley was born in 1971. I do not want to discredit his research as the basis for disagreement because my writing is based on research. My dispute stems from what I saw in 1968. I was a kid at that time and can say that whatever improvements Riley claims occurred during this era are imaginary. The Kerner Commission Report was released on February 26, 1968. Martin Luther King was killed on April 4, 1968, 1 month and six days after the report was released.

"In 1960, just 7% of blacks between 20 and 24 were enrolled in college; by 1970, that percentage had more than doubled, to 16%. College enrollment among whites also rose during this period, but not by as much. These educational gains allowed more blacks to lift themselves out of poverty and access better-paying jobs. Between 1940 and 1970, the proportion of families living below the poverty line fell by 40 percentage points among whites and by 57 points among blacks. White-black gaps in homeownership, life expectancy, and white-collar employment also were shrinking in the postwar era, contrary to the pessimism of the Kerner Commission."[8]

    What Riley wrote was misleading. Riley shows that the percentage of blacks between 20 and 24 who enrolled in 1960 and 1970 doubled while white enrollment did not. While this is accurate, Riley leaves out the percentage of whites who enrolled. According to the National Center for Education Statistics, non-Hispanic white college enrollment increased from 45.8 percent in 1960 to 52 percent in 1970.[9] Riley argues that since black poverty dropped more than white poverty, the Kerner Commission was wrong, and racism was not the problem. He paints a pretty picture of a 57-point drop in black family poverty, and in his view, since whites had a 40 point drop, the Kerner Commission findings were somehow wrong in their conclusion. He doesn't say that in 1970 all those significant improvements reduced black family poverty to 32.2 percent, while poverty for white families was 8.1 percent. [10] [11]

> *"We can't hope to address effectively the social pathology on display in so many black ghettos by playing down the role of culture and personal responsibility so as to keep the focus on white racism. What blacks were doing on their own to develop human capital and to narrow racial gaps in the first half of the 20th century has a far better record of success than any government program. This history is seldom discussed among politicians in search of votes or activists in search of relevance, but it ought to be part of any serious national debate about racial inequality today."*[12]

If you consider that black poverty dropped 57 percentage points from 1940 to 1970, and it was still 32 percent, it borders on delusional not to assess the impact of white racism. Riley adopted the far-right opinion of how government cannot do anything right. His assessment of what happened in the first half of the 20th century is incorrect. His view that blacks advanced further without the government is debunked by the fact that a Civil Rights Act was necessary. His claim misses the point that Federal government executive actions made it possible for blacks to be more than custodians in places like the Wall Street Journal. I say he adopted white standards because he regurgitates the white "conservative" narrative of how they did things without government help. History shows a long and storied record of government assistance for whites. He ignores that the past 50 years have been a prime example of blacks enforcing, preaching, and teaching personal responsibility. If anyone thinks not, sit in a black church next Sunday morning.

I will paraphrase Riley's internalization of racism: *"things have improved, so we cannot blame white racism for every problem blacks have."* The problem with that position is that white racism still exists, and we have most certainly come to see just how strong it still is during the past decade or so in America. Riley finishes off with the classic white racist cultural pathology argument. Everything he writes ignores one thing, and it is paramount, the cumulative effect of continuing white racism on black people since the Kerner Commission report. After all, that racism has impacted him to such an extent that he internalizes it. When people such as him talk about cultural responsibility, the evidence shows that the failure is on our American culture that fosters racism to such an extent that whites on the right will pay blacks top dollar to regurgitate white racist beliefs.

Certain groups openly accept individuals such as Riley in the dominant culture because his views can be used to validate the dominant culture's beliefs. These people do far more harm than good to the black community and general society. Allowing such individuals prominence in the national discourse on race is distasteful. They are only conferred status by the racist subculture to further its agenda. Internalized racism creates conflict within and between racially subordinated groups to suppress all attempts at a united effort to combat racism. The problems we are dealing with start with white racism, and there are many ways blacks have learned to deal with that racism, both good and bad. What must be understood is the impact of racism on blacks instead of dismissing that impact as some inherent black cultural flaw.

Findings from large-scale national studies indicate that, while African Americans have a lower risk for many anxiety disorders, they have a 9.1% prevalence rate for PTSD, compared to 6.8% in Whites. That means that **almost one in ten Black people**

becomes traumatized, *and I think these rates may actually be higher since diagnosticians are usually not considering the role of racism in causing trauma.*[13]

As in any other form of abuse/trauma, some things trigger the stressors which bring back the negative experiences felt because of racism. I have a simple layman's understanding of psychology. I am no expert on PTSD. I have learned that when a person has this disorder, there can be events that trigger the old terror the individual went through due to the past abuse. Therefore, as people of color continue to see acts of racism in various iterations, it is vital to recognize how these events trigger a reminder to people of color of the bad experiences they had due to racism. It is even more important to understand what those bad experiences mean regarding behaviors that might arise or resurface instead of making racial judgments. Simply put, every act of racism causes PTSD in black people. So when 47 million blacks continue to experience or watch racist actions, these things start happening according to the Mayo Clinic:

- *Recurrent, unwanted distressing memories of the traumatic event*
- *Reliving the traumatic event as if it were happening again (flashbacks)*
- *Upsetting dreams or nightmares about the traumatic event*
- *Severe emotional distress or physical reactions to something that reminds you of the traumatic event*
- *Trying to avoid thinking or talking about the traumatic event*
- *Avoiding places, activities or people that remind you of the traumatic event*
- *Negative thoughts about yourself, other people or the world*
- *Hopelessness about the future*
- *Memory problems, including not remembering important*

aspects of the traumatic event
- *Difficulty maintaining close relationships*
- *Feeling detached from family and friends*
- *Lack of interest in activities you once enjoyed*
- *Difficulty experiencing positive emotions*
- *Feeling emotionally numb*
- *Being easily startled or frightened*
- *Always being on guard for danger*
- *Self-destructive behavior, such as drinking too much or driving too fast*
- *Trouble sleeping*
- *Trouble concentrating*
- *Irritability, angry outbursts or aggressive behavior*
- *Overwhelming guilt or shame* [14]

"Why I just can't believe that white racism caused those black people to riot and burn up their entire community!" The stress and trauma caused by racism can create a lot of things. Many of them are negative. Yet we must endure opinions from those outside the black community and black elitists that do not match reality. It is vital to reduce or end the events or stressors that make people adapt by using harmful coping mechanisms. There are also positive mechanisms where blacks use racism as a motivator to achieve things that the dominant group has refused to allow blacks to do. I cannot speak for him, so I will not say that racism motivated Barack Obama to get to the point where he was able to run and succeed in becoming the first black president in America. Still, I wouldn't be surprised if racism was one motivator that created the internal drive to refuse to be stopped.

We must begin to look deeper at the overall damage caused by racial abuse as a country. Because when you look at racism as a form of abuse, it is easier to understand how one can say that white racism creates various behaviors. So instead of the failure of the black culture argument used to condemn certain behaviors by blacks, maybe we begin to take a more complex look at the failure of American culture relative to race. This should not be taken as an excuse to appease those who use destructive coping mechanisms. Hopefully, it is a way to reduce and prevent such behaviors from increasing in the future. Some whites refuse to look at racism in this manner because they do not want to be looked upon as abusers, but if you practice racism, that is what you are. If you go along in silence, ignoring the racism, you enable the abusers.

We have entered a time where many whites have adopted the colorblind claim of non-racism. The declaration of being colorblind is fake news. People of all colors exist who do not hold racial bias, but the lack of racial bias is not what colorblind is. Colorblind racism is basically when a person dismisses the existence of racism in modern American culture while simultaneously being a racist. One of the main problems with the belief in colorblindness coming from whites is that it ignores some 400 years of history. We could all go colorblind relative to race tomorrow, but the damage created by centuries of color-coded abuses will still exist. Whites will be colorblind then continue not hiring blacks because blacks do not have work experience. That lack of work experience would have been due to racism before everybody turned colorblind. But now that we are colorblind, we can ignore those years because we do not see color and only hire based on "merit."

If this is not already done, racial abuse requires creating support groups and networks for victims. No one should be shamed or belittled for complaining about racist treatment. Racism is not just a mean word; it is a series of actions that cause great harm. I will repeat, the victims of racism will struggle with this abuse for the rest of their lives just like victims of other forms of abuse.

Racial gaslighting is another abusive behavior used by a segment of the white community to create doubt or dismiss the lived experiences of all people of color. Racial gaslighting is: *"the political, social, economic and cultural process that perpetuates and normalizes a white supremacist reality through pathologizing those who resist."*[15] In short, this is where whites try to create an impression that blacks or nonwhites are the ones with the problem because we point out the racism in white America.

Part of America has developed an alternate reality whereby they claim that people of color who point out past and present forms of white racism are racists because they define all whites because of race. This is not the case. Opinions on whites by people of color are generally not based on false, untrue stereotypes of a race of people or assumed genetic, moral, cultural, intellectual, and human superiority, but opposition to the way people of color continue to be treated by members of the white community.

> *"Usually, the black racist has been produced by the white racist. In most cases where you see it, it is the reaction to white racism, and if you analyze it closely, it's not really black racism... If we react to white racism with a violent reaction, to me that's not black racism. If you come to put a rope around my neck and I hang you for it, to me that's not racism. Yours is racism, but my reaction has nothing to do with racism..."*
>
> **—Malcolm X**

The World Health Organization defines health as: *"a state of complete physical, mental, and social well-being and not merely the absence of disease or infirmity."*[16] The great Michelle Obama has spoken about the toll consistently living with racism takes upon black people by detailing her battle with low-grade depression. On August 6, 2020, the governor of Michigan declared racism a public health issue by executive order.[17] This is a significant development. The Center for the Study of Racism, Social Justice and Health defines Public Health as: *"the collective efforts of a society to create the conditions in which people can be healthy."*[18] These definitions, when applied to racism, place it on the list of public health issues.

"Racism is part of the fabric of life for African Americans and is among the causes of enduring negative health outcomes. There is really nothing new or startling in the assertion that social circumstances encountered as part of day-to-day experience influence physical health. At the turn of the last century, W. E. B. Du Bois (1906) and Kelly Miller (1897) proposed in separate manuscripts that oppressive social conditions encroaching on the lives of African Americans contributed to poor health and premature death.

Fifty years later, Frantz Fanon's classic studies (1967, 1968) examined the effects of oppression and included a recognition of "psychosomatic"— that is physical— consequences. Currently, social epidemiologists, health psychologists, and medical sociologists have extended the insights of these important early scholars by showing how racism generates systems and practices that contribute to persistent disparities in health outcomes.

Estimates indicate that the failure to erase these disparities costs tens of thousands of African American lives each year. As long as the rates of the leading causes of death differ along racial lines, the specter of racism will haunt the United States. The persistence of racial health disparities and of racism in any form calls scholars, therapists, activists, and political leaders to vigorous action." [19]

Racism causes chronic stress. Understanding this has severe implications for health in the black community. While I am not a doctor, what I have read written by medical professionals explains how constant stress creates unhealthy outcomes. The continuing racism blacks face keeps blacks stressed out and creates chemical imbalances within our bodies, causing many health problems. Increasing evidence supported by research shows that racism shortens lives. On June 3, 2020, SAMHSA's Office of Behavioral Health Equity published a report titled: *"Trauma, Racism, Chronic Stress and the Health of Black Americans."* They found that racism contributed to poor mental health and chronic physical health problems.

"Racism and associated trauma and violence contribute to mental health disorders, particularly depression, anxiety and PTSD, and chronic health conditions such as cardiovascular disease, hypertension, diabetes, maternal mortality/infant mortality and morbidity in African Americans. Racism is considered a fundamental cause of adverse health outcomes for racial/ethnic minorities and racial/ethnic inequities in health. The primary domains of racism - structural/institutional racism, cultural racism, and individual level discrimination— are linked to mental and physical health outcomes. Racism and violence targeting a specific community is increasingly associated with complex trauma and intergenerational trauma, all of which have physical and behavioral health consequences."[20]

Studies show that consistent exposure to adversity and marginalization causes early health declines in black Americans.[21] Racism is a stressor that triggers the body into allostasis or better understood, racism forces the body to adapt to stress. Allostasis is the process that helps us adapt to stress.[22] Allostatic load is compiled damage to the body due to constant pressure.[23] Such stress leads to allostatic overload, which is the point when the overall amount of stress causes health problems or death.[24] For example, allostatic processes lead to increases in blood pressure, a leading cause of death in the black community. Allostatic overload created by stress caused due to constant exposure to racism increases the occurrences of myocardial infarction in blacks.

Simply put, a myocardial infarction is a heart attack. In 2014, *"Structural racism and myocardial infarction in the United States,"* a study by Alicia Lukachko, Mark Hatzenbuehler, & Katherine Keyes, was published in Social Science and Medicine Journal. Their research showed that structural racism was one cause of heart attacks in black people.

"This study demonstrates adverse effects of structural racism—specifically state-level racial disparities disadvantaging Blacks in political representation, employment, and incarceration —on past 12-month myocardial infarction. These adverse effects, however, were specific to Blacks, and among Whites, indicators of structural racism appear to have a benign or even beneficial effect on cardiac health. It is important to note that individual-level risk factors including age, sex, education, income, and medical insurance do not account for these findings. Furthermore, lending support to the construct validity of our measures of structural racism, the effects persist above and beyond those of state-level racial disparities in poverty.

Measures of structural racism pertaining to job status did not follow the expected pattern of association, and were inversely associated with myocardial infarction among Blacks. While this finding was unexpected, it is in line with results from previous studies that have documented that Black Americans in high status positions report greater exposure to interpersonal discrimination. This increased exposure, coupled with potential pressures to assimilate and to defy negative racist stereotypes, may in turn place high status Blacks at greater risk for adverse health outcomes. Our results similarly suggest that Black Americans in states with greater representation of Blacks in high status positions are at higher risk for heart attack."[25]

There seems to be a state of confusion among members of the racist subculture as to what racism is. They have made racism into a few bad words or a claim that denies behavior and limits it to thoughts. I have been told by other people that everyone can have racist thoughts. When people believe such things, they give credence to those who want to dismiss what racism has been. While everyone can have racist thoughts, everyone's racist thoughts did not turn into a system governed by the rule of law. Everyone's racist thoughts did not turn into public policy that denied rights and opportunity based on beliefs derived from those same thoughts.

"Essentially racism is a 'thought crime.'....penalizing some people based on what they allegedly think or believe.... enforced not by our system of jurisprudence but by the media."
—White internet forum poster, 2021

Racism is more than thoughts and spoken slurs. The practice of racism relative to the treatment of people is illegal only on paper. It still goes on in America right now. Racism is an abusive behavior based on an individual's race that causes lifelong harm. Racial abuse can lead to self-destructive and societally destructive violent behavior. Racist whites led by former President number 45 ran their mouths loud and long about the looting and rioting they falsely blamed solely on Black Lives Matter during the summer of 2020. Those blacks that did commit such acts are prime examples of what happens when people are continually traumatized by racial abuse or see instances of such abuse. The murders of George Floyd, Brianna Taylor, Ahmaud Arbery, and others reminded people of color of their bad experiences in America due to racism. Denial is no longer an option. It is too late to ask us to keep accepting small amounts of incremental progress. Perhaps it is time to recognize the holistic nature of damage caused by centuries of racism imposed upon blacks and all people of color in the United States of America.

"I for one believe that if you give people a thorough understanding of what confronts them and the basic causes that produce it, they'll create their own program, and when the people create a program, you get action"
—*Malcolm X*

Racism is Not a Thing of the Past

"For these anti-anti-racists, accusations of racism are a greater concern than actual discrimination and prejudice against blacks and other minorities. It's not that they support racism, but that they see it as largely irrelevant to contemporary life. Any problems with minority communities, in their eyes, have more to do with cultural dysfunction, not racial inequality. Moreover, if there's a racial problem in America, it's not against minorities, it's against whites: "Caucasian is not one of the colors getting helped," said Fox contributor Todd Starnes, attacking President Obama's My Brother's Keeper initiative.

As rhetoric, anti-anti-racism is popular in the conservative movement. You saw it in Andrew Breitbart's obsession with ACORN and Shirley Sherrod and Fox News' obsession with the New Black Panthers, and you see it in some attacks on Attorney General Eric Holder, alleging discrimination against whites."

-Jamelle Bouie

Today, members of a white subculture call blacks and members of other non-white populations racists because we mention a continuing pattern of behavior from the colonial days until the very second you read these words. That particular subculture tries to create an equivalence between pointing out that pattern of behavior and false stereotypes created about black people. A black person is now a racist just for detailing things whites have done.

The one thing the internet does is show you how wide the variety of intelligence is in this world. There are some mean, hateful, and stupid people out there. I am neither Jesus nor Einstein, but wow, my goodness, some of my conversations on the internet! If we could only have been at the Comedy Shop. I started posting in forums way back in the mid-1990s. I started at a "conservative" discussion forum. I did so because I worked in a city run by "conservatives" and had to understand how they thought when it was time to make presentations or advocate.

During these conversations, I heard almost every type of stereotype and racist description used about black people known to humans. I guess I set myself up for this by telling these people I was black while trying to discuss the impact of racism upon blacks. But of course, these white people knew far better than I, a black man, how and why blacks are in our position. The reason had nothing to do with a legacy of racist laws and policies; only that blacks decided we did not want to work and wanted only to lay around, have illegitimate children, do drugs, and wait for the government to give us free stuff. The racism was astounding, and even after making racist comments, these same people declared that racism by whites no longer existed.

However, the problem is bipartisan and crosses the lines of ideology. I was invited to join a presumably more progressive forum. I thought these so-called white progressives who at least understood that racism exists would be willing to discuss how racism has impacted the black community. Instead, I found that most of these were white people who claimed to have marched in the 1960s to protest for civil rights. Because they did, their general attitude was that black folks owed them gratitude. To them, the best way to combat racism was to sit on the internet and complain about how racist conservatives were.

I read this complaining each time I entered the forum, so one day I asked if they were willing to confront racism because it takes more than talk to bring about change. I also stated that whites must work harder and take more of a leadership role for racism to end. Those self-declared "progressive, liberal, anti-racist, colorblind" whites did not like that. I was immediately attacked by a 69-year-old white man and a 67-year-old white woman. The white man informed me that he does not say blacks should take the lead on black-on-black crime, which had nothing to do with the conversation. The white woman decided I challenged her whiteness by making that comment. I then got a 2-day vacation because I said whites need to take a leadership role in stopping racism. I guess I did not genuflect sufficiently enough in recognition of their efforts in the sixties. The woman who got so angry did not lead. She did not stand face to face with leaders forcing them to change the way things were. Neither did the man. If they attended any marches, they were young faces in the crowd who took a day out of class to protest. Sincere people do these things without asking for gratitude.

"The Native Americans blended into the Caucasian culture well."
—white internet forum poster 2018

Some people in this nation have descended into what you can only call purposeful forgetfulness. Even though whites tried wiping out the indigenous nations because they refused to assimilate, this is what some in the racist subculture think. In one forum, I was told that blacks did not deserve reparations because, at the time of slavery, blacks were not citizens of this nation. I guess that means since we were not citizens at the time, the oppression never happened, and since the enslavement was legal, it infers there was somehow an agreement between the U.S. government and blacks in America to be enslaved. There are many examples of the crazy world of online racial discussions or debates. Let us check out a few examples that should allow us to understand that we still have a serious problem as a nation.

Some say racism is in the past. But we are here in the 21st century still looking at examples of racism in person, on television, or in social media and online forums. Racism is done differently today. Some people think that because we do not see any "no blacks allowed" signs that racism cannot exist. Modern racism is covert which allows racists to lie about its continuing existence. Modern types of racism will be looked at in chapter 13. Please continue reading.

Wonderlic test scores leaked for NFL draft qb's, black qb is at bottom of barrel
—white internet forum poster 2018

Here we see a statement made the 21st Century where a white person felt he had to declare that a black QB got a low score on a test used by the NFL that has nothing to do with playing football. This player had proven in his college career that he could play football at a level less than 100 men in college football history ever have. Instead of recognizing his incredible skills, we must know how dumb this guy is supposed to be for a low score on a test that had nothing to do with reading defenses. And we certainly had to be informed how a black player scored lower than whites.

There were many blacks at this particular the combine who scored high on the Wonderlic. Yet there were other stories at this event that showed the great resolve these young black men had and the desire to work towards accomplishing the goal of being picked to play football at the highest level on earth. This man failed to mention Shaquem Griffin, who was in the same combine. Griffin was a young brother from Central Florida who played linebacker with only one hand. He could not mention how this young man benched 225 pounds 20 times basically with one hand. A weight that white man probably could not have done once with both hands. Instead of talking about the many stories like Griffins, he felt he must say blacks are dumb. Today we see and read the same stuff people believed in the 1700s and 1800s while being told that racism is a thing of the past.

> *"People like you are so fucking racist that you don't even realize that had it not been for WHITES, blacks would still be slaves today. Not all "whites" are as racist as you apparently are."*
> **—white internet forum poster, 2018**

This response is from a man shown continuing acts of racism by whites. According to some in today's world, this amounts to racism. So, this guy reacts by replying with a classic racist line and thinks what was said is not racist. Such is the delusion some have fallen into with this belief in ending "political correctness." I find it ironic that almost everything these individuals claim is fighting political correctness has to do with the ability to express racism openly or to say insulting things in general. I guess this is "what needs to be said." We will see how that works shortly.

> *"Cognitive dissonance, first described by the psychologist Leon Festinger in the late 1950s, occurs when conflict emerges between what people want to believe and the reality that threatens those beliefs. The human mind does not like such inconsistencies: They set off alarms that spur the mind to alter some beliefs to make the perceived reality fit with one's preferred views."* [1]

For those who may not know what cognitive dissonance

is, let's just put it this way, this is where the brain creates a false reality when faced with conflicting beliefs. Regarding race, cognitive dissonance is the ruling mindset in the white racist subculture. This subculture feels victimized because they cannot impose what they believe is their rightful claim to America. They have something that needs to be said. According to them, this message must be heard, and it is not racist.

*"There are black extremists and there are white extremists. The ones in between do not speak out. This thread could have been done as a poll and what I'm going to say might not have become necessary. So, this is the first of a couple of posts. **THIS IS WHAT NEEDS TO BE SAID.**"*

*When my forefathers left the tyranny of King George, they came to the United States seeking **Liberty**. The **FIRST** governing document of the New World was the Mayflower Compact. It opens as follows:*

*"**IN THE NAME OF GOD, AMEN**. We, whose names are underwritten, the Loyal Subjects of our dread Sovereign Lord King James, by the Grace of God, of Great Britain, France, and Ireland, King, Defender of the Faith, &c. Having undertaken for the Glory of God, and **Advancement of the Christian Faith...**"*

Those colonists saw themselves as the Israelites of the Bible and they sought to build a homeland - a New Jerusalem. As a matter of fact, up until the time that Ronald Reagan was president, it was common to have presidents and other politicians give a speech invoking John Winthrop's famous sermon about a "shining city on a hill."

Although the entire world probably knows that America is the New Jerusalem mentioned in the Bible (see Zechariah chapter 2 - especially verse 12 and then check out Matthew 23: 37 - 39) NONE will admit it. It's simply not in vogue to admit the root of the race issue. But I digress.

—white internet forum poster 2018

Matthew 23: 37 – 39. 37.) *"Jerusalem, Jerusalem, you who kill the prophets and stone those sent to you, how often I have longed to gather your children together, as a hen gathers her chicks under her wings, and you were not willing. 38.) Look, your house is left to you desolate. 39.) For I tell you, you will not see me again until you say, 'Blessed is he who comes in the name of the Lord.'"*[2]

Never mind that the twenty-third chapter of Matthew was a warning to people about hypocrisy whereby Jesus warns the people to not do as the rabbis who only do what they do for a show. The verses mentioned are at the end of a chapter where Jesus expressed his displeasure and put a curse on that generation. Nothing in chapter 23 provides anything mentioned by the individual quoted. Zechariah Chapter 2, Verse 12 says, *"The Lord will inherit Judah as his portion in the holy land and will again choose Jerusalem."*[3] How this came to mean that America was the new Jerusalem only for whites to inhabit strains logic. Especially when more than 100 nations were already here.

"So, here is part 2 of what I had to say. We will soon see if all of it makes the cut... no more judging me without reading the applicable posts."

THIS IS WHAT NEEDS TO BE SAID PART 2

*"When America was founded, it was founded on Christian principles, not as a theocracy, but upon Christian principles. **Virtually every early state constitution** had some references to things such as only white Christians being able to vote and / or hold public office. In our first immigration statute, federal law limited citizenship to White persons of good character. And, as such, our race became a part of our culture."*

"For example, it was Justice Roger Taney, a Democrat, that wrote the ruling in the Dred Scott v Sanford decision that African-Americans, having been considered inferior at the time the United States Constitution was drafted, were not part of the original community of citizens and, whether free or slave, could not be considered citizens of the United States."

"Now, let us be totally honest and realistic. Taney was at least partially right. The Preamble to the Constitution reads:"

*"We the People of the United States, in Order to form a more perfect Union, establish Justice, insure domestic Tranquility, provide for the common defence, promote the general Welfare, and **secure the Blessings of Liberty to ourselves and our Posterity**, do ordain and establish this Constitution for the United States of America."*

I bolded that fragment of a sentence to show that the Constitution was designed to secure the blessings of Liberty to ourselves (the founders) and our Posterity (meaning their children and their offspring - aka the white race.)" Then there was this in the Constitution:

"Article I, Section. 2
Representatives and direct Taxes shall be apportioned among the several States which may be included within this Union, according to their respective Numbers, which shall be determined by adding to the whole Number of free Persons, including those bound to Service for a Term of Years, and excluding Indians not taxed, three-fifths of all other Persons."

"3/5th Clause in the Constitution. What is it and why was it put in?

I'm not going to overwhelm you any single post, but here is the bottom line: The whites who came here originally saw themselves as a separate culture, chosen of God, to establish a New Jerusalem. Building on those principles, America became the greatest nation in the annals of history. If you're going to understand the race issue in America it is imperative that you understand this reality.

"Today, we find ourselves in very precarious predicament. The Preamble of the Constitution states, unequivocally, **WHO** that document pertains to along with the first Naturalization laws saying that in order to become a citizen, one had to be a white person of good character. That is all fact. Then history records that the Dred Scott decision confirming that inspired the Republicans to pass the 14th Amendment... which was done illegally:"

"**IF** the 14th Amendment was not legally ratified, then the black people who are claiming citizenship are no more "citizens" than migrant worker who slid under the wall from Mexico."

"Today, black people can be citizens (via an illegally passed Amendment), but they are obsessed with punishing the whites for the black peoples perception of history. And so, they are conducting a subtle form of genocide against the whites, preying upon programmed emotions related to slavery... an institution NOT initiated by the whites. And the most telling of this, blacks are **NOT** grateful to the white race for being the ones to be the first to stop slavery. Oddly, I have never seen where the Bible condemns slavery per se, but if it's wrong, then the black people should step up to the plate, admit their role in being the first to start it, and hold themselves accountable *for participating and profiting off of selling their brethren to the slave traders as it relates to America."*

You have read the reflections of a white man in the 21st Century. He maintains that nonwhites are not citizens, and the 14th amendment *was* not legally ratified. According to him, blacks have made up an incorrect perception of history. Reality shows us the 14th Amendment was ratified on July 28, 1868. Blacks first ended slavery in Haiti. American history is documented; therefore perception has nothing to do with how blacks see history. His words were written in the 21st century, and this guy is not the only one living today with such views.

"Listen, because of the provisions provided to the blacks over the years, and this in order to get them up to speed in everything that is available as American, we have had many whites over these years who had to sacrifice a huge amount in order to make it all happen for them. Fact !!!!"
—white internet forum poster 2018

When people declare that systemic racism does not exist, they don't recognize the existence of individuals such as the ones in the prior quotes. Millions of these individuals are employed within the institutions that move our society. These people teach. People with this belief hire, terminate, determine salaries, raises, and promotions. They work as lenders in banks. They are police officers. They rent property, sell houses, insurance, and investments. They provide medical care. They make city, state, and federal policy. They are judges and attorneys in the legal system. We know that there was at least one on the modern supreme court.

"There are those who contend that it does not benefit African Americans to get them into the University of Texas where they do not do well, as opposed to having them go to a less-advanced school, a slower-track

school where they do well.*"[4]*
—The late Supreme Court
Justice Antonin Scalia, 2015

Scalia is not with us anymore, so I'm not going to pile on. Judge Antonin Scalia did not make his comments during the civil rights cases of the late 1800s. He made them in 2015. Here we see an example of racism from a member of our highest court. Just how far have some of our justices come from the ignorance of Taney?

"Now, I'm no expert but I will offer my thoughts on the matter. Racism stems from an inherent idea that one's group is unique and special and a fear and mistrust of other groups outside of our own that may be a threat to our uniqueness or survival. It is one of the defining characteristics of mankind and is manifested in many ways, including the two most often seen throughout history: war and conquest; enslavement. There are examples too numerous to cite but the ones that readily come to mind the Spanish conquest of South and Central America; the wars and enslavement between the Mesoamerican tribes before that; the Roman conquests; the warring tribes in Africa, including the more recent war in Rwanda between the Hutu and Tutsi; the Holocaust; the Japanese invasion of China in the late 30s and of course the enslavement of Africans throughout the Western world.

Black racism in America stems from the same causes: fear and mistrust of whites. Sometimes it is misplaced, sometimes it is not."
—white internet forum poster, 2019

In the above quote, the poster mentions the conflict between the Hutu's and Tutsis in Rwanda. He believed he was making a thoughtful insight into racism. He was trying to build an argument based on human similarities. It was a noble try. His attempt failed because he really didn't know the entire story.

> *"From 1894 until the end of World War I, Rwanda, along with Burundi and present-day Tanzania, was part of German East Africa. Belgium claimed it thereafter, becoming the administering authority from 1924 to 1962. During their colonial tenure, the Germans and Belgians ruled Rwanda indirectly through Tutsi monarchs and their chiefs. The colonialists developed the socalled Hamitic hypothesis or myth, which held that the Tutsi and everything humanly superior in Central Africa came from ancient Egypt or Abyssinia. The Europeans regarded Hutu and Twa (about 3% of the population) as inferior to Tutsi. Sixty years of such prejudicial fabrications inflated Tutsi egos inordinately and crushed Hutu feelings, which coalesced into an aggressively resentful inferiority complex."*[5]

The entire world was shown the horrors of attempted genocide in Rwanda. Here in America, many of us received a half story about the Hutus and Tutsi's that makes it look like one side woke up one day and decided to erase the other side. Unless you go to scholars who study Africa or talk to a Rwandan, the American half story is all you know.

Rwanda and Burundi had existed for centuries without European assistance, but due to the Berlin Conference in 1884, whites decided that Germany could have Rwanda and Burundi. In 1916 Belgian took control of Rwanda and Burundi due to a League of Nations mandate.[6] Once Rwanda was colonized by Europeans, the colonizers invented a fake racial hierarchy whereby the Europeans deemed themselves superior, decided that the Tutsis were closer to white than the Hutus, and gave Tutsis preference over the Hutus.[7] Under this fake hierarchy, Tutsis were deemed more intelligent and were born to rule, while Hutus were second class citizens .[8]

Once put in force, this European construct limited the employment opportunities and educational attainment of the Hutus. Because the colonizers considered the Tutsis the preferred group, Tutsis were given positions Hutus were not allowed to have. To enforce this preference system, the Belgian colonizers introduced identity cards labeling each individual as Tutsi, Hutu, Twa, or Naturalised.[9] Before that time, it had been possible for some Hutus to become "honorary Tutsis,"[10] but the implementation of identity cards eliminated that possibility, thereby cementing Hutu second-class status.

This Belgian belief of superiority was based on the Hamitic Hypothesis, which claims that blacks are the cursed descendants of Ham and whites the descendants of Shem and Japheth.[11] Using Genesis 9:25, where Ham was cursed because he looked upon Noah's nudity, white supremacists have claimed biblical justification for slavery and black second-class status. Besides the fact that would have made one of Noah's sons black and the other two white, the point is that Europeans created a false history and fake racial superiority between African tribes to control a nation and colonize the people living there. Belgium's rule favoring the Tutsi created hatred and animosity. Tensions grew between the groups, and in 1959 Rwanda had a revolution whereby the Hutus killed Tutsis, destroyed Tutsi property, and made the Tutsis flee the country.[12]

To make a long story short, Rwanda gained independence in 1962. It's funny how I say that when they had been independent before the Berlin Conference. Africans are not perfect, and over the centuries before the Berlin Conference, there were wars in Africa just like there were everywhere else. However, the 58 years of colonization created periods of strife after Rwanda gained independence. Sporadically Tutsis living in surrounding countries would attack and Hutus would retaliate until the 1990 civil war that resulted in the near genocide of the Tutsis.[13] All this was the result of the colonization of Rwanda by Europeans. When some white Americans start preaching about the ills of Africa as a whataboutism relative to race, it will benefit them mightily to research the history of whatever country they choose to try using to excuse the racism in America. Later in this book, I will present another example of how colonization created modern problems in Africa.

Some people have a fantastic ability to ignore essential things to believe what they choose to. This person claims that whatever he sees as black racism is due to the same things as whites who practice racism. Not that we were enslaved, lynched, murdered, forced into second-class status, and still face white racism today, but the same fear and mistrust whites had about the Africans they encountered and knew nothing about when they created the lie of white supremacy. Such deliberate and willful denial is one of the main reasons we cannot have an honest conversation about race. The racist subculture is OK with lecturing blacks on life. He represents a significant problem- paternalism. Paternalism allows them to assume they know better than other races what is good for them. It is a belief that continues to be held by the members of the racist white subculture.

> *"How does me thinking a black person resembles a monkey mean i think the black race is inferior?"*
> **—white internet forum poster, 2018**

This was asked in a thread of a "conservative" internet forum populated mainly by the alt-right. It was titled *"Why is saying that a Black Person looks like a monkey racist?"* It was created shortly after the infamous Roseanne Barr tweet. The person who posted this question squeals like a stuck hog about how a black person is racist for saying anything about racist acts by whites but calling a black person a monkey? He's perplexed. He just cannot understand how that is racist. It is trifling, but it exemplifies the attitude of the racist subculture. This subculture wants to return to the days when they could be blatantly racist with no consequences.

For the last 20-30 years, this same subculture has decided to tell us how there is no racism, that it's all in the past, and that somehow we are wrong for talking about the problem. The online world is a crazy place. I remember a book I read back in the 1980s titled *"Megatrends."* The writer predicted the high-tech society we would live in today. In the book, there was a category called high tech /high touch, meaning that as a world, we would interact less with each other because of technology and that we would need more high touch social activities to offset this. I think we are there now. The device-free commercials are evidence of just how correct John Naisbitt was. We now live in a world of disinformation whereby people can click a link and be told what they want to be told. However, there is such a thing as fact. Anyone can create a website. Crazy Clyde can build one full of opinions, and people who have similar beliefs as Crazy Clyde will use his opinions as fact. At the same time, legitimate and respected agencies, universities, and federal, state, and local government entities compile data. These sources are responsible for collecting the data to resolve issues. Crazy Clyde does not have that responsibility.

We have seen the proliferation of so-called news websites that claim to be presenting information the so-called "MSM" is too afraid to show. There is a reason for that. The so-called news they "report" is generally disingenuous. This "news" comes from sites like Project Veritas, run by a man who has gone to court for questionable reporting on multiple occasions. Places like the Daily Caller by Tucker Carlson and other fountains of disinformation include: Ben Shapiro's lunacy on the Daily Wire, Dennis Prager's madness, PJ Media, the Epoch Times, Infowars, the list of loon sites is long. People read this stuff and the often-virulent racism coming from those sites and then move to various forms of social media to discuss the crazy they just heard or read.

Blacks should pay us for the privilege of living in a better civilization than they could build on their own. They should pay us for all the crimes they commit. We would be better off without them. They would be lost without us.
—white internet forum poster 2018

"The criminal justice system favors Blacks. The public schools favor Blacks. Government favors Blacks. The fact that Blacks are so far behind Whites in IQ while excelling at savage behavior has nothing to do with Whites (and some Asians, some Jews, and some Indians from India, etc.) being way more advanced for the most part. You cannot change DNA, at the present time. And programs to help Blacks only makes things worse, since they are destined to fail, and non-Blacks get annoyed that they are being discriminated against for no reason."
—white internet forum poster 2018

These are examples of what kind of crazy ideas the sites I mentioned have people believing and expressing online. All you have to do is enter a social media forum or use Facebook, Instagram, or whatever, and you don't have to go far before you see a comment that looks like it came straight out of the 1700s. What's sad is the fact these forums are not regulated. They call themselves having staff, but most of them are blatantly racist. Something must be done. The events of 1-06-2021 are a prime example of why we need to regulate internet-based media.

"The right has turned the proud institution of American journalism into an instrument that causes and reinforces a state of paranoid psychosis. It's great for

their politicians who never have to do anything good for the voters but it's made the American right into a mob of mentally unstable maniacs who demand an end to everything good, honest and empathetic in government. Look at this crap OP has posted. They believe this hogwash 100%. How do you argue with paranoid delusions on a scale like this?"
—**Anonymous white internet forum user 2021**

The quotes you have read in this chapter are from The United States Message Board forum. I believe it is incumbent on ISPs and hosting services to monitor who are using their services. At USMB I have read extreme neo nazi beliefs that continue to be allowed while opposition to them gets bullied or banned. America now is at a breaking point mainly because we have allowed this kind of thing to linger. I have received threatening personal messages from people in this forum. I am not the only one who has faced these threats. Because of events we have seen, it should be a top priority that we begin to clamp down on forums purposefully promoting hate and extremism using the first amendment as a shield such as the United States Message Board.

These forums and so-called opinion or news websites are used as media by those who dismiss the so-called mainstream media. They should be held to the same rigid standards as every other form of media. They should be required to pay all applicable FCC fees and be regulated. Because of the vast array of "news sites," we must reestablish the Fairness Doctrine or create a new policy governing online communications. Whatever you call it, the misinformation or disinformation that ruled the last few years in this nation and worldwide must be controlled. Freedom of speech in the public square does not grant anyone the freedom to lie or create disingenuous garbage some call news by taking half of what is said then creating what you want from the rest. Nor does it cover a person making things up, posting it, then calling it news.

The opposition to the hate and disinformation allowed to circulate because algorithms keep directing people to that hate and disinformation is increasing. Companies like Facebook/Meta and X (formerly Twitter) are under fire because their platforms seem to push people toward hate and disinformation. Lawsuits were filed against individuals who used social media to organize white supremacist rallies and to intimidate a student of color on a college campus. Hopefully, this continues until the problem of freely pushing misinformation is solved.

I write all this to illustrate a real and serious problem that is not new to the issue of race. As a black man or as a person of color, I do think I can best speak to the experience I have lived through with more accuracy than someone who has not. If you tell some white people nowadays how they are not black and don't know, they want to come back with you don't know how it is to be white as if everything is the same. For nonwhites, our survival in a white-dominated culture depends on our understanding of white people. Too many whites have never tried to understand us; this is apparent in the 400 years of American history.

"A bigot traditionally is anyone who has intolerant views towards their opposition, and the racial qualifier was added further down the line. To assume that one needs to be a racist to be a bigot is simply a product of race peddling and a cottage industry that wants to co-opt whatever it can in negative mechanisms.

As it was traditionally, racists, and those who fervently oppose them, would both be bigots because neither group is tolerant of their opposition's views."
—white internet forum poster 2018

"At this point, the whole race thing is over . . . it doesn't matter anymore. We've transcended it. Now we have a black president, so clearly we are not racist," stated one young woman after the first election of Barack Obama as president of the United States.
—white internet forum poster 2018

These are prime examples of how crazy things have become. To some, a person is a bigot because they are intolerant of white racism. What's next? Shall we be called bigots for not tolerating fascism? Are we now bigots for being intolerant of totalitarianism? Is it now bigotry if we are intolerant of misogyny? LGBTQ+ phobia? What else can you call a statement like that but lunacy? A person is not a bigot for opposing bigoted views. The mere election of a black president did not end racism, nor was it going to. It did not represent any transcendence. Too many of us want a simple solution to the problem. I remember the night of Obama's victory. I saw his victory as one last chance for our nation to get right on matters of race. Instead, things got worse, and some whites blamed it on Obama. For them, Obama created the riot in Ferguson, not the prosecuting attorney who felt the murder of Mike Brown was not an indictable offense. To that same troublesome subculture, Obama increased racism because as a light-skinned black man, he claimed that if he had a son, he would look like a light-skinned black teenager murdered for no reason. Somehow to such people, the United States had become racially unified until Obama spoke out against racism.

"Propaganda is cheap to produce on the web. And a purposeful lie in an age of "viral content" not only can race around the world in a day but resurface time and time again with surprising resiliency."
—Alex Amend

What I have presented here is but a fraction, a very minute one, of the racism allowed online. More significant than this being allowed online is a reality most Americans want to sweep under the rug and deny. During these conversations I was not communicating with imaginary beings; these were real humans. These conversations show that racism exists today just like it did in the past. Some in the white community hold the same age-old racist attitudes and beliefs as yesteryear. Just because racism is not painted on signs or overtly carried out does not mean it is gone. This means everything that goes with racism exists. You have read all of the quotes and despite the overt racism contained in words written, not one time did any of the whites believe the comments were racist or they were. Even worse, after reading these opinions and looking at more and more acts of old-time overt racism in our culture today, some whites claim the term racism is overused.

> *I agree that the word Racism has been overused to the point, EVERYTHING is now RACIST. I guessed it's really all the left has to use as an excuse to "make them satisfied".*
> **- white internet forum poster 2020**

We have endured a presidency that began with a campaign by a man floating down an escalator to declare that Mexicans are rapists and murderers. People excused that by claiming that Mexicans are not a race. During his presidency, number 45 called black nations shitholes, told four women of color to go back to where they came from, spewed racist rhetoric at his hate rallies, and implemented one of the cruelest policies in American history on our Southern border. But according to millions, none of these things were racist.

As this was going on, we have seen increases in the numbers of white supremacist groups and associated acts of terror. In August 2019, the most significant act of terror on Hispanics was inflicted on our Hispanic brothers and sisters in El Paso, Texas.[14] Twenty-two were killed. 61 shot in all. This was done by a white racist who drove 635 miles from Dallas to El Paso just to hunt Hispanics. In the year 2020, due to a virus that originated in China, the racist description of the virus by President number 45 caused over 3,800 racial attacks against Asian American citizens.[15] A new phenomenon was created called the Karen. Police get called on black children selling lemonade. When a black citizen can get stopped for "walking while black," as was done in San Clemente, California, resulting in the death of a homeless black man who supposedly was jaywalking,[16] or the 2022 murders in Buffalo by a white supremacist, no one can sanely believe that racism is an overused term. I now present the following words from white American men and women in the 21st century:

"This is pipe dream shit meant to feed the n-I-g-g-e-r-s and the s-p-I-c-s because they're stupid enough to believe that shit."

"Today blacks act like animals because they are BARELY evolved past the Ape and need a strong central figure (the white man) to keep them in place and acting like normal people."

"Sick of their shit and we should not hide it anymore. When they call me a fucking racist, and I say you damn right I am!!! Fuck those fucking people!"

"Why do Browns ("people of color") feel compelled to steal, assault, rape, murder Whites, their obvious superior beings? Browns should be worshiping Whites instead of being jealous douchebag criminals."'

"Blacks... prone to violence, think they're still in the jungle, low IQ blacks."

"How can you look at the world and not see that ALL ADVANCEMENTS came from Europe and America? Yeah, we're the superior race on the earth. All others developed because of whites"

"Look, he is actually intelligent and an actual person of color! How often does that happen?"

"We swear muthafuckers, you take our beaners from us and we'll come for your guns one day Filthy

fucks!"

"MAGA! This is great news! Everything is falling into place so we can build the Wall and thwart this invasion of brown diseease ridden third worlders who are a threat to our sovereignty, culture and American traditions."

"Being the elected representative of a bunch of dumbass ghetto Jungle Monkeys doesn't take intelligence. It take a ghetto dialect and a promise to get them more welfare."

"Valerie Jarrett.... Is she that light skinned negro who looks like that ape in Planet of the Apes (negroes?)

I thought she was an ape...Next you'll be telling me Mooch isn't really a shaved wookie."

"The asians made fun of obama.....the asians refer to negroes as 'monkey people' and not in jest....they are serious....and why shouldn't they be?"

"Pay the pavement ape or he will get very angry and burn his house down."

"Yawn, Kambala wants every African American crack addict to have their own home while White, Red, and Yellow Americans some disabled vets rot on the street."

"Nigga's acting like a Nigga...must be part of the Thugery... most blacks don't act like that!"

"Engage me and die, n'gr."

"Folks, you couldn't today pay me enough to live anywhere near a large black population."

"I believe the black race is inferior to both the white and yellow races....I can prove it by taking a look at the world map and income, innovation/scientific discoveries, and prison populations. Maybe you have some other mysterious way of defining the word but you never seem to say what it is".

"Most intelligent people understand how stupid blacks are....average i.q. of 85.....being one you should know."

"Fuck off House Negro. Shine my boots bitch."
"Monkey's are more civilized than many blacks - Quit insulting monkeys."
"You're talking about balkanization. I'm all for it. I'm also for restoring the 1790 Naturalization Act, the very first legislation by the first Congress making only White people U.S. Citizens."
"Hasn't it been proven, in the last few days, that blacks are incapable of living in the environment of civilization? Send them back to Africa."
"Why do blacks behave the way they do?"
"Genetic deficiencies...proven the world over. Dark people need whitey to lead....PERIOD just like Africa is the shithole of the world, the black US communities mirror that"
"Video emerges of the carjacking that killed an Uber Eats driver this week. The girls were arrested and are ages monkey and chimp."
"You can take a negro out of the ghetto. But you can't take the ghetto out of the negro."
"Ever wonder why blacks are so sensitive about being compared to monkeys? hehheh obviously the truth can be painful."
"See, coloreds like that monkey have no value. They're worthless. It should be legal for the cop to simply draw his weapon and shoot him in his fat fucking face..."
"Just White peoples existence is a constant reminder to blacks that they are very inferior."
"Everybody knows black people fuck everything up and make the value go down.
If only you could just quit being black.
But you can't.....DARKIE!!!"

In a poll taken by the Washington Post after Charlottesville, nine percent of Americans said holding neo-Nazi or white supremacist views is acceptable. That 9 percent potentially equals 22 million Americans.[17] According to a 2017 IPSOS poll *"Thirty-one percent of Americans polled strongly or somewhat agreed that 'America must protect and preserve its White European heritage."* [18][19] Those are the same views held by white supremacists. White racism is a thing of the past? "Yeah, that's the ticket."

> *"If you stick a knife nine inches into my back and pull it out three inches, that is not progress. Even if you pull it all the way out, that is not progress. Progress is healing the wound, and America hasn't even begun to pull out the knife."*
>
> **-Malcolm X**

Entitlement Mentality

"From its inception, the country's legal foundations, political architecture, and civic fabric were designed to privilege the well-being of those who declared themselves white at the expense of Native Americans, African Americans, and other people of color. Generation after generation, as the baldest tactics were challenged, white America creatively renewed and reworked this pact to protect ourselves from political disempowerment, economic uncertainty, legal jeopardy, and physical violence. When the weight of the blood spilled by over 750,000 Americans shattered outright slavery, white America picked up the shards, fashioning them into a ramshackle but effective system of sharecropping, lynching, convict leasing, segregationist Jim Crow laws, restrictive immigration policies, appeals to "states' rights," voter suppression, and mass incarceration."

-Robert P. Jones

Recently I was up late and saw a commercial where Pat Boone was trying to sell a book titled "I See the Future, and it looks like Baltimore." The title alone shows how much many whites have ignored in America because of racial preferences they have received as part of white privilege. How did Baltimore come to be? Racist government public policy is the answer. But to the racist white subculture, the answer is people living there created the problems because blacks endorse a lazy criminal subculture where everyone wants to sell drugs, have babies out of wedlock and collect government welfare checks instead of working. This is just how ignorant many American whites have been to longstanding racist policies designed to create slums and impoverished areas populated by blacks.

We are going to look at this from a different perspective. This chapter will cover terms like entitlement and dependence on government. Generally, when we talk about entitlement, it is with disdain because we have informed ourselves that no one is entitled to anything but the right to work hard and earn your place on the merits. I watched the news one day and listened to Senator Joe Manchin moaning about how he doesn't want America to become an entitlement society. Well Senator Manchin, you're at least 2 centuries too late. On top of that, Senator, you were born during segregation and entered college about the time the Civil Rights Act was passed. So you may have been allowed to do things that blacks and other people of color couldn't.

Maybe now that we have reached the 21st century and are well into it, we start being truthful. The racist subculture within the white community blames minority groups for having an entitlement mentality because of laws that eliminated segregation and racist policies, or at least reduced them in practice to such a level that nonwhites can at least try competing in the system. These are not entitlements. They are policies and laws to guarantee equal protection for nonwhites who were not getting those protections before the laws were made. Entitlement is a little different from that. Per Merriam Webster, the full definition of entitlement is **"A state or condition of being entitled. A right to benefits specified by law or contract. A government program providing benefits to a specific group. The belief that one is deserving of or entitled to certain privileges."**

62

Let us start with the first part of the definition: **"State or condition of being entitled."** The system in America is built upon a belief in white racial superiority. What made whites believe they were superior and therefore entitled to things that others were not? What made the whites from Europe decide they had the right to invade different continents and create governments where governments already existed?

After doing a lot of reading, it appears that we must take ourselves back to the era of what was called the Age of Enlightenment. I don't know just exactly who was enlightened by these ideas because to some, the period had nothing to do with being "enlightened." This time is called the Age of Reason, but much of what came out of this age does not fit the description. This era is credited with forward-moving concepts like liberty, constitutional government, as well as the separation of church and state. Such "reason and enlightenment" came equipped with philosophies steeped in racism. Half of the story has not been told to promote some great ideal of the superiority of thought and reason based on European doctrines. However, the top thinkers of the time held ideas or beliefs such as this from David Hume:

"I am apt to suspect the negroes and in general all other species of men (for there are four or five different kinds) to be naturally inferior to the whites. There never was a civilized nation of any other complexion than white, nor even any individual eminent either in action or speculation. No ingenious manufactures amongst them, no arts, no sciences. On the other hand, the most rude and barbarous of the whites, such as the ancient GERMANS, the present TARTARS, have still something eminent about them in their valour, form of government, or some other particular. Such a uniform and constant differences could not happen in so many countries and ages, if nature had not made an original

distinction betwixt these breeds of men. Not to mention our colonies, there are Negroe slaves dispersed all over Europe, of which none ever discovered any symptoms of ingenuity, tho' low people, without education, will start up amonst us, and distinguish themselves in every profession. In JAMAICA indeed they talk of one negroe as a man of parts and learning; but 'tis likely he is admired for very slender accomplishments like a parrot, who speaks a few words plainly."[1]

Cleopatra, Hannibal Barca, and Mansa Musa might have disagreed with this assessment. So would have multiple leaders in Asia and indigenous leaders in what is now North and South America. Hume was not the only one with this flawed belief. Immanuel Kant was one of the earliest advocates of what is now called scientific racism and was considered the greatest thinker of his time. The excuse of *"that is how they thought at the time"* has been used to defend his racism. We have been misguided relative to our education in this and other western societies.

"In three separate works Kant claimed that the Negro is, in most respects, the lowest of all races. He also referred to blacks as the "bad race" and whites as "the good race," argued that the white race contains "all incentives and talents," and felt that whites were the "only ones who always progress toward perfection."

To my knowledge, Kant never repudiated any of these explicitly racist claims."[2]

Murder was wrong in those days, but no one will excuse people who murdered others during the so-called age of enlightenment because that's just how they did things then. Bloodletting was a medical procedure, but no one today will doubt the medical ignorance of such a practice. As I read what was believed, if this was enlightenment, how dark were the dark ages? Excuses must stop being made because it is from these ideas that many of the problems we face today relative to racism or ethnocentrism come from.

Kant's idea that the white race was the only race capable of self-improvement and the highest level of civilization were very popular in Europe.[3] These ideas created the belief in European superiority that we still see today in a newer descriptive term called Western civilization. Kant and Hume were not alone in this belief. My goal here is not to go into a deep discussion of enlightenment philosophy or scientific racism. However, the term scientific racism itself explains the prevailing thought in Europe during this time.[4][5] Therefore, its basic premise should be exposed and understood as to how it created a belief of entitlement and privilege among whites that continues until the present.

Scientific racism is nothing more than racist B.S. The term defines itself. It is the use of science to justify racial supremacy. This belief or ideology has been a problem for more than four centuries. A long line of European thinkers during this period supported scientific racism. These views still exist today among specific segments of the worldwide white community. It is now called racial realism.

"It is a serious question among them whether they [Africans] are descended from monkeys or whether the monkeys come from them. Our wise men have said that man was created in the image of God. Now here is a lovely image of the Divine Maker: a flat and black nose with little or hardly any intelligence. A time will doubtless come when these animals will know how to cultivate the land well, beautify their houses and gardens, and know the paths of the stars: one needs time for everything."[6]

These words are from Voltaire in "Les Lettres d'Amabed" written in 1769. Voltaire is given credit as an advocate for civil liberties, yet as we see, Voltaire had problems. Benjamin Rush, one of the so-called founding fathers of this country, believed that people born black had leprosy.[7] In every instance of trying to provide this "scientific" understanding of cultural differences and skin complexion, whites always gave themselves top billing as more advanced, more intelligent, and more civilized.

Scientific racism has been a considerable part of the American experience. On March 12, 1851, Dr. Samuel Cartwright read a report he was appointed to do for the Medical Association of Louisiana titled, *"Report On The Diseases And Physical Peculiarities Of The Negro Race."* Dr. Samuel Cartwright was the guy who made up the disease called Drapetomania to claim blacks running away from slavery suffered from a mental disorder. People believed Drapetomania was a legitimate mental disorder, and Cartwright was considered one of the leading doctors of his time.

Hoss Cartwright could have written a better report. Cartwright claimed Blacks had been running around in Africa with no medical facilities or medical study.[8] I think Imhotep and a few others would disagree with Cartwrights' opinion. Cartwright claimed that the brain size of blacks is a "ninth or tenth less than in other races of men."[9] He goes on to use the skeletal, vascular and nervous systems of blacks to claim that blacks are like children and that blacks can only prosper in a situation where a controlling force governs them.[10] In his report, Cartwright asserted that blacks were incapable of self-rule, that blacks gravitated towards slavery and enjoyed being under such rule.[11] While reading this report, I was reminded of Damon Wayans character Oswald Bates from *"In Living Color."* The report is 23 pages with many big words making no sense.

Then we have Madison Grant. While some in the study

of the environment may see Grant as a great man, had he stuck to his work in that field, perhaps I could agree. But he didn't. Grant was hailed as one of the great progressives of his time. Progressivism was a far different thing at the turn of the 19th century because the founder of the American Renaissance also praised Grant as a tireless advocate for racialism.

Madison Grant promoted scientific racism his entire adult life. He was active in the eugenics movement of that time. Grant wrote a book titled *"The Passing of the Great Race: Or, The Racial Basis of European History"* in 1916. The ideas expressed in the book influence us even today. He wrote the book to dispel the American notion of the melting pot.[12] In this book, Grant promotes the Nordic Theory of racial supremacy. This theory assumes that Caucasians are a superior race, and the Nordic "sub-race" is the most eminent of all Caucasians. This theory is one of the main philosophies in modern white supremacist culture.

"Africa should be given back to the white man, because it's clear the blacks can't do anything with it."
- white internet forum user, 2020

Near the end of the 19th century, European countries and the United States came to believe they had the right to go into Africa and control the natural resources on that continent. Their belief led to the Berlin Conference on November 15, 1884. Countries attending the conference were: Austria-Hungary, Belgium, Denmark, France, Germany, Great Britain, Italy, the Netherlands, Portugal, Russia, Spain, Sweden, Norway, Turkey, and the United States of America. African nations were not in attendance. The countries at this meeting decided to divide the continent of Africa up among themselves. Some whites have considered this decision as a benefit to Africa. But in reality, the decision destroyed African prosperity. That decision is the genesis of much of the ethnic strife and divisions plaguing the continent today.

Still, according to some, no African today should be angry or resentful of whites for their decision or the resulting damage created by that decision. To do that makes them racist.

The colonization of the continent of Africa is well documented. The participating nations raped, pillaged, stole, and plundered, taking the money back to Europe and America, getting rich while draining African economies everywhere they went. Perhaps no one detailed the destruction of Africa better than the great Walter Rodney. Despite the finest legends about Africa told by white supremacists or whites who are generally ignorant of Africa, the fact is that African nations during this period were just as developed as Europe before Europeans "discovered" Africa. In chapter 6 of his book, *"How Europe Underdeveloped Africa,"* Rodney debunks the European tale of how colonization was beneficial in the development of Africa. *"For the first three decades of colonialism, hardly anything was done that could remotely be termed a service to the African people."*[13] He uses the Portuguese, who occupied parts of Africa for five centuries, as one of many examples. *"At the end of shouldering the white man's burden of civilizing African natives, the Portuguese had not managed to train one African doctor in Mozambique, and the life expectancy in eastern Angola was less than thirty years."*[14]

The "Scramble for Africa," ruined the continent, and it is still rebuilding. Today in South Africa, whites still control much of that nation's economy more than thirty years after apartheid. They stole the land through murder and plunder, enacted laws making it illegal for black South Africans to own land, controlled the black population with authoritarian force while killing countless blacks for fighting the oppression. Now that blacks want their land back, a particular segment of the American white community wants us to all forget about the atrocities black South Africans endured and complain about how wrong it is for the blacks to want land stolen from them back. Whites here and in South Africa are whining to the world about how Afrikaners are victims of cruel racism.

"I'm fully aware of what apartheid was. It's not an excuse to persecute a "race" of people. Or to sit by and do nothing while a vengeful segment of the population plays out their hateful fantasies"
-white internet forum user, 2020

In this example, we had discussed the current South African situation. Instead of looking at the situation objectively and considering the history of South Africa, this guy began ranting and raving inaccurately about how the black South African government was promoting racial violence because the government was giving blacks back their ancestral lands. I suggested he might do some study and analysis of the laws and policies that existed during Apartheid to understand how the conditions in South Africa today result from those laws and policies. Instead of looking at such things, he made the quoted comment. How does a person make such a comment? The definition of apartheid is *"a system based upon discrimination on the grounds of race."* For whites like this to complain because blacks want to get ancestral lands back, or to whine about how blacks don't like them after over 100 years of white imposed terrorism, makes one conclude some whites believe they are entitled to everything no matter how they get it.

In the mid-1800s, white Americans decided they had God's permission to expand west. Manifest Destiny, a phrase made up in 1845, drove this territorial expansion. According to the American government, Manifest Destiny was God telling them that the United States was to expand to spread democracy and capitalism across North America. I am no biblical expert, but I have read nothing in the bible saying that. So then, according to the American government, God permitted them to wipe out millions of citizens in the indigenous nations already living on those lands. Wasn't there something written about coveting what is not yours? How about killing?

As we look at Europe and America, the descendants of the same people today are complaining about illegal immigration. They have decided to block out of their memories how they have done what would today be considered illegal immigration all over the planet. It appears that no one set boundaries or citizenship requirements on whites as they entered a country. Judging by what went on, the European Doctrine of Discovery was not agreed to by the countries they claimed to "discover." Non vetted illegal immigrants came here without permission of the indigenous people of this continent who had existing governments and decided their governments did not count. What's worse is that our government, created by what would be considered illegal immigrants today, decided they could make rules on who could come here. Why are these nations of primarily white people now complaining about immigration into their countries? It cannot be due to a concern of assimilation because colonization does not contain assimilation as part of the package. This is a prime example of the **"State or condition of being entitled."**

The second part of the definition is **"A right to benefits specified by law or contract."** I will continue to say that whites who do so have no room to talk about how others have an entitlement mentality. I am now about to present a few examples to support my claim. Whenever the conversation is about race and privilege, inevitably, we get a lecture. I have been told how blacks should do things more like whites. People tell me that blacks need to pull themselves up by the bootstraps as various white ethnic groups have done. History shows these comments to be, at best, a misstatement. Anyone making such a comment needs to assess how whites really accomplished what they have. I am not sure they want us to do things the same way. Doing so would include creating laws to confiscate all property and money whites have, making it illegal for whites to educate themselves, and passing laws making whites chattel. These are just a few things to consider because there are many more, and none are good. Some folks might want to slow down on the lectures. Let us look at: **"A right to benefits specified by law or contract."**

In 1618, the Virginia colony passed "the Great Charter of privileges, orders, and laws." Among these laws was a provision that any person who settled in Virginia or paid for the transportation of another person to settle in Virginia would get fifty acres of land per person. "The right to receive fifty acres per person, or per head, was called a headright."[15] It got even better for colonists as those who "imported" slaves also got 50 acres per slave. The practice was continued by the government of Virginia, for 161 years, ending in 1779.[16] Headrights were not only limited to Virginia. The headright system was used in all the original 13 colonies.[17] Headrights were the first of many government handouts of free stuff or guarantees providing whites with economic development assistance.

"They [Locke, Rousseau, and Hobbes] brought the important news that by nature all men are free and equal and that they have rights to life, liberty and the pursuit of property. But the American colonists, having accepted these ideas while at the same time enslaving the Africans and dispossessing the Native Americans, found themselves in a dilemma wherein they wished to continue these ideas, to identify with key ideals, but at the same time to continue to profit from the anti-ideal, which the Lockean belief in self-interest led them to believe in equally. The result was the American 'trick': the surrender of morality and higher aspirations to self-interest... By ignoring the equal humanity of its minorities[sic], America began the long process of denying the reality of its history." **-Y.N. Kly, The Anti-Social Contract**

The Constitution of the United States is the supreme

law of this land. Included in the constitution is the three-fifths compromise. The Three-Fifths Compromise is found in Article 1, Section 2, Clause 3 of the United States Constitution. It says: *"Representatives and direct Taxes shall be apportioned among the several States which may be included within this Union, according to their respective Numbers, which shall be determined by adding to the whole Number of free Persons, including those bound to Service for a Term of Years, and excluding Indians not taxed, **three-fifths of all other Persons.**"*

Stories tell us how the so-called founders struggled for several years to figure out how much of a person blacks would count as a human. Starting in 1783, our wise and omniscient founders began to try figuring out how to count enslaved people as a population for representation. By 1787, they figured it out. This ridiculous "conclusion" blacks did not agree to allowed humans to count as 3/5th of a person because they were slaves. Whites still counted as whole people. Yet there were free blacks, so the compromise could not have conferred entitlements just on whites, right? This renders my claim as simply a black man whining according, to right-wing logic.

> "This unfortunate difference of color, and perhaps of faculty, is a powerful obstacle to the emancipation of these people."
> **-Thomas Jefferson**[18]

Let me keep on crying and show you another example. On March 26, 1790, the United States of America decided who could be a citizen of this country for the first time. The Naturalization Act of 1790 states: *"any alien, being a free white person,"* could apply for citizenship, so long as they lived in the United States for at least two years and in the state where the application was filed for at least one year. This law allowed *"children of citizens of the United States that may be born... out of the limits of the United States shall be considered as natural-born citizens.*" Please notice the first seven words. Only whites were entitled to be citizens of this country. Never mind the Native American nations already here. Blacks could forget about it.

One of the greatest miscarriages of justice in this nation's history was a direct rebuttal to the claim that all men are created equal called Dred Scott v. Sandford. I am not going into all the particulars of this case. The court's opinion says all you need to know. "A black man has no rights a white man is bound to respect." The result of Dred Scott v. Sandford was that whites were given rights and status blacks were denied. Based on this decision, blacks had no rights or constitutional protection by law. Therefore the United States Constitution did not apply to blacks at that time.

> *"At the very same time that America refused to give the Negro any land, through an act of Congress our government was giving away millions of acres of land in the West and the Midwest, which meant it was willing to undergird its white peasants from Europe with an economic floor."*
> **-Rev. Martin Luther King Jr.**

Passed in 1862, the Homestead Acts gave away 246 million acres of land. To qualify for Homestead land, a person had to be a citizen of the United States, and blacks were not given citizenship until 1866. This alone should provide evidence of the limited benefit this act had for blacks in America. Research shows that 99.73 percent of that land went to whites, including white immigrants.[19] 1.5 million white families were given free land, the equivalent of a minimum of $500,000 per family.[20] Today 93 million whites still benefit from the Homestead Act,[21] this is about 40 percent of the current white population in America. This land has helped those whites accumulate the wealth they have today.

"Whites are the ones who traveled a thousand miles in covered wagons and claimed the land, as usual your people failed to take advantage of opportunity."
-White internet forum user-2021

When shown evidence, there is a consistent flow of excuses or attempts to justify the wrongs committed by part of the white American population. One major impediment for blacks concerning homesteading was the lack of documentation. Many states had literacy laws that made it a crime for blacks to be taught to read and write. Because of this, it should surprise no one how newly freed blacks would have difficulty understanding the legal terminology or process involved in land acquisition. After a lifetime of slavery it should be noted that many freed blacks did not have the documents necessary to prove their identity. Once freed, blacks could get the documentation after registering for citizenship, but that documentation was not always considered proof by whites. The inability to show documents proving identity made it difficult for newly freed blacks to file homestead claims.

"As early as 1865, certain white Southerners put legal obstacles in place to prevent ex-slaves from acquiring property. In the provisional state governments under President Johnson's protective leniency, planters not only prohibited black landownership but enacted extreme measures of social control that virtually restored slavery. The black codes struck directly at freedmen striving to escape their subordination and to obtain their communities. It was class and race legislation."[22]

On March 3, 1865, the Freedmen's Bureau Act was passed by congress. The Freedman's Bureau was supposed to be a temporary agency with the mission to provide "the supervision and management of all abandoned lands, and the control of all subjects relating to refugees and freedmen from rebel states."[23] The Freedmen's Bureau was the beginning of a long line of half measures using public policy to create solutions to assist black people. The bureau was supposed to help blacks acquire what was necessary to live successfully as free American citizens. But as in every other effort of its kind, the agency was understaffed and underfunded. What made things even worse was that it was managed by individuals who either had paternalistic beliefs or had no genuine interest in helping the newly freed blacks.

The primary indicator of the lack of importance placed on the agency was that it was temporary. Initially, the bureau was supposed to be open for one year. Think about that for a second. The United States government believed that it would take one year to solve a problem created by 246 years of actions by colonial and federal governments. In 1866 the charter came up for review. Lincoln was gone, and in his place was Andrew Johnson. Johnson opposed the continuance of the Freedmen's Bureau after only one year. His reasons sounded much like some today, claiming that it would make blacks dependent on the same government that had depended on their free labor for nearly 100 years and because the bureau provided services to blacks that poor whites could not get. Johnson "conveniently" ignored that poor whites had not been enslaved since 1619.

Johnson vetoed the charter to keep the bureau open after just one year. His veto was overridden. Southern members of Congress then went to work weakening the bureau. It was supposed to be funded by Congress and rent paid by freedmen for land. Thanks mostly to its southern members, Congress never provided enough funding for the Bureau. The revenue that was supposed to come from rent didn't because President Andrew Johnson pardoned southern planters in 1865 and gave the land back to them. The bureau stayed understaffed and underfunded.

"During a period where many citizens were given

public land by the government, Blacks who wanted to be small farm owners had to pay for their land and struggle against obstacles that most of their White counterparts did not."[24]

Freedmen also faced the "pull yourself up by your bootstraps" attitude of people the freedmen's labor helped to live comfortably while ignoring how the government had been THEIR bootstraps.[25] During those times, that was called the Free Labor Philosophy.[26] The Free Labor Philosophy was a northern belief about labor. As it pertains to the newly freed blacks, the northern whites in charge of the Freemans Bureau believed that blacks should earn the land they wanted by working to make money to buy it. These northern whites thought that if the government gave the land away, blacks would not respect work and would get used to living off the government. Sound familiar? We are talking about people who worked from dark to dark seven days a week without wages for 246 years before the beginning of the bureau. This thinking was going on while the government was giving away free land to whites. But this was not the worst. I'll show you the worst in the next chapter. By 1872 the Freedman's Bureau was closed, it lasted just seven years.

"But not only did they give them land, they built land grant colleges with government money to teach them how to farm. Not only that, they provided county agents to further their expertise in farming. Not only that, they provided low interest rates in order that they could mechanize their farms."

"Not only that, today many of these people are receiving millions of dollars in federal subsidies not to farm, and they are the very people telling the black man that he ought to lift himself by his own bootstraps. And this is what we are faced with, and this is the reality."

-Rev. Martin Luther King Jr.

As Dr. King so eloquently described, the government saw th need to provide education and services to assist whites moving west to help them survive on the free land the government was handing out. Because of that, the United States Congress passed the Morrill Act of 1862, better known as the Land Grant Act. The act gave each state 30,000 acres of land per senator to be used for educating homesteaders in the professions available during that time in America.[27] The grants were used to build colleges making land grant colleges one result of the Morrill Act.

Blacks were not allowed to attend many Morrill Act institutions. To combat this, the U.S Congress came up with the Agricultural College Act of 1890 (26 Stat. 417, 7 U.S.C. § 321 et seq.) or easier remembered as the Morrill Act of 1890.[28] The second Morrill Act allowed blacks to attend Land Grant Colleges. States having separate colleges for blacks and whites were required to train black students in the same professions of the time as whites. This law created some of America's legendary HBCU'S, but until desegregation became the law, black land grant colleges were woefully underfunded. These land grants established white economic advancement, and as Dr. King said, they built an economic floor for the European immigrants that entered America. Blacks were freed from slavery, but their economic base was limited due to Black Codes and apartheid.

On April 16, 1895, the United States Supreme Court rendered another one of the sorriest decisions in American history. It is known as Plessy vs. Ferguson. From this decision came the principle of separate butequal. The Supreme Court ruled that racial segregation was acceptable as long as equal facilities existed for blacks. So while whites believed blacks were inferior, they were supposed to make sure that blacks and whites had similar facilities even if the races were to stay apart. States made sure to enforce the separate part, but the equal never came. Not for blacks. Black public facilities were often cheaply built, and black schools were underfunded. Black communities lacked the amenities white communities had. I saw this in my life because the neighborhoods I lived in as a youngster had dirt streets, white neighborhoods had cement streets. That was the case until the 1970s. These are just a few examples of *"A right to benefits specified by law or contract."*

"I'm careful not to attribute any particular resistance or slight or opposition to race. But what I do believe is that if somebody didn't have a problem with their daddy being employed by the federal government, and didn't have a problem with the Tennessee Valley Authority electrifying certain communities, and didn't have a problem with the interstate highway system being built, and didn't have a problem with the GI Bill, and didn't have a problem with the [Federal Housing Administration] subsidizing the suburbanization of America, and that all helped you build wealth and create a middle class — and then suddenly as soon as African Americans or Latinos are interested in availing themselves of those same mechanisms as ladders into the middle class, you now have a violent opposition to them — then I think you at least have to ask yourself the question of how consistent you are, and what's different, and what's changed."
-Former President Barack Obama

America has a history of providing whites with the necessary assistance programs to help them prosper. This nation was built by such programs. Right-wing whites gladly talk about how they made it based on those programs. MAGA is an appeal for a return to the time when America funded white progress only. The whining began when other races were allowed to get the same assistance. Once that happened the government was too big, too intrusive, and our tax money shoul not go to such programs because they foster dependency.

The third part of the definition is: **"A government program providing benefits to a specific group."** Whites in America have benefitted from affirmative action programs throughout American history. However, some have not seen it that way. It is difficult to review the history of this country and not come to that conclusion, but that is all part of the madness. Racial preferences were codified by American law basically until 1965. Understanding our history means reasonable people can conclude no rational argument exists about the unfairness of considering race as a qualification.

The National Housing Act was passed by Congress and signed by President Franklin D. Roosevelt in 1934.[29] This law created the Federal Housing Administration or the FHA. The National Housing Act is the policy that may have had the most impact on wealth accumulation in modern America. This law increased the federal government's capacity to monitor and fix the economy when necessary. Many of today's republicans and others complaining about how government expansion is wrong benefitted from this policy. I say this because the FHA was able to create a guaranteed home loan program whereby potential homebuyers could get bank loans guaranteed against default by the government. But the government had standards, and most of those standards were based on racist beliefs.

Between 1934 and 1968, the FHA implemented and put into practice a policy that still negatively impacts communities today.[30] The FHA Underwriting Manual set the guidelines real estate agents used to assess home values in American neighborhoods. This manual promoted racist real estate practices. It was done by defending racially restrictive covenants and segregated communities. Due to this manual, the FHA established a neighborhood grading system based purely on false racist perceptions.

Redlining was the name of that grading system. Redlining has been well documented, so there is no need for me to go into a lengthy analysis of the policy. I will say that redlining was based on a premise of neighborhood decline caused by blacks that has never been proven. Growing up in a small town, the majority-black neighborhood I lived in until I was 15 was considered a ghetto when it wasn't even close. To this day, blacks are still accused of depreciating neighborhood values without proof.

Furthermore, the biggest eyesore in our community was a house owned by whites. If there had been COVID19 masks in the 70s, we would have been required to wear them if we passed by that house. My point here is the FHA was a government agency whose policies specifically provided whites with opportunities to increase wealth through homeownership. The formation of the FHA and its guaranteed loan program only worked to increase white advantage. *"Of the $120 billion worth of new housing subsidized by the government between 1934 and 1962, less than 2 percent went to nonwhite families."*[31] Black creditworthiness was no excuse for banks because the federal government guaranteed payment of the loans.

The Social Security Act of 1935 created the Social Security program, state unemployment insurance, and assistance to single women with children.[32] Today most Americans love the program. However, when the act was signed, the law excluded occupations mainly done by blacks.[33] When President Roosevelt signed the law, approximately two-thirds of the blacks in America were ineligible.[34] For years, most blacks were excluded from social security savings and could not get unemployment.

"According to economic research, race has been the single most important predictor of support for American welfare programs. In other words, black

poverty has been viewed as a moral failing, whereas white poverty had been viewed as a systemic problem."
-Mehrsa Baradaran- The Color of Money, Black Banks and the Racial Wealth Gap

Time out! Hold up! Whoa! Let's take a short break from the action to talk about the assistance to single women with children part of the Social Security Act. Title 4 or IV provided grants to states as Aid To Dependent Children. Eventually the name of the program was changed to Aid to Families with Dependent Children. This was welfare folks. Assistance for single moms with children and no daddy at home. In 1935. Blacks were excluded. Aid to Dependent Children functioned mainly to provide federal grants to help the states with mothers' aid laws that began in 1910.[35]

The ADC plan was written by two ladies who had been former directors of what was at the time called the U.S. Children's Bureau. The Children's Bureau's goal was to provide aid to all children whose mothers had no support from a husband no matter how they got into that position. From the Children's Bureau in 1910 until 1965, no one talked about how the welfare state was wrong and created the disintegration of the white family. I read no lectures about the irresponsible white father. The program was not denigrated as something creating dependence on government; Aid for Dependent Children was seen as essential assistance needed to help women without husbands who had children. Only when the law required that others besides whites be included did the story change to how the welfare state was wrong and destructive.

The Fair Labor Standards Act of 1938 created the minimum wage and time and a half overtime pay for working over forty hours a week.[36] Child labor was eliminated by this act. All these were good things, but... In every law that was passed as part of The New Deal, Roosevelt had to compromise with southern representatives to get the votes he needed. In the case of the FLSA, due to pressure from southern congress members, he decided that industries would be excluded from the regulations where the majority of workers were black.[37] Because of this, blacks were paid less than the minimum wage.

> *"I'm the beneficiary of the biggest affirmative action program in American history: A free education, a loan for a house. But black veterans didn't get it. We got made middle class by our government program."*
> **-The Rev. Jim Wallis**

Earlier I mentioned that our society had allowed low lives into our national discourse on race. These liars and disingenuous opinion-makers have sold many in modern America a race-baited tale of opportunity lost and failure of black Americans that when examined, fails every fact check known to humanity. In the history of this country, I, an ordinary average Joe, can point to at least four specific instances where whatever government was in power, colonial or constitutional republic, provided direct economic stimulus or assistance primarily for whites: The Headright Program, The Homestead Acts, The New Deal, and The Servicemen's Readjustment Act.

On June 22, 1944, President Roosevelt signed the Servicemen's Readjustment Act, better known as the G.I. Bill.[38] This law provided benefits for veterans returning from World War Two. This act included funds for college tuition, low-cost home loans, and unemployment insurance. As in every other program during this time, southern members of Congress fought the passage of these laws unless there were provisions that limited access to blacks. The G.I Bill was no different.

Democratic congressmen in the south fought against provisions of the GI Bill out of fear that returning black veterans would use their status as war heroes to end the dependence on cheap black labor and the white racial preferences better known as "the southern way of life." Like the New Deal, Southern Democrats pressured Northern Republicans to create policies allowing states to administer benefits. Southern Democrats knew doing that would let southern states to do what each state had been doing since the Civil Rights Cases. That would be states implementing policies full of loopholes and restrictions they would enforce on blacks but not whites, thereby ensuring the GI Bill would primarily benefit whites. As in every other case, Northern Republicans gave Southern Democrats what they wanted.

The reality of the G.I. Bill is that black veterans were sabotaged at nearly every opportunity.[39] Due to the racism in our society that overflowed into the military, blacks were disproportionately dishonorably discharged. Dishonorable discharge disqualified veterans from benefits, so that stopped some black veterans. Whites tried intimidating black veterans with acts of terror. Some black veterans survived the war, came home, tried to use the benefits they so rightfully earned, and ended up getting lynched. Due to segregation, black veterans often could not enroll in the same classes or training as their white counterparts. When the VA wasn't trying to send black veterans to vocational schools, it was sending the large majority of them to black colleges that had been underfunded since the 1890 Morrill Act and the Plessy decision.

Over 1 million returning black soldiers were unable to get GI benefits. My father was one of those soldiers. *"After World War II, blacks wanting to attend college in the South were restricted to about 100 public and private schools, few of which offered education beyond the baccalaureate and more than a quarter of which were junior colleges, with the highest degree below the B.A."[40]* Blacks could not look north for help either. *"In 1947, some 70,000 African American veterans were unable to obtain admission to crowded, under-*

resourced black colleges. The University of Pennsylvania—one of the least-discriminatory schools at the time—enrolled only 40 African American students in its 1946 student body of 9,000."[41]

During the 20th century, numerous programs and policies were designed that provided race-based advantages by law for whites by every level of government in the United States. The policies excluded those who were not white; most excluded all who were not white and male. These were programs that provided benefits to a specific group, and that group was whites. When we talk about government dependence, whites have depended on government for almost two- and one-half centuries. Americans of all races far greater than I have made mention of the programs the American system of government provided for whites that excluded all others from the same benefits, specifically during the 20th century. They have detailed how public policy created negative situations in many non-white communities and how they have adversely affected blacks and other people of color over the past century.

"What I'm concerned about it how the current race preferences are such a disservice to African American professionals in various fields who have Harvard degrees. Its gets patients wondering- is my black surgeon qualified or not as he has a Harvard degree? There is a real good chance he isn't so you might want to pick another surgeon who doesn't have a Harvard degree but instead went to Georgetown or Bologna."
-Anonymous white internet forum poster 2019

This comment has been made without thinking about how the history of AMERICAN race-based policies has helped whites. Do people who make this type of comment ever stop to give the same consideration that every white graduate of Harvard might only have gotten accepted because of legacy? Have they questioned every white professional who has worked in this country for the last two and one-half centuries because they achieved due to opportunities available because of white racial preference? This cognitive dissonance is what non-whites have to deal with.

I will present a policy here that many will not believe benefitted whites. That policy is Affirmative Action. Statistics regarding white wealth from the initial time of policy implementation show that this program has benefitted white families more than anyone else by creating more high-earning double-wage families. Yes, that's right, Affirmative Action has helped whites more than anyone else.

"Hoping to create in white men and women a shared sense of victimization at the hands of people of color, conservatives have made sure to ignore whatever gains have come to women through affirmative action and have sought to "racialize" the debate and its attendant imagery."

-Tim Wise

"How do you figure, wasn't affirmative action made for blacks?" NO! Affirmative Action was created to combat discrimination, and blacks have not been the only ones discriminated against. So here we introduce another protected group, women. That includes white women. Do not get confused about this, women deserved this protection. While we know that white women could not vote by law until 1919, we have to recognize a "small" matter called the Law of Coverture.

While we blacks were in slavery, white women were in another type of bondage. That bondage was called Coverture. [42],[43] This was an English law that immigrated to America with the British colonists. Under this law, married women had no rights her husband was bound to respect. In this law, a married woman's rights were tied to her husband. A married woman or "femme covert" could not own property, sign contracts, decide how to spend her own money, or write a will. Unmarried women, or women categorized as "femme sole" could do all those things. The Law of Coverture was based on a belief that when a woman got married, she and her husband became one person. When you hear right-wingers talking about individualism, understand that individualism did not apply to white females.

Between 1839 and 1895, Married Women's Property Acts were passed in every state.[44] The first U.S. Married Women's Property Act was passed in Mississippi in 1839.[45] This law allowed married women to earn money from their property, but the law still gave the husband control of basically everything else. While the wife could earn an income, the husband was running the business. By 1900, laws were written that formally ended Coverture in every state. I said the word formally because things didn't end by 1900, and there are some men still running around today with the coverture mentality. The Law of Coverture is one of many reasons women, including white women, rightfully became a protected class.

On June 17, 2013, Sally Kohn wrote an article in Time titled, *"Affirmative Action Has Helped White Women More Than Anyone."* Kohn provides this historical backdrop for the implementation, including the reasons why President Johnson added women: *"Originally, women weren't even included in legislation attempting to level the playing field in education and employment. The first affirmative-action measure in America was an executive order signed by President Kennedy in 1961 requiring that federal contractors "take affirmative action to ensure that applicants are employed, and employees are treated during employment, without regard to their race, creed, color, or national origin." In 1967, President Johnson amended this, and a subsequent measure included sex, recognizing that women also faced many discriminatory barriers and hurdles to equal opportunity."*[46] Kohn continues by stating that while Affirmative Action has helped people of color, it has disproportionately benefitted white women.

> *"While people of color, individually and as groups, have been helped by affirmative action in the subsequent years, data and studies suggest women — white women in particular — have benefited disproportionately. According to one study, in 1995, 6 million women, the majority of whom were white, had jobs they wouldn't have otherwise held but for affirmative action."*
>
> **-Sally Kohn**

The National Womens Law Center did a study on Affirmative Action and found that: *"Women of color have lagged particularly far behind in both employment and education. For example, in 1998, the median weekly salary for Black women was $400 compared to $468 for white women and $615 for white men. Hispanic women earned a median weekly income of only $337. Even in sectors where women have made inroads into management, minority women continue to be underrepresented. In the banking industry, only 2.6% of executive, managerial and administrative jobs were held by Black women, and 5% by Hispanic women, compared to 37.6% by white women. In the hospital industry, Black and Hispanic women each held 4.6% of these jobs, while white women held 50.2%. At the top, women of color represented only 11.2% of all corporate officers in Fortune 500 companies. Women of color also earn fewer college degrees than white women. In 1997, white women made up 39% of college undergraduates and 42% of graduate students; minority women were only 16% of undergraduates and 10% of graduate students."*[47]

Tim Wise had a paper published in the National Women's Studies Association Journal in the fall of 1998 titled, *"Is Sisterhood Conditional?: White Women and the Rollback of Affirmative Action."* His paper was about the reluctance of some white women to advocate for Affirmative Action despite the gains white women had achieved from the policy over the 30 years at that time, due to the policy.

"Thanks in large measure to affirmative action and civil rights protections that opened up previously restricted opportunities to women of all colors, from 1972-1993:

• The percentage of women architects increased from 3% to nearly 19% of the total;

• The percentage of women doctors more than doubled from 10% to 22% of all doctors;

• The percentage of women lawyers grew from 4% to 23% of the national total;

• The percentage of female engineers went from less than 1% to nearly 9%;
• The percentage of female chemists grew from 10% to 30% of all chemists; and,

• The percentage of female college faculty went from 28% to 42% of all faculty.

Furthermore, since only 1983, the percentage of women business managers and professionals grew from 41% of all such persons, to 48%, while the number of female police officers more than doubled, from 6% to 13% (U.S. Department of Commerce, Bureau of the Census 1995, Table 649). According to a 1995 study, there are at least six million women — the overwhelming majority of them white — who simply wouldn't have the jobs they have today, but for the

inroads made by affirmative action (Cose 1997, 171).
-Tim Wise[48]

The increased number of white women graduating college then entering into higher-paying fields formerly dominated by men raised the earnings of white women. Since white men were already disproportionately represented in high-paying positions, as white women married those men, their earnings combined with his further increased white household wealth. White women have been the number one beneficiary of Affirmative Action. At the same time, white women have been some of the fiercest in opposition to the policy.[49] There are white women in this country who recognize their confusing history in this regard and are working to fix it. But some don't seem to understand that affirmative action has helped them.

> *"It isn't Affirmative Action when a woman decided she needed or wanted to work outside of the household. If a woman isn't qualified she will not hold a position long at a job. Women have fought for their rightful place in the workforce, equal pay for equal skills, etc. You talk of laws that should have been given to blacks long before they were, I agree, but women were also denied many things in the past. Giving them the same rights as men is not being given an advantage, such as AA."*
> **-Anonymous white internet poster**

This is an example of the denial a portion of the white population has displayed pertaining to matters of race and overall American equal rights. Here is an example of a white female described by Tim Wise. These women gladly ride in the white grievance wagon, and then when a person of color begins breaking down white racism, she becomes the poor downtrodden colorblind female victim of sexism. Women like this who try playing both sides are no different than black "uncle toms." They only help keep things divided and hurt the efforts of white women who legitimately fight for social justice.

In America, we have sold ourselves the big lie of egalitarianism. At the most elementary level, egalitarianism would mean everybody was enslaved. It would mean Jim Crow laws denied everybody opportunity. But that's not the way it happened. Nor is it a part of modern America. If Critical Race Theory asserts that race is a construct created by whites used to further their interests, the American history of public policy destroys any opposition to this contention. Because of what was done, racism is embedded into or inherent in all American institutions. As I have tried showing in this chapter, there have indeed been legal decisions and public policies that advanced the interests of whites while denying blacks and members of other nonwhite groups. Critical Race Theory, as assumed by the American right, is entirely accurate in its analysis of the American system and how it has operated. For those who claim that Critical Race Theory is un-American, I beg to differ. If Critical Race Theory states what has been claimed, evidence shows it is as American as the Bald Eagle and the flag. The policies I presented are examples of: **"A government program providing benefits to a specific group."**

Per Merriam Webster, the full definition of entitlement is: **"A State or condition of being entitled. A right to benefits specified by law or contract. A government program providing benefits to a specific group. The belief that one is deserving of or entitled to certain privileges."** Our system has a problem that begins with an attitude not just of racism but the belief of white entitlement that comes with it. This entitlement mentality has those on the right complaining about cancel culture because people want to get rid of symbols that represent atrocities. This entitlement mentality has members of the American right refusing to recognize that a narrow segment of whites in America have demanded that people cancel their cultures to blend into a culture defined only by that same little segment. This is what assimilation has become.

This same entitlement mentality also has people complaining about the woke culture, which again is something that has come about for us to understand that we do live in a diverse society. One group does not get sole definitive power over what it means to be American. "Wokeism" also challenges traditional systems and does so to remake those systems to meet the needs of a diverse, multicultural society. We are that society whether the right-wing likes it or not. Assimilation in the future will require recognizing and accepting that while deconstructing and then rebuilding systems created under the old order to meet the modern reality of America.

> *"But lack of clarity about history is also a tragedy for greater society, because it leads to a false confidence about the simplicity of rectifying racial injustice through appeals to personal goodness rather than structural intervention."*[50]
>
> **-Emily Walton**

Africans Sold Other Africans!

"Africans sold their own people as slaves is a stock argument White Americans use when the subject of slavery comes up."

-Queen Adira

You cannot discuss racism without that one white person telling you how Africans enslaved and sold other Africans. This claim is supposed to absolve whites of their role in the slave trade or somehow equally implicate blacks for modern American racism. This is at best, a disingenuous claim. Blacks have not been perfect and African nations had conflicts just like every other nation or tribe on this planet during the history of the world. Many European cultures killed those who they captured in wars. Most African tribes enslaved prisoners of war. Slavery was used to pay off debt. Slavery was also a punishment for criminal behavior. There were sex slaves also. None of this is good or right but neither is the Africans sold other Africans' argument.

The problem with this narrative is there are two sides to this situation, but we primarily get told only one. Some here in America have dismissed the African side of the story, except to blame Africans for selling each other. Many whites also use the Trans Saharan slave trade or Arab trader argument to justify American slavery. The Arab Trader argument is that Muslims enslaved people in Africa, and because of this, whites cannot be held responsible for making slavery legal in America. I tried this type of argument with my mother as a child and found out how it does not have merit.

When I was 10, I went bike riding with some friends. We rode into an apartment complex and saw a pop machine sitting wide open, so we each took a can of soda pop and rode off. When I got home, I opened the soda and started drinking it. Enter mom, who knew we did not have any money when we took off. She asked me how I got the soda. Looking back, it would have ended better if I had lied and said I found a dime lying on the ground. In 1971 you could still buy pop in a machine for a dime. I did not do that. I told mom the truth. You could have fried an egg on my derriere about five seconds later.

As this was happening, I told her that other kids did it too, like that made it right. My mom did not have any of that. She informed me that we all were stealing, and she held me responsible for what I did. What the other kids did was of no concern to her as I was her child. The Arab trader argument uses the same "logic" I used with my mom to deny American racism. The Trans Saharan slave trade existed, but going back to the Pleistocene epoch to find an excuse to say that other nations did it too or how slavery has been practiced since the beginning of time is weak. While it is true that slavery existed in Africa before Europeans got there, the lie begins with the nature of African slavery while ignoring the fact that whites made slavery legal in America.

Before European colonization, it is written that Africa had up to 10,000 states or nations with different languages and customs. There have been numerous kingdoms and dynasties on that continent. Dr. Cheikh Anta Diop wrote that the ancient name of Africa was Alkebulan. [1],[2],[3] According to Dr. Diop this is what the continent was called by the Moors, Nubians, Numidians, Carthaginians, and Ethiopians. All of

93

these were nations in Alkebulan. The name Africa itself is said to have come from the Greeks and Romans. I write this so that we understand how distorted the European tale about Africa has been. Africa was not some barren land where everybody ran around in loincloths. We learn about the significant accomplishments of Egypt, but Egypt is in Africa. When Europeans arrived, Alkebulan was full of nations containing cities with universities, businesses, trade, and governments. The comment that Africans sold each other into slavery is disingenuous because these nations did not consider themselves Africans; they were citizens of their respective kingdoms. No different than the French, the Spanish, the Germans, and the Norwegians.

> *"Well if y'all are so advanced and superior how in the hell did blacks end up enslaved and oppressed by the evil ignorant inferior whitey like you claim!"*
> **-Anonymous White internet forum user 2018**

You are about to read an account from an African about what happened when Europeans showed up in Africa. His ancestors passed this story to each generation, and it was told to him by his elders.

> *"Even in this modern world, there are wars and rumors of war almost everywhere you go. There were wars in Europe in those days and there were wars in America. There were wars almost everywhere in the world. There were tribal wars in Africa too. The difference between the tribal wars in Africa and the wars in the outside world was that, in the outside world, the conquered were often butchered (due in part to the highly sophisticated weapons of war used) whereas the conquered in Africa (excluding Arabs/ Muslims in the north) became part of the conqueror. In other words, while no enemy was left standing in the outside world, the conquered enemies were left to*

live and serve in Africa.

So it is true there were some "slaves" in Africa in those days before the white man came. However, those "slaves" were not taken purposely to become "slaves" of another kingdom or empire. They were just victims of tribal wars and it was somehow "better" than what was happening in the outside world where no enemy was allowed to live.

Was Africa one nation? Were Africans one people? Were the Europeans in Africa just to trade? If Africans willingly participated in the "trade" then why would the Europeans bring battle troops and weapons of war all the way from Europe to Africa? Why the so many "Europeans against Natives" wars in African history and what were the Europeans fighting for in Africa? Were the European currencies of any value to Africans? Was there a common currency in Africa? Which currency was used to buy slaves in Africa? Did Africans willingly trade ship-loads of "valuable" slaves for just bottles of wine? Does the Bible permit slavery and slave trade? Why did the church participate in the slave trade?

I read an article online today and I was shocked to read so many people believe Africans sold their own brothers and sisters into slavery just like that. I wanted to comment on the article but the comment section had been disabled and that is why I am making this post to let people know that we Africans (my ancestors) weren't that stupid to have sold our own brothers and sisters into slavery just like that. We were stupid to have allowed ourselves to be manipulated by the foreigners (my people used to refer to the white men as "white strangers" so pardon me if you see a "white stranger" in my post). We were stupid to have trusted the "white stranger" in the first place and we were stupid to have allowed the "white stranger" into our land. My people allowed the white strangers into our land because they (the white strangers) said they "come in peace".

Before I continue, I am not a historian and I don't claim to be one. However, I am an African and I cherish our oral traditions. I did study history in school (in Africa) and I was taught by someone who actually knew what he was talking about.

In continuation, please note that there were 2 types of slave trading in Africa. The one introduced mostly by the coming of Islam through the Arab raiders and traders from the Middle East and North Africa or the Trans-Saharan slave trade and the one introduced by the coming of the Europeans or the Trans-Atlantic Slave Trade (the one I am talking about). The Trans-Saharan Slave Trade is deeply rooted in the Islamic cultures of several countries in the North (especially in the Maghreb region or the "Berber world") and still practiced although "silently" by Muslim-dominant countries such as Mauritania and Libya.

According to my grandfather, In those days when there were no Christianity and no modern day government systems in Africa, Kings, Queens, and other traditional rulers ruled their kingdoms as heads of state and judged cases according to the rules and regulations of the land. Those who disobeyed the laws of the land were punished and those who obeyed and sacrificed for the land were rewarded accordingly. Although every land had some "prison" facilities, those prisons weren't meant for large groups of criminals so those who killed were killed. Those who stole paid dearly for it. Those who slept with people's wives were banished from the land. Children who disobeyed elders were punished accordingly. And so on.

My country Ghana in West Africa was a major Slave Trading Post (Headquarters) where slaves from different parts of Africa were brought and arranged before shipping abroad.

When the white strangers first came to Africa, We (my ancestors) were not sure about their intentions so most communities drove them away from their land. However, the white strangers managed to convince some of our traditional rulers that they had not come to cause any harm but just to preach the good news (the Bible) and also to trade with the local people. It was barter trading where goods were exchanged for goods. My country Ghana was called "Gold Coast" because gold was in abundance. Although my ancestors valued gold as a precious metal, the white strangers valued it more as a precious mineral worth more than blood in some cases. In other words, my ancestors had the gold and the white strangers needed the gold and had to trade things like bottles of wine, clothing and textiles, guns and ammunitions, etc. for pieces of gold. That was how the "trade" started.

Some of the local chiefs along the coast started accepting the white strangers by giving them place to stay. The white strangers started building missionary centers where they stayed and preached the gospel and also traded with the local people. The white strangers later on expanded those missionary centers (including churches and cathedrals) into forts and castles where they packed slaves before shipping them abroad.

The white strangers did not understand the local language and the local people did not understand *a word the white strangers were saying so it made communication very difficult. To help break the language barrier, the white strangers went to the local rulers and asked the local rulers to give them some of the local people to train so they could speak the foreign language which would make communication easier but none of those local rulers were ready to give their people out to go stay with strangers.*

Later on, some of the local rulers came up with an idea that, instead of killing those criminals, they could actually give those criminals to the white strangers so the white strangers could preach the good news they said they came to preach to those criminals, change them into good people and also train them in the foreign language in order to aid communication which was better than killing those criminals. So the traditional rulers gave those criminals out to the white strangers and to show appreciation, those white strangers gave gifts like textiles, bottles of wine, mirrors, etc. to the traditional rulers. That was how the white strangers got their first "local servers."

Those local people (the criminals) lived and served the white strangers in the castles and forts and learned the foreign language which enabled them to serve as mediators translating the local language for the white strangers and the foreign language to the local people. This helped a lot in communication.

As I mentioned earlier on, those local servers living with the white strangers were the criminals in the society and although they served as mediators and made communication a whole lot easier, they also made life a living hell for the local people (some as a form of revenge). For example, when the white strangers sent them to go collect taxes (lets say 5 pieces of gold), those criminals added their own taxes and made it 8 pieces of gold. At times too, they mis-translated just so they could get more power. Some of those criminals even became more powerful than the traditional rulers. In other words, the white strangers, after preaching the good news to those criminals, turned them into even far more dangerous monsters than they were before. Why? Because only the white man had guns at that time and they shot anyone the criminals considered "criminals."

Those criminals were the few "Africans" who helped the white strangers to get more slaves. However, don't forget the fact that they were criminals condemned to death in their various societies for being "Un-African."

Those local people living with the white strangers served and "worshiped" them so well to the point where the white strangers began asking for more. Because of the benefits they derived from those local servers, some of the white strangers took some local servers with them on their return home. Back home (abroad), they found those local servers (the black men from Africa) very useful and decided to come back for more. They realized they could use them to work on their plantation farms back home to make more money. They also realized they could sell some of those 'local servers' to their friends and countrymen and make more money and that was why most of them (the white strangers but this time around slave traders) returned with the intention of picking more local servers (this time around, slaves).

So they returned for slaves but no local ruler was ready to give their people out except those criminals I mentioned earlier on and prisoners of war (tribal wars). In my country for example, the Ashantis and *those living in the interior parts of the country did not want to have anything to do with the white strangers. In fact, the first white stranger that set foot on the Ashanti empire did not return.*

However, the white strangers needed slaves and more slaves but there was no easy way of getting slaves in Africa. So what they did was that, they created confusion among the various tribes so that there would be more tribal wars and more war prisoners so they could get more "slaves" and that was exactly what they did.

Before the white man came to Africa, tribal wars were mostly fought with swords, spears, bows and arrows. Although these weapons were lethal they were nowhere near as quick and fatal as the gun. The problem here was that, only the white strangers had guns and decided which tribal group to support in times of battle. Any tribal group the white strangers supported with their powerful cannons, guns and ammunitions, easily conquered their enemies. This also created another major problem. The white strangers did not support any tribal group for free. In fact, the white strangers started demanding taxes (which included pieces of gold and prisoners of war) and total submission after victory. Any tribal group or community which failed to submit to the Europeans and pay taxes were wiped out. Sometimes the leaders of those communities were executed publicly as a form of warning to neighboring communities. Most communities in Africa were turned into concentration camps with European authorities in place.

Although not often mentioned in history books, there were well trained and well equiped European troops all across Sub-Saharan Africa and they fought several battles with native tribes who refused to submit to European authority and that explains the several "European against natives" wars in the African history.

In other words, my ancestors were not ready to give their own brothers and sisters out into slavery. In fact, most fought and died in battle just to save their communities from the hands of those white strangers. Rather, the white strangers were the ones who "demonically" manipulated my people by creating so much confusion between the various tribes and creating so many tribal wars all in an effort to get slaves.

In Ghana for example, because the Ashanti empire was so powerful to defeat, the white strangers created so much confusion and so many wars between the Ashantis and the neighboring tribes and in most cases supplied some of those neighboring tribes with guns to enable them defeat the Ashantis. The white strangers continued this until they were able to defeat the Ashantis and took away the king of the Ashantis (Nana Prempeh I) and the queen mother (Nana Yaa Asantewaa) and several others into exile just to break the Ashanti kingdom apart even after slavery so they could colonize and control the Ashanti gold,etc.

To conclude, my ancestors did not sell their own brothers and sisters into slavery just like that. They were deceived and "demonically" manipulated by those white strangers who visited our land."[4]

The Schomburg Center for the Research of Black Culture has excellent information about the African slave trade that provides a stark contrast between what happened and what some use as an excuse to discount the experiences of blacks in America. The website is named *"The Abolition of the Slave Trade-African Resistance."* The information contained in this collection debunks the race baited tales presented by some in America today.

> *"Africans started to fight the transatlantic slave trade as soon as it began. Their struggles were multifaceted and covered four continents over four centuries. Still, they have often been underestimated, overlooked, or forgotten. African resistance was reported in European sources only when it concerned attacks on slave ships and company barracoons, but acts of resistance also took place far from the coast and thus escaped the slavers' attention. To discover them, oral history, archaeology, and autobiographies and biographies of African victims of the slave trade have to be probed. Taken together, these various sources offer a detailed image of the varied strategies Africans used to defend themselves from and mount attacks against the slave trade.*
>
> *The Africans' resistance continued in the Americas. They ran away, established maroon communities, used sabotage, conspired, and rose against those who held them in captivity. Freed people petitioned the authorities, led information campaigns, and worked actively to abolish the slave trade and slavery.*
>
> *In Europe, black abolitionists launched or participated in civic movements to end the deportation and enslavement of Africans. They too delivered speeches, provided information, wrote newspaper articles and books. Using violent as well as nonviolent means, Africans in Africa, the Americas, and Europe were constantly involved in the fight against the slave trade and slavery."*[5]

Africa's role in the slave trade as told by a segment of white society is incomplete and lacking in fact. It was not so simple as blacks capturing each other and selling them to whites. Europeans did not just waltz into Africa and overwhelm a bunch of backward, naked, dumb savages. They were in a fight for 400 years. Many Europeans entered Africa, and Africa ended up being their final resting place.

"Some leaders actively worked against the transatlantic slave trade. One of the most famous was Abdel Kader Kane, the Muslim leader of the Futa Toro region in northern Senegal. Kane had succeeded in peopling his kingdom by retaking by force his people who had been kidnapped and by forbidding slave caravans from passing through his territory. After the French took three children from Futa, Kane sent a letter to the governor:

"We are warning you that all those who will come to our land to trade [in slaves] will be killed and massacred if you do not send our children back. Would not somebody who was very hungry abstain from eating if he had to eat something cooked with his blood? We absolutely do not want you to buy Muslims under any circumstances. I repeat that if your intention is to always buy Muslims you should stay home and not come to our country anymore. Because all those who will come can be assured that they will lose their life."[6]

We get told stories about the shackles and chains, but not really why they were necessary. It is just "you sold your own into balls and chains." But things just did not happen as some have chosen to believe.

"As the slave trade expanded, resistance to it grew as well, and the need for shackles, guns, ropes, chains,

iron balls, and whips tells an eloquent story of continuous and violent struggle from the hinterland to the high seas. As one slave trader remarked:

For the security and safekeeping of the slaves on board or on shore in the African barracoons, chains, leg irons, handcuffs, and strong houses are used. I would remark that this also is one of the forcible necessities resorted to for the preservation of the order, and as recourse against the dangerous consequences of this traffic."

"Wherever possible, such as in Saint-Louis and Gorée (Senegal), James (Gambia), and Bance (Sierra Leone), the Europeans' barracoons were located on islands, which made escapes and attacks more difficult. In some areas, as soon as local people approached the boats, the crew is ordered to take up arms, the cannons are aimed, and the fuses are lighted . . . One must, without any hesitation, shoot at them and not spare them. The loss of the vessel and the life of the crew are at stake."

"The heavily fortified forts and barracoons attest to the Europeans' distrust and apprehension. They had to protect themselves, as Jean-Baptiste Durand of the Compagnie du Sénégal explained, from the foreign vessels and from the Negroes living in the country."

"These precautions notwithstanding, in the eighteenth century, Fort Saint-Joseph on the Senegal River was attacked and all commerce was interrupted for six years. Several conspiracies and actual revolts by captives erupted on Gorée Island and resulted in the death of the governor and several soldiers. In addition, the crews of quite a few slave ships were killed on the River Gambia; in Sierra Leone, people

sacked the captives' quarters of the infamous trader
John Ormond. Similar incidents occurred in other
parts of the African coast. Written records document
how Africans on shore attacked more than a hundred
ships.

Some Western slavers maintained occult centers
in their barracoons, staffed by men they paid to work
on the captives, sometimes with medicinal plants.
The objective was to kill any spirit of rebellion, to
tame the detainees, and make them accept their fate.
The existence of these centers shows the extent of the
precautions taken by slavers to prevent rebellions on
land and during the Middle Passage: shackles and
guns controlled the body, while the spirit was broken.

But revolts on slave ships, although extremely
difficult to organize and conduct, were numerous.
**About 420 revolts have been documented in
slavers' papers, and they do not represent the
totality. It is estimated that 100,000 Africans
died in uprisings on the coast or during the
Middle Passage. The fear of revolts resulted
in additional costs for the slavers: larger
crews, heavy weapons, and barricades. About
18 percent of the costs of the Middle Passage
were incurred due to measures to thwart
uprisings, and the captives who rose up saved,
according to estimates, one million Africans
from deportation by driving up the slavers'
expenses."**[7]

Let me stop right here with this. The narrative of the
African running up to whites on the African coast yelling, "We
got slaves for sale," is untrue. Many have written in detail
about the resistance Africans waged against slavery. The
claim that whites ended slavery is false because slavery was

first ended in Haiti thanks to Jean-Jacques Dessalines and Toussaint L'Ouverture. The tired diversion of "Africans sold each other into slavery" is used as an out by the same white subculture that has always had problems with race. Africans did not make the laws in America. It is time to look at what the American government allowed to be done to the Africans that ended up here.

America could have avoided the problems created by slavery; instead, there were a series of choices made by those in power to create divisions to maintain that power. They used race to get it done. In 1970, Ebony magazine published an article by Lerone Bennett titled *"The Road Not Taken."* It is from a book Bennett wrote called "The Shaping of Black America." This is a fascinating article detailing how America made decisions that created the racism or racial hierarchy that still exists in our country. In 1619 whites unofficially invented the race card in America. Whites, specifically wealthy elites, invented this card to maintain power and control.

"The race problem in America was a deliberate invention of men who systematically separated blacks and whites in order to make money"
-Lerone Bennett[8]

When people start talking about race, there are just some simple realities that cannot be denied. If you are white and don't like how whites are portrayed, start thinking about how unpleasant it is for us who are not white to be described as weak inferior people who got conquered by a supposedly superior race and culture. It is not a pleasant subject. For this to end we all must face the unpleasantness.

The doctrine of **Partus Sequitur Ventrem** comes from European civil law. It means, "That which is brought forth follows the belly."[9] This principle determined the status of children born by slave women in America.

December, 1662. Act XII: Negro women's children to serve according to the condition of the mother. Whereas some doubts have arisen whether children got by any Englishman upon a negro woman should be slave or free, Be it therefore enacted and declared by this present grand assembly, that all children borne in this country shall be held bond or free only according to the condition of the mother, And that if any Christian shall commit fornication with a negro man or woman, he or she so offending shall pay double the fines imposed by the former act.[10]

Partus Sequitur Ventrem removed male slave owners from any obligation he may have for children born resulting from his "relations" with enslaved women. It gave the slaver the ability to sell children by taking them away from their biological parents at any time. **Partus Sequitur Ventrem** was the doctrine that created the first family separation policy in America. This principle does not appear to have been a part of the system of African slavery. It is now time for me to stop wasting words explaining or defending anything against the excuse primarily right-wing whites in America have used to diminish what was done here sanctioned by American law. Let us now look at what happened once the Africans landed in the so-called "New World."

"The historian Kenneth Stampp, in his remarkable book "The Peculiar Institution," has a fascinating section on the psychological indoctrination that was necessary from the master's point of view to make a good slave. He gathered the material for this section primarily from the manuals and other documents which were produced by slaveowners on the subject of training slaves. Stampp notes five recurring aspects of this training.

First, those who managed the slaves had to maintain strict discipline. One master said, "Unconditional submission is the only footing upon which slavery should be placed." Another said, "The slave must know that his master is to govern absolutely and he is to obey implicitly, that he is never, for a moment, to exercise either his will or judgement in opposition to a positive order." Second, the masters felt that they had to implant in the bondsman a consciousness of personal inferiority. This sense of inferiority was deliberately extended to his past. The slaveowners were convinced that in order to control the Negroes, the slaves "had to feel that African ancestry tainted them, that their color was a badge of degradation." The third step in the training process was to awe the slaves with a sense of the masters' enormous power. It was necessary, various owners said, "to make then stand in fear." The fourth aspect was the attempt to "persuade the bondsman to take in an interest in the master's enterprise and to accept his standards of good conduct." Thus, the master's criteria of what was good and true and beautiful were to be accepted unquestionably by the slaves. The final step, according to Stampp's documents, was "to impress Negroes with their helplessness: to create in them a habit of perfect dependence upon their masters."

Here, then, was the way to manage the slaves. Accustom him to rigid discipline, demand from him unconditional submission, impress upon him a sense of his innate inferiority, develop in him a paralyzing fear of white men, train him to adopt the master's code of good behavior, and instill in him a sense of complete dependence."

-Dr. Martin Luther King Jr.[11]

Slavery came equipped with a company "orientation" program. This "orientation" was called seasoning. In this program, slaves did not learn about the company's history, employee policy, workplace safety, vacation time, or company benefit packages. The slave orientation program was between 1 to 7 years.[12] During "seasoning," Africans were robbed of their names, language, culture, mores, history, spirituality and forced to assimilate into a European-style culture. They were forced to adapt to o'dark to o'dark working hours, poor nutrition, and miserable, unsanitary living conditions. If disease didn't kill them, slaves endured physical and psychological torture so brutal that it is estimated that between 7 and 50 percent of the slaves in this "orientation" program died.[13] The object of this training program was to prepare the slaves for work on the plantation. "Seasoning" was the original cancel culture.

> *"Many died in the first few weeks or months from dysentery, malnutrition, several types of worm infections, change of diet and climate, and the White man's diseases. One reason is that the Slaves were terribly weakened by the trauma of the Middle Passage voyage and the addition of exposure to diseases, inadequate nutrition, bad water, work exhaustion from being unaccustomed to the "sunrise-to-sunset gang labor," and cruelty were simply overwhelming. Immediately, new owners and their overseers obliterated the identities of their newly acquired Slaves by breaking their wills and by severing any bonds with their African past. Such occurred while the Slaves were being forced to adapt to new and horrendous working and living conditions; to learn a new language; and to adopt new customs."[14]*

Again, America had every chance not to implement slavery. We are told how the so-called founders of this country created the way to end slavery when they wrote the constitution.

Many will cite the fact they made the importation of slaves illegal by 1808 as evidence. But refusing to stop importing slaves did not end the slaving business in the United States. What it produced was an original American industry-slave breeding.

> *"During the fifty-three years from the prohibition of the African slave trade by federal law in 1808 to the debacle of the Confederate States of America in 1861, the Southern economy depended on the functioning of a slave-breeding industry, of which Virginia was the number-one supplier."*[15]

If America had continued to import slaves, it would have diluted the market, thereby driving down the price of slaves. Slave sellers could not have this. So instead of the truth, we are told that "our nearer to God than thee" founders, in all their benevolent glory, looked towards a future whereby slavery would be no more. According to some, the so-called founders had a dream whereby little black boys and little black girls would no longer be enslaved because of the color of their skin. This is the story we are supposed to believe. However, reality does not show that.

> *"In fact, most American slaves were not kidnapped on another continent. Though over 12.7 million Africans were forced onto ships to the Western hemisphere, estimates only have 400,000-500,000 landing in present-day America. How then to account for the four million black slaves who were tilling fields in 1860? "The South," the Sublettes write, "did not only produce tobacco, rice, sugar, and cotton as commodities for sale; it produced people." Slavers called slave-breeding "natural increase," but there was nothing natural about producing slaves; it took scientific management. Thomas Jefferson bragged to George Washington that the birth of black children*

was increasing Virginia's capital stock by four percent annually."[16]

To be blunt, America had slave breeding "factories" where enslaved people were forced to breed. I call them actories, but they are described as farms in most cases. These "farms" generally had at least a 2:1 female to male ratio.[17] In some states, slave production was the number 1 industry. Virginia led the nation in slave production, and PRESIDENT Thomas Jefferson was one of the leading producers. The slave breeding industry has been ignored by many in the discussion of American exceptionalism.

After reading about this "industry," it becomes very easy to see why. There are just some wrongs that cannot be excused. The bottom line here is that the slave breeding industry manufactured human beings to be sold into labor. It is tough to read the atrocities associated with such a practice and not get angry. To hear people today dismiss the entire enterprise of slavery like it was just some short-term inconsequential inconvenience this country experienced for a little while that we as blacks should forget is crazy. For someone black to mimic that opinion is just pure accommodationist lunacy. If you think that is a radical opinion, consider the stories from former slaves you are about to read.

My master often went to the house, got drunk, and then came out to the field to whip, cut, slash, curse, swear, beat and knock down several, for the smallest offense, or nothing at all.

He divested a poor female slave of all wearing apparel, tied her down to stakes, and whipped her with a handsaw until he broke it over her naked body. In process of time, he ravished her person and became the father of a child by her. Besides, he always kept a colored Miss in the house with him. This is another curse of Slavery concubinage and illegitimate connections which is carried on to an alarming extent in the far South. A poor slave man who lives close by his wife is permitted to visit her but very seldom, and other men, both white and colored, cohabit with her. It is undoubtedly the worst place of incest and bigamy in the world. A white man thinks nothing of putting a colored man out to carry the fore row [front row in field work] and carry on the same sport with the colored man's wife at the same time.

I know these facts will seem too awful to relate, but I am constrained to write of such revolting deeds, as they are some of the real "dark deeds of American Slavery." Then, kind reader, pursue my narrative, remembering that I give no fiction in my details of horrid scenes. Nay, believe, with me, that the half can never be told of the misery the poor slaves are still suffering in this so-called land of freedom.

-WILLIAM J. ANDERSON, Life and Narrative of William J. Anderson, Twenty-Four Years a Slave, 1857[18]

[Patsy] had a genial and pleasant temper and was faithful and obedient. Naturally, she was a joyous creature, a laughing, light-hearted girl, rejoicing in the mere sense of existence. Yet Patsy wept oftener and suffered more than any of her companions. She had been literally excoriated. Her back bore the scars of a thousand stripes not because she was backward in her work, nor because she was of an unmindful and rebellious spirit, but because it had fallen to her lot to be the slave of a licentious master and a jealous mistress. She shrank before the lustful eye of the one and was in danger even of her life at the hands of the other, and between the two she was indeed accursed.

In the great house, for days together, there were

high and angry words, pouting and estrangement, whereof she was the innocent cause. Nothing delighted the mistress so much as to see her suffer, and more than once, when Epps had refused to sell her, has she tempted me with bribes to put her secretly to death and bury her body in some lonely place in the margin of the swamp. Gladly would Patsy Have? appeased this unforgiving spirit if it had been in her power, but not like Joseph, dared she escape from Master Epps, leaving her garment in his hand. Patsy walked under a cloud. If she uttered a word in opposition to her master's will, the lash was resorted to at once to bring her to subjection. If she was not watchful when about her cabin, or when walking in the yard, a billet of wood or a broken bottle, perhaps, hurled from her mistress' hand, would smite her unexpectedly in the face. The enslaved victim of lust and hate, Patsy had no comfort of her life.

-SOLOMON NORTHUP, Twelve Years a Slave: Narrative of Solomon Northup, 1853[19]

I was regarded as fair-looking for one of my race, and for four years a white man I spare the world his name had base designs upon me. I do not care to dwell upon this subject, for it is one that is fraught with pain. Suffice it to say that he persecuted me for four years, and I became a mother. The child of which he was the father was the only child that I ever brought into the world. If my poor boy ever suffered any humiliating pangs on account of birth, he could not blame his mother, for God knows that she did not wish to give him life. He must blame the edicts of that society which deemed it no crime to undermine the virtue of girls in my then position.

-ELIZABETH KECKLEY, Behind the Scenes: Or, Thirty Years a Slave, and Four Years in the White House, 1868[20]

This industry included the first "employer"-based health care program. Enslaved women were the first people in America to get free health care. I do not say this to be funny because the reason why that happened was both sad and simple; after the importation of slaves was made illegal, dependence on slave labor hinged on the continued births of children by healthy slave women. The only way left to maintain the system was by increasing the number of slaves through births. Due to this, a black woman's ability to reproduce was of the utmost economic importance to southern planters and slave breeders. Because of that, slave owners had to monitor the health of slave women. But since the overall goal was the mass production of human beings, slave women often began "breeding" while very young and were forced to have numerous children. Most slave women could "retire" after 10-15 births. If they lived.

> *"The blacks are immeasurably better off here than in Africa, morally, socially & physically. The painful discipline they are undergoing, is necessary for their instruction as a race, & I hope will prepare & lead them to better things. How long their subjugation may be necessary is known & ordered by a wise Merciful Providence."*
>
> **-Robert E. Lee**[21]

I think we need to understand how depraved things were during these times. The range of crimes went from rape to castration.[22] A practice called Buck Breaking was used to control slave uprisings.[23] If an enslaved man was considered a troublemaker, the slave master would give that slave a severe beating. Once the slave was beaten basically unconscious, the slave master made the other slaves lay him over a tree stump where his pants would be taken off, and the slave owner would perform sodomy on that slave. Enslaved men were forced to have sex with each other in front of their families and they were also raped in front of their sons.[24] Many of these men would kill themselves or run away after this happened to them. However, buck breaking was not the only abuse suffered by slaves.

Gay people are not a product of modern "liberals." Gays and lesbians have always been part of the world community. Gay slave owners existed. Gay slave owners bought male slaves. Gay slave owners raped their slaves. Black men were raped for pleasure. "Sex Farms" were created to breed black men for gay white men to have sex with.[25] Gay white men would travel from plantation to plantation for "sex parties." in order to rape slaves. I really do not know any other way to describe this because the black men involved really had no choice in what was happening to them.

As I wrote earlier, breeding factories were in business to increase the population of black people by forcing them to have sex to maintain slave labor. The derogatory term "motherfucker" derives from this practice. In many cases, black men had to sleep with their daughters, mothers, or sisters. Refusal to do so could end up in death.[26] Black women were forced to sleep with their fathers, sons, and brothers. They were also routinely raped by slave owners. This went on in the southern United States, South America, and the Caribbean. Still, with all this happening, whites believed it was blacks who lacked sexual self-control and morals.

"By a conservative estimate, in 1860 the total value of American slaves was $4 billion, far more than the gold and silver then circulating nationally ($228.3 million, "most of it in the North," the authors add), total currency ($435.4 million), and even the value of the South's total farmland ($1.92 billion). Slaves were, to slavers, worth more than everything else they could imagine combined."[27]

In today's money, slaves were worth over 127 billion

dollars. That is a conservative estimate, meaning the amount could be even more. In 1860 the total value of slaves was 17- and one-half times more than the money circulating in the economy. Slaves were worth more than the gold, silver, total U.S. currency, plus all the farmland in the South combined in 1860, but did not receive a dime. Remember that enslaved people were considered property. Because they were, the following activity could occur.

During slavery, wealthy slave owners securitized slavery. That's right. I said they securitized slavery. Slave owners created and sold slave-backed securities. Your eyes are not playing tricks on you. Let me repeat, slave owners securitized slavery, and the securities were sold internationally. Wall Street should be called Slavery Street; this is the cold reality on which American capitalism has been built. Cornell professors Edward E. Baptist and Louis Hyman detailed how it was done in an article published by the Chicago Sun-Times on its website dated March 7, 2014. This is from the article:

> *In the 1830s, powerful Southern slaveowners wanted to import capital into their states so they could buy more slaves. They came up with a new, two-part idea: mortgaging slaves; and then turning the mortgages into bonds that could be marketed all over the world.*

> *First, American planters organized new banks, usually in new states like Mississippi and Louisiana. Drawing up lists of slaves for collateral, the planters then mortgaged them to the banks they had created, enabling themselves to buy additional slaves to expand cotton production. To provide capital for those loans, the banks sold bonds to investors from around the globe — London, New York, Amsterdam, Paris. The bond buyers, many of whom lived in countries where slavery was illegal, didn't own individual slaves — just bonds backed by their value. Planters' mortgage*

payments paid the interest and the principle on these bond payments. Enslaved human beings had been, in modern financial lingo, "securitized."

As slave-backed mortgages became paper bonds, everybody profited — except, obviously, enslaved African Americans whose forced labor repaid owners' mortgages. But investors owed a piece of slave-earned income. Older slave states such as Maryland and Virginia sold slaves to the new cotton states, at securitization-inflated prices, resulting in slave asset bubble. Cotton factor firms like the now-defunct Lehman Brothers — founded in Alabama — became wildly successful. Lehman moved to Wall Street, and for all these firms, every transaction in slave-earned money flowing in and out of the U.S. earned Wall Street firms a fee.

The infant American financial industry nourished itself on profits taken from financing slave traders, cotton brokers and underwriting slave-backed bonds. But though slavery ended in 1865, in the years after the Civil War, black entrepreneurs would find themselves excluded from a financial system originally built on their bodies.
-Edward E. Baptist and Louis Hyman, American Finance Grew on the Back of Slaves[28]

As I read the accounts from the slaves, the stories of buck breaking and sex farms, it made me sick to my stomach. Then reading again about the callous nature of such people to create interest-bearing financial tools backed by human lives made me angry. How could one not be? Yet some in America right now have decided it is wrong for blacks today to be upset about this. We are told to forget about it. NEVER!

"What happened is beyond comprehension. It was

horrendous and wrong. Why do you continuously post these things? History can't be changed. No white guilt, we didn't participate."
-White internet forum poster 2020

I sometimes understand how white extremists can get tired of hearing how the belief in their supremacy is a bunch of psychosis-riddled babbling. Perhaps I could have more sympathy for the extremists that hijacked conservatism if they had not spent the last 40 years preaching about a return to the nation of our so-called founders, complete with Christian nationalist theology, along with lectures to us as blacks about personal responsibility. The quote above was made by a person who read a post about sex farms and buck breaking. Like many other whites in the racist subculture, she had words to say about Africans selling Africans. But when confronted by what Africans did not do, she produced the "I wasn't there, I didn't do it," defense.

"According to database-backed estimates by David Eltis and David Richardson, only about 389,000 kidnapped Africans were disembarked in the ports of the present-day United States, the majority of them before independence."[29]
"By 1860, those few hundred thousand Africans had given way to four million African Americans."
-Ned & Constance Sublette,
The American Slave Coast: A History of
the Slave-Breeding Industry[30]

According to the Sublette's, 389,000 slaves landed on the shores of what is now America. By 1860 there were 4 million slaves living here. The importation of slaves was made illegal in 1808. So from 1808 until 1860, the number of slaves increased by at least 1,000 percent. If we allow for the Africans selling each other, Africans would be responsible for approximately 389 thousand slaves. What about the 3.1-4 million additional slaves? Africans did not create them. This was done by forced slave breeding for business, pleasure, and entertainment. The depth of this atrocity matches anything spoken about Hitler. We are talking about babies taken from their mom and sold, mulatto children murdered by jealous wives, or sold away from their mothers by a husband who wanted to keep his cheating or raping a female slave a secret. If you saw the movie Mandingo, understand that such things really happened.

If I buy drugs from a drug dealer, it is not the drug dealer's fault I became an addict. I chose to purchase the drugs. In the same way, Europeans decided to invade Africa and purchase African war captives. I have not been able to find research whereby Africans loaded up slave vessels that landed in Europe to sell slaves. I see no record of any West African shipping company that sailed the Atlantic, dropping off slaves in South America, the Caribbean, and then America. As I wrote earlier, things are not as simple as "Africans sold other Africans into slavery." It is not as simple as blacks invented slavery and that we should be forever grateful to whites for being so kind as to end it. I was told as a child that half the truth equals a lie. Half the truth is what the tale of Africans selling other Africans is. You cannot make a sale if no one buys. I learned that the hard way years ago while trying to sell insurance. Africans did not own the shipping companies that carried the slaves to America, nor did they swim across the Atlantic to get here. Finally, Africans did not make U.S. laws.

This book is about racism in America, and it is way past time for the whites who make excuses to face the truth. We are far beyond talking about slavery. Slavery is only part of the issue. To waste time explaining how slavery was different in Africa than what became the Trans-Atlantic Slave trade has been done and will continue to be done by people far greater than I. Everything is not the same as slavery, and not everybody has had the same experience as blacks in America. *Awww...the poor snowflakes. Who the hell isn't "wounded"? Hundreds of thousands of Irish people came here under indentured servitude, which wasn't much better than slavery.*

-Anonymous white internet poster

That is one of the greatest falsehoods that has manifested itself in the discourse about racism in America. For years I even believed that. I remember reading a book titled *"Trinity"* written by Leon Uris, about a fictional hero of the Irish resistance named Conor Larkin. The story detailed the treatment of the Irish from the 1700s until the 1916 uprising. After reading that book, I was convinced that the Irish had it just as bad as blacks. Yes, the Irish were treated terribly in Europe and when they first came to America. But they were not slaves. Irish historians such as Liam Hogan have made this crystal clear.

"I conservatively estimate that tens of millions of people have been exposed to 'Irish slaves' disinformation in one form or another on social media."

-Liam Hogan[31]

The intent here is not to dismiss the history of Irish citizens of this country but to destroy a popular white supremacist meme that has plagued social media and American culture for years. From 2015 until 2019, Liam Hogan compiled some 52 different articles debunking the tale of Irish slavery. According to Hogan and other Irish historians, the Irish were indentured servants and not slaves. The fallacy in the white supremacist argument lies in the fact that indentured servitude was a contractual agreement made between 2 or more parties. One party agreed that for payment of passage to America, the individual(s) would work for a specified term to repay the cost of passage. Generally, when servitude was done, the former indentured servant received a headright. Slavery was permanent. There were no headrights for slaves.

> *"The tale of the Irish slaves is rooted in a false conflation of indentured servitude and chattel slavery. These are not the same. Indentured servitude was a form of bonded labour, whereby a migrant agreed to work for a set period of time (between two and seven years) and in return the cost of the voyage across the Atlantic was covered. Indentured servitude was a colonial innovation that enabled many to emigrate to the New World while providing a cheap and white labour force for planters and merchants to exploit. Those who completed their term of service were awarded 'freedom dues' and were free. The vast majority of labourers who agreed to this system did so voluntarily, but there were many who were forcibly transplanted from the British Isles to the colonies and sold into indentured service against their will. While these forced deportees would have included political prisoners and serious felons, it is believed that the majority came from the poor and vulnerable. This forced labour was in essence an extension of the English Poor Laws, e.g. in 1697. John Locke recommended the whipping of those who 'refused to work' and the herding of beggars into workhouses. Indeed this criminalisation of the poor continues into the 21st century. In any case, all bar the serious felons were freed once the term of their contract expired."*
>
> **- Liam Hogan**[32]

The general argument to dismiss or derail conversations about the treatment of blacks is that everybody had it tough. That is true, but everybody else CHOSE to come to America. It does not appear that the majority of the more than 12 million Africans shipped across the Atlantic made any contractual agreement to perform labor in return for passage. So yes, the Europeans that chose to come here with little or nothing did struggle. Indeed, the Irish did endure difficulties. But the various European ethnic groups had one thing they used to lift themselves—the race card.

"Whiteness is a social construct, and one with concrete benefits. Being white in the U.S. has long meant better jobs and opportunities, and an escape from persecution based on appearance and culture. Although these structural advantages remain, the meaning of whiteness is still hotly debated."
-Sarah Kendzior, How do you become "white" in America?[33]

Many people claim to have suffered like blacks. Native Americans have a legitimate claim based on the genocide committed by the American government. Chinese were prevented from coming here by written law. But others? I will cite two groups, the Irish and the Polish. Upon coming to this country, both groups were considered lesser and inferior. Irish and blacks competed for the same jobs in the north and were relegated to low-wage, menial labor. Irish and blacks in the north lived in the same communities. Both groups mixed socially, intermarried, and had biracial children.

"In the early years of immigration the poor Irish and blacks were thrown together, very much part of the same class competing for the same jobs. In the census of 1850, the term mulatto appears for the first time due primarily to inter-marriage between Irish and African Americans. The Irish were often referred to as Negroes turned inside out and Negroes as smoked Irish. A famous quip of the time attributed to a black man went something like this: "My master is a great tyrant, he treats me like a common Irishman." Free blacks and Irish were viewed by the Nativists as related, somehow similar, performing the same tasks

in society. It was felt that if amalgamation between the races was to happen, it would happen between Irish and blacks. But, ultimately, the Irish made the decision to embrace whiteness, thus becoming part of the system which dominated and oppressed blacks. Although it contradicted their experience back home, it meant freedom here since blackness meant slavery.

An article by a black writer in an 1860 edition of the Liberator explained how the Irish ultimately attained their objectives: "Fifteen or twenty years ago, a Catholic priest in Philadelphia said to the Irish people in that city, 'You are all poor, and chiefly laborers, the blacks are poor laborers; many of the native whites are laborers; now, if you wish to succeed, you must do everything that they do, no matter how degrading, and do it for less than they can afford to do it for.' The Irish adopted this plan; they lived on less than the Americans could live upon, and worked for less, and the result is, that nearly all the menial employments are monopolized by the Irish, who now get as good prices as anybody. There were other avenues open to American white men, and though they have suffered much, the chief support of the Irish has come from the places from which we have been crowded."

Once the Irish secured themselves in those jobs, they made sure blacks were kept out. They realized that as long as they continued to work alongside blacks, they would be considered no different. Later, as Irish became prominent in the labor movement, African Americans were excluded from participation. In fact, one of the primary themes of How the Irish Became White is the way in which left labor historians, such as the highly acclaimed Herbert Gutman, have not paid sufficient attention to the problem of race in the development of the labor movement.

And so, we have the tragic story of how one oppressed "race," Irish Catholics, learned how to collaborate in the oppression of another "race," Africans in America, in order to secure their place in the white republic. Becoming white meant losing their greenness, i.e., their Irish cultural heritage and the legacy of oppression and discrimination back home."

-Art McDonald, Ph.D., "How the Irish Became White"[34]

The Polish had a similar experience. As you read the following paragraphs, you will see a pattern that has been used in modern America against another group of immigrants today. "The more things change, the more they remain the same."

"Here it is important to understand how, exactly, Americans 'become white'. The history of Polish-Americans is an illuminating example. Upon arriving in the U.S. en masse in the late 19th and early 20th century, Poles endured discrimination based on their appearance, religion and culture. In 1903, the New England Magazine decried the Poles' "expressionless Slavic faces" and "stunted figures" as well as their inherent "ignorance" and "propensity to violence". Working for terrible wages, Polish workers were renamed things like "Thomas Jefferson" by their bigoted Anglo-Saxon bosses who refused to utter Polish names.

The Poles, in other words, were not considered white. Far from it: they were considered a mysterious menace that should be expelled. When Polish-American Leon Czolgosz killed President William McKinley in 1901, all Poles were deemed potential violent anarchists. "All people are mourning, and it is caused by a maniac who is of our nationality," a Polish-American newspaper wrote, pressured to apologize for their own people. The collective blame of Poles for terrorism bears great similarity to how Muslims (both in the U.S. and Europe) are collectively blamed today.

But then something changed. In 1919, Irish gangs in blackface attacked Polish neighborhoods in Chicago in an attempt to convince Poles, and other Eastern European groups, that they, too, were "white" and should join them in the fight against blacks. As historian David R. Roediger recalls, "Poles argued that the riot was a conflict between blacks and whites, with Poles abstaining because they belonged to neither group." But the Irish gangs considered whiteness, as is often the case in America, as anti-blackness. And as in the early 20th century Chicago experienced an influx not only of white immigrants from Europe, but blacks from the South, white groups who felt threatened by black arrivals decided that it would be politically advantageous if the Poles were considered white as well. With that new white identity came the ability to practice the discrimination they had once endured.

Over time, the strategy of positioning Poles as "white" against a dark-skinned "other" was successful. Poles came to consider themselves white, and more importantly, they came to be considered white by their fellow Americans, as did Italians, Greeks, Jews, Russians, and others from Southern and Eastern Europe, all of whom held an ambivalent racial status in U.S. society. Also, intermarriage between white ethnic groups led some to embrace a broader white identity."

-Sarah Kendzior, How do you become "white" in America?[35]

In both instances, these groups stepped on blacks when they had the chance to unify and end the oppression of both sides to advance themselves. What we are looking at here is literally white privilege. No matter how people argue or complain, this is what our history records. Today there are descendants of European immigrants holding overtly racist views. Not one of these groups can honestly claim how they have had it just as bad as blacks, so blacks need to stop complaining and pull themselves up by the bootstraps like the Irish, Italians, Polish, etc.

"Blacks should follow the model of Asian determination. Of course, they have been and still are discriminated against to some degree. That has never deterred them at all. Being American is not about skin color. It is about believing in the concept of America, working hard, and relying on yourself."
-Anonymous white internet forum poster 2020

The black experience here is a prime example of determination from where I stand. It seems easy for members of the racist subculture to blurt out delusional racist lunacy. Aside from the fact that the person who made that quote does not understand what determination is, some whites have deemed themselves racial spokespeople for Asians. Members of the racist subculture have tried using Asians to justify their racism for quite a while. I would be pretty angry if I were Asian listening to some idiot like this. I am not arrogant enough to believe I speak for the Asian people in America. I will say this one thing, Asians and blacks must understand that civil rights for blacks are civil rights for Asians and vice versa. It is time to stop falling for the European divide and conquer over issues such as Affirmative Action.

One of the great speeches I have read was delivered at the Asian Law Caucus Banquet in April 1990 by Dr. Mari J. Matsuda. I read it one day online. It was a powerful speech, a call out to the pride and history of her people. The title was: *"We Will Not Be Used: Are Asian-Americans the Racial Bourgeoisie?"* I have cited excerpts from this speech.

> *"Living in 19th century Europe, Marx thought mostly in terms of class. Living in 20th century America, in the land where racism found a home, I am thinking about race. Is there a racial equivalent of the economic bourgeoisie? I fear there may be, and I fear it may be us.*
>
> *If white, historically, is the top of the racial hierarchy in America, and black, historically, is the bottom, will yellow assume the place of the racial middle? The role of the racial middle is a critical one. It can reinforce white supremacy if the middle deludes itself into thinking it can be just like white if it tries hard enough. Conversely, the middle can dismantle white supremacy if it refuses to be the middle, if it refuses to buy into racial hierarchy, if it refuses to abandon communities of Black and Brown people, choosing instead to form alliances with them."*[36]

She continues:

> *When Asian-Americans manage to do well, their success is used against others. Internally, it is used to erase the continuing poverty and social dislocation within Asian-American communities. The media is full of stories of Asian-American whiz kids. Their successes are used to erase our problems and to disavow any responsibility for them. The dominant culture doesn't know about drug abuse in our communities, about our high school dropouts, our AIDS victims.*
>
> *Suggestions that some segments of the Asian-American community need special help are greeted with suspicion and disbelief. External to our*

communities, our successes are used to deny racism and to put down other groups. African-Americans and Latinos and poor whites are told, "look at those Asians — anyone can make it in this country if they really try." The cruelty of telling this to crack babies, to workers displaced by runaway shops, and to families waiting in line at homeless shelters, is not something I want associated with my genealogy.[37]

There is more:

Yes, my ancestors made it in this country, but they made it against the odds. In my genealogy and probably in yours, are people who went to bed hungry, who lost land to the tax collector, who worked to exhaustion and ill-health, who faced pain and relocation with the bitter stoicism we call, in Japanese, "gaman." Many who came the hard road of our ancestors didn't make it. Their bones are still in the mountains by the tunnels they blasted for the railroad, still in the fields where they stooped over the short-handled hoe, still in the graveyards of Europe, where they fought for a democracy that didn't include them. Asian success was success with a dark, painful price.

To use that success to discount the hardship facing poor and working people in this country today is a sacrilege to the memory of our ancestors. It is an insult to today's Asian-American immigrants, who work the double-triple shift, who know no leisure, who crowd two and three families to a home, who put children and old-folks alike to work at struggling family businesses or at home doing piece-work until midnight. Yes, we take pride in our success, but we should also remember the cost. The success that is our pride is not to be given over as a weapon to use against other struggling communities. I hope we will not be used to blame the poor for their poverty.[38]

Still, there is more:

Nor should we be used to deny employment or educational opportunities to others. A recent exchange of editorials and letters in the Asian-American press reveals confusion over affirmative action. Racist anti-Asian quotas at the universities can give quotas a bad name in our community. At the same time, quotas have been the only way we've been able to walk through the door of persistently discriminatory institutions like the San Francisco fire department.

We need affirmative action because there are still employers who see an Asian face and see a person unfit for a leadership position. In every field where we have attained a measure of success, we are underrepresented in the real power positions. And yet, we are in danger of being manipulated into opposing affirmative action by those who say affirmative action hurts Asian-Americans.[39]

She goes on to say:

What's really going on here? When university administrators have secret quotas to keep down Asian admissions, this is because Asians are seen as destroying the predominantly white character of the university. Under this mentality, we can't let in all those Asian over-achievers and maintain affirmative action for other minority groups. We can't do both because that will mean either that our universities lose their predominantly white character, or that we have to fund more and better universities. To either of those prospects, I say, "why not?" And I condemn the voices from our own community that are translating legitimate anger at ceilings on Asian admissions into unthinking opposition to affirmative action floors needed to fight racism.

In a period when rates of educational attainment for minorities and working class Americans are going down, in a period when America is lagging behind other developed nations in literacy and learning, I hope we will not be used to deny educational opportunities to the disadvantaged and to preserve success only for the privileged.[40]

The crescendo:

I love my Asian brothers, but I've lost my patience with malingering homophobia and sexism, and especially with using white racism as an excuse to resist change. You know, the "I have to be Bruce Lee because the white man wants me to be Tonto" line. Yes, the J-town boys with their black leather jackets are adorable, but the pathetic need to put down straight women, gays, and lesbians is not. To anyone in our communities who wants to bring their anger home, let's say, "cut it out." We will not be used against each other.

If you know Hawaiian music, you know of the ha'ina line that tells of a song about to end. This speech is about to end. It will end by recalling echoes of Asian-American resistance.

In anti-eviction struggles in Chinatowns from coast to coast and in Hawaii we heard the song, "We Shall Not Be Moved." For the 90's, I want to sing, "We Shall Not Be Used." I want to remember the times when Asian-Americans stood side-by-side with African-Americans, Latinos, and progressive whites to demand social justice. I want to remember the multi-racial ILWU (International Longshoremen and Warehousemen's Workers' Union) that ended the plantation system in Hawaii. I want to remember the multi-racial sugar beet strikes in California that brought together Japanese, Filipino and Chicano workers to fulfill their dreams of a better life. I want to remember the American Committee for the Protection of the Foreign Born that brought together progressive Okinawan, Korean, Japanese, Chinese, and European immigrants to fight McCarthyism and deportation of political activists. I want to remember the San Francisco State College strike, and the Asian-American students who stood their ground in a multi-racial coalition to bring about ethnic studies and lasting changes in American academic life, changes that make it possible for me, as a scholar, to tell the truth as I see it. [41]

Dr. Matsuda broke 'em off something as it is said. This speech is one that many Americans need to read. Asians are to be heard; they are not just quiet, hardworking people who sit there and accept white racism. Within the Asian diaspora are some of the world's oldest cultures. Cultures there were long battle-tested before the United States of America was "founded." Just like Africa. Just like the Middle East. Just like the Indigenous peoples of the so-called North and South American continents. It is time some of our white citizens here stopped trying to use Asians as a racial wedge.

There have been times where I and probably several million other blacks have tried talking to a white person about what has happened, and they come back with the "Irish were slaves too" or "look at the Asians what's wrong with blacks" tripe. They fail to understand what happened in the nearly 160 years since the end of slavery was written on a piece of paper.

We need to understand the depths of the white resistance in the almost 160 years since slavery ended.

I will say this more than once, blacks' grievance with America left slavery as the sole issue pretty much the day after blacks were informed of emancipation. We were freed from slavery even though we received no compensation for the economic damage caused. Today's grievances include not just slavery but the 100 years after emancipation and modern forms of racism. Simply put, human rights violations against blacks did not end after slavery. Dr. Carol Anderson points this out in detail in her book, *"White Rage."* While I shall explore white backlash in a later chapter, I will cite some examples in this chapter. This must be done to debunk the age-old excuse of how everybody had it tough used to dismiss what blacks have endured.

Dr. Anderson chronicles the many methods whites used in the years after slavery to restrict the right for blacks to move around freely in America. Whites in the south used any means necessary to discourage blacks from moving north. In the north, whites terrorized blacks competing for jobs with better pay and those trying to live in majority white neighborhoods. According to Anderson's research, *"at the time of emancipation 80 percent of Americas GNP was tied to slavery."*[42] This comment refers to the entire nation of America, not just the south. As shown earlier, enslaved people were the most valuable commodity in America; the net worth of enslaved people surpassed all cash in America and assets in the south. Again, blacks got none of the money. As a result of emancipation, in January of 1865, Special Field Order 15 was issued.

I. The islands from Charleston south, the abandoned rice-fields along the rivers for thirty miles back from the sea,and the country bordering the Saint John's River, Fla., are reserved and set apart for the settlement of the negroes now made free by the acts of war and the proclamation of the President of the United States.

II. At Beaufort, Hilton Head, Savannah, Fernandina, Saint Augustine and Jacksonville the blacks may remain in their chosen or accustomed vocations; but on the islands, and in the settlements hereafter to be established, no white person whatever, unless military officers and soldiers detailed for duty, will be permitted to reside; and the sole and exclusive management of affairs will be left to the freed people themselves, subject only to the United States military authority and the acts of Congress.

By the laws of war and orders of the President of the United States, the negro is free, and must be dealt with as such. He cannot be subjected to conscription or forced military service, save by the written orders of the highest military authority of the Department, under such regulations as the President or Congress may prescribe; domestic servants, blacksmiths, carpenters, and other mechanics will be free to select their own work and residence, but the young and able-bodied negroes must be encouraged to enlist as soldiers in the service of the United States, to contribute their share toward maintaining their own freedom and securing their rights as citizens of the United States. Negroes so enlisted will be organized into companies, battalions, and regiments, under the orders of the United States military authorities, and will be paid, fed, and clothed according to law. The bounties paid on enlistment may, with the consent of the recruit, go to assist his family and settlement in procuring agricultural implements, seed, tools, boats, clothing, and other articles necessary for their livelihood.

III. Whenever three respectable negroes, heads of families, shall desire to settle on land, and shall have selected for that purpose an island, or a locality clearly defined within the limits above designated, the inspector of settlements and plantations will himself, or by such subordinate officer as he may appoint, give them a license to settle such island or district, and afford them such assistance as he can to enable them to establish a peaceable agricultural settlement.

The three parties named will subdivide the land, under the supervision of the inspector, among themselves and such others as may choose to settle near them, so that each family shall have a plot of not more than forty acres of tillable ground, and when it borders on some water channel with not more than 800 feet waterfront, in the possession of which land military authorities will afford them protection until such time as they can protect themselves or until Congress shall regulate their title. The quartermaster may, on the requisition of the inspector of settlements and plantations, place at the disposal of the inspector one or more of the captured steamers to ply between the settlements and one or more of the commercial points, heretofore named in orders, to afford the settlers the opportunity to supply their necessary wants and to sell the products of their land and labor.

IV. Whenever a negro has enlisted in the military service of the United States he may locate his family in any one of the settlements at pleasure and acquire a homestead and all other rights and privileges of a settler as though present in person. In like manner negroes may settle their families and engage on board the gun-boats, or in fishing, or in the navigation of the inland waters, without losing any claim to land or other advantages derived from this system. But no one, unless an actual settler as above defined, or unless absent on Government service, will be entitled to claim any right to land or property in any settlement by virtue of these orders.

V. In order to carry out this system of settlement a general officer will be detailed as inspector of settlements and plantations, whose duty it shall be to visit the settlements, to regulate their police and general management, and who will furnish personally to each head of a family, subject to the approval of the President of the United States, a possessory title in writing, giving as near as possible the description of boundaries, and who shall adjust all claims or conflicts that may arise under the same, subject to the like approval, treating such titles altogether as possessory. The same general officer will also be charged with the enlistment and organization of the negro recruits and protecting their interests while absent from their settlements, and will be governed by the rules and regulations prescribed by the War Department for such purpose.

VI. Brig. Gen. R. Saxton is hereby appointed inspector of settlements and plantations and will at once enter on the performance of his duties. No change is intended or desired in the settlement now on Beaufort Island, nor will any rights to property heretofore acquired be affected thereby.[43]

In July 1865, Circular 13 was issued by General Oliver Howard fully authorizing the lease of 40-acre plots of land to the newly freed blacks.

All confiscated and abandoned land, and other confiscated and abandoned property, that now and or that may hereafter come under the control of the

Bureau of Refugees, Freedmen & Abandoned Lands, by virtue of said acts and Sections of Acts and order of the President, are and shall be set apart for the use of loyal refugees and freedmen and as much as may be necessary, assigned to them as provided in Sect 4.of the act establishing the Bureau viz: "to every male citizen, whether refugee or freedman, as aforesaid, there shall be assigned not more than forty acres of such land, and the person to whom it was so assigned shall be protected in the use and enjoyment of the land for the term of three years at an annual rent not exceeding six per centum upon the value of such land, as it was appraised by the state authorities in the year eighteen hundred and sixty, for the purpose of taxation, and in case no such appraisal can be found, then the rental shall be based upon the estimated value of the land in said year, to be ascertained in such manner as the commissioner may by regulation prescribe. At the end of said term, or at any time during said term, the occupants of any parcels so assigned may purchase the land and receive such title thereto as the United States can convey, upon paying therefor the value of the land, as ascertained and fixed for the purpose of determining the annual rent aforesaid."[44]

As a result of these actions, 40,000 formerly enslaved people began work on land that now belonged to them. But President Andrew Johnson killed these two orders and removed those 40,000 blacks from that land while destroying any income they could make. He gave the land back to whites. Johnson pardoned most of the confederate leaders, allowing them to regain power. By doing this, Johnson unleashed a reign of terror on blacks that was nothing short of attempted ethnic cleansing.

That was not all. The Freedman's Bank was incorporated on March 3, 1865, due to the passage of the Freedman's Bureau

Bill by Congress.[45] Freedman's bank was created to provide a place for blacks to begin saving the money they were earning as a result of winning their freedom. The Freedman's Bank provided a place for blacks to deposit money that they could trust. The bank also provided jobs and financial training, which helped the formerly enslaved people understand the American financial system and monetary policy.[46] However, the bank was controlled by a white board of directors. Eventually, this became a significant problem.

Freedman's Bank was widely popular. The creation of the bank immediately improved the lives of blacks; however, the benefits ended up being short-lived.[47] The institution grew due to the large numbers of depositors. The bank grew fast, holding millions of dollars with 37 branches in 17 states. Freedman's Bank eventually built its headquarters in Washington D.C. in a state-of-the-art facility. These were critical mistakes. Building branches depleted bank resources. The Washington facility was top of the line, a real source of pride, but it cost real source of pride money as well. The facility cost more than 200 thousand dollars in 1874 which is equivalent to 5 million dollars today. This further depleted bank resources. Congress was supposed to provide oversight in the affairs of Freedman's Bank but did little to none.

Another problem was the Freedman's Bank Board of Trustees. A 50 member board of Trustees and a three-man finance committee governed the affairs of Freedman's Bank.[48] I use the term governed, but none of those charged with that responsibly ever really did anything. Some of them would not even show up for meetings.[49] All were white until the bank was almost dead. Near the end, the board of trustees asked Frederick Douglass to save the bank. No one paid attention to what was going on because in what has become an American tradition, this whole endeavor was a symbolic show of care by people who had no intention of doing the work it took for the newly freed blacks to gain equal footing.

The Freedman's Banks customers were small depositors who made many withdrawals. Due to the nature and number of transactions, Freedman's Bank had higher operating costs than similar banks. Eventually the trustees and finance committee asked congress to amend their charter to allow the bank to make more risky loans.[50] At the start, Freedman's Bank could only invest in government-backed securities, but once congress amended the banks charter in 1870, it allowed more risky investments. The bank began speculating on railroads. In addition, several members of the board who ran other banks transferred liabilities their banks had to Freedman's Bank.[51] The board of trustees squandered the deposits of newly freed blacks on wild speculation schemes that ended up dying and leaving the Freedman's Bank in the lurch.

'The failure of this bank has done more to harm the future of freed black slaves than 10 additional years of slavery."

-Frederick Douglass

The timing of the bank creation required Congress to make a serious effort to ensure the success of Freedman's Bank. The financial picture in America after the civil war was unstable. From the end of the Civil War until 1873, the American economy experienced great turbulence. This turbulence reduced the value of government-backed securities. Due to being heavily invested in such securities, Freedman's Bank took a hit. Finally, the Panic of 1873 caused a massive run on the banks. Due to bogus loans, rampant speculation using bank funds, and transferring white bank debt to Freedman's Bank, the bank could not meet its obligations. Freedman's Savings and Trust Company was forced to close in 1874 after only nine years of operation. As a result, 60,000 former slaves, black veterans of the civil war, and other black citizens of this country were robbed of 68.2 million dollars in today's money.[52]

There was no FDIC in 1874, so those deposits were not insured. However, Congress decided they would repay the black depositors 60 cents back for every dollar they lost.[53] Despite this, most of those who deposited their hard-earned money in this bank never got it back. Congress was in charge of oversight of the bank, but oversight did not happen. The Congress of the United States allowed the board of trustees of the Freedman's Bank to rob the newly freed blacks of their savings. What was done was illegal, but no one was ever indicted.

Whites were killing Blacks with no crimes charged while the Supreme Court rendered the 13th, 14th, and 15th amendments ineffective with a series of rulings. Due to a series of barbaric acts by whites, and with no protection, southern blacks felt they had to go north. When blacks started moving north, southern business and government leaders enacted laws to stop free people from going where they could earn a decent living. But even under the threat of jail or death, millions of blacks headed north where they believed they'd be treated right. If they had known what was waiting, the great migration would have bypassed the northern states and ended in Canada.

There were a series of massacres, bombings, lynchings, and other acts of terror against blacks by whites due to the northern migration of blacks trying to escape massacres, bombings, lynchings, and other acts of terror against blacks by whites in the south. As southern blacks went north, they found that geography was the only difference between a southern white and a northern one. When blacks went north, so did lynchings. The great northern migration resulted in years of rioting by angry whites. Such historical amnesia makes it hilarious to listen to the disingenuous fake outrage of the racist white subculture about blacks and riots today.

On the evening of Saturday, July 19th, 1919, in Washington D.C., a mob of mad drunken white World War 1 veterans invaded a black neighborhood because of a rumor spread about a black man assaulting the wife of a white navy man.[54] Those mad white men proceeded to beat all the blacks they found. They snatched blacks out of streetcars or off sidewalks and beat them for no reason. Where were the police? Donuts had been around for 72 years, so... The violence lasted four days. Random blacks got beat down on the streets of Washington. The rioting happened even in front of the White House.

The Omaha Race Riot occurred on September 28–29, 1919. Three conditions: black property acquisition, economic anxiety, and black male sexual aggression claims have been the standard for white violence against blacks throughout American history. The Omaha Riots met at least 2 of the three conditions. The eventual lynching of Will Brown began with reports in local media about the alleged rape of a woman on September 25, 1919. The following day, the police arrested Brown. Brown was accused of the crime without the victim making an identification. There was an attempt to lynch Brown on the day of his arrest, but it failed.

The *Omaha* Bee publicized the incident claiming it was part of a series of alleged attacks on white women by black men in Omaha. The *Bee* was owned by Edward Rosewater, a friend of a man named Thomas Dennison. Dennison ran a political machine that controlled Omaha. To be blunt, Dennison was a crook. He ruled Omaha for 18 years before the city elected someone not directed by Dennison as mayor named Edward Smith. The election of Smith angered Dennison. To make Smith look bad, Dennisons men ran wildly throughout the town wearing blackface, assaulting women and blaming blacks for it. Dennison orchestrated the incidents while Rosewaters paper pumped up the fake news. Thanks to his buddy at the Omaha Bee, the Dennison gang race baited the people of Omaha and incited the Omaha Riots. On the night of the lynching, Omaha Police even caught one of Dennison's men on the street in blackface. No one was charged or convicted for what happened. Will Brown was not so fortunate. Brown was lynched, shot up after he was dead, dragged through the streets of Omaha, and set on fire.[55] He had committed no crime.

White mob violence did not end in 1919. One of the worst acts of domestic terrorism in America happened in two days of American history, beginning on May 31st, 1921, in Tulsa, Oklahoma. This riot is better known as *"The Tulsa Massacre."*[56] One may as well say this was an act of war waged on the black citizens of Tulsa, Oklahoma. I say this because blacks were attacked on the ground and by air. In a manner best described by the scene of Ben Richards being told to shoot the people during a food riot in *"The Running Man,"* whites in private planes flew over the black community shooting down on blacks and bombing black homes and businesses.

> *"I could see planes circling in mid-air. They grew in number and hummed, darted and dipped low. I could hear something like hail falling upon the top of my office building. Down East Archer, I saw the old Mid-Way hotel on fire, burning from its top, and then another and another and another building began to burn from their top,"*
>
> **-B.C. Franklin**[57]

The excuse by city law enforcement officials was that the planes were reconnaissance used to protect against a Negro uprising. Still today, an accurate accounting of the number of dead varies. More than 6,000 people were admitted to hospitals. More than 10,000 blacks were left homeless. The bombings and ground attacks destroyed 35 city blocks of Tulsa, resulting in damages that equaled over 32 million dollars in today's money.[58]

I don't think people understand just exactly how bad things have been for blacks when they start trying to blame blacks for the slave trade or slave ownership. I am waiting for the day somebody white tries to say that blacks created the black codes, sundown towns, and Jim Crow. Such is the state of the madness here in America at this time. Members of the racist subculture have complained about "political correctness," yet when "political incorrectness" is applied to them, suddenly things must be forgotten, revised, altered, or kept quiet.

On December 23, 1945, Mr. and Mrs. H. O'Day Short and their two little children were burned to death in Fontana, California. The description was; *"A fire of incendiary origins set by persons who did not want them to move into the white community."*[59] Before they were murdered, the family was threatened but got no protection from the police. According to the report, the Shorts had no electricity and were using gas lamps when they moved in. On the day of the murder, with the Shorts gone, people broke in their house and sprayed an explosive chemical all inside of the residence. When the Shorts got home and started lighting their lamps, their home went up in flames.[60]

On August 6, 1948, 6 young black men were convicted of murder and given the death sentence in Trenton, New Jersey. The witness accounts stated that the killers were *"two or three white or light-skinned Negro teenagers."*[61] The suspects taken in by police did not contain one teenager. Out of the 6, only one was light-skinned.[62] Four of the men had alibis. They were held without warrants and interrogated for days until they confessed after being drugged. The doctor who examined ended up getting convicted of perjury for testifying that the men had not been coerced. His penalty? A fine and probation. The trial was a sham, and the men were sent off to die. But unlike similar cases this during this period, some of these young men got saved.

Bessie Mitchell, the sister of one of the six men, wrote everybody she could ask for help because she knew her brother was innocent. She contacted the ACLU and NAACP, no use. The NAACP said they did not do murder cases, and the ACLU could not find any racism in the case. But in what can only be described as an act of God, Mitchell found a piece of paper in a gutter about the Civil Rights Congress.[63] The Civil Rights Congress was a communist organization, but Mitchell was out of options.

With the help of a communist organization, Bessie Mitchell was able to bring the necessary attention to the plight of the Trenton 6. Celebrities joined the cause, the NAACP and the ACLU joined forces with the Civil Rights Congress to save 4 of the six men.[64] My point here is not to denigrate The Civil Rights Congress for its communist political views but to provide an example of where so-called American democracy and its claim to the rule of law has failed blacks and all people of color.

Some whites resorted to terrorism to intimidate blacks so they would not move into white communities. For the first five years after WW2 in Chicago alone, there were over 300 documented acts of terror by whites against blacks who tried living in or near majority-white neighborhoods.[65] In 1951, a black man named Harvey Clark and his family tried to move into the Cicero neighborhood of Chicago. A white mob vandalized his home and burned his furniture in the front yard. The police did nothing.[66] In 1955, there were more than 200 recorded acts of violence against blacks by whites in Philadelphia alone.[67] In 1964, blacks again tried renting an apartment in Cicero, their apartment was vandalized. Police acted this time. They entered the apartment, took out the furniture, and told the people they were evicted.[68] During the same period in Detroit, there were over 200 acts of terror to stop black families from moving to the suburbs.[69] In 15 years from 1950 to 1965, more than 100 recorded bombings of black-owned homes occurred in Los Angeles.[70] In 1987, another black family tried moving into Cicero. They got gunfire and firebombs.[71] Again, that was in 1987, not 1887.

Consistently since the end of slavery, there has been a section of the white community who violently resisted the efforts of blacks to live successfully in America. During this time, prosperous blacks faced acts of terror while thriving black communities got destroyed by mobs of angry whites who felt they were losing out because blacks had acquired the same things whites had. This kind of terrorism has gone long ignored in understanding the brutality and hardcore resistance to black freedom in America. Forgotten is that blacks worked hard to get what they had, but that did not matter because blacks were always to be lesser than whites, and the caste was to be maintained by any means necessary. White immigrants, whose descendants will say today how they are not responsible because their ancestors did not enslave people, committed violence against blacks.

"Again and again, African-American individuals and families have worked hard to produce wealth, but American finance, whether in the antebellum period or today, has snatched black wealth through bonds backed by asset securitization."
-Edward E. Baptist and Louis Hyman,
American Finance Grew on the Back of Slaves

I began this chapter with the all-too-common refrain spoken today by a portion of the white community that preaches personal responsibility but takes none themselves. It is the claim of Africans selling each other. History is recorded, but we have only received one side of it about the slave trade. Yes, some people were citizens in one African tribe who sold members of other African nations to Europeans. Europeans were not forced to buy Africans, but Africans were forced to sell other Africans in many cases. Nearly 400,000 Africans ended up on these shores and turned into 4 million by atrocities that rank with the worst in human history. Africans did not do that.

After slavery ended, southern whites went on a campaign of what can only be called ethnic cleansing. The federal government turned tail and ran by establishing a legal principle whereby the federal government did not have to enforce the 13th, 14th, and 15th amendments by using states' rights. Apartheid became the law of the land due to the Plessy decision. Blacks tried to escape the oppressive conditions in the south by coming north, but they found just how united the states were relative to white supremacy. Africans did not do that. At every turn, whenever blacks tried reaching for what this country claims to promise, we have run into a brick wall, or more accurately, a white mob. Africans did not do that.

"One major author on the slave trade (appropriately titled Sins of Our Fathers) explained how many white people urged him to state that the trade was the responsibility of African chiefs, and that Europeans merely turned up to buy captives- as though without European demand there would have been captives sitting on the beach by the millions!

- Walter Rodney

The 13 Percent Excuse

"The truth? As the largest racial group, whites commit the majority of the crimes in America. In particular, whites are responsible for the vast majority of violent crimes. With respect to aggravated assault, whites lead blacks 2-1 in arrests; in forcible-rape cases, whites lead all racial and ethnic groups by more than 2-1. And in larceny theft, whites lead blacks, again, more than 2-1.

-Edward Wyckoff Williams
Don't White People Kill
Each Other too?

When we black folks start talking about what police have done to us, we have to get the lecture about our supposed lack of concern about black-on-black crime from the usual suspects. If you look at the Uniform Crime Reports filed by the FBI every year, whites account for between 65-70 percent of all arrests annually. They commit between 45-51 percent of the murders depending upon the year. They account for over 60 percent of arrests for rapes and assaults for most years. These are violent crimes.

In early 1995, I began organizing an all-night vigil to protest the violence in a particular black section of a city when a long-time resident who was black heard of what I was trying to do and read me the riot act. I listened to that person and said nothing, but I spent the following two weeks living in that community. I walked those streets late at night. I wandered through the neighborhoods all day. I talked to members of the community. I watched the activities as school began and let out. I visited after school programs in that community. I saw people needing resources that the local government would not give to them trying to make it, trying to help kids succeed and not one time did I see an act of violence. We held the all-night vigil standing at the intersection of two busy streets in a community claimed to be the most dangerous area in a city ranked in the top ten nationally in murder. I am still alive.

But still, I heard the mounting cries of how we black people needed to stop black-on-black crime. I lived in that city for several years, watching the killing and crime on the news. I saw how most of those things went on outside of the black community. When it happened, there was no describing the crimes by race. Rarely were community citizens asked about their concerns relating to white-on-white crime. But when it happened in the black community, black leaders were asked all kinds of questions about what they would do. Maybe it is time the lectures ended from those who rant incessantly about back on black crime while ignoring the more significant white-on-white crime problem in America. I find it funny that some whites are so concerned about how all crime matters after whites in authority have committed blatant atrocities. They always are the trusted characters you can depend on to start off on rants about crime in the black community. It is always the same racist garbage that starts with unwed births.

"For the past two decades, the country has been talking about phantom police racism in order to avoid talking about a more uncomfortable truth: black crime. But in the era of data-driven law enforcement, policing is simply a function of crime. The best way to lower police-civilian contacts in inner-city neighborhoods

would be for children to be raised by their mother and their father in order to radically lower the crime rate there."[1]

This came from a bout of madness titled *"The Lies told by the Black Lives Matter Movement,"* written by Heather MacDonald on September 6, 2016. First, let us understand that the New York Post is part of the American Media. You know, that so-called liberal media controlled by democrats. You do not have to think hard to wonder why a news source such as the Post would entertain this kind of rhetoric. Here McDonald skews all manner of information to make an invalid argument. The right-wing media and "conservative" individuals inside of the media have promoted a narrative of Black-on-Black crime, then try tying it to unwed births or the lack of two parents in the house.

Charles Blow wrote an article in the New York Times titled, *"Black Dads Are Doing Best of All."* McDonald should have read it. This article takes apart the tale of black fathers not being around for their kids. The issue of unwed births has no relation to whether two parents are around. An unwed birth is a child born while the couple is not married. That does not mean a man and a woman are not together raising the child. The single mother narrative got destroyed long ago because a single mother does not mean a man will not be around to influence the child as it grows up. Most of these women have boyfriends. Many of these women eventually marry. One fantastic example of this is Shaquille O'Neal's story about his relationship with Sergeant Phillip Harrison, who raised him with his mother. Finally, the appearance of former President Barack Obama on the world stage allows me to say once and for all that a single-parent family is not the cause of the problem. Articles have been written showing that most black children in this country live with their fathers or their fathers are active participants in their lives. In reality, a mother and father ARE present in the majority of black homes.

Josh Levs points this out in his new book, "All In," in a chapter titled "How Black Dads Are Doing Best of All (But There's Still a Crisis)." One fact that Levs quickly establishes is that most black fathers in America live with their children: "There are about 2.5 million black fathers living with their children and about 1.7 million living apart from them."

-Charles Blow[2]

The Centers for Disease Control published a report titled *"Fathers' Involvement With Their Children: United States, 2006–2010,"* in the National Health Report on December 20, 2013. The findings dispute the opinions of those in the white racist subculture who have decided they can paint black culture in moral terms those same whites have refused to live by themselves. The findings in this study debunk the standard racist white narrative to the point that it is miseducation, misinformation, lies, or whatever word you want to give to the purposeful deception provided to describe a race of people. Some of the findings are as follows:

• *A higher percentage of fathers who lived with their children under age 5 fed or ate meals with them daily—72% compared with 7.9% of fathers with noncoresidential children. A higher percentage of fathers living apart from their children did not feed or eat meals with them at all in the last 4 weeks—43% compared with 0.8% of fathers with coresidential children (Table 2). Variation by Hispanic origin and race was seen in the percentages of coresidential fathers who ate meals with their children every day. Specifically, Hispanic fathers were less likely to eat meals with their children every day (64%) than were non-Hispanic white (74%) or non-Hispanic black (78%) fathers.*

• *There was a significant difference by Hispanic origin and race among fathers with coresidential children: Black fathers (70%) were most likely to have bathed, dressed, diapered, or helped their children use the toilet every day compared with white (60%) and Hispanic fathers (45%).*

• *A higher percentage of Hispanic fathers aged 15–44 (52%) had not played with their noncoresidential children in the last 4 weeks compared with white (30%) and black (25%) fathers.*

• *Larger percentages of Hispanic (82%) and white (70%) fathers had not helped their noncoresidential children with homework at all in the last 4 weeks compared with black fathers (56%).*[3]

Pew Research estimates that 67 percent of black dads who do not live with their kids see them at least once a month, compared to 59 percent of white dads and 32 percent of Hispanic dads.[4] Evidence shows that many black dads live apart from their kids because of inequality and poverty.[5] The research showed that black men placed high importance on being a father who provides emotional support, discipline, guidance, and financial help for his children. The racist assumption that African American men place less or no value on parenting is just one more excuse used to deny problems created by racism.

"As late as 1950, only 18% of black households were single parent. From 1890 to 1940, a slightly higher percentage of black adults had married than white adults. In 1938, black illegitimacy was about 11% instead of today's 75%. In 1925, 85% of black households in New York City were two-parent. Today, the black family is a mere shadow of its past."
-Walter Williams[6]

In 1939 during this time of great black two-parent families, the poverty rate for employed married black couples was 89 percent.[7] In 1959, the poverty rate for that same couple was 54.9 percent.[8] These sky-high rates of poverty occurred during the time "conservatives" rant about. Today due to the " liberal welfare state breaking up the black family by giving them welfare," black poverty is half of what it was in 1959 and more than 1/3 of what it was in those imaginary grand old glorious days of the two-parent black family. Again, the unwed single mom and absent black father are not the cause of problems in black communities.

Whites commit more crimes, and that includes violent crimes. The question NEVER asked by anyone like McDonald is why whites lead every year in arrests in 90 percent of crime categories listed in the Uniform Crime Report. I have seen, read, and heard many misguided opinions about black crime from people like Heather McDonald. The rhetoric from such individuals is way past old. Perhaps it is time some whites started talking a good long look into their communities instead of continuing the fine racist tradition of making up stories about how violent and criminal other races are.

"'Starting with black crime and not with racism, is always the major flaw in Mac Donald's work. Still, she remains an opponent to both learn from and take oh so seriously. Thankfully, Mother Jones is among the few progressive organizations which work as hard as Mac Donald does to disprove the notion that blacks have no one to blame but themselves. It's just that we're going to need a lot more folks doing work at this level to drown out the MacDonalds."
-Debra J. Dickerson[9]

I have looked at the Uniform Crime Reports every year since 1994. Every report I have read shows that whites get arrested the most for crimes in the United States. The excuse for this is there are more white people. I say this is an excuse because more whites are taking college entrance exams too, but that is not considered by the members of the racist subculture when the discussion favors whites. McDonald's claim about blacks needing to have daddy and mommy at home is not supported by reality. Using right-wing logic, since most white families have mommy and daddy at home, why are they arrested for approximately 70 percent of all crimes in America annually?

> *"From 1994 to 2015, white-on-white violence (down 79%) and black-on-black violence (down 78%) declined at a similar rate."*[10]

This information comes from a report issued in October of 2017 by the U.S. Department of Justice, Office of Justice Programs, Bureau of Justice Statistics. The title is *"Race and Hispanic Origin of Victims and Offenders, 2012-15."* This report shows that from 1994 to 2015, while people like McDonald, the Fox News prime time lineup, and most American media were promoting a narrative of high black-on-black crime, the reality is that black-on-black crime decreased. It also shows that most crimes are intra-racial and that whites were victimized primarily by other whites in similar percentages.

> *"During 2012-15, there were no differences among white, black, and Hispanic intraracial victimizations reported to police."*[11]

These facts show the utter nonsense McDonald and others like her share relative to the issue of black-on-black crime. This information kills the claim by the racist subculture that blacks don't take responsibility for crime due to the arduous work of unknown, not-so-famous blacks toiling in obscurity in cities/towns all over this country. These are the stories that rarely get told by the media. Instead, space is wasted with the opinion of MacDonald and that ilk.

On August 15, 2013, The Center on Juvenile and Criminal Justice published a paper by Mike Males titled, *"Why the Gigantic, Decades-Long Drop in Black Youth Crime Threatens Major Interests."* Americans tend to create nostalgia about the past. The fact is that the good old days never were. I say this as a black citizen of this country, but the "good old days" never existed for anyone. Males points this out in his report. *"For nearly all serious and minor offenses, including homicide, rates among black teenagers nationally were lower in 2011 than when racial statistics were first collected nationally in 1964. Black youths' murder arrest rates are considerably lower today than back when Bill Cosby was funny (long, long ago)."*[12]

He states: *"We don't associate Jim and Margaret Anderson's 1950s cherubs with juvenile crime—but that's based on nostalgia and cultural biases, not fact. Back then, nearly 1 in 10 youth were arrested every year; today, around 3 in 100. Limited statistics of the 1950s show juvenile crime wasn't just pranks and joyriding; "younger and younger children" are committing "the most wanton and senseless of murders... and mass rape," the chair of the Senate Subcommittee on Juvenile Delinquency warned in 1956."*[13] Whoa! Hold up! Stop! Does this mean that "super predators" existed in the 1950s? I guess this explains Eddie Haskell. Or perhaps Maynard G. Krebs. Males makes a point here that requires further investigating.

Congressional committees and subcommittees met in the 1940s and 1950s to discuss youth violence resulting from reading stories in comic books. Superman, Spiderman, Aqua Man, Captain America and whoever else was a member of the Justice League were held responsible for the outrageously high rate of violent juvenile delinquency during that period. I blame The Hulk. I heard he was jealous because Flash and

Wonder Woman were in a relationship, and we all know it's not good to make The Hulk mad. Okay, I get it. That was not funny. So let's get back to the subject.

On June 1, 1953, the United States Senate adopted Senate Resolution 89. This resolution created the Senate Judiciary Committee on Juvenile Delinquency in the United States to study youth crime. The primary focus of this study: *"(1) determining the extent and character of juvenile delinquency in the United States and its causes and contributing factors, (2) the adequacy of existing Federal laws dealing with youthful offenders, "(3) sentences imposed on, or other correctional action taken with respect to, youthful offenders by Federal laws dealing with youthful offenders, and (4) the extent to which juveniles are violating Federal laws relating to the sale or use of narcotics."*[14]

Let us take a look at some of the findings. *"In the 8-year period, from 1948 through 1956, juvenile court cases more than doubled while the child population of that age group increased only 19 percent. As in previous years, the increase is at a much greater rate in rural areas than in urban areas, and the ratio of 5 boy delinquents to every 1 girl delinquent is still in evidence."*[15]

"In the year 1956, there were upwards of 1,300,000 boys and girls coming to the attention of local law-enforcement officers. Approximately one-fourth of the police cases are referred to juvenile courts. The remaining juvenile court cases are referred from individuals and other agencies in the community."[16]

From 1948 until 1956, juvenile crime rose in rural areas. Juvenile crime was rising faster than juvenile population growth. This was primarily happening in white communities. With mom and pops at home, before the sexual revolution. Back in the day, as we say, the switchblade knife was the cause of a lot of deaths and suffering. There are similarities to the proliferation of switchblade knives in the 1940s and1950s and the increase in military-style weapons used on our streets today.

"Of the robberies committed in 1956, 43.2 percent were by persons under 21 years of age. A switchblade knife is frequently part of the perpetrator's equipment in this type of crime. In New York City alone in 1956, there was an increase of 92.1 percent of those under 16 arrested for the possession of dangerous weapons, one of the most common of which is the switchblade knife.

Out of several hundred questionnaires sent by the subcommittee to purchasers of switchblade knives, whose names were derived from a distributor's mailing list, 133 responses have been received. Seventy--five percent of the purchasers were under 20 years of age, and of this group, 43 percent were between 11 and 15 years of age. Of the persons responding to the questionnaire, only a small portion claimed that the knives were secured for a constructive purpose.

In addition to the interviews with manufacturers and distributors and the receipt of information from questionnaires, staff contact was made with some of the purchasers in the immediate area and numerous retail stores. The proprietors of these stores conceded that the bulk of the demand for switchblade knives came from juveniles, some as young as 8 or 9 years of age.

A major outlet for the switchblade knife are military supply stores which are located near military installations."[17]

E-commerce via the internet was 40-50 years in the future at this time. Yet kids could order switchblades by mail or purchase them in military supply stores. This is similar to the easy manner in which assault weapons can be purchased now. In 1956, not 1996, or the period of "American Carnage" inaccurately described by president number 45, 43 percent of the robberies in this country were committed by people under the age of 21. With mom and dad at home. When the family consisted of Ward, June, Wally, and The Beaver, not Adam and Steve or Joni and Jane.

Over 1 million incidents between youth and police. Over 500,000 cases in juvenile courts. From 1948 through 1956, there were annual increases in juvenile cases heard before the courts. These increases in juvenile crime were by kids from 8 to 18. The owners of the military supply stores stated to members of the judiciary committee that most switchblade purchases in their stores were made by youth. High school children were walking American streets carrying switchblades. These were the good old days. These conditions existed before the Great Society programs that have been blamed for the decay of American society and deemed responsible for the destruction of the black family.

"Trayvon Martin had a father. Jordan Davis had a father. Michael Brown had a father. Tamir Rice had a father. Having a father won't protect black boys from America."
- Mychal Denzel Smith

Mike Males article provides evidence of how a racist society builds a strawman then tries turning that straw into skin and bones. This information displays just how some members of this society have chosen to accept a fictional account of this country. This fiction has been accepted to such an extent that our police departments have become militarized despite a national decrease in crime. It is a lie so tough that innocent blacks posing no threat to anyone end up in funeral homes.

"Since the sainted Fifties, America has seen rapid teenage population growth and dramatic shifts toward more single parenting, more lethal drugs and weapons, increased middle-aged (that is, parent-age) drug abuse and imprisonment, decreased incarceration of youth, decreased youthful religious affiliation, and more violent and explicit media available to younger ages. Horrifying, as the culture critics far Right to far Left—including Obama, who spends many pages and speeches berating popular culture as some major driver of bad youth behavior—repeatedly insist.

And after 50 years of all these terrible changes in American culture? Today's young African Americans display the lowest rates of crime and serious risk of any generation that can be reliably assessed.

In the last 20 years in particular, the FBI reports, rates of crime among African American youth have plummeted: All offenses (down 47%), drug offenses (down 50%), property offenses (down 51%), serious Part I offenses (down 53%), assault (down 59%), robbery (down 60%), all violent offenses (down 60%), rape (down 66%), and murder (down 82%)."

-Mike Males[18]

There continues to be a subculture in the white community where people believe in the white race's inherent superiority and human perfection. This subculture has consistently promoted a narrative of inherent black violence. Much like the rest of racism this narrative is unfounded; quite frankly, given the history of America, it's projection. Where that belief came from cannot be based in reality. I guess since slaves tended to resist their enslavement and white slaveowners believed that blacks actually enjoyed being slaves, the assumption was made that slaves who fought were just naturally prone to violence. This belief ranks right up there with Drapetomania in the annals of crazy, but let's go on.

In August of 1896, a book titled *"The Race Traits and Tendencies of the American Negro,"* written by Frederick Hoffman, hit the streets of America. Hoffman was a statistician for Prudential Insurance. He wrote the book to justify higher life insurance premiums charged to African Americans at that time. Here is his reason:

"All the tables for various states and cities confirm the census data and show without exception that the criminality of the negro exceeds that of any other race of any numerical importance in this country."
-Frederick Hoffman[19]

In this book, Hoffman used the racial proportion argument as basis for his claims of black criminality. His claim was that due to traits inherent to blacks, the black race was dying off faster, was more violent, committed more crime, and had a higher rate of illegitimate birth rates than whites. Please remember that his study was published in 1896, and in 1896, black codes, vagrancy laws, and convict leasing were in full effect. But that didn't matter to Hoffman; blacks simply had a natural propensity for crime and immoral behavior. He presented what is now the age-old claim of high black violent crime and rape. Never mind that in 1896 a black person could get accused of crimes they did not commit, get arrested, tried, and found guilty even when evidence showed they were innocent of the crime. He even denied that race had anything to do with lynchings. Black leaders of that time almost immediately criticized his findings.

W.E.B. DuBois wrote a scathing critique of Hoffman's work in a review published in the January 1897 volume of "Annals of the American Academy of Political and Social Science." Dubois found severe errors in Hoffman's work.

He begins by questioning the source Hoffman used for his analysis, the Eleventh Census of the United States. *"In the Eleventh Census, Mr. Hoffman expresses great faith, and thinks it as reliable as any of the previous enumerations. There nevertheless exists in the minds of many scholars grave doubts as to the accuracy of a large part of this census, and a disposition to base few important conclusions on its results. To this extent, therefore, many of Mr. Hoffman's conclusions will be discounted. The anthropological material collected at war-time is of undoubted value, if, as Dr. Gould himself points out, the student remembers that they relate to one sex only, and to the most healthful years. Finally, in all deductions drawn from the vital statistics of large cities, the student must know that only in recent years are these figures reliable, and that they give little or no clue to conditions in the country where over three-fourths of the Negroes live."*[20]

In his review, Dubois found numerous errors in sampling and logic. He points out Hoffman's mistakes in understanding the impact of slavery on blacks and the response young blacks had at that time to the obstacles put in front of them due to white racism. Hoffman argued that what was happening was due to traits inherent in the black race. Dubois argued that circumstances and conditions were the cause. His argument boiled down to this: the root cause of the problems blacks faced was white racism. Dubois contrasted the death and illegitimacy rates of American blacks presented by Hoffman to rates in European cities. Dubois debunked Hoffman's claim by showing that black death and illegitimacy rates in the American cities Hoffman used for his study were lower than, Paris, Rome, Munich, Vienna, Stockholm, Paris, and Brussels. Like some in the white community today, Hoffman ignored the systemic racism of that time as a causal factor. DuBois concluded:

"To comprehend this peculiar and complicated evolution, and to pronounce final judgment upon it, will take far greater power of analysis, niceness of inquiry, and delicacy of measurement than Mr. Hoffman brings to his task. In the absence of such an investigation, most persons will persist in seeing in the figures which Mr. Hoffman himself adduces, grounds for great hope. Rome, Munich, Vienna, Stockholm, Paris and Brussels have all shown in recent years more startling percentages of illegitimacy than the Negroes of Washington; while the Negroes of Rhode Island showed a rate of only five per cent of illegitimate births in 1890. The criminal statistics raise the whole question as to how far black and white malefactors are subjected to different standards of justice. The record of poverty is not startling for a people who started practically penniless a generation or two ago. On the other hand how much of toil, self-denial and patience does the fifteen millions of Negro property in Georgia represent, or the 833,000 acres of Virginia soil?

To sum up briefly, the value of Mr. Hoffman's work lies in the collection and emphasis of a number of interesting and valuable data in regard to the American Negro. Most of the conclusions drawn from these facts are, however, of doubtful value, on account of the character of the material, the extent of the field, and the unscientific use of the statistical method."[21]

Another black leader, Kelly Miller, also evaluated Hoffman's study and had similar criticisms. Again, he cites that the significant error in Hoffman's work was that he assigned the cause of the problems to an inherent racial trait in blacks rather than the circumstances and conditions blacks faced at that time. Miller made the following conclusions of Hoffman's work:

The author's conclusion will not stand the philosophical tests of a sound theory.

1. It is based upon disputed data. The accuracy of the eleventh census is not acceptable either to the popular or the scientific mind.

2. It is not based upon a sufficient induction of data. The arguments at most apply to the Negroes in the large cities, who constitute less than 12 per cent of the total population.

3. It does not account for the facts arranged under it as satisfactorily as can be done under a different hypothesis. The author fails to consider that the discouraging facts of observation may be due to the violent upheaval of emancipation and reconstruction, and are, therefore, only temporary in their duration.[22]

Hoffman's findings are part of a long tradition of denying the overall impact of racism upon people of color, specifically blacks. His claims sound eerily similar to "black culture" claims made by today's white racist subculture. Hoffman's racist views on blacks further mainstreamed a belief that crime and violence are inherent traits in black people. The remnants of such madness continue in books such as *"The Bell Curve,"* studies such as *"The Color of Crime,"* or the belief that black men are violent and dangerous. While they continue teaching their children the same racists beliefs as their grandparents, we hear the wailing primarily from the right about how they should not be blamed for what their grandparents did. This belief of inherent black violence has been maintained for so long that information such as what Males discovered remained outside the so-called liberally biased mainstream media. For example, when Males published his findings in 2013, he wrote: *"FBI clearance and arrest tabulations now indicate black youths under age 18 account for just 2% of the nation's homicides."*[23] The data was ignored, even by President Obama. You would think this would be cause for celebration. This information needed to be widely known by the general public. "How did America miss this?"

While people like McDonald and most of the right-wing were expressing racist opinions, young blacks were described   by Males in this manner: ***"Today's young African Americans display the lowest rates of crime and serious risk of any generation that can be reliably assessed."***[24] Our country chose to ignore facts. Because that was done, we have seen needless deaths in the black community. George Zimmerman was able to get away with murder because he believed he could push a tale of the young, violent black thug who endangered his life, so he had to stand his ground. It allowed a 6'4, 220 pound, 25-year-old cop named Darren Wilson to claim he felt like a child compared to the strength of a teenage boy.

"Black people - more than any race in America - are more prone to committing crime. Why this is important, but I don't want to go too deep into the subject besides saying it is because they are discriminated against which creates more poverty for their population AND because many African Americans as a subculture are violent, disruptive people... kind of naturally. I don't of course want to generalize black people as being all the same. There are a lot of great black people I've met over the years as well as there being great, black public figures we all know. It's just that I can't help but think the left is in denial to an extent about black people as well as they are toward Muslims. Black people need to take more responsibility for their role in society. Part of the problem is repulsive gangster rap that many black people are raised on. That's worth noting.

On the flip side, police who may be bored on patrol will target black people because they can assume the black person has done something illegal or has a warrant. The problem is that they target law abiding black people as well who understandably feel as though the police are racist. It's completely unfair and it make the race debate more complicated.

My overall point is that both sides need to take responsibility for their actions. It also makes me speculate on the chicken or the egg argument."
- white internet forum poster, 2020

One Sunday years ago, I was watching a Sunday morning talk show. The guests in the particular set I refer to were Rudy Giuliani and Dr. Michael Eric Dyson. On several occasions, Mr. Giuliani had spoken about how blacks should be more concerned with black-on-black crime. He was able to recite all the statistics. Giuliani gladly recited how another black person kills 93 percent of blacks who are killed. He basically told blacks to shut up complaining about white police murdering unarmed citizens. Giuliani dared to argue with the honorable Michael Eric Dyson, a warrior who has been front and center studying these issues trying to bring solutions to the black communities Giuliani lied about saving. Giuliani refused to provide equal time to the equally serious problem of white-on-white crime. I will repeat, on an annual basis, whites make up more than TWO-THIRDS of all arrests for crimes in this country. Another white person kills over 80 percent of all whites who are killed. For years, whites have lamented about an American epidemic of black-on-black crime. For some whites to ignore the crime in their communities to lecture others is like the gin drinker calling a beer drinker an alcoholic.

"American Black culture glorifies criminal acts. A person who engages in crime is stigmatized by American culture, thug life obviously has a different view."
- Anonymous white internet forum poster

I guess the Sopranos were black. Between 1980 to 2008, a majority (53.3 percent) of gang-related murders were committed by whites, the majority of the victims were white. According to the US Department of Justice statistics, in 2011 there were more cases of whites killing whites than there were of blacks killing blacks. "American culture" ...

"If blacks are killed by officers at a rate higher than their population numbers, economist Ted Miller told The Guardian, "it's the excessive arrest of minorities that's the problem. We need to bring down the numbers of [blacks] being arrested in the first place." (Unless blacks themselves bring their crime rate down, however, the only way to lower their arrest rate is to eliminate criminal statutes or to ask the police to ignore crime.)"[25]
- Heather MacDonald, "Black Lies Matter"

MacDonald qoutes this even as whites are getting arrested the most. I used information from the 2010 through 2020 FBI Uniform Crime Reports for this book. From 2010 through 2020, whites averaged 69 percent of all arrests in America while blacks averaged 28 percent. On an annual basis, whites led in arrests by large margins in 27 out of the 30 categories of crime defined by the FBI. Again, the excuse used to defend such high numbers is there are more whites. We'll take a look at this shortly.

"People who look like you are far more violent than people who look like me. Sponsored by powerful tyrants within the White race, Blacks are allowed to be uncontrollably quick-tempered and to go postal over what they are told by the Whiteys Hating Whitey is "prejudice."

You are totally dishonest for not blaming the common behavior of your own race for any reaction to that, which you have to pay for. You better reform those thugs or we will soon crush you totally, the good with the bad, because blaming us and not them makes you an accessory to crime. Others who look like you act in an anti-social manner; the more you try to deflect from the behavior that rationally justifies racism, the guiltier you are.

The only way we can stop you from making scapegoats of Whites instead of admitting that your own kind give you a bad name is to directly attack the whole class that sponsors your unearned civil rights, which, in a free country, your uncivilized behavior would have long ago forfeited forever. You are just pawns and decoys; your insulting attitude is preached at us to prevent us from eliminating those who write all your dialogue for you."

- white internet forum poster

The quote shows the type of lunacy that some in this country believe. Although whites have killed millions during American history, a black person has to hear and read stuff like this. The departure from reality is evident here, yet there are millions with this departure. As a black man, I have become the number one enemy of the state just for living here. There are some very dangerous beliefs held by a section of the white community about us, and in my view, it is time these opinions ended. Since whites think we are so adept at killing, we will kill a favorite line right wing whites use to look at crime and race in this part of the book. That would be the 13 percent excuse.

"Blacks make up approximately 13% of the US population while they commit 52% of crime. In 2014 according to the FBI, 90% of black homicide victims were killed by other black people."

Back in the day before calculators, when we had to add, subtract, multiply and divide by writing with a number 2 pencil on a Big Chief tablet, the larger number meant things occurred more. Playing sports, for example, the team who had the most points at the end of the game was the winner. Two hamburgers were always more than one. We had symbols that made things clear, such as 9 > 1 or 2< 7. But today, among some types of people, the larger number is no indication of a bigger problem. 2 million now is > 7 million because if we divide that 2 million into a per 100,000 rate, then the 2 million produces the higher rate. Now less than has become more than to satisfy the confirmation bias of a particular section of the white community. The racists.

People who deny the high crime existing in white communities often try justifying their denial by using per capita. Per Capita is an excuse and a weak one at that. Per Capita is determined by dividing the number of occurrences by the population then multiplying that fraction by 100,000 or whatever number is decided. This number twisting is what members of the racist subculture do to make claims about the black crime rate. I will use the FBI Uniform Crime Report crime offender data for 2020 to make my point. According to the 2020 Uniform Crime Report, there were 7,173,072 crime offenders in the United States.[26] 3,642,932 whites,[27] 2,122,038 blacks.[28] Clearly, the numbers show that 1.5 million more whites were offenders than blacks. Whites were 51 percent of the criminal offenders in 2020. Blacks were 30 percent. In any circumstance, 51 percent is a majority. Instead of facing the problem of crime among whites, this is the answer:

3,642,932 #white offenders / 235,400,000 #American white population(2020) = 0.0154754970263381 x 100,000= 1,548 white offenders per capita.

2,122,038 #black violent offenders /46,900,000 #American black population(2020) = 0.045246012793177 x 100,000= 4,524 black offenders per capita.

Poof! As if by magic, a group that had 1.5 million more offenders suddenly now has less of a crime problem because instead of looking at the total number of crimes, crime is broken down into units of 100,000. If this is being done to guess the probability of the commission of a crime, logic shows us that if there are more whites than blacks, the probability of a crime committed by someone white is greater than it being done by someone black. If the crime in your community is so high that you must divide two numbers to get a percentage, then multiply it by 100,000 to claim that you don't have serious problems, you have serious issues. Who decided that occurrences must be divided by 100,000? Why couldn't it be 1? What happened to individualism? Members of the problem subculture are good at looking for excuses, but none exist. The excuse begins with whites being five times the population of blacks. I was told that since whites have five times the population, they must commit five times the number of crimes for the problem to be equal to what blacks are doing. "We are allowed to commit more crime because there are more of us." If this is not lunacy, then what is?

The problem with this opinion is if you multiply things by 5 to make the populations the same, there are things that no longer exist for blacks. We would have more economic opportunities. We would have equal representation relative to numbers of police, lawyers, judges, and political representatives. Increased black representation affects public policy formation, law enforcement, and legislation. Crime would reduce because of the increased opportunities; wealth would increase, and poverty would be dramatically reduced. Long-needed community improvements would be initiated in blighted communities, which increases property value, creating additional funding for schools in those communities. The number of blacks entering and graduating college now rises to the same level as whites. These increases result in a more highly trained and qualified black workforce. Blacks would have the same number of businesses, and those businesses would be staffed with black employees. This increase in jobs lowers black unemployment to the same rate as whites. Fewer blacks would be on government assistance because they now have stable employment. Things would be dramatically different. Yet to the racist, nothing else changes except that crime increases. The racist subculture continues arguing this ridiculous per capita idiocy no matter what. The use of per capita fails miserably and is used by the racist subculture to deny a severe crime problem THEY need to address instead of trying to preach to us.

During the George Floyd protests, the right-wing media went to town telling the nation how police shoot more whites to dismiss the claims of racism in law enforcement. Christopher Tremoglie of the Washington Examiner wrote an article about the death of a white man at the hands of police that happened four years before George Floyd.[29] As usual, the whining went on about liberals and the media wanting to stoke racial tensions by not covering this man's death because he was white. Tremoglie mentioned how police kill blacks at a higher percentage than the black population, then tried justifying police shooting blacks at such a rate by using the 13 percent excuse. He cited an FBI victimization survey where 39 percent of known offenders in homicides were black. In his eyes, 39 percent represented three times the percentage of blacks relative to the black population, which made everything OK. His argument is weak.

The argument coming from the right is that since blacks are 13 percent of the population, blacks should be committing 13 percent of the crime. The problem with this claim is that percentages come attached with real numbers, and when you use those real numbers, the 13 percent excuse has no merit as an argument. In 2020, whites made up 51 percent of all criminal offenders.[30] According to Tremoglies logic, this would justify the higher rates of white deaths at the hands of police. At 51 percent, there would be more interaction between white police and white criminals than the 29.5 percent that were black. We aren't playing lotto or poker, guessing based on probability. The fact that there are more whites means that white violence and crime is the more significant threat. However, a deeper look into this claim reveals its weakness.

Let's return to the 2020 Uniform Crime Report Crime data I just presented. Again, in 2020, there were 7,173,072, crime offenders in the United States. That 7.1 million is 100 percent of the offenders in America. In 2020 according to the census, the U.S. population was 331,449,281.[31] That number is 100 percent of the U.S. population. Out of 331,449,281 citizens, 7,173,072 people or 2.16 percent of the American population were criminal offenders. The 3,642,932 white offenders were 1.09 percent of the American population. The 2,122,038 black offenders were 0.6 percent of the American population. This is where the 13 percent excuse fails. Simple math shows the misuse of percentages. The 13 percent excuse uses the percentage of blacks committing a crime against the percentage of the black population instead of it being used to reflect the percentage of blacks committing a specific violation. The numbers here show that 13 percent of the American people are not committing 50 percent of the crime. Furthermore, they show that 1 percent of the population is 51 percent of the criminal offenders and they are not black.

The 13 percent excuse is a lazy analysis. We have the numbers. They show us the number of crimes and the number of people by race that commit them. The 13 percent excuse must stop. Math exists we can use to be more accurate, and it is elementary. Since all people of any race do not commit crimes, we can only assess crime and race by looking at the number of people who commit or are arrested for crimes in each race. If we want to talk about population, we should measure the number of participants in crime as a percentage of the population. That is done by making subsets of the population who are arrested or participating in crimes then dividing their number against the overall population to create a more accurate claim.

Racist whites have consistently whined about what the media doesn't show. Christopher Tremoglie complained in his article about how the media doesn't show whites being killed by police because the media wants to stoke racial tension. Yet he ignores how the media does not cover white on white crime with the tenacity it does about blacks. Mass shootings in recent years have happened at predominantly white locations, yet no discussion of an epidemic of white-on-white crime. It's always a lone wolf with a mental problem.

Furthermore, the fanatical obsession with guns mainly by whites is never discussed as the enabler of white-on-white crime. Instead, we get the "guns don't kill people, people kill people" line, defense of the second amendment, then calls for thoughts and prayers instead of the critique of white-on-white crime. When Michael Milken was running around saying "Greed is Good" and robbing whites of billions, there was no mention of white-on-white crime. As blacks, we get lectured about black-on-black crime, but in 2020 blacks led in arrests in 2 categories in the Uniform Crime Report, murder and robbery. I am not going to pretend this is a good thing, but let's look at the arrest categories whites led in:

Rape, Aggravated assault, Burglary, Larceny-theft, Motor vehicle theft, Arson, Violent crime, Property crime, Other assaults, Forgery and counterfeiting, Fraud, Embezzlement, buying, receiving, and possessing stolen property, Vandalism, carrying, possessing, Weapons, Prostitution and commercialized vice, Sex offenses besides rape

and prostitution, Drug abuse violations, Gambling, Offenses against the family and children, Driving under the influence, Liquor laws, Drunkenness, Disorderly conduct, Vagrancy, All other offenses (except traffic), Suspicion, Curfew and loitering law violations.[32]

It is time some in the white community started looking at themselves. We all know who they are, so the complaints about this being about hatred of everybody white is just another dishonest dodge. Work on the violence and crime in the white community. This fake news narrative based on racially biased misuse of percentages has led to unnecessary deaths in the Native American, Hispanic American, and African American communities. I must be crazy, but I used to think the most accurate indicator of things was total numbers. But in the world of the white racist, per capita is the only "valid" measure.

"No, black people are definitely the more violent community. History has proven that."
-Anonymous white internet forum poster

Apparently, that person was taught drunk history. I can point to whites' attempted genocide of the indigenous people of this land as proof of how wrong that individual is. Sociologists and criminologists have stated that violent crime is a complex issue. Research shows that regardless of race, poor people commit the most violent crime. According to the Bureau of Justice Statistics, from 2008 through 2012, "persons in poor households at or below the federal poverty level had more than double the rate of violent victimization as persons in high-income households. This pattern of poor people having the highest rates of violence was consistent for both whites and blacks."[33]

171

For the period 2008-12:

- *Persons in poor households at or below the Federal Poverty Level (FPL) (39.8 per 1,000) had more than double the rate of violent victimization as persons in high-income households (16.9 per 1,000).*

- *Persons in poor households had a higher rate of violence involving a firearm (3.5 per 1,000) compared to persons above the FPL (0.8- 2.5 per 1,000).*

- *The overall pattern of poor persons having the highest rates of violent victimization was consistent for both whites and blacks. However, the rate of violent victimization for Hispanics did not vary across poverty levels.*

- *Poor Hispanics (25.3 per 1,000) had lower rates of violence compared to poor whites (46.4 per 1,000) and poor blacks (43.4 per 1,000).*

- *Poor persons living in urban areas (43.9 per 1,000) had violent victimization rates similar to poor persons living in rural areas (38.8 per 1,000).*

- *Poor urban blacks (51.3 per 1,000) had rates of violence similar to poor urban whites (56.4 per 1,000).*[34]

Notice the numbers per capita when all else is the same. Across the board, poor whites had higher per capita violence rates than poor blacks. More than eighty percent of whites who get killed are killed by other whites in America. This continues not getting the attention it needs. People like Tremoglie were the ones running around with the "All Lives Matter" signs, yet police killed the man in his article, and four years later we see someone whining about the media he is a part of, not covering a police killing. Was Tremoglie really interested in fighting police brutality or was he race baiting while using the death of a white citizen of this country to air his opposition to blacks protesting racism in law enforcement? If the problem of police killing whites is so significant to people like Tremoglie, then I suggest they either join with Black Lives Matter and start marching or organize marches on their own.

Blacks have been fighting this for a long time. Those who like to preach to blacks need to understand is that we have taken responsibility. People in our community have been in the trenches for decades working to reduce black-on-black crime. For years, people have been asking those in control for the necessary funds to help them eradicate or reduce problems but never getting what they need. Fixing the overall damage caused by the centuries of racism against blacks and other people of color cannot be done on the cheap. Whites spared no expense to say they live in low-crime communities, even if that is shown not to be true. They built these communities with tax dollars blacks also put in the pot. It is time for those who fake concern about black crime because they have an agenda to start asking themselves: **"What about white on white crime?"**

People at the New York Post appear to have a problem with the black community's grievances. Before I end this chapter, let me put things in a more easy perspective for those who deny the situation to understand. We started this chapter with some mental illness from Heather McDonald, and I will end it by citing more silly season ranting from an article written by Rav Arora titled, *"These Black Lives Didn't Seem To Matter In 2020."* In this article, Arora sings the same racist tune we have all come to know.

Arora writes this mumbo jumbo calling himself mocking Black Lives Matter. But when we look at reality, his opinion is lacking. His beef appears to be with blacks protesting being murdered by police. He is trying to denigrate BLM because he falsely believes there is a lack of concern for the number of blacks not killed by police. He points out that over 8,600 blacks were killed in 2020 and that 90 percent of those were killed by another black. He then goes on to say this: *"Since more than 90 percent of black homicide victims are killed by black offenders, the ghost of endemic white supremacy cannot be invoked to push racial grievance narratives. As a result, the media turns a blind eye. Black lives only seem to matter when racism is involved."*[35]

Arora is right; the media, including him, turn a blind eye to the biggest killer of black people. For years we as black people have heard the constant lectures about black-on-black crime. People like Arora, McDonald, Carlson, Shapiro, and others have written extensively on blacks murdering blacks. Arora cites 8,600 homicides of blacks with 90 percent of those homicides committed by other blacks and believes he is making a compelling argument while calling out black organizations such as BLM to take responsibility for what he views as THE problem in the black community. So let me help Mr. Arora and others who hold similar beliefs understand the real problem.

According to the American Heart Association, hypertension-related deaths in the black community increased from 171,259 to 270,839 annually from 2000-2018.[36] These numbers are 20 and 31 times the number of blacks who were murdered in ways that "bother" people like Arora. Most of these people died from hypertension caused by the stress of living with white racism. Racism was outlawed on paper by 1965. That makes racism a crime. Racism is a crime that continues to be perpetrated against blacks and all people of color in the United States. According to Arora, at least 90 percent of those 8,600 murders of blacks were by blacks. If you use Aroras claim as the basis, at least 7,740 blacks were killed by other blacks in 2020. He and others claim this is a number that blacks must immediately address. More than 270,000 blacks died due to hypertension in 2020, judging by the trends shown by the American Heart Association. If we are generous and conclude that just 10 percent of these deaths are directly attributed to racist actions by whites, over 27,000 such deaths in 2020 were caused by white racism. That means 3.5 times more black people died from stress induced by white racism than blacks murdering each other on the streets of America. That is white-on-black crime, and it's a real problem that must be solved by the white community. Maybe it's time to stop wasting newspaper space and bandwidth with the bs we see authored and posted by the American right.

Blacks get most of the blame for crime, and it is not justified. In 2020, Whites were 51 percent of the offenders for all crimes committed in America. A white offender committed Fifty-four percent of the crimes against persons.[37] Whites committed most property crimes (42%) and crimes against society (65%).[38] Seven out of every ten arrests for crimes in America is on someone white. Whites have a history of criminal behavior that started at the very beginning of this country. Whites have elected numerous criminals to make laws in this country. Whites organized crime and made it a corporate business. Whites control the manufacturing, shipment, and distribution of drugs in this country. Whites made two of the most destructive drugs legal, creating millions of addicted citizens. I am talking about alcohol and nicotine. Whites have embezzled and scammed people out of trillions of dollars in the years America has been a country. Whites control the manufacturing, shipping, sales, and distribution of deadly weapons in this country. I am not trying to blame all whites for these things. Americans with good sense should understand that I am just stating the truth based on history. People can make up all the fancy equations they want, but in the end, one person = 1 person. The record shows that in 2020 3.6 million whites were criminal offenders, that is more than the 2.1 million black offenders in the same year. Percentages have their place, but when used in a disingenuous manner that causes needless harm and death, it may be time to stop making the 13 percent excuse.

"And because I had been a hustler, I knew better than all whites knew, and better than nearly all of the black 'leaders' knew, that actually the most dangerous black man in America was the ghetto hustler. Why do I say this? The hustler, out there in the ghetto jungles, has less respect for the white power structure than any other Negro in North America. The ghetto hustler is internally restrained by nothing. He has no religion, no concept of morality, no civic responsibility, no fear--nothing. To survive, he is out there constantly preying upon others, probing for any human weakness like a ferret. The ghetto hustler is forever frustrated, restless, and anxious for some 'action'. Whatever he undertakes, he commits himself to it fully, absolutely. What makes the ghetto hustler yet more dangerous is his 'glamour' image to the school-dropout youth in the ghetto. These ghetto teen-agers see the hell caught by their parents struggling to get somewhere, or see that they have given up struggling in the prejudiced, intolerant white man's world. The ghetto teen-agers make up their own minds they would rather be like the hustlers whom they see dressed 'sharp' and flashing money and displaying no respect for anybody or anything. So the ghetto youth become attracted to the hustler worlds of dope, thievery, prostitution, and general crime and immorality."

-Malcolm X

Where are the Good Cops?

"There has been a long-standing scourge of white supremacy and racial capitalism, as well as slavery and its legacy, in the U.S. in which two systems of law exist: one for white people and another for people of African descent. Under color of law, Black people are targeted, surveilled, brutalized, maimed and killed by law enforcement officers with impunity, as being Black is itself criminalized and devalued. Invariably, when a police killing of a person of African descent is known to have been unjustified, it is dismissed as merely the action or collective actions of "a few bad apples." This excuse obscures the real problem, however, which is structural racism, embedded in the U.S. legal and policing systems."

-Report of the International Commission of Inquiry on Systemic Racist Police Violence against People of African Descent in the U.S.

I will not begin this chapter with the disclaimer that not all cops are bad cops. That is a statement that should not have to be said. I will not be using that smokescreen to downplay what has been done by bad cops. This is about the bad cops, and if there are good ones, step up and stop the killing. From the Department of Justice: *"84% of police officers have stated in a recent survey that they have directly witnessed a fellow officer using more force than was necessary." "52% of police officers report that it is not unusual for law enforcement officials to turn a blind eye to the improper conduct of other officers." "61% of police officers state they do not always report serious abuse that has been directly observed by fellow officers." 43% of police offers agree with this sentiment: "Always following the rules is not compatible with the need to get their job done."*[1]

"From 2006 to 2012, there were approximately 51,000 emergency department visits per year for patients injured by law enforcement in the United States."[2] "On average police kill 1,000 people annually, but less than 2 percent of the police doing the shooting are prosecuted for murder."[3]

"The right of the people to be secure in their persons, houses, papers, and effects,[a] against unreasonable searches and seizures, shall not be violated, and no Warrants shall issue, but upon probable cause, supported by Oath or affirmation, and particularly describing the place to be searched, and the persons or things to be seized."
-Fourth Amendment, United States Constitution

"All persons born or naturalized in the United States, and subject to the jurisdiction thereof, are citizens of the United States and of the State wherein they reside. No State shall make or enforce any law which shall abridge the privileges or immunities of citizens of the United States; nor shall any State deprive any person of life, liberty, or property, without due process of law; nor deny to any person within its jurisdiction the equal protection of the laws."
-Fourteenth Amendment, Section 1, United States Constitution.

The due process clause is supposed to protect us from what we have seen being done by police today. The original understanding of the clause was that the government or should I say the state, was not supposed to deprive the rights of citizens without a trial. Both the Fourth and Fourteenth Amendments are used to assess police conduct because of their focus on due process. Courts have modernized their thinking over time and have split due process into three categories: (1) "procedural due process;" (2) the individual rights listed in the Bill of Rights, "incorporated" against the states; and (3) "substantive due process."[4] I am going to focus on procedural due process in my amateur attempt to be Perry Mason.

Procedural due process is "the process or procedures government must follow before they deprive a citizen of life, liberty, and property."[5] I may not be a lawyer, but I can read words and see actions. Now I recognize that the Fourth amendment was not intended for blacks when the words were written. Justice Taney made that very clear in his opinion in Dred Scott v. Sandford. Ratification of the 14th amendment meant blacks were supposed to be included, thereby covered as citizens by all constitutional rights. What has been written on paper has not been followed, especially by those in law enforcement. Police have consistently violated the constitutional and human rights of black people.

Tennessee vs. Garner gave police the right to kill if they determined the suspect was a threat.[6] This was a case taken to the Supreme Court by the father of Edward Garner, who was killed by police as he was running unarmed with a purse that had 10 dollars in it. Here are the facts of the case:

"During a chase, police officer Elton Hymon shot 15-year-old Edward Eugene Garner with a hollow tip bullet to prevent Garner from escaping over a fence. Garner was suspected of burglarizing a nearby house. Hymon admitted that before he shot he saw no evidence that Garner was armed and "figured" he was unarmed. The bullet hit Garner in the back of the

head. Garner was taken to the hospital where he died a short time later.

Garner's father sued seeking damages for violations of Garner's constitutional rights. The district court entered judgment for the defendants because Tennessee law authorized Hymon's actions. The court also felt that Garner had assumed the risk of being shot by recklessly attempting to escape. The U.S. Court of Appeals for the Sixth Circuit reversed, holding that killing a fleeing suspect is a "seizure" under the Fourth Amendment and such a seizure would only be reasonable if the suspect posed a threat to the safety of police officers or the community at large."[7]

The question presented to the Supreme Court was if a state statute allowing police to use deadly force violated the Fourth Amendment. By a 6-3 decision, the court said yes. But...

"The Fourth Amendment prohibits the use of deadly force unless it is necessary to prevent the escape of a fleeing felon and the officer has probable cause to believe that the suspect poses a significant threat of violence to the officer or the community."[8]

Let's look at several of these situations. We know the story of Michael Brown. He was hit with 6 bullets by officer Darren Wilson who claimed his life was in danger when an unarmed 300-pound teenage boy wearing flip flops and pants sagging was supposedly sprinting at Usain Bolt world-class speed towards Wilson snarling and snorting fire. Come on, man! Really? I didn't know Brown or his parents, and I don't mean any disrespect here, but the type of agility Brown would need to have to be running at full speed with his pants sagging below his butt cheeks while wearing flip flops (as shown on the store videotape released by the FPD) makes me wonder why a major college football team did not recruit Brown. For Brown to be running in the manner Wilson made up, he would have needed to have the ability to fully extend his legs in order high step into such a sprint. The fact his pants were sagging below his butt erased that possibility. So was the fact that he was some 20 yards away from Wilson as he was shooting. That passed as a serious threat to Wilson's life.

When you watch videos of the Alton Sterling murder, the question arises about the lack of humanity in law enforcement. I saw two police officers walk up to a man who was selling CDs, tackle him, and start firing bullets into his chest at point-blank range as he struggled against what was an unjust police action. The claim was that Sterling was reaching for a gun, so the officers were in danger of losing their lives. I've watched the video countless times, and I didn't see that. They had the man pinned down, two on 1. They had tasers and nightsticks. Yet they chose to fire bullets into Sterling's chest until he died. Where was the threat?

Philando Castile was stopped according to police reports because he looked like a crime suspect, but the officer began by warning him about a busted taillight.[9] The officers on the scene then asked Castile for ID. Castile told the officer that he had a gun and that he was licensed to carry it. It seems that immediately officer Jeronimo Yanez went into panic mode, yelling, "Don't reach for it," while Castile was reaching into his pocket to get the ID as Yanez requested. According to reports, Castile told the officer that he was not going for his gun, but that didn't matter. Yanez opened fire on Castile. Yanez had been there less than one minute before he felt his life was threatened by a man sitting in a car behind a steering wheel.

Please remember that Castile was stopped at 9:05 pm on July 6, 2016.

9:05:52 p.m: Castile calmly informed Yanez: "Sir, I have to tell you that I do have a firearm on me." Before Castile completed the sentence, Yanez interrupted and calmly replied, "OK," and placed his right hand on the holster of his own holstered weapon. 9:05:55 p.m.: Yanez said, "Okay, don't reach for it, then ... don't pull it out." Castile responded, "I'm not pulling it out," and Reynolds also said, "He's not pulling it out."9:05:59 p.m.: Yanez repeated, raising his voice, "Don't pull it out!" as he quickly pulled his own gun with his right hand and reached inside the driver's window with his left hand. Reynolds screamed, "No!" 9:06:00 p.m.: Yanez removed his left arm from the car and fired seven shots in the direction of Castile in rapid succession.[10]

Jonathan Ferrell was in a car accident on September 14, 2013. He was injured and went to a nearby house to ask for help. The people he contacted called the police complaining about an attempted break-in that was not happening. Ferrell's murder is a prime example of what the belief in things like the 13 percent excuse written about in the previous chapter can cause. In this case, Ferrell had been in a car accident. His car was damaged so severely that he had to kick out a window to get out of it. It was an injured limping man, no doubt bloody also, who walked up to the residence of Sarah McCartney asking for help. Instead of help, he got a door slammed in his face, and McCartney called 911.

"I need help. There's a guy breaking into my front door, he's trying to kick it down." "Oh my God," McCartney says over and over. "He's in the front yard yelling."

"I need help," she said, crying.

When McCartney saw the police outside of her home, she's heard on the 911 tape saying, "Oh, please let them get him."[11]

Ferrell was not even close to breaking into McCartney's house. Her excuse for the police call was that she feared for her and her child's life. What was that belief based on? The racist notion that black men are violent and dangerous. Ferrell had been in a car accident, and he needed medical help, not the police. Because of racism, the police showed up and ended Farrell's life. The killer was named Randall Kerrick. When the police arrived, Ferrell walked toward the officers, probably hoping to tell them about the accident and how he needed help. Officer Kerrick fired 12 shots, hitting Ferrell 10 times. Ferrell was dead at the scene. There was no indication of alcohol and drugs.

"Police say that Ferrell was unarmed at the time of the shooting and was no robber at all--just someone looking for help at the first house he saw."[12]

Samuel Dubose was sitting in his car after being stopped by a campus officer who then shot him in the head after Dubose refused to get out of his vehicle on police demand. Dubose was killed instantly. The killer, Officer Raymond Tensing of the University of Cincinnati Police Department, claimed he shot Dubose in self-defense after Dubose dragged him with his car.[13] Unfortunately for Tensing, his body cam could not edit the film to cover his lie. Aside from the fact that the film shows that Dubose did none of what Tensing claims, Tensing shot an unarmed man. Tensing was a campus police officer but made this stop off campus on a man who had not been on campus and had not committed a violation. Basically, Tensing shot him because he would not get out of his car, which Dubose had the right to do.

Tensing consistently claimed he fired in fear for his life as he was being dragged. The video was shown to the jury, experts testified that Tensing's tale of being dragged was not so, and still, the jury could not come to a unanimous vote. Tensing ended up getting away with murder because of 2 hung juries.[14] Tensing got his job back and over 300,000 dollars in back pay for wrongful termination. Samuel Dubose however, did not get to come back to life.

Here is one more. I read a story about a deaf man killed by police in Oklahoma City. Once again, the claim was that police believed their lives were in jeopardy. The victim had a 2-foot pipe. The police had guns, tasers, nightsticks, and multiple cars dispatched to the scene. Police began yelling at the man, but people at the scene who knew the man were trying to tell the police that the man was deaf. Before I go further, the victim's neighbors stated that when the deaf man took walks, he carried the pipe with him to defend himself against attackers. In other words, the deaf man posed no threat to the police.

People were screaming at police not to shoot. The police decided to ignore the people and the man who could not hear started walking towards them. The excuse for why they shot him despite the yells was this from OKC Police Capt. Bo Mathews: *"When you have a weapon out, you can get what they call tunnel vision,"* he said, *"or you can lock into just the person who has the weapon, the threat against you."*[15] The police claimed they felt their lives were in danger, so they gunned him down. He could not hear their commands, but he's now dead because as his friends were yelling at police, "He can't hear you!"

The Oklahoma City Police Department is the same police department that hired Daniel Holdsclaw who raped black women while on police duty and got sentenced to 263 years in prison.[16] The Holdsclaw case shows an attitude that we have seen in the police who are white and patrol mainly in black communities. Some seem to think less of the citizens in these communities and don't like working in them. If you hate your work environment, you're going to hate your job and those you are dealing with on that job. Not good if you are given a badge, nightstick, taser, gun, and permission to use deadly force.

Apparently, Holdsclaw was trained by Alonzo Harris and believed King Kong had nothing on him, so he would ride into primarily poor black communities and sexually assault black women on stops. Since some of them had priors, he would take full advantage of his uniform and badge to force them to perform sexual acts. He made them perform oral sodomy on him as well as raping them. I guess he figured that no one would listen to black women who had records. How many Holdsclaws, Chauvins, and Panteleos exist in police departments?

Bad police are recycled in the law enforcement system. In 2010, Timothy Loehmann began applying for law enforcement jobs. After being turned down several times, he finally got a job at the Independence Ohio Police Department. During his time there, he suffered from emotional issues. His supervisor wrote that Loehmann "could not follow simple directions, could not communicate clear thoughts nor recollections and his handgun performance was dismal."[17] Technically, Loehmann resigned from the Independence Police Department citing personal reasons. More on this shortly. He eventually was hired by the Cleveland Police Department on March 3, 2014.[18] Eight months later, he shot 12-year-old Tamir Rice, who ended up dying.

Words cannot describe the sadness writing those words made me feel. Tamir Rice was a little boy. I might be an old man now, but I remember being 12. Considering all that I would have missed good or bad if I died at that age is just something I can't comprehend. Then I started thinking of all the things Rice cannot do because some unstable individual was allowed to wear a uniform and given permission to use deadly force. But I know that the way I feel is minuscule compared to the never-ending pain Tamir Rice's family still lives with. The belief of the young dangerous black male was debunked by Mike Males report in 2013. That report should have been required reading by EVERYONE in law enforcement.

The personnel records of the Independence Police Department document an emotionally unstable man who eventually was given a choice to resign.[19] Loehmann's file is 62 pages, starting on page 56 until the end there is documentation of problems Loehmann had emotionally and his inability to do his job. Despite the questionable circumstances of the Tamir Rice shooting, Officer Loehmann and his partner were never indicted.[19] The situation was deemed "a perfect storm of human error."[20] People get fired for messing up orders at the drive-through window. **THAT** is an error. The death of another human being because of bad judgment is a lot more than an "error." Loehmann got suspended but kept his job until he was fired in 2017 for putting false information on his application. The unnecessary death of a child was written up as an error, but a mistake written on an application got him fired. But that wasn't the end of Loehmanns law enforcement career. The Bellaire Ohio police department hired Loehmann as a part-time officer in 2018.[21]

Loehmann's case is just one example of how law enforcement recycles bad cops instead of getting rid of them. The Jennings Missouri Police department employed Darren Wilson before he worked for the Ferguson Police Department. The Jennings Police Department was so racist and corrupt that the city of Jennings "defunded the police" by disbanding the department.[22] Wilson then went 3 miles northwest and got hired by the Ferguson Police Department. Daniel Pantaleo had at least seven complaints before he used a hold BANNED by the New York Police Department that killed Eric Garner.[23] Derek Chauvin had numerous excessive force complaints before he killed George Floyd.

I saved the best for last. Franklin County, Ohio's Deputy

Sheriff Jason Meade. Meade's attitude about his job is summed up in this statement: "I hunt people; it's a great job."[24] He gave a speech in church service about using deadly force on citizens citing the examples of David and Jesus. In this speech, he called the use of deadly force a form of "righteous release."[25] It is clear that Meade had flown a jet over the cuckoo's nest. Meade was not only able to maintain employment, but the department also assigned him to work with U.S Marshalls. Jason Meade murdered Casey Goodson on December 4, 2020. He shot him three times in the back, then claimed Goodson had a gun and his life was being threatened.[26] Meade was indicted, but that doesn't bring Goodson back to his children.

"I felt my life was threatened" is a song located on page 1 of the police hymnal. On February 18, 2022, Officer Kim Potter of Brooklyn Center Minnesota was sentenced. As of this writing, Officer Kim Potter has been sentenced to 2 years in prison for the killing of Daunte Wright. The judge had mercy calling it a sad case. But Potter decided she would play tough cop and pull somebody over for hanging air freshener on a rearview mirror. Potter served 16 months in prison and the last 8 months of her sentence she was on supervised release. Mistakes like this cannot continue getting slaps on the wrist. Maybe the Potter case will finally make those working in the American justice system take an honest hard look at Tennessee vs. Garner again because too many police are killing people, claiming they saw weapons or felt threatened.

We hear how the police are scared. What about us? We are the ones who are scared on stops knowing that we could be facing the end because a police officer decides that no matter how old we are, we pose a threat to their lives. We are 68-year-old Kenneth Chamberlain, who accidently hit his life alert and when police showed up at his door, says he doesn't need them, but they barge in any way and shoot him.[27] We are the 5-year-old threatened by police because she wrote something on Facebook about them killing people.[28] We are the woman playing on the Xbox with her nephew when police shot through her window and killed her.[29] We are Botham Jean peacefully sitting in his apartment that somehow was mistaken for another one.[30] We are Freddy Gray. We are Brianna Taylor. We are George Floyd. We are Elijah McClain. We are Sondra Bland. We are Daunte Wright. We are Senior Airman Roger Fortson. I can keep going with the names of the people who are dead because police "felt" they were threatened.

"Vast numbers of the country's 17,000 police departments don't file fatal police shooting reports at all."[31]

Police are given a couple of problematic options relative to both the Fourth and Fourteenth Amendments. These options are called pretextual stops and qualified immunity. Both give police too much authority to restrict individual freedom, and both allow police to conduct themselves in a manner that would be criminal if they were not in uniform. A pretextual stop is when police stop a person for a minor crime because they believe the person stopped has committed a more serious offense. As it pertains to race, this is where the belief in blacks' inherent criminality turns into a problem when a white individual who has problems with racial bias is given employment in law enforcement. Pretextual stops such as what happened to Philando Castile have been done on millions of blacks, including me. The Report of the International Commission of Inquiry on Systemic Racist Police Violence against People of African Descent in the U.S. found that such stops are often the beginning of a process that leads to the use of deadly force by police against blacks in the United States.

"The Commissioners find that pretextual traffic stops are a common precursor to police killings and uses of excessive force against people of African descent. Indeed, 6 of the 44 cases heard by the Commissioners

involved police use of deadly force during a traffic stop. This figure is consistent with national trends. According to a study conducted by National Public Radio, more than a quarter of the police killings in 2018 occurred during traffic stops. The use of force against civilians, however, is not commensurate with the level of risk confronted by law enforcement during stops. According to a study by legal scholar Jordan Woods, "the rate for a felonious killing of an officer during a routine traffic stop was only 1 in every 6.5 million stops." Conversely, a report by ProPublica found that Black men were killed at a rate of 31.17 per every one million stops."[32]

Time Out! It seems that we have a little problem here. The report points out that a police officer faces a potential murder 1 in every 6.5 million stops. I believe you have a better shot at winning the lottery than that. Yet police are killing people at routine stops because they claim they are in danger. Jordan Woods did a 10-year study of police stops, and it is considered one of the most in-depth studies on this issue. The findings were published in 2019 and are available at the Michigan Law Review repository website. Here are his words:

"To summarize, the findings do not support the dominant danger narrative surrounding routine traffic stops. Based on a conservative estimate, I found that the rate for a felonious killing of an officer during a routine traffic stop for a traffic violation was only 1 in every 6.5 million stops. The rate for an assault that results in serious injury to an officer was only 1 in every 361,111 stops. Finally, the rate for an assault (whether it results in officer injury or not) was only 1 in every 6,959 stops. Less conservative estimates suggest that these rates may be much lower. In addition, the vast majority (over 98%) of the evaluated cases in the study resulted in no or minor injuries to

the officers. Further, only a very small percentage of cases (about 3%) involved violence against officers in which a gun or knife was used or found at the scene, and the overwhelming majority of those cases resulted in no or minor injuries to an officer. Less than 1% of the evaluated cases involved guns or knives and resulted in serious injury to or the felonious killing of an officer."[33]

The findings speak for themselves. The actual threat level to police appears to be less than the authority to kill police are given. Based on this information, do we not have the right to be scared for our lives when we see the police? Or are we just supposed to send out hopes and prayers that this is one of the good ones? We are dealing with a situation where people are dying for no reason at the hands of the police. We have given the police the ability to kill at their discretion, given them qualified immunity, and those we elect refuse to end that immunity.

"Qualified immunity is a judicially created legal doctrine that shields government officials performing discretionary duties from civil liability in cases involving the deprivation of statutory or constitutional rights. Government officials are entitled to qualified immunity so long as their actions do not violate clearly established statutory or constitutional rights of which a reasonable person would have known."[34]

Qualified immunity was supposed to protect police and other government officials only if they acted according to rights granted by the constitution. When courts determine qualified immunity they look for *"whether the complaint being made is based on a violation of the constitution and if that right was clearly established"* when the alleged violation occurred.[35] Like almost everything else, qualified immunity has been expanded, and that expansion has allowed police to misuse it. The courts have been enablers. *"From 2005 to 2007, 44 percent of courts favored police in excessive force cases. That number jumped to 57 percent in excessive force cases decided from 2017 to 2019."*[36] It appears that police and courts are confused about what constitutes an established violation. It is hard for me to understand this. Looking at the actions by police that we have seen, it is clear. Police and police departments have consistently violated the constitutional rights of citizens in this nation. Since law enforcement has violated this privilege nationwide, a serious assessment of this policy is necessary. A portion of America is fine with police violating the constitution. As long as the violations are committed against the "proper people."

To hear "law and order" right-wingers talking, you would think they would want to take away the right of police to break laws and be immune from punishment. Senator Tim Scott stood in the senate chambers giving a tear-filled speech about being a senator stopped for driving while black. Yet he could not summon the fortitude to press the Republican Party to support an end to qualified immunity. He saw a police officer in his state murder Walter Scott then try planting his taser on him so he could make up a story about his life being in danger to cover his murder. If not for a camera phone, Officer Slager would have used qualified immunity and the claim that Scott took his taser in a fight so he had to use deadly force to get away with it. Despite seeing the video, Senator Scott determined that ending qualified immunity was a nonstarter for much-needed law enforcement reform.

There are far too many citizens who never question decisions made by police and do not appear to see the problem existing within police culture when they feel they cannot be questioned, and if a citizen does, they can threaten their life. Or, if you don't do what they tell you, they can use deadly force. There are way too many Daniel Holdsclaws out there for people to just blindly follow police orders. Serpico is not just a movie starring Al Pacino. Frank Serpico was a real police officer exposing real police corruption. America is not supposed to be a police state, but we have allowed the police to believe they are personally above the law.

As police killings started getting increased national attention, police had difficulty understanding the growing backlash against their tactics. They were dumbfounded. "Cops are hurt." "They don't understand what's going on." "Every cop in America is on their guard." Are police just that dumb? What do we have here, 900,000 Dawson and Downeys in a "Few Good Men" who get told to commit code reds while not understanding they are committing murder? Is every police chief Colonel Jessup or something?

Don't they know what's going on? Two cops walk up to a man, tackle him, put a gun to his chest and fire six bullets into it, and they do not know why people are angry? Three police hold a man face down while a fourth has his knee in his neck and will not take it off when he tells them he cannot breathe? Police storm into the wrong house and open fire? A male police officer beating a woman on the side of a highway? Another taking down a teenage girl in a swimsuit and pulls his gun on her? I have seen videos of police bullying children on bicycles. An unarmed mother and her children were told to lie face down in a parking lot, and police drew guns on them. The police would have received the benefit of the doubt in almost every instance if not for camera phones. They have beaten, bullied, and killed American citizens and then filed false stories that the public accepted.

On June 8, 2020, several families of unarmed blacks who were killed by police took their case to the U.N. Human Rights Council. They asked for a Commission of Inquiry to investigate police violence and systemic racism that violate the human rights of blacks in the United States according to international law. The U.S. government refused to be held accountable for such violations. Due to U.S pressure, the Council did not pass a resolution to investigate the United States by itself; instead, the Human Rights Council passed a resolution to investigate police brutality against citizens of African descent worldwide.[37] This is standard American operating procedure that allows our government and the members of the racist subculture to point fingers at everybody else to excuse the behavior of Americans.

Because of the unwillingness of the U.N. to investigate the U.S. exclusively, the National Conference of Black Lawyers, the International Association of Democratic Lawyers, and the National Lawyers Guild started their own commission to conduct an independent inquiry into:

1.   Cases of victims of police violence, extrajudicial killings and maimings of people of African descent and entrenched structural racism in police practices throughout the U.S.

2.   Structural racism and bias in the U.S. criminal justice system that results in the impunity of law enforcement officers for the violations of U.S. law and international human rights standards.[38]

Here are some of the conclusions:

"The Commissioners find that the use of force against unarmed people of African descent during traffic and investigatory stops is driven by racial stereotypes and racial biases resulting in U.S. law enforcement agencies routinely targeting people of African descent for questioning, arrest and detention based on racist associations between Blackness and criminality. Because law enforcement authorities are constitutionally enabled to engage in pretextual stops, Black drivers are targeted by police officers

who suspect them of crimes for no reason other than the color of their skin. The Commissioners find that pretextual traffic stops are a common precursor to police killings and uses of excessive force against people of African descent."[39]

"While the Fourth Amendment could serve as an important bulwark against police violence in Black communities, the Supreme Court has interpreted the Fourth Amendment in a manner that expands state power to inflict violence against Black people. After the landmark Civil Rights legislation of the 1960's, the Court gave police nearly unfettered power, which they employ liberally to stop people whom they assume to be criminals, with little or no evidence."[40]

"Nevertheless, the Commissioners find a pattern of police violations of the Fourth Amendment rights of Black people to be secure in their persons, houses and effects from unreasonable searches and seizures. These violations include the securing of warrants that lacked probable cause due to reckless disregard for the truth of the allegations, including some based on information from unreliable informants. The Commissioners find a proliferation of the use of risky no-knock warrants. Police illegally entered the homes of many Black people without a valid warrant or exigent circumstances. And police repeatedly stopped Black people with no reasonable suspicion of criminal activity. These Fourth Amendment violations invariably led to the use of excessive force, and ultimately, to police killings of Black people."[41]

"In case after case, the Commissioners find evidence of an alarming pattern of destruction, loss and manipulation of evidence, coverups, obstruction of justice, and collusion between various arms of

law enforcement in connection with the unjustified killings of unarmed persons of African descent. Police officers and their unions, prosecutors, coroners and "independent medical examiners" are accomplices in the service of impunity. The Commissioners also find a troubling pattern of creating false narratives and smear campaigns directed at victims and their families."[42]

Here is an example. What you will read next is what the police issued as a press release regarding the death of George Floyd. How many other murders have police been able to cover up with stories like this?

May 25, 2020 (MINNEAPOLIS) On Monday evening, shortly after 8:00 pm, officers from the Minneapolis Police Department responded to the 3700 block of Chicago Avenue South on a report of a forgery in progress. Officers were advised that the suspect was sitting on top of a blue car and appeared to be under the influence.

Two officers arrived and located the suspect, a male believed to be in his 40s, in his car. He was ordered to step from his car. After he got out, he physically resisted officers. Officers were able to get the suspect into handcuffs and noted he appeared to be suffering medical distress. Officers called for an ambulance. He was transported to Hennepin County Medical Center by ambulance where he died a short time later.

At no time were weapons of any type used by anyone involved in this incident.

The Minnesota Bureau of Criminal Apprehension has been called in to investigate this incident at the request of the Minneapolis Police Department.

No officers were injured in the incident.

Body worn cameras were on and activated during this incident.[43]

Police have mastered the cover your ass technique. They have used it consistently over the years to get away with brutality and murder. We, the public, enable them to do so by defending their misdeeds on the job they have chosen and have been trained to perform. We accepted the lies because we automatically trust that police are saints that are here only to protect us. "Oh, the police have such a tough job; we have to support them even when they are wrong." No, we do not! Police will say, "You don't know what it's like out there on those streets." How do you figure? We live on the same streets.

Where are the good cops? The 2019 Global Burden of Diseases, Injuries, and Risk Factors Study published in The Lancet estimated that from 1980-2018, a span of 38 years, that police in the United States killed 30,800 people.[44] During the same period, the study estimated that police killed 293,000 people worldwide.[45] The study found that despite the U.S. having only 4 percent of the global population, American law enforcement was responsible for more than 13 percent of all police killings on planet earth.[46] The per capita people missed this one.

"The burden of police violence fatalities in the USA is known to fall disproportionately on Black, Indigenous, and Hispanic populations. Recent studies suggest that over the life course, about one in every 1000 Black men are killed by the police in the USA, making them 2.5 times more likely to be killed by police than White men. Black women are about 1.4 times more likely to be killed by police than are White women. Systemic and direct racism, manifested in laws and policies as well as personal implicit biases, result in Black, Indigenous,

and Hispanic Americans being the targets of police violence.[47]

It seems to me that many of us in America have decided that when a person puts on a blue uniform, they become nonbiased, non-racist, and lose all bigotry. Yet they are human. If a person is raised in a racist environment and become a police officer, they are a racist wearing a blue uniform. A significant problem with this is now they have the rule of law they can use to bludgeon people they believe are somehow lesser human beings.

In 2006, the FBI warned America about the infiltration of white supremacists into police departments.[48],[49] The supremacists could do so by using people hiding their affiliation with white supremacist groups who apply for jobs in police departments. They are known as ghost skins. A ghost skin is a white supremacist who hides his/her beliefs to blend into society and covertly help further a racist agenda.[50] These ghost skins operate in every occupation in American society, such is why claims of racism being in the past remain untrue. Even worse is that police are now volunteering to help white supremacists.

"Although white supremacist groups have historically engaged in strategic efforts to infiltrate and recruit from law enforcement communities, current reporting on attempts reflects self-initiated efforts by individuals, particularly among those already within law enforcement ranks, to volunteer their professional resources to white supremacist causes with which they sympathize."[51]

As we are now in the 3rd decade of the 21st century, there are some harsh realities we must face. One such truth is that blacks are being killed by police in numbers that equal or surpass the number of blacks who were lynched during Jim

Crow. On July 17, 2016, Annalisa Merelli wrote an article on the quartz.com website titled, "More black people were killed by US police in 2015 than were lynched in the worst year of Jim Crow." The title speaks for itself. Take a look at some of the facts she presents:

"According to the historic record "Lynchings, white and negroes" kept by Alabama's Tuskegee University, a total of 2,911 black Americans were lynched between 1890 and 1965, when the so-called Jim Crow laws were enforced. Beginning in the 1890s, these racist laws segregated black Americans in several states until about 1965. During this time, black Americans were often victims of unspeakable violence, and infamous extrajudicial lynchings."

"On an average, 39 black people were lynched per year under Jim Crow. In 1892, the worst year, 161 black Americans were lynched."

"More than a century later, the numbers have hardly improved. In 2015, 258 black people were killed by US police, representing over 26% of deaths."

"For 2016, the trend seems similar. As of July 7, US police have shot dead 509 people this year, of whom 123 were black."

"Even counting only the deaths of black people who were unarmed, the results are staggering. A conservative count puts that death toll at 38, right in line with the average during Jim Crow."[52]

The evidence of police racism is more than anecdotal. We aren't talking about 1-2 rotten apples. Racism in law enforcement is a systemic problem. History shows us that one constant occurrence remains seemingly fixed as a natural part of American culture, the act of a heinous racist crime that happens to a person of color by law enforcement. There has been a continuous downpour of unarmed blacks killed by police. At the same time, a part of white America in every instance tries criminalizing the dead black victim to justify murder.

"While it is somewhat cruel to suggest, Floyd's Black life didn't really matter much for many people. Indeed, the world is a somewhat better place without him in it."

- White internet forum poster 2020

Protect and serve has become protect the police from prison and serve the funeral home director an increased flow of income. The most excellent example of the reality of the preceding sentence is what happened to George Floyd. As we all now know, George Floyd was detained by police for allegedly trying to use a counterfeit 20-dollar bill. As I watched the videotape, I saw a man peacefully complying with the police. He offered no resistance. He did not try to fight. He did not try to take the officer's gun. He was handcuffed. The video continued, and for some reason, the police felt the need to lay him face down in the street.

Floyd is face down on the street while one officer has his knee on his neck. You could hear Floyd tell the police he could not breathe during the video. He pleads with the officer to let him breathe. He was heard asking for his dead mother. Then before he tried to take his last breath, he told his kids he loved them. After this murder, America went up in flames, and right on time, that singular sorry trifling section of America began denigrating the rioters. I am not condoning rioting, but the people doing the criticizing are the same people who are quick to tell somebody black about Dr. King.

"Now I wanted to say something about the fact that we have lived over these last two or three summers with agony and we have seen our cities going up in flames. And I would be the first to say that I am still committed to militant, powerful, massive, non¬-violence as the most potent weapon in grappling with the problem from a direct action point of view. I'm absolutely convinced that a riot merely intensifies the fears of the white community while relieving the guilt. And I feel that we must always work with an effective, powerful weapon and method that brings about tangible results. But it is not enough for me to stand before you tonight and condemn riots. **It would be morally irresponsible for me to do that without, at the same time, condemning the contingent, intolerable conditions that exist in our society. These conditions are the things that cause individuals to feel that they have no other alternative than to engage in violent rebellions to get attention. And I must say tonight that a riot is the language of the unheard. And what is it America has failed to hear? It has failed to hear that the plight of the negro poor has worsened over the last twelve or fifteen years. It has failed to hear that the promises of freedom and justice have not been met.** And it has failed to hear that large segment of white society are more concerned about tranquility and the status quo than about justice and humanity."[53]

These words are from a speech by Martin Luther King given on March 14, 1968. It was titled, "The Other America." Today there are people in the white community who still do not listen. Over the years, we have seen videos of police beating and killing black people in high definition. The instances have been well documented and discussed. The police need to stop acting like they are innocents who are getting picked on and victimized by people who just hate them or have chosen to wage war on the police for no reason. They have been allowed to kill people under a flimsy set of criteria where they alone get to judge what is reasonable use of deadly force.

In the recent past, we had cases where police were gunned down, and leaders preached to us about the appalling violence done to each officer. I feel for anyone who must suffer through that experience, but generally, when somebody is caught on video killing a police officer, they go to prison. They don't get to use the "I feared for my life" excuse, they don't get qualified immunity, and they don't get Attorney Generals like Daniel Cameron who decide to protect people who barged into the wrong apartment and killed somebody. What about the people murdered by police? These killings have created intolerable conditions for the citizens of this country who happen to pay the salaries of the same police that are killing us. In the book "We Charge Genocide," author William Patterson details gruesome police murders of blacks beginning after World War 2. Police have been murdering blacks ever since police departments were first created. How many more do they get to kill? How many funerals must we endure? Too many black people are asking the Goldberg question: "Who's next?"

> *"I don't condone the rioting, but you simplifying this down to one incident is just stupid and shows you have no concept of what is going on. Floyd's death is part of a pattern of behavior by the police against black people. These people are fed up and don't believe peaceful protest can make any real institutional change. Rioting gets their point across for better or for worse."*
> **-Anonymous white internet forum poster 2020**

The death of George Floyd began a series of nonstop daily protests in America and worldwide. The American protests were heavily policed. During the summer of 2020, the administration of President number 45 tried presenting a narrative of Black Lives Matter violence in coordination with ANTIFA. President number 45 sent secret police to a city claiming to be using them to protect federal property. His secret police detained citizens unconstitutionally, riding in unmarked vehicles and snatching people off the streets. He tried pressuring cities with the threat he would send in troops to set things straight with a quickness. This sounded good to the racist subculture in the white community because a story was set that described the stereotype of the violent black looter. But a funny thing happened, the protests were tracked and documented.

> *"The vast majority of demonstration events associated with the BLM movement are non-violent In more than 93% of all demonstrations connected to the movement, demonstrators have not engaged in violence or destructive activity."*[54]

The Armed Conflict Location & Event Data Project documented the summer protests. They recorded over 7,500 protests and found that more than 93 percent were peaceful. ACLED documented over 2,400 locations and found that violence occurred in less than 220. The violence ranged from *"fighting back against police" to vandalism, property destruction looting, road-blocking using barricades, burning tires or other materials."*[55] This report also found that the government response from President number 45 contributed to the violence. The federal response increased tension and violence. For example, in Portland Oregon, violence increased by 9 percent after President number 45 sent troops to that city.[56] ACLED also found that the government intervened more in BLM demonstrations than any other demonstration or protest.

"ACLED also highlights a violent government response, in which authorities use force more often than not when they are present at protests and that they disproportionately used force while intervening in demonstrations associated with the BLM movement, relative to other types of demonstrations."[57]

Another funny thing was discovered during these protests (well, actually not so funny). The violence in many of these protests was from people not associated with Black Lives Matter. The evidence from ACLED shows that much of the violence came from infiltrators and counter-protesters, many associated with white nationalist and paramilitary organizations. These groups had an ally that often helped escalate the situation, then used violence to settle things down. That ally was law enforcement.

"Since Floyd's killing, dozens of car-ramming attacks by individual perpetrators — in some cases acting independently with no reported affiliation, and in others linked to hate groups like the Ku Klux Klan — have been reported at demonstrations around the country. Other cases have involved those affiliated with the government, such as the military and law enforcement, including an on-duty police officer at a demonstration in Anaheim, California on 25 July; an off-duty police officer at a demonstration in Seattle, Washington on 4 July; an army sergeant at a demonstration in Austin, Texas on 25 July; and an off-duty jail correctional officer at a demonstration in Kokomo, Indiana on 30 May."[58]

In another study of the protests, the Radcliffe Institute at Harvard found that 96.3 percent of the BLM protests had no property damage or police injuries.[59] In 97.7 percent of events, no injuries were reported at all.[60] In fact, the study determined that most of the violence was directed at BLM protesters. There were arrests in 5 percent of the protests.61 Protesters/bystanders were reported injured in 1.6 percent of the protests.[62] Police were reported injured in 1 percent of the protests.[63]

The George Floyd protests were the perfect place for accelerationists. The ideology or belief in accelerationism was not a topic covered in detail by the so-called "highly liberal biased" mainstream media. For accelerationists, the riots were evidence of the breakdown in society they believe is taking nations like America into a policy of white genocide.[64] Accelerationists with this belief saw the riots as a perfect opportunity to move the country towards the race war they want to see in the hopes of creating a white ethnostate. Knowing these protests were led by Black Lives Matter, accelerationists committed acts of violence, including looting and burning, knowing it would be blamed on Black Lives Matter. This is not to say that no blacks participated in these activities, but again, according to most of the documentation I read, much of the violence came from people who were not associated with Black Lives Matter.

In the first chapter, I wrote about the Kerner Comission findings. The Kerner Commission was created in response to a situation such as the events following the murder of George Floyd. One conclusion by the commission was that the riots happened because of "accumulated grievances by the black community and the failure of local governments to correct the conditions."[65] In 2020 and right now, the same thing can be said, not only for local governments but also for state and federal governments in respect to their failure to adequately address the decades-old problem of law enforcement's poor relationship with communities of color.

In 1968, the Kerner Commission issued this warning:

"The Commission believes there is a grave danger that some communities may resort to indiscriminately and excessive force. The harmful effects of overreaction are incalculable. The Commission condemns moves to equip police departments with mass destruction weapons, such as automatic rifles, machine guns and tanks. Weapons which are designed to destroy, not to control, have no place in densely populated urban communities."[66]

Law enforcement did not listen. Our police departments became militarized. The record of many city police departments is precisely what the Kerner Commission predicted. Over the 52 years between the warning given by the Kerner Commission and the death of George Floyd, police behavior did not change. There have been countless beatings and at least 30,000 deaths. That the George Floyd policing bill died because of the Republican refusal to end qualified immunity shows us how deaf the party members are to the call for change in policing. Chris Hayes, in his book, *"A Colony In A Nation,"* describes most black communities as colonies ruled by the iron fist of law enforcement based on white fear. The "colonization" has gone on far too long. If congress does not do what is necessary, this issue has nowhere else to go but to The Hague.

The quote below is written by members of the National Conference of Black Lawyers, the International Association of Democratic Lawyers, and the National Lawyers Guild as part of the Report of the International Commission of Inquiry on Systemic Racist Police Violence against People of African Descent in the U.S., on page 16:

"The Commissioners find a prima facie case of Crimes against Humanity warranting an investigation by the International Criminal Court (ICC). The crimes under the Rome Statute include: Murder, Severe Deprivation

of Physical Liberty, Torture, Persecution of people of African descent, and other Inhumane Acts, which occurred in the context of a widespread or systematic attack directed against the civilian population of Black people in the U.S."[67]

Where are the good cops?

"In the Nation, there is law; in the Colony, there is only a concern with order. In the Nation, you have rights; in the Colony, you have commands. In the Nation, you are innocent until proven guilty; in the Colony, you are born guilty."
Chris Hayes, "A Colony In A Nation"

America Has Taken a Knee on Us!

"What to the American slave is your Fourth of July? I answer, a day that reveals to him more than all other days of the year, the gross injustice and cruelty to which he is the constant victim. To him your celebration is a sham; your boasted liberty an unholy license; your national greatness, swelling vanity; your sounds of rejoicing are empty and heartless; your shouts of liberty and equality, hollow mock; your prayers and hymns, your sermons and thanksgivings, with all your religious parade and solemnity, are to him mere bombast, fraud, deception, impiety, and hypocrisy - a thin veil to cover up crimes which would disgrace a nation of savages. There is not a nation of the earth guilty of practices more shocking and bloody than are the people of these United States at this very hour."

-Frederick Douglas

Some people have an excuse that says we cannot hold Americans who lived in the past to today's standards. I could understand if this standard was applied to all past events, ideas, beliefs, and philosophies, but it seems that this excuse is only used when racial injustices are discussed. For example, we have the political ideology called conservatism, whose members will proudly quote statements from the founders about the role of the American government today. None of the founders are here now. They are people of the past. The right credits them for ideas they had. They can

207

assess today's standards to their words. We get told how we need to return to those standards consistently. Yet if you say, "No, I can't do that because they owned slaves, which means they did not truly believe the words they spoke," suddenly you can't hold people from the past responsible, or you cannot place today's standards on their beliefs. The record shows how the people of that time assessed "today's" standards on themselves. Almost every one of them spoke out against slavery. Ben Franklin and Ben Rush formed an abolition organization. John Quincy Adams was called the "hell hound for Abolition."[1] Don't believe me, here are their words.

"Why keep alive the question of slavery? It is admitted by all to be a great evil."

Charles Carroll, Signer of the Declaration[2]

"I am glad to hear that the disposition against keeping negroes grows more general in North America. Several pieces have been lately printed here against the practice, and I hope in time it will be taken into consideration and suppressed by the legislature."

Benjamin Franklin, Signer of the Declaration, Signer of the Constitution, President of the Pennsylvania Abolition Society[3]

"That men should pray and fight for their own freedom and yet keep others in slavery is certainly acting a very inconsistent, as well as unjust and perhaps impious,"

John Jay, President of Continental Congress, Original Chief Justice U. S. Supreme Court[4]

"I hope we shall at last, and if it so please God I hope it may be during my life time, see this cursed thing [slavery] taken out. . . . For my part, whether in a public station or a private capacity, I shall always be prompt to contribute my assistance towards effecting so desirable an event."

William Livingston, Signer of the Constitution; Governor of New Jersey[5]

"The whole commerce between master and slave is a perpetual exercise of the most boisterous passions, the most unremitting despotism on the one part, and degrading submissions on the other. . . . And with what execration [curse] should the statesman be loaded, who permitting one half the citizens thus to trample on the rights of the other. . . . And can the liberties of a nation be thought secure when we have removed their only firm basis, a conviction in the minds of the people that these liberties are of the gift of God? That they are not to be violated but with His wrath? Indeed I tremble for my country when I reflect that God is just; that his justice cannot sleep forever."

Thomas Jefferson[6]

Thomas Jefferson talked a good game. His rhetoric opposing slavery was soaring and majestic, but Jefferson froze up when it came to action. Many of our heralded founding fathers enslaved people. Sixty-four men are credited with the "founding" of America. Out of the 64 so-called founders, 49 owned slaves.[7] The slave owners were:

George Washington, James Madison, Thomas Jefferson, Benjamin Franklin, Patrick Henry, James Monroe, John Jay, Alexander Hamilton, John Marshall, Samuel Chase, John Hancock, Benjamin

Harrison, John Dickinson, William Floyd, George Mason, Joseph Hewes, John Penn, Edward Rutledge, Thomas Heyward, Thomas Lynch, Jr., Arthur Middleton, William Paca, Thomas Stone, Charles Carroll, George Wythe, Richard Henry Lee, Thomas Nelson, Jr., Francis Lightfoot Lee, Carter Braxton, Button Gwinnett, Lyman Hall, Robert Morris, Benjamin Rush, George Taylor, Caesar Rodney, George Read, Philip Livingston, Francis Lewis, Lewis Morris, Richard Stockton, John Witherspoon, Francis Hopkinson, John Hart, Abraham Clark, Josiah Bartlett, William Hooper, William Whipple, Stephen Hopkins, and Oliver Wolcott.[8]

We are on President number 46 as of this writing. Out of these 46 presidents, it is a fact that 12 of them enslaved people.[9] More than ONE-FOURTH of all U.S presidents owned slaves. Nine of the twelve either owned or "hired" slaves to work in the white house while in office.[10] It would actually be ten because Washington's presidency began when the U.S. capital was in Philadelphia while the white house was under construction. While many want to make this so clean and easy, I will not do that. It must be made clear that ten presidents of this country conducted the business of slavery in the white house or in whatever facility served as presidential living quarters. They bought and sold slaves in the white house. They beat their slaves in the white house. Whatever slavery entailed, it was done in the white house. The twelve slave owners while president were:

Our nation's "father," George Washington, owned over 300 slaves. Thomas Jefferson owned 600 slaves. His slave mistress even had children with him. Think about that each time you see a black person with the last name Jefferson or Hemmings. James Madison owned more than 100 slaves. My last name is Madison. Hmmmm! James Monroe owned 75 slaves. Andrew Jackson owned 200 slaves. Martin Van Buren owned one slave. I guess he would be considered a friendly and humane slave owner. After all, he could have owned 600. William Henry Harrison owned 11 slaves. John Tyler owned 70 slaves. James K. Polk owned 25 slaves. Zachary Taylor owned 100 slaves. These ten men enslaved people as duly elected presidents of the United States. Only one president freed his slaves, George Washington. That sounds good until you learn that he did not release them until he died. Andrew Johnson and Ulysses S. Grant owned slaves, but not when they served as president.

When a black person or a person of color starts detailing our American experience, we get the "I was not there, I was not alive" excuse. These are the people telling us as blacks living today, how we weren't enslaved. This disingenuous tactic is used to dismiss what are legitimate grievances. Because we were not enslaved according to this argument, we have no right to use that enslavement as an argument addressing the issues we face today that result from a system that began with slavery. In this logic, since whites today didn't enslave, they are not responsible for fixing the damage created that started with slavery. Slavery is still part of the black experience for millions of us. I will describe this in the next chapter.

Let me see if I can make sense here. People tell us that we have never been slaves and that whites today never enslaved people. We get told how the past doesn't matter today while simultaneously making deities of the so-called founders of this nation. Then as we talk about modern racism, people start talking about not being blamed for the past because they weren't there. Nobody today was alive on July 4th, 1776. But every year, we fire up the barbeque, shoot off fireworks and declare how the past is why we are a free nation today.

July 4th is fake news for blacks, poor white men, women, Native Americans, Asians, and Hispanics. Here is when the talk of not holding people of the past to modern standards looks and sounds crazy. I don't think freedom or human rights are just twentieth and twenty-first century standards. If past standards do not apply now, why do we refer to a document written in the past and ratified by people who are not here now? None of us attended the constitutional convention, nor did we vote to ratify the constitution, so if past standards are irrelevant, then so is this document. If the past doesn't have anything to do with today, we need a new set of laws that do. This sounds crazy, doesn't it? It is no crazier than the excuses blacks and others of color must hear when we talk about America's true history.

"But the truth is that what so often passes for American history is really a record of white priorities or conquests set as white achievement."
-Michael Eric Dyson

It's funny how certain whites see the right to free speech. To me, it appears that free speech is limited for blacks. For example, in writing this book, I briefly allowed a third party to read some of the writings and asked basically for a grammar evaluation. The book was fine when that person read the introduction, but everything changed when the first chapter hit. I was told not to place all whites in a basket. But I started the book by writing that not all whites are responsible for racism. The person then said to me that I needed to rephrase some things as I didn't want to lose those I was trying to reach. This is the problem with trying to speak on race as a person of color. Far too many whites want us to talk about the issue in a way they want to hear it. Political correctness becomes of paramount importance when we speak to some whites about race.

The "we'll talk about it, but you must talk to me nicely" attitude doesn't recognize one simple thing, racism is not nice. We who live with racism live in an unpleasant situation. We did not ask to live in a racist society, we have asked for that to stop, but it doesn't. We have asked nicely in the way many whites have said they want us to, but little has changed. So why should we tone down how we feel about it?

Tone policing is when members of the dominant culture focus on the language and emotion of marginalized or underrepresented groups when discussing things like race then use that emotion to dismiss their experience. Although tone policing has been primarily defined as an internet phenomenon, the reality of American social interactions about race shows us a history of tone policing as a tool used to maintain white supremacy. Throughout American history, various tone policing tactics have been used to dismiss grievances expressed by marginalized groups. This book is about race, but tone policing happens to women in the same way.

Some in America have gone to extremes to tone police. Tone policing suppresses our first amendment rights. People of color have been imprisoned, beaten, or killed so the dominant majority can maintain power and control. If you doubt that ask Medgar Evers, Malcolm X, countless Native Americans, and Martin Luther King. I will go as far as to say that the opposition to Colin Kaepernick's peaceful act is another example of tone policing. None of that represents what America says it stands for. Yet we are supposed to take it and express our undying support of anything or any symbol representing America.

In 1942 the West Virginia Board of Education passed a resolution requiring that students in public schools salute the flag. We must understand the times when this decision was made to understand the folly of the modern argument about protests by black professional athletes.

On December 7, 1941, America was attacked by the Japanese at Pearl Harbor. Our nation lost over 2,400 men, and more than 1,100 were wounded. If there was a time to remember the sacrifices of those who serve, it was then. After the attack, America began preparing for one of the worst wars in the history of humanity. The buildup of the military was massive. Sixteen million men were sent into battle. War was imminent, and it had become necessary to use any means to support the war effort. Saluting the flag had become mandatory, but some Jehovah's Witnesses decided not to salute. Certainly, the Jehovah's Witnesses loved America, but their teachings say to only honor God. The Jehovah Witnesses refused to salute. Due to what they endured by refusing, they went to the federal courts. In 1943, during World War 2, the Supreme Court rendered its verdict:

"If there is any fixed star in our constitutional constellation, it is that no official, high or petty, can prescribe what shall be orthodox in politics, nationalism, religion, or other matters of opinion, or force citizens to confess by word or act their faith therein."[11] That was part of the opinion in West Virginia v. Barnette, one of the Supreme Court's most significant cases, furthermore:

"Nevertheless, we apply the limitations of the Constitution with no fear that freedom to be intellectually and spiritually diverse or even contrary will disintegrate the social organization. To believe that patriotism will not flourish if patriotic ceremonies are voluntary and spontaneous, instead of a compulsory routine, is to make an unflattering estimate of the appeal of our institutions to free minds."[12]

It's funny how the "it is my personal choice" people pertaining to vaccination to save us from potential death were fine with mandating that we stand while playing a song. The choice to salute or not to is our right. To stop that and force a required ritual denies Americans our right to freedom of expression. The anthem and flag should stand for more than just our military. Did Harriet Tubman not fight for freedom? How about Sojourner Truth? W.E.B. Dubois? Mary McCloud Bethune? James Reeb? Schwerner, Chaney, and Goodman? Fannie Lou Hamer? Leonard Peltier? Russell Means? Fred Korematsu, Richard Aoki and members of the Yellow Power Movement? How about Ceasar Chavez and Delores Huerta? What about the suffragettes and the ladies of the women's lib movement? Do these people not count as patriots?

So precisely who and what are we disrespecting by protesting the current forms of racism blacks and nonwhites face in this nation? The problem subculture needs to learn that their opinion of things is not the only one. What they think of as patriotism is not the only definition. Often there have been people who have been late to the party or show up when the party has been over for years. We all now love Martin Luther King, but when King was murdered, nobody was repeating words from his "I Have a Dream" speech. But now you have all kinds of people who are "experts" on King's life, repeating one line in a speech. More about this later in the book. Keep reading please. Muhammad Ali went to his grave as a legendary American some 50 years after taking his stand against the Vietnam war, which cost him millions. That's how late some people have been.

I hate to state the obvious, but I must due to deplorables we have allowed into the national discourse. Nonwhite people are Americans. As such, we have the right to air our grievances peacefully. If we peacefully take a knee during the anthem, we are wrong. If we organize to peacefully march to protest the killings of unarmed people of color, we are wrong. If we speak out against white racism in any way, we are racists and wrong. When we ask peacefully, no one listens. So what is the proper manner we nonwhites are to protest? Must we genuflect expressing our gratitude for being allowed to live here before we protest? I don't think so.

People who have been afforded everything the constitution enumerates and then some are mad about nothing but tell those of us who have been on the other end how we should be grateful. For what? The chance not to get a job? Having to work twice as hard as a less qualified white person to get less pay? To be denied housing where we might want to live? To be murdered by police for no reason? To look monuments honoring people who committed an atrocity equal to or surpassing what Hitler did for a much longer duration? Somebody tell me. Because what freedom do people of color really have when every time we try using our constitutional right to free speech and expression, there are whites who are quick to use any means necessary to discredit us?

> *"We in America believe in freedom of speech. We have a tradition of it."*
> **- Anonymous white internet forum user 2019**

Do we? The story of the Black Americans says most of us were slaves on July 4th, 1776. My family has been here far longer than most of the descendants of European immigrants who came here through Ellis Island. Our primary "crossing point" was farther south, but the fact remains that we are Americans. As Americans, our story and beliefs are central to American culture; it is time some citizens here understood that we do not have to fall in line with how they tell the story. We have the right to speak the truth of our experience. We do not have to celebrate July 4th. Why should we? That is what Frederick Douglas was asking. How much of a sham is it for us to be celebrating a day when all we did was work upon command of enslavers while under the worst tyranny there was?

I am again going to step into the realm of true political incorrectness. Certainly, this point of view will be roundly criticized by the usual suspects. But this book has not been written to please them. It's written because many of us, regardless of our skin tone or genitalia, are tired of the usual suspects. It's easy for us to sit back and condemn the people who support the maintenance of symbols celebrating the confederacy while using the excuse they are only remembering southern heritage. Slavery was part of that heritage, but that's where the disconnect always occurs when discussing such matters.

We blast the confederacy and have ranted about flying the confederate flag. I oppose the continued display of confederate symbols, but what about the American flag? The US flag flew during slavery that existed before there was a confederacy. It flew during the period of American Apartheid. The same flag flew while dispossessing the original inhabitants of their homelands. The same flag flew as our government passed laws excluding Chinese and sending decent, hard-working Japanese-Americans to internment camps. Why should we stand for the anthem? A song that was sung in segregated stadiums that blacks could not enter to watch a game and where blacks were not allowed in the competitions. It was sung when the United States government was rounding up Mexican immigrants to spray them with Zyklon B. For those who don't know, the United States government used the same chemical on Mexicans that Hitler used on the Jews in Auschwitz.

"Beginning in the 1920s, U.S. officials at the Santa Fe Bridge deloused and sprayed the clothes of Mexicans crossing into the U.S. with Zyklon B. The fumigation was carried out in an area of the building that American officials called, ominously enough, "the gas chambers." I discovered an article written in a German scientific journal written in 1938, which specifically praised the El Paso method of fumigating Mexican immigrants with Zyklon B. At the start of WWII, the Nazis adopted Zyklon B as a fumigation agent at German border crossings and concentration camps. Later, when the Final Solution was put into

effect, the Germans found more sinister uses for this extremely lethal pesticide. They used Zyklon B pellets in their own gas chambers not just to kill lice but to exterminate millions of human beings."

-David Dorado Romo[13]

Can we stop fantasizing about symbols? For symbols are not real. We need to begin thinking strongly about what these symbols represent for everyone. First off, we are not to worship any graven image. The flag is a graven image. The flag flies while the national anthem is played as we continue to see numerous racist incidents by people who then deny that what happened was racist. We see the flag flying and the anthem playing loud and proud while white supremacy is still a supported doctrine by some citizens in this country. Today blacks, other nonwhites, and anti-racist whites are constantly attacked by the racist subculture for using our right to free speech.

So if a black person, nonwhite person, a woman, a member of the LGBTQ community, or anyone else decides to take a seat and not sing the anthem, understand the reality that the flag and that song are symbols of an ideal that has not been completely met as of this time. Until we meet those ideals, that song and that flag do not represent freedom for everyone. The same should be said for the Fourth of July. America has taken a knee on us, and until America can stand for us, why should we stand for the flag or anthem? For those who want to force-feed a version of America that everybody sees does not exist: "Start working on ways to make it so the flag and anthem represents what you claim." When that is done, we all can stand up as proud Americans. **But until that day, June 19, 1865 and July 2, 1964 are my Independence Days.**

"I'm a human being, I'm not anyone's mascot! And I am America's conscience. And that's what they don't want to look at. They would rather look at a cartoon character than at the deceit of this country and this government."

-Russell Means

He Hates White People

Whiteness, within sociology, is defined as a set of characteristics and experiences that are attached to the white race and white skin. In the U.S. and European contexts, whiteness marks ones as normal, belinging and native, while people in other racial categories are perceived as and treated as unusual, foreign, and exotic. Sociologists believe that what whiteness is and means is directly connected to the construction of people of color as "other" in society. Because of this, whiteness comes with a wide variety of privileges.

-Nicki Lisa Cole, Ph.d.

Recently there has been a trend on college campuses to create courses that discuss the concept of whiteness. Once that began, the usual suspects crawled out from under the rocks and started whining about racism against whites. Never mind that black studies departments exist, the American right must whine. Hence the current right-wing movement to cleanse our history books of everything they believe makes European descendants look bad.

In the 21st century, we must move beyond memes created by mostly far-right loudmouths. These types have some whites believing we all chose to come over here on the Mayflower. Some believe it is unfair how whites get portrayed in modern teachings. Unfair is revising history to leave out the factual record. Teaching our children the mistakes we made should not mean we are teaching them to dislike whites or being white. I and generations of other blacks endured the annual K-12 section of history about black slavery, and it did not make me hate being black. In recent years we have seen a consistent well-funded, politically supported movement by the right-wing to enforce gaslighting as a way of educating today's students. In this movement, anything that negatively shows whites must be censored. Meanwhile, whites on the right teach their children racist beliefs at home.

"Actually, its ignorant to claim that all slaves were unhappy as slaves. And there were positive aspects to being a slave---lower crime rate and no welfare pop to mind. Being a slave in America--was far far better than being a slave in south America, Africa, or on the islands.

The slaves in America growing up as a slave on plantations knew nothing else. And hell even when given the chance to be free, many did not want to be----see my favorite over hyped story of slaves HARRIET TUBMAN---she went back to FREE her family as she was paid by the head by abolitionists to "free" slaves. Many of her own family refused to leave and opted to return to the plantation. Her daddy by the way, was given a house and lands by his owner and was freed... like a retirement package. Many who owned slaves did not wish to abuse their slaves and often treated them quit well (I know we aren't supposed to know this but it is historic fact, but you know the libs would have a melt down if the truth was posted.) MANY MANY slave owners released their slaves, while Many others felt slavery was evil but could not find a way to release the slaves and make it possible for them to support themselves if they were free. Slavery in America was like no other place and certainly not always as portrayed by the race pimps of now. There were very abusive slave owners--but there were many who didn't have malice--they just grew up with slavery as a way of life but held no malice against the slaves."

-Anonymous white internet forum poster, 2021

It is painfully apparent that we must teach our children the truth. Most whites aren't going to hate being white for learning the truth. The teaching of race and history as it stands has us where we are now. I went to school from K-12 while being taught Critical White Supremacy Theory. CWST can only be what getting taught that whites did everything great in this country can be called. All the founders were white. All the presidents were white. All the great inventions and acts of heroism were done by whites, except Crispus Attucks and George Washington Carver. All blacks contributed was being slaves until whites bravely fought and died to free us from slavery. When I got to college, I found a place in the university library with information on the history and accomplishments of nonwhite people. I missed so much knowledge because of what was not taught to me that it made me angry. Anger is the outcome when people of color are shown their accomplishments get canceled to learn CWST. The continued teaching of CWST by force will make things worse.

According to CWST, there was a riot in Boston. Oops, I mean, the Boston Tea Party took place on December 16, 1773.[1] I was taught this event is what started the Revolutionary War. We learned about the death of Crispus Attucks an enslaved Black person who is said to have been the first to die for American independence. All this is fantastic but left out is the story of another slave. His name was Onesimus, and without him, there may not have been a Boston to have that riot; oops, I mean the protest against the unfair taxation of American colonists by Britain.

In 1721 Boston was hit by a smallpox epidemic. The epidemic began with a sailor infected with the virus. By the time he was quarantined, it was too late. *"Between April and December 1721, 5,889 Bostonians had smallpox, and 844 died of it."[2]* Bostonians were looking for anything that would stop the spread of smallpox. Onesimus, a slave owned by Cotton Mather, a prominent Bostonian of the time, told Mather about an inoculation procedure he had while in Africa.[3] Mather then went to a doctor named Zabdiel Boylston, who listened to Mathers suggestion and experimented with the process by inoculating his son and two slaves.[4] Boylston saw that it worked, so he and Mather went to area doctors advocating for inoculation as a solution to stop the spread of the virus. Since the idea originated from a slave, there was great skepticism about the actual effectiveness of the procedure. In the end, those doctors had to rest their racism for a moment since people were dying and what Onesimus presented was the only proven solution. So facing the choice of using it or watching people die, the doctors decided to try the technique Onesimus suggested. Boston was saved. CWST taught that Cotton Mather was the father of inoculation in America, but as more is known, there are increasing writings coming out with references to Onesimus.

CWST teaches us of great patriots such as Paul Revere, Patrick Henry, and George Washington. Indeed these men were great patriots who helped white colonists gain independence from Britain. Despite opposition to black soldiers fighting in the revolutionary war by all the great patriots taught to us as part of CWST, the fact is that at least 5,000 black soldiers fought in the Revolutionary War.[5] The reason for the opposition was that white slave owners, one of which was General Washington, feared that giving blacks weapons would give slaves a way to gain freedom by using weapons to rebel. The truth of those times is the slave owners feared a slave revolt more than they did the British. Each state was required to provide a certain number of soldiers to help fight. However, the attrition of war was taking its toll, and state militias could not meet those numbers with white soldiers.

While the colonists could not find enough white soldiers, the British allowed slaves to fight. Washington had two choices, lose, or take black soldiers. That probably would have been his end if Washington had failed, so guess what?

Salem Poor was born into slavery. I read his story as written on the site I used as a reference, and it made me laugh. Here is a quote: *"Salem Poor was born into slavery in 1747 on a farm in Andover, Massachusetts owned by John Poor and his son John Poor Jr. Many New England families treated their slaves as live-in servants and near family members, which may have been the case in the Poor family. Salem Poor purchased his freedom on July 10, 1769, from John Poor Jr. for 27 pounds, a year's salary for an average working man at the time."*[6] Folks, the man was a slave. It doesn't matter if he got to live in the house or how "near" he was considered as family. The Poors were so kind to him that he had to pay them a considerable sum of money for freedom. Can those who do so stop pretending about slavery?

Salem Poor joined the military in 1775. The soldiers who fought with him wrote this to the Massachusetts legislature:

"To the Honorable General Court of the Massachusetts Bay: The subscribers beg leave to report to your Honorable House (which we do in justice to the character of so brave a man), that, under our own observation, we declare that a negro man, called Salem Poor, of Col. Frye's regiment, Capt. Ames' company, in the late battle at Charlestown, behaved like an experienced officer, as well as an excellent soldier. To set forth particulars of his conduct would be tedious. We would beg leave to say, in the person of this said negro, centers a brave and gallant soldier. The reward due to so great and distinguished a character, we submit to the Congress."[7] Poor is the only colonial soldier to get this kind of recognition in the Revolutionary War.

CWST teaches us about Nat Turner, Denmark Vecsey, and John Brown. Schools taught about the victories of white slavers and those who supported slavery against anyone rising against it. Many Blacks endured going from kindergarten through 12th grade learning that blacks were just too weak to fight, and those who couldn't run away just accepted being enslaved. We were taught how runaway slaves were caught and sent back or killed. I was 16 when the original movie Roots was first aired. That was the first time I saw a somewhat balanced version of what happened during slavery.

On September 11, 1851, a federal marshal led a raid into the home of William Parker. Parker was an escaped slave who was hiding four other slaves owned by a man named Edward Gorsuch.[8] Gorsuch wanted his slaves returned, and according to the Fugitive Slave Act, he had every right to use any means necessary to get them back. Gorsuch and his raiders then descended on Christiana, Pennsylvania, to recapture his slaves. If Gorsuch could speak to us today he would tell us he made the wrong decision. Gorsuch and his raiders attacked the house and ran into bullets returned by the escaped slaves inside the house. The life of Edward Gorsuch ended on September 11, 1851, as a result of his decision. His raiders ran away. Most of the blacks involved in the shooting escaped to Canada.

Later that year, the United States government tried charging 41 people who resisted the attempted re-enslavement for treason. The charges were dropped.[9] This is known as The Christiana Resistance. There were other similar acts of resistance, but such things did not get taught as part of CWST. The failure of teaching accurate history has allowed many adults today to be ignorant about black resistance to enslavement which is an essential part of American history.

I don't think white children will grow up hating themselves to learn that blacks have done some great things in America too. But think about the impact on a young black child to know that Onesimus saved Boston from a smallpox epidemic while hearing the story of Paul Revere? Why can't we be taught about Salem Poor and George Washington? How about teaching the complete story of the heroism of blacks who resisted slavery? What's wrong with teaching about the First Kansas Infantry Unit along with stories of other civil war heroes? How about teaching about the Gullah Wars, where blacks in Florida waged a more than 100 year battle against the U.S. Military for freedom? Teaching these things should not make white kids hate themselves, and it shows black kids that blacks have accomplished much more than being slaves who were freed because white men died to save us. It will also teach white children that they are not the only ones that contributed to the building of this nation so they won't grow up repeating the type of idiocy coming from adults as illustrated in chapter 4. That idiocy is the result of the Critical White Supremacy Theory.

I can continue going on, but much of what I would present would repeat what others have written. Many of us have been educated based on a foundation of falsehoods. The lies have allowed the white racist subculture to create a paternal attitude towards other races and are the beginning source of cancel culture in this country. Critical White Supremacy Theory created a false history that ignores significant accomplishments of almost everyone who was not white.

> *"When you've had as much freedom to do what you want to do and think what you want and say what you want and act as you please, then you get irrationally rankled at having to curtail your life and your thought in any way,"*
> **- Peggy McIntosh**

Don Gonyea wrote an article for NPR titled: *"Majority*

Of White Americans Say They Believe Whites Face Discrimination." The article cited a poll from NPR, the Robert Wood Johnson Foundation, and the Harvard T.H. Chan School of Public Health. Fifty-five percent of the whites participating in that poll believed whites were discriminated against.[10] When asked if they had ever been personally discriminated against, no more than 19 percent could say they had personally been discriminated against.[11]

The Washington Post did a poll in 2016 asking blacks and whites to compare how much of a problem racial bias had been since the 1950s. Both groups determined anti-black bias had been reduced since 1950, but whites felt that anti-white bias had increased. It is interesting to read the opinion of whites that led to this claim. I was born in 1961 and I really cannot understand how they came to this conclusion.

"White respondents agreed that anti-white bias was not a problem in the 1950s but reported that bias against whites started climbing in the 1960s and 1970s before rising sharply in the past 30 years."[12]

It can be no coincidence that whites claim anti-white bias began to increase starting with the civil rights movement. There is a difference between bias and refusing to accept continuing racism. I believe whites in this poll confused the two issues regarding their opinion. The belief that anti-white bias was the basis for resistance avoids the reality of overt racism and legalized segregation during that time. It also is evidence of the lack of education in our society about this era and how blacks felt. We get taught about Rosa Parks, Brown vs. Topeka, and things of that nature, but this poll raises questions about how educated some whites are relative to prevailing attitudes blacks had of whites during those years. The following comments are from a man who believed Malcolm X taught racial hatred in the sixties. He was asked to explain, and this was his response:

1. *A man who indicted white America in the harshest terms*
2. *He went to prison for larceny and breaking and entering*
3. *He later wrote, Little was the name that "the white slavemaster ... had imposed upon [his] paternal forebears"*
4. *Promoted black supremacy, advocated the separation of black and white Americans, and rejected the civil rights movement for its emphasis on integration*

Until he finally came to his senses and disavowed the nation of Islam and other tools of racism and racial hatred. Too late for him. He eventually got the right idea that people are more alike for what they share in common, rather than the pinheaded notions like fools who live in polarity seeking to divide himself from others for any superficiality he can find different.

- white internet forum poster 2019

Overt racism practiced in the 1960s was not what caused Malcolm X to criticize whites, according to this person. He ignores that it was WHITES who wanted to live separately. That was written law in the United States. Malcolm advocated separatism because whites refused to accept us as equals. The shame in this commentary is that some whites see things in this manner. His opinion is a false depiction of Malcolm X along with a complete denial of the times in which he lived. He continued his explanation with this comment:

"For one thing, he uses language that racists or collectivists use, instead of viewing people as individuals, viewing them solely as members of a group. "White men this" "white men that". Also, in most of the quotes I have seen of his, I can tangibly feel his bitterness, anger, and "us against them" attitude

in regard to whites. Even if it is not explicitly stated in his words. If that was in reverse, you would call it racism, or at the very least bigotry."

- white internet forum poster 2019

It is difficult to understand how some whites can look at what was going on in the 1960s and make these kinds of comments. Yet these are the types who would have taken part in that Washington Post poll. They felt that less racial bias existed against whites instead of understanding that what was coming from blacks was not bias but an angry reaction to overt white racism created by white bias. The racist subculture has developed a phantom discrimination where they claim a bias exists they cannot describe experiencing.

Blindness to racism is a pathology that has been a consistent part of a portion of the white population. According to anti-racist advocate and lecturer Tim Wise, a survey was done in the 1960s during the civil rights movement. The results indicated whites did not think race relations were bad. Today we see the same attitudes as white racism is dismissed as a thing of the past, while those pointing it out get described as victims and whiners or accused of race hustling.

"If you had actually done as I asked you would see that 9 times out of 10 when the news media references the phrase "white men" it is a negative story which invalidates everything you just said about white people not being held to account for the actions of individuals that they had nothing to do with. Conversely if you google "black men" you will see few mentions of the crimes they perpetrate and the people they kill, instead you will see a laundry list of black men who are supposedly victims including Tamir Rice who according to you has been forgotten and swept under the rug."

- white internet forum poster 2018

Today, some whites have taken the art of victimization to a new level. Criticism of whites becomes a whining session Paul Masson or Julio Gallo would appreciate. Any mention of white racism turns into a pity platform of "not all whites" or "you can't hold a whole race accountable for the actions of a few." These excuses deny that since 1776, there have been whites who practice racism. Fortunately, some whites are aware of this. They see racism as continuing and want to stop it. They begin with attempts to educate whites. But they get criticized for doing so by members of the white community who suffer from amnesia.

Members of the racist subculture call the attempt to educate other whites about the damage racism causes anti-white racism. I disagree. Teaching white supremacy is anti-white racism. This idea gets debated among Americans in person-to-person social interactions, internet forums, and social media. In my opinion, there is something wrong with this thinking. Teaching whites to end white supremacy is about as pro-white as it gets. So precisely what is anti-white racism?

"Anti-Racist is a Code Word for Anti-White"
- Bob Whitaker[13]

This opinion comes from an essay titled *"The Mantra."* Written by Bob Whitaker, the essay exposes an apparent inability to remember how whites have colonized most of the world. His complaint is a common one stated these days by the right-wing about how whites are losing a perceived place on the world stage. However, my point here is not that whites have invaded every nation; it is to question where someone came up with the belief that if you oppose racism, you are anti-white.

"What's always interesting to me is the degree to which you've seen created in Republican politics the sense that white males are victims."
- Former President Barack Obama

We must understand how complete the madness is. There are whites promoting the belief that teaching whites to stop being racists creates more white supremacists. This belief is promoted by so-called alt-right "intellectuals" and self-declared "conservatives." They cite articles written and classes taught by anti-racists as the cause. In the May 23rd, 2016, online edition of The Federalist, an article titled, *"How Anti-White Rhetoric Is Fueling White Nationalism"* was written by David Marcus. As you read this article, the writer's premise must be questioned.

Marcus complains about 5 "articles *"The White Guy Problem," "White Men Must be Stopped: The Very Future of Mankind Depends on It," "I Don't Know What To Do With Good White People," "Ten Things White People Need To Stop Saying,"* and *"Dear White People: Here's a List of Things We'd Wish You'd Stop Doing."*[14] After I read his article and the five others, it took some time to gather the proper thoughts on what I read. I asked myself what Marcus was complaining about. The articles only detailed the truth of what white men have done. I find it amazing that a group of people choose to deny documented events in such a way.

"It's a very particular performance I'm seeing more and more of, and it's always the same: the Defensive White Guy makes a racist or misogynistic statement, is called out for it, then immediately begins claiming he's the victim, either in the discussion, in American culture, or both. He claims that he is not racist or sexist. He labels any oppositional commentary, no matter how bland, as an attack, often conflating the commenter with entire groups, such as "liberals,"

"feminists," or "SJWs." Often he will double down on the original racist/misogynistic statement by posting more of the same, even while claiming not to be racist or sexist. His attacks are filled with horrible insults. He claims perfect entitlement to the usage of those terms because he is being "attacked," or because the people who disagree with him "deserve" it."
-From: The White Guy Problem[15]

A classic example of this "performance" happened during the reign of President number 45. During the summer of 2019, President number 45 decided to tell four women of color that they could go back where they came from if they did not like America. It was a blatantly racist comment. Once President number 45 was called on it, he performed as described by the writer I cited above. He doubled down, insulted the women more, asserted the comments were not racist, and claimed the four ladies were disrespecting America. To him, they deserved the attack because of this imaginary disrespect. The main problem with his tantrum was that these women were sitting members of congress. Not only were they U.S citizens, but they were elected officials charged with providing oversight on the Executive branch. Their criticism of the President was not disrespectful to America. It was what we call a constitutionally mandated duty.

Marcus used the sad, sorry argument that white men today are angry because they get blamed for things done in the past. The problem is they still benefit from that past. Individuals like Marcus are the first to use the "content of character" line in discussing the role whites have as it pertains to race in America. When we look at what Marcus wrote based on the content of character, we see that men like him lack character. I am far from perfect myself, and I say that to balance my criticism of what Marcus wrote. Still, to be so arrogant as to think white men can demand accountability from others for things they have not done while threatening others with how white men will turn racist if they are held accountable is a display of unmitigated gall. If white men today do not want to be held to account, end the racism. Some white men know how to end it and work to do so. They get ostracized by whites such as Marcus, blamed for teaching people to hate whites, teaching whites to hate themselves, or forcing whites to feel guilty about things they did not do, even as some continue doing them.

> *"Aggrieved whiteness is a white identity politics aimed at maintaining white socio-political hegemony through challenging efforts to combat actual material racial inequality, while supporting heavily racialized investments in policing, prisons, and the military, and positing a narrative of antiwhite racial oppression loosely rooted in an assortment of racialized threats."*
> **Mike King**[16]

Aggrieved whiteness is a trait shown mainly by right-wing white men. They have problems reconciling how people are holding them accountable for the creation and maintenance of a system here in America and most of the world that has benefitted many of them by exploiting others. An op-ed was written in the July 3, 2017, edition of the Boston Globe titled "In Defense of the White Male" By Roland Merullo. In this article, we see the most common argument used by the white grievance crowd when the topic is racism. Here the author complains about how he thinks white men are mistreated, suggests that white males have done no more or less evil than anyone else, and wonders why in his view, everybody is picking on the poor oppressed white male. He then points out specific examples of nonwhites who committed dastardly wrongs. He brings up Idi Amin, Pol Pot, Baby Doc Duvalier, and Hirohito.[17]

The problem with his thinking here is not his assertion that these were evil men. They most certainly were. However, in any discussion of racist acts by whites, and specifically by white males, I have not heard anyone contend that nonwhites are sinless. The second problem lies in his refusal to recognize the political conditions that allowed these men to gain power. For example, he mentions Idi Amin. Our media does story after story on the atrocities committed by those like Amin, but many of us appear not to understand the complete story. Nobody sane will excuse what Amin did, but where the writer fails is in his recognition of how Amin eventually was able to come to power in Uganda.

When you look at Uganda, you see a nation that had been self-governed for centuries until the British decided they wanted to make money off the plentiful resources in Africa. During the "Scramble for Africa" in the 1800s, England decided they would make Uganda a British protectorate. The British gained control because of the signing of the first Buganda agreement.[18] A representative of the King signed the first Buganda agreement because the King was a baby at the time. The Kings representative took advantage of the situation by agreeing to reduce the King's power while increasing the power of his advisory council. This agreement gave the final say in all matters to the British, who could veto decisions made by the King.

That first agreement created many problems. Eventually, there was a second Buganda agreement. But my point here is that the existence of a King signifies a line of succession, showing us that Uganda was a sovereign nation governed by a monarchy. Uganda had been so ruled for at least 800 years before the Buganda agreement. From 1894 until 1962, a span of 68 years, Britain colonized land that had been occupied for over 50,000 years. British colonization created division among the people of Uganda. In 1962 Uganda gained independence and passed a constitution. At that time, the Uganda Peoples Republic was voted into power under Prime Minister Milton Obote. One of Obotes friends was named Idi

Amin. Four years later, Obote did away with the constitution. Obote remained in power until 1971, when he was overthrown in a military coup by Amin.[19] The rest is well known.

The author of this article ignored these significant events so he could complain about the persecution of white men. No record exists of nonwhites colonizing a nation of whites in modern times. Despite this fact, Merullo argues that since white men have done no worse than Idi Amin, it is unfair that white men are blamed for bad things. Had it not been for the colonization of Uganda, instead of allowing Uganda to govern itself as it had been doing for 800 years before the British decided they had the right to control that country, it is very possible there would have been no rule by Idi Amin. White men have held men like Amin, Mobuto Sese Seko, Mugabe, and others to account for their evil acts. So why can't they be held to the same account?

The policies of imperialism and colonialism by white nations, better known as the west, have been an enormous problem and a cause of consistent destabilization. These policies have been enacted based on western interests, primarily understood as the profit margin. Usually, these interests have involved extracting natural resources in other lands that can create income for businesses in western countries. The maintenance of western interests has come at a high cost for the countries western nations have "interests" in. Millions have died in those countries because of western interest in what they could extract. Western governments have gone so far as to use military force to install governments that would be friendly to western corporate interests. Because white men have primarily ruled western countries, white men are responsible for enacting policies that created the problems.

"From Jews to African-Americans to homosexuals to Irish, Italian, and now Middle Eastern immigrants, hatred began by tossing all of them into a group,

235

and attributing to that group the most unattractive characteristics imaginable. What is being done to "white males" now, it should go without saying, is not on a par with what was done to those people. But the instinct to label and blame is born of the same kind of group-think."

Roland Merullo[20]

White males tossed all the people he mentioned into those groups and attributed those unattractive labels that many of us still face coming from members of the white male population today. This reality is what men like Marcus, Merullo, Whitaker, former president number 45, and other white men with this mindset willfully ignore. Therefore, they can write such articles and believe they have a legitimate grievance. To them, being held accountable is unfair blame. Yet they can hold anyone they want responsible even if it is made up. Again, this is part of the entitlement mentality that encompasses white male privilege. This kind of amnesia has allowed a part of the white community to embrace a position of white victimhood.

Anti-White Racism is just a talking point the far right has raised to the level of a belief.
-white internet forum user 2019

Webster defines anti-racist as: "opposed to racism." It is just that simple. So how can anti-racist come to mean a person is anti-white? Are we to assume that whites are inherently racist? By Webster's definition, that's racism. Is racism a qualification for whiteness? This makes no sense. But this is a view now held by a segment of the white population. Whites, and most specifically white men, believe they are being replaced or systematically eliminated. This madness has been given some legitimacy because of a rise in white racial extremism expressed at the leadership level in media, politics, and business.

The Great Replacement is a right-wing conspiracy theory created by a Frenchman named Renaud Camus. The "theory" is based on the premise that whites are being replaced in a organized genocide. Members of the American right have also adopted this theory. Evidence does not support this opinion. In America, white males are 31 percent of the population. More than 2/3's of the American people are not white males. Where are they being replaced? White males have the most jobs, own the most businesses, run all the institutions that control this country, earn the most money, and have the most accumulated wealth. Where is the anti-white racism or discrimination?

> *"Why would I waste my time? Your allegiance seems to be elsewhere than the U.S.A. and its people. It seems to be with white straight males who play identity politics, race cards, gender cards, and the rest of us Americans be damned. You rely on laws passed by a group of white men hundreds of years ago who first made sure that no others were included in the deliberative body that passed them. Pure identity politics. How many women and minorities deliberated, voted for, and signed the Constitution? Why did women of all backgrounds and non-white men have to fight to get to vote and participate in democracy?"*
> **-Anonymous white female 2020**

The major problem with much of this modern-day whining by so-called white "Christian" men misses a timely truth that preachers have spoken since Jesus ascended. Jesus told us long ago that God is not to be mocked; what a man sows, he shall also reap. White Europeans replaced indigenous populations all over this planet by invasion and murder. Now they complain about the outcome of 4-500 years of sowing colonization. Today white men on the right want to brag about their accomplishments, but to paraphrase what Robert McCall said to Nicolai as he sat across from him in the Equalizer, "When you pray for rain, you've got to take the mud." Those of us who have been consistently dragged in the mud say NO MORE!

"Telling white people how racist they are (incidentally bc of their race) isn't going to do shit to fix racism... if fact, it might just fuel it."
- Anonymous white internet forum user 2019

The comment above is another example of the white subculture that wants to demand everyone else understand the consequences of poor choices while not willing to be held to account for their poor decisions. People expressing this view claim to be angry because the history being taught implicates whites. Never mind the fact that whites made racist policies to make sure **EVERY** white person was granted rights, not just a few. For example, the Plessy case was decided by seven white men. These seven men voted in favor of separate but equal: Melville Fuller, Stephen J. Field, Horace Gray, Henry B. Brown, George Shiras Jr., Edward D. White, and Rufus W. Peckham.[21] Their vote made segregation possible. Their votes allowed millions of whites to participate in the denial of equal opportunity for blacks and other nonwhite INDIVIDUALS AND GROUPS by law for 58 years after their decision.

"You have 12 year old kids talking about being slaves. They have been raised to hate all races from birth, but specifically whites. Then you have stupid white kids in their 20's that are raised by society to feel guilty for doing absolutely nothing wrong. Such bullshit. Anybody that has issues with someone because of their race, creed or nationality is racist. But people shouldn't be made to feel as if they are responsible for things that happened 80 years ago."
- white internet forum user 2018

It is exceedingly difficult to believe that some people are this dumb. This is how far the lunacy has gone. Here is an individual who believes blacks get trained to hate whites. That blacks are "institutionalized" or "conditioned" to blame all whites for the problems in the black community based only on past events whites of today had nothing to do with. Their frame of reference in cases regarding race relations begins and ends with slavery. They did not enslave people, so they should not be made to feel guilty for it. They created a meme they call white guilt and condemn all whites who understand the continuing racism today as self-loathing people who hate being white and are teaching other whites to hate themselves.

Rational thought has never really been a part of racism, and it is apparent when you hear people talk about white guilt. Issues of racism in America go far past slavery and have not been resolved. I printed the years with the quoted comments to show that "old time" racism exists now. If blacks are angry at whites today, it has nothing to do with slavery or the past. It has everything to do with the continuing racism of today and the attempts to insult our intelligence with the constant gaslighting done by right-wing media, writers, and thought leaders.

"There are plenty of black people who are racist against whites and therefore believe whites should feel bad bc they're white. There are also brainwashed white people who believe white people should feel bad for being white.

I think the above image is a good example of someone experiencing white guilt. Also this article: How Can I Cure My White Guilt?

What do you mean by "false narrative" regarding white guilt? Seems pretty real to me. Thinking white people are racist solely bc they're white (which some

239

*people DO think) is an extreme POV and may anger
some white people and such flawed logic may make
them discriminate against POC—this is just a guess on
my part. I never said you can't tell whites anything as
long as it comes from a respectful place and isn't laced
with condescension."*
    - Anonymous white internet forum user 2019

In 1954, Gordon Alpert developed a theory of prejudice based on what is called contact hypothesis. To paraphrase what I learned in a very simple way is that prejudice comes from applying a broad brush to describe or stereotype an entire group of people based on a **lack of information** about that particular group.[22] In America, we have information that shows 400 years of white racism. Given the record of racism by whites, we just cannot assume there are no whites who are racists. Blacks get called racists because we recognize American history's information. Are we supposed to instinctively know which white person is a racist and which one is not? How do we identify this? So while some want to declare how they are not going to feel guilty about continuing to be racists, we are to feel guilty for not trusting that all whites are not racists based on documented history.

The issue of whiteness has never been about losing white pride. Pride is different than a belief in superiority. From the beginning of U.S. history, Whiteness has been about the overall superiority of white people. With that has come something which can only be described as fascism. While whites gave themselves freedom, they operated in an authoritarian manner regarding nonwhite people. That is not an extreme statement. The denial of rights, the attempt to eliminate the original inhabitants of this land, and the exclusion of citizenship by law to nonwhites are all evidence. If you believe you are superior, pride already exists. Therefore, we are talking about something entirely different than the ability of whites to be proud of their heritage. It appears those who believe in the right to celebrate white supremacy believe that white supremacy is white heritage. In a society consisting of more than whites, this cannot be accepted.

Whites are a combination of ethnic groups; they all have celebrations that display pride in their achievements. British, Irish, Scottish, Welsh, Italian, Polish, German, French, Norwegian, Swedish, and Dutch are "white people." All of them have pride, all of them celebrate their heritage. And I am glad to say that I celebrate with them. There's nothing like a good festival. The racist subculture needs to join whites who celebrate their heritage without opposing the rights of other heritages to exist. Because of what was done, blacks cannot do the same. We did not get to know our ethnic traditions because there were whites who killed, tortured, or punished blacks that attempted to retain their ethnic traditions.

So now that we try doing this as blacks, the racist subculture complains about this being racist. Just how much more stupid can this situation become? I am not just black, I descend from a specific tribe and nation. Members of the racist white subculture are crying about how they cannot have white pride, but I am unable to celebrate pride in my authentic culture because of white racism in the past some do not want to recognize has an effect on today. This has been what whiteness has represented, whether whites like it being said or not. To us as people of color, whiteness has meant the complete deconstruction of our heritage and forced assimilation into whiteness. I mentioned earlier that my last name is Madison. That is an English name. This name is evidence of how my true ancestry has been canceled. It shows that a family with the last name of Madison owned some of my ancestors on my father's side of the family. My last name is an example of how slavery still touches us now.

"Whiteness is what I call the "transcendental norm," which means that whiteness goes unmarked. As

unmarked, white people are able to live their identities as unraced, as simply human, as persons. And this obfuscates the ways in which their lives depend upon various affordances that black people and people of color don't possess."[23]

George Yancey puts the finger on the cause of the amnesia that seems to exist in parts of the white community. When this subculture sees a mental picture of an American, they see a white person. Ask Mitch McConnell if you don't think so. His comments about blacks voting just like Americans were not slips of the tongue or gaffes. Part of the white community has conflated the word American to mean white and claim they do not see race when that is all they see. They do not think twice about how that is racist. Then as the complete story of how things happened is revealed, some whites complain because there are whites who have been depicted justifiably as villains for doing criminal things. Right-wing whites are angry, blaming the left for teaching hate because they tell the actual story instead of the revised one.

"The whites are in charge because they know how to do things, how to make things, etc. You become their equals not by killing them or doing atrocities to them but by becoming as good as them by learning things they know so they no longer have the exclusive knowledge of the things that make your world work. Grow food, build, provide goods and services to others. Learn to be what it is that makes them what they are."
-white internet forum user 2017

Here you have a comment made from absolute ignorance of reality. If whites are in charge, it is not for any reason this person stated. What was said is based on pure fiction. This is a prime example of historical revisionism. No other civilization but white ones knew how to make things? Only whites knew how to do something? We all have been miseducated, and the attempt to correct this miseducation should not be construed as a negative. As this comment shows, the whites doing the most whining about not being able to express their "white pride" do not lack any pride in the fact they are white. Fortunately, there are whites who refuse to follow the program.

> *"The problem with white supremacists although their intention is to stand up for whites and make things better for whites they actually do the opposite and make things much worse for whites in America.*
>
> *White supremacists instead of uniting us they divide us and by their ignorant actions just intensify hatred and divisions between whites, blacks, and Latinos. I hear the complaints of many of my friends who are black and Hispanic and even from my own wife who is half American Indian and part Mexican.*
>
> *Thank you so much ignorant white supremacists, you make living in this country as a white man a lot harder due to your own stupidity."*
> **-white internet forum poster 2019**

Some white people meander through life without seeing the difficulties racism places on people of color. Due to this, some of them have a somewhat altered view of reality whereby they discount the effects of racism. As we see from many of the preceding quoted statements and beliefs, whites without that experience cannot accept, understand or recognize why others criticize what has been done. Instead of looking at this as a matter of constructive criticism made with the hopes of ending racism to bring the races closer, they see it as a reverse racist attack on whites. Because of this, they feel cornered or trapped, get their backs arched, and retreat deeper into racism. Dr. Robin D'Angelo has studied the reactions of whites over years of leading anti-racist education. What she says is confirmed by the opinions in many of the preceding quotes.

*"**White people in North America live in a social environment that protects and insulates them from race-based stress.** This insulated environment of racial protection builds white expectations for racial comfort while at the same time lowering the ability to tolerate racial stress, leading to what I refer to as White Fragility. **White Fragility is a state in which even a minimum amount of racial stress becomes intolerable, triggering a range of defensive moves.** These moves include the outward display of emotions such as anger, fear, and guilt, and behaviors such as argumentation, silence, and leaving the stress-inducing situation. These behaviors, in turn, function to reinstate white racial equilibrium."*

Dr. Robin D'Angelo[24]

I always wondered why some whites would react to any discussion of racism with such defensiveness. After all, if I am talking to a white person about that subject, it is because I know that person is not a racist. This is how many blacks and others of color generally try to discuss the reality of how the racism that has plagued this nation affects us. You cannot reason with an outright racist. Instead, we try talking to whites who say they are not.

"Any white person living in the United States will develop opinions about race simply by swimming in the water of our culture. But mainstream sources—schools, textbooks, media—don't provide us with the multiple perspectives we need. Yes, we will develop strong emotionally laden opinions, but they will not be informed opinions. Our socialization renders us racially illiterate. When you add a lack of humility to that illiteracy (because we don't know what we

don't know), you get the break-down we so often see when trying to engage white people in meaningful conversations about race."

- Dr. Robin D'Angelo[25]

"Racism is just a hateful form of collectivism where humans are seen as members of groups rather than Individuals. That's really all it is. The solution is rather simple. Stop encouraging Americans to adopt a group mentality."

- white internet poster 2018

Understanding the concept of discourse and the discourse of individualism shows me that "individualism" is just another method used in white supremacy. As I read and re-read writings on the discourse of individualism, I find that for people to consistently talk about how we should look at each other as individuals and not as races is an insult. Whites who believe strongly in individualism may not see it that way, but that is not my concern here. This belief says that we must ignore our experiences and history. What we have experienced as blacks did not happen to us individually.

"The Discourse of Individualism is a claim that we all act independently from one another and that we all have the same possibility of achievement and are unmarked by social positions such as race, class, and gender. As Mill states, however, "The reality is that one can pretend the body does not matter only because a particular body... [white] is being presupposed as the somatic norm." The Discourse of Individualism posits race as irrelevant. In fact, claiming that race is relevant to one's life chances is seen as limiting one's ability to stand on one's own; standing on one's own is both the assumption and the goal of Individualism. Because it obscures how social positioning impacts opportunity, the Discourse of Individualism is a dominant discourse that functions ideologically to

reinforce and reproduce relations of unequal power."
- Robin DeAngelo[26]

The argument of individualism, when used to excuse personal responsibility to erase racism from this society is disingenuous. Individualism removes the collective responsibility whites have to end racism in their communities because "they are an individual and did not do it, so find those who did," is the attitude you get from whites who use individualism as a denial. Those who argue about individualism would have a case if racism was practiced in a way that harmed a few individuals while being done by just a few people. Racism is a macro-level problem. Individualism is a micro-level philosophy. At its most elementary level, the definition of American is a GROUP of people living in the United States. Group identification doesn't seem to be a problem for those who use the flag as a shield.

White privilege is an institutional (rather than personal) set of benefits granted to those of us who, by race, resemble the people who dominate the powerful positions in our institutions. One of the primary privileges is that of having greater access to power and resources than people of color do; in other words, purely on the basis of our skin color doors are open to us that are not open to other people.
-Francis E. Kendall[27]

The definition of Zero Sum is *"of, relating to, or being a situation (such as a game or relationship) in which a gain for one side entails a corresponding loss for the other side."* This is what some whites have come to think that laws and policies coming from the Civil Rights Movement have been for whites. Despite controlling representation in a democratic form of government and measuring favorably in every metric involved in a capitalist economic system, some whites feel they are losing out. What rights are whites losing by allowing people of color the same constitutional rights as they get?[28]

Allowing others who are not white equal rights and protections as granted by the constitution is not taking anything away from whites but the right to be racists. Please stop listening to white race pimps spinning the lie that anti-racist is anti-white. The claim of anti-racism being anti-white infers that racism is pro-white. Those who believe this assert that being white cannot be celebrated or pride in being white taken without the right to be racist. Those making this claim apparently believe that racism is an inherent right that comes with being white. I don't think, actually I know, that most whites do not believe in this "inherent" right.

> *"Justice for black people will not flow into this society merely from court decisions nor from fountains of political oratory...White America must recognize that justice for black people cannot be achieved without radical changes in the structure of our society.*
> **-Martin Luther King, Jr.**

Playing the Victim

Gaslighting *is a form of psychological manipulation that seeks to sow seeds of doubt in a targeted individual or in members of a targeted group, making them question their own memory, perception, and sanity. Using persistent denial, misdirection, contradiction, and lying, it attempts to destabilize the victim and delegitimize the victim's belief.*

Gaslighting is a prime tactic used by the racist subculture in America. It is dishonest and ruins any attempt at decent debate or discussion. Furthermore, when we speak of race relations, all this technique does is create animosity against whites by non-whites who continue to face the racism the person says we make up as they try to gaslight. Abusers use this technique in relationships to make the abused person blame themselves for the abuse.

White racism exists today. Nobody is making it up, and no one wants things to be this way except the racists. My challenge to those who claim that whites are discriminated against is: show me how any policy you say does so. Show where these policies have had any adverse impact on the population of whites and white men in particular. Let's see if you can find any evidence without stalling and gaslighting. I am tired of hearing and reading stupidity that comes in all colors, from the late Rush Limbaugh to Dr. John McWhorter, that says blacks are playing the victim.

"I fear we are witnessing the "death of expertise": a Google-fueled, Wikipedia-based, blog-sodden collapse of any division between professionals and laymen, students and teachers, knowers and wonderers – in other words, between those of any achievement in an area and those with none at all."
-Tom Nichols-"The Death of Expertise"

Nichols has articulated a home truth. Where did this stump stupid thinking come from? I say it started when the Reagan administration decided to get rid of the Fairness Doctrine. Suddenly you had all manner of radio talk shows with idiots making fact-less comments. Years ago, I heard some guy on the radio ranting about blacks playing race cards, race hustling, and playing the victim. Or, "Blacks are pretending racism exists just to feel persecuted," along with other genuinely ignorant comments. Rush Limbaugh was allowed to influence at least a couple of generations with his race-baiting. He encouraged the racist subculture in the white community who used his words to claim that they were not racists but were being politically incorrect.

Limbaugh was able to preach his racist mumbo jumbo day in and day out for over 30 years. He got millions of people to buy into his message, and when you examine his rhetoric, it was pure unadulterated hate. The lunacy of his argument was apparent and what has been evident is that we must be a nation of dunce caps to have allowed this man to become a serious part of our national discourse. Unfortunately, Limbaugh passed away while I was writing this. I feel for his family. Despite how deplorable he was, he had people who cared for him. But what he did during his time here was shameful. He became a multi-millionaire by making a career out of fostering white racial resentment.

"You are the perfect example of "you will find what you look for." You lift every rock and think there's a

racist under every one, son. And so there is. Tough way to go through life, but that's on you. Thank Jesus it's not on me."

- white internet forum poster 2018

We have people running around telling us blacks that we are always looking for racism. Now think about this for a minute. Blacks who want to get rid of racism spend all their days looking for racism so they can stay upset, mad and stressed out. How stupid is that? Some whites have told me that I wake up only to go looking for racism. This kind of thinking strains the definition of sanity. So I wake up every morning, drink my coffee, then leave home to begin my daily search for a reason to be miserable, unhappy, and angry.

I would rather pass by the amusement park to find that Klan rally. I would rather sell my ticket to a pro football game to find a Richard Spencer seminar. I would bypass a date with a beautiful woman to watch a Jared Taylor lecture. At work, I will clock in and spend my day looking for examples of ways to be insulted by race so that I can spend all day long mad and miserable. I'm accusing the company of racism because they provide white-out but not black pens. If I am having a conversation with someone white, I can't wait to hear them say something racist, so I can have hurt feelings and anger that I must hold inside of me for the rest of the day until I get home. When I watch TV, instead of being entertained, I watch TV only to look for examples of racism so I can stay angry and bitter toward whites. If I go to a restaurant, I will complain that it is a racist establishment because it serves white milk but not chocolate. I think black ice is a racist designation for ice, so I am mad at the weather person for making racist comments. This is the idiotic garbage some people came to believe by listening to Limbaugh each day on the radio.

Limbaugh even invented a card. Jennifer Garner and Samuel Jackson do not advertise for this card. He left Sean

Hannity, blacks like Kevin Jackson, Jesse Peterson, or Larry Elder, nonwhites such as Dinesh D'Souza, and others to advertise for this card company. It is called The Black Benefits Company, and they have a card these people imagine provides extra rights and privileges to those holding the company card. I remember this white individual telling me how I was playing a race card as I described public policies initiated by whites that created damage in the black community that people face today. This person wanted to lecture me about all this free stuff blacks get because we have this card. I never received all this free stuff, so I asked him to provide me the website and address to the United States Free Black Stuff Administration to apply for my no-cost black benefits. I am still waiting.

People of color like Jackson, D'Sousa, and others give this fictional card credence among the whites who imagine that today blacks get all of these extra things that whites don't get by simply stating our race. If you look at the reality of America's past and present, whites are the only ones who own this card. As stated earlier, cognitive dissonance seems to be a tradition in some parts of the white community. As the south was seceding, those states had whites that believed the negro was happy being a slave. As American Apartheid became a way of life, blacks who got angry and physically fought back when mistreated were considered violent. It was deemed a natural trait that we were violent, not how blacks might just be a little upset with how they were treated. During the civil rights movement, southern whites thought blacks enjoyed how things were and believed that if those northern "agitators" left blacks alone, blacks would continue to live happily in shacks on dirt streets.

Today, this type of madness exists in a belief that we are using race to play the victim because racism is no longer supposed to exist. That leaders in the modern black struggle for equality make up racism to line their pockets and get rich. That blacks do not want equality, they want revenge. That blacks want to enslave whites just as we were enslaved. All this is lunacy, but some whites, nonwhites, and blacks who have internalized racism believe this. I was once asked would I complain if things were different and blacks were the ones doing what I protested.

When you think about these 240 plus years as a black person, it makes no sense to fight for all this time to end a system of oppression and then restart the same oppression because you are in charge. Logically what would be the outcome of this so-called revenge? A nation of whites fighting against us as we fought, a country of unrest, mistrust, and hatred just like we have now, with the same constant division among the citizens of this nation. Yeah, that's what we black folks want. To reverse the violence and hate so that we can say we won. Just think about how stupid that sounds, and yet people believe this because of idiots like Coulter, Kirk, Prager, Savage, Cernovich, and others who have consistently baited white racial fears based upon lunacy. These people were unknown, and now they are rich. So just exactly who are the people lining their pockets by using racism?

"The spectacle of members of a racial demographic that comprises 75% of the nation's populace and dominates both the political and economic spheres whining that they are oppressed is pathetic."
-white internet forum user 2021

Let us understand what this so-called victim mentality is. The victim is not the person who says whites continue to practice racism, that it's wrong, and we need to stop it. The victim is not the black person who fights for equality whites have denied us, which has created tremendous damage that black communities face. The victim is the one who has given up, the one who tells us not to rock the boat, ignore racism, work harder, and all will be well. The victim is the person who makes up things that don't happen, such as anti-white discrimination, or who proclaims that anti-racism means you are anti-white. The victim is the person who has all the preferences and advantages of a society but complains that somehow they are being forgotten and left out.

The victim is the type who believes that somehow another group's fight for equality means their group loses rights. The victim is the person who thinks they are being discriminated against because the university is 70 percent white instead of 75 percent because it accepts people of color. The victim is the person who cries about "merit" without considering that whites, who are the majority of the population, end up with the applicants with most of the high SAT scores mainly because more of them are taking the test, not because they are inherently more intelligent. A victim whines about how whites are getting passed over based only on those test scores when the university's stated admissions policy says that race is but one factor a university considers.

The victim is the white employee complaining that they have gotten passed over for a "quota" that does not exist unless the company is in violation of federal law and still practices racism in hiring and promotion. How many years did Limbaugh whine every day about how terrible things are for whites, how everyone is against whites, and how the world hates whites? That's whining. That's playing the victim.

"Because most whites have not been trained to think with complexity about racism, and because it benefits white dominance not to do so, we have a very limited understanding of it. We are the least likely to see, comprehend, or be invested in validating people of color's assertions of racism and being honest about their consequences. At the same time, because of white social, economic, and political power within a white dominant culture, whites are the group in the position to legitimize people of color's assertions of racism.

Being in this position engenders a form of racial arrogance, and in this racial arrogance, whites have little compunction about debating the knowledge of people who have thought deeply about race through research, study, peer-reviewed scholarship, deep and on-going critical self-reflection, interracial relationships, and lived experience. This expertise is often trivialized and countered with simplistic platitudes, such as "people just need to see each other as individuals" or "see each other as humans" or "take personal responsibility."

White lack of racial humility often leads to declarations of disagreement when in fact the problem is that we do not understand. Whites generally feel free to dismiss informed perspectives rather than have the humility to acknowledge that they are unfamiliar, reflect on them further, seek more information, or sustain a dialogue."

- Dr. Robin DiAngelo[1]

I read an article written by Zaid Jilani in the New York Times titled, *"John McWhorter Argues That Antiracism Has Become a Religion of the Left."*[2] There are too many blacks that want to bend over backward to accommodate. I have great respect for how Dr. McWhorter has represented himself and in return, the black community, but I disagree with his opinion on this matter. Maybe it is because I haven't seen everything Dr. McWhorter has seen. Perhaps it's because I am not working in the same environment, but I don't see the things McWhorter or Jilani claim. As a black man who spent a few years working in the black community, I didn't see the people making anti-racism a religion. I saw black mothers, fathers, grandmas, grandpas, aunts, and uncles working to encourage the succeeding generations to do better. I saw drug dealers telling kids who were straight-A students to get away from them because they had a chance to do better. I saw community meetings where people strategize and organize to stop or reduce crime. I don't see blacks who don't hold black killers of other blacks to account, and I have seen plenty of candlelight vigils to protest black-on-black killings. I have been involved in protests against such violence myself.

I think it's time to face reality. This is not about what the left believes; it is what the facts show. As pointed out in chapter 1, in 2018 The Economic Policy Institute compared the situation of blacks today to the time the Kerner Report was published in 1968 and it revealed little change. That's not making anti-racism a religion. It is called truth. It's time we stopped lying to ourselves. The facts of history are documented. Blacks in America have survived slavery and Jim Crow Apartheid. There is no black victimhood. We have worked far harder, far longer than whites, and for far fewer rewards.

Finally, you get the racist who says we are jealous of how whites have been able to accomplish things. I have these words for those who think this way: I see no reason to be jealous of a group of people so weak they made laws excluding everyone else then brag like it's a gigantic accomplishment because they achieved more than those they did not allow to compete. Blacks and other nonwhites have been able to "equally" compete in this system for just over 60 years. At 60 years of existence on this continent, whites were still in a colony dependent on Britain.

"We live in a society of an imposed forgetfulness, a society that depends on public amnesia."
-Angela Davis

Sellouts and Uncle Toms

"The concept of an "Uncle Tom" as that term is used in the Black community is a slave who is given prestige & comfort by the master, using his position to tread on the slaves abused by the master."

-Pam Keith

T hroughout history, blacks in America have developed many philosophical views on how to deal most effectively with the racism used against us. I know there is the separatist view and others under the guise of black nationalism, but I will focus on two. W.E.B. Dubois's philosophy of protest, agitation, and political action and Booker T. Washington's philosophy of accommodation and patience. I describe these philosophies in this manner because Washington's perspective is claimed to promote hard work and self-reliance, but so did Dubois. There is no black philosophy I have ever read or known of that did not demand that we value hard work and self-reliance.

"There is another class of colored people who make a business of keeping the troubles, the wrongs, and the hardships of the Negro race before the public. ... Some of these people do not want the Negro to lose his grievances, because they do not want to lose their jobs ... There is a certain class of race-problem solvers who don't want the patient to get well."

Booker T. Washington[1]

Some say that Booker T. Washington is the father of black conservatism. I'm not sure this is true, but his ideas and what some modern black conservatives say are close. Washington wanted blacks to work hard, learn trades and not challenge whites. It was hoped this would gain the respect of whites. Washington's philosophy created more artisans and tradespeople, which is a positive. But did it work? No. We did not get the right to vote, civil rights, or equal opportunities because of the Booker T. Washington plan. Some blacks falsely identified as conservatives but are right-wing must understand this. Appeasing and going along with the whites who are racists hoping for change DOES NOT WORK! Washington's plan did not work for one primary reason. Ta-Nehisi Coates points this out in his 2009 article, "The Tragedy And Betrayal Of Booker T. Washington."

> *"The dominant logic of the post-Reconstruction era held that the real problem wasn't white racists, but carpetbaggers and meddlers from up North who'd elevated illiterate blacks above their station. The white Southerner, presumably, had no existential objection to blacks, they just didn't want to live next door to them or have an illiterate and morally degenerate population electing their politicians. To this Washington, and much of black America, said Fine. Cease fire. You let us be, we'll let you be.*

> *In retrospect, this was a grievous error. In point of fact, whites actually did have an existential objection to black people. Their beef wasn't that illiterates and moral degenerates might get too much power. Quite the opposite. Their beef was that blacks would prove to not be illiterates and moral degenerates, and thus fully able to compete with them."*[2]

Washington's idea or plan did not work out because he dismissed one essential truth. Southern whites hated blacks.

They did not want blacks to succeed; all they wanted was for blacks to get out of the way and return to slavery. He seems to have paid no attention to how many southern whites did not like blacks being free. Like a few of today's black "conservatives," Washington looked past the rhetoric whites kept speaking or the laws and policies they passed and thought that perhaps if we accept the way things are, we will gain their respect one day. Eventually, if we do it this way, racism will end. If we leave them alone and do what we do, if we ignore the racism, they won't bother us, and we won't bother them. It is possible to believe his thinking was not this simple in its conclusion. It may also be unfair to compare Washington with some of today's black "conservatives."

Washington lived when blacks did not genuinely have constitutional protection. We could not vote in the south. We were overtly denied opportunities by law. No matter how loud Republicans of today get with how they are the party of Lincoln, blacks at that time did not have much support from either the Republican or Democratic parties. Whites would sneak up on your family and harm you if you got too "uppity." The KKK was in full effect. The military was of no help. The police were killing blacks, lynching was legal, and there was really no justice system for blacks at that time. Black "conservatives" now do not face such limitations. Today there is no reason to say, "let's give them time" or "let's not be too loud about this racism stuff." There is no excuse for anyone black today to be telling other blacks that we need to be quiet about racism so that we will stop dividing the country.

"Most persons do not realize how far [the view that common oppression would create interracial solidarity] failed to work in the South, and it failed to work because the theory of race was supplemented by a carefully planned and slowly evolved method, which drove such a wedge between the white and black workers that there probably are not today in

the world two groups of workers with practically identical interests who hate and fear each other so deeply and persistently and who are kept so far apart that neither sees anything of common interest.

It must be remembered that the white group of laborers, while they received a low wage, were compensated in part by a sort of public and psychological wage. They were given public deference and titles of courtesy because they were white. They were admitted freely with all classes of white people to public functions, public parks, and the best schools. The police were drawn from their ranks, and the courts, dependent on their votes, treated them with such leniency as to encourage lawlessness. Their vote selected public officials, and while this had small effect upon the economic situation, it had great effect upon their personal treatment and the deference shown them. White schoolhouses were the best in the community, and conspicuously placed, and they cost anywhere from twice to ten times as much per capita as the colored schools. The newspapers specialized on news that flattered the poor whites and almost utterly ignored the Negro except in crime and ridicule."

-W.E.B DuBois[3]

The other philosophy is that of W. E. B. Du Bois. Dubois advocated for civil rights and increased political representation. He faced the same things as Washington, and he was trying to figure out a way to change the situation to create peaceful coexistence with whites here in America. Dubois stressed advanced education and helped found what would become the premier civil rights organization in American history, The National Association for the Advancement of Colored People. While the accommodation strategy did little, the NAACP helped end Jim Crow apartheid. Dubois's approach has been the most successful in securing blacks' rights today. His strategy was a blueprint to successfully organize, giving blacks power to advocate, lobby, and present our case to the nation. The formation of various organizations also allowed blacks greater ability to gain access to federal and state governments, where they could create pressure on legislators to end unjust laws and policies.

Martin Luther King and other black leaders may not have succeeded without organizations that built consensus through membership support. The sit and be quiet philosophy has not worked. It will not work. Even with the formation of today's organizations allowing group consensus to organize protests and advocacy campaigns, there is still much work to be done on racial equality. For us to sit, wait, and accommodate is not the strategy. Ignoring the problem expecting it to go away magically, or even denying its existence is nothing but enabling racism to continue.

Many modern black "conservatives" consistently ignore that we would still be either enslaved people or living without equal rights under the law if not for the FEDERAL GOVERNMENT. Therefore, given the reality of how we have been able to get what we have, we must stop listening to the narrative coming from right-wing whites of how they have done things and then trying to appropriate that into our strategy. Any party preaching less government and states' rights will not be popular with blacks regardless of how many blacks repeat silly right-wing rhetoric. Liberal whites do not control blacks to keep blacks dependent. When Republicans say that we don't need the federal government and that we need to allow states to make decisions, so-called black "conservatives" miss the fact that states have had difficulties enacting equal opportunity policies until forced to by the federal government. In other words, Blacks vote Democrat for an excellent reason. The next chapter will look at the Republican record pertaining to blacks. Keep reading, please.

These so-called black "conservatives" have not studied history because they miss this essential aspect of black history to talk about some untrue tale white conservatives made up about some fake plantation the democratic party made for blacks. They use the words plantation, slavery, and slave dishonestly, knowing that will conjure up negative images of the past in a black person's mind and then tell blacks how republicans freed the slaves and how the Democratic party formed the KKK. Again, most Republicans are for states' rights. The principle of states' rights allowed the KKK to run free and allowed apartheid to be effective in America.

"And to my black brothers, if you do not have anything positive to say about our social challenges, please keep your mouth shut."
- Champ Bailey, 2019 NFL Hall of Fame Induction

Some blacks have chosen to repeat and believe every harmful meme about blacks that can be expressed. Then they cry, whine and complain about how other blacks call them sellouts. But that is what they are. It's high time this got shut down. We cannot get the needed changes if some people agree with racist whites on why blacks face what we do while ignoring what caused it. It's time we got something straight, folks. No one wants more government, black, white, green, or otherwise. No one wants the government to reduce freedom or more intrusion. From the first escaped slave, the goal has been self-reliance to produce what is needed to succeed in the American system.

Hard work, self-reliance, personal responsibility, strong family values, everything white "conservatives" claim blacks don't have, has always been part of black culture. Even after slavery was made illegal, blacks ventured out and built communities, trying to create the things needed to prosper in this country. So then who died and made people like Ben

Carson, Thomas Sowell, Star Parker. Rev. Jessie Peterson, James Manning, David Clarke, Alan West, or Clarence Thomas, the spokespeople on issues that affect the back community? Why is what they say so important to hear?

What semblance of reality for blacks do these people speak on? James Manning thinks blacks are animals. Jesse Peterson says racism is made up. Clarence Thomas opposed affirmative action, the same policy that got him into Yale law school. Star Parker is a former welfare recipient who used it because she fell upon hard times and now blasts welfare. Thomas Sowell claims blacks are starting a race war against whites. David Clarke was a police officer who saw racism in police departments and denigrated black organizations fighting to end the racial bias in the justice system. Ben Carson said we should ignore race because we are dividing the country as we try asking for equality. All this is garbage. So what do these people present to us as black people that we need to hear? What real positives do they bring to America? How are these people with such attitudes bettering the relations between the races here in America?

These are the type of people who complain about being called sellouts, Uncle Toms, and other names. They just can't understand how other blacks do not like them. While other blacks oppose these people for the damage they cause, they get embraced by a specific segment of the white community. Instead of examining the error in their thinking, it has been easier for that segment to decide those opposing the sellouts are the problem.

"You can rise above racism if you work hard. I did."[4] I paraphrased this, but this mealy-mouthed madness is why I can't stand Ben Carson. We don't need Carson's lectures on what blacks can do for themselves. We already know. Blacks are doing that and have done it since we got here. The belief that we cannot blame whites when whites put laws and policies in front of us that did inhibit, stall or eliminate opportunities is simply stupid. He was in a position to create solutions. Instead, he made things worse. In his role, he needed to be informing those in power how laws and policies were designed that created long-lasting damage that has never been adequately addressed or fixed.

Carson talks about being individuals. That view ignores reality. Men like my father volunteered to enter WW2 because he wanted to show America that he was an individual. Still, when he came back after taking a bullet for this country, he was told that it didn't matter if he wore the uniform. He had to sit in the back of the bus. Martin Luther King, among many, stood up and said to America that we are men and women, individuals who deserved the right to use public facilities and vote. Still, until 1965 the very people who continue today crying about identity told him that because he is black, he did not have all the rights and privileges Americans are supposed to have as endowed by our creator. According to the laws, his identity made him less than instead of equal to.

This is what bothers me about some of these blacks on the right. They live in the same country as the rest of us. They face the same racism, yet they want to preach to people that such racism doesn't exist or is irrelevant. They act like it is a badge of honor because racists are accepting them as they condemn blacks who oppose their anti-black rhetoric. What kind of mentality exists in these men and women to desire acceptance from a racist subculture that hates them? Why not instead make friends with the millions of whites who aren't racists and are genuine in wanting a fair society?

Right-wing whites quickly push blacks and other nonwhites out to the forefront who they think can advance their beliefs. To support my opinion, I'll tell you a personal story. I attended a 1996 Republican victory function in the state capital of Kansas. It happened by accident as we were bored and saw that Republicans were holding a watch party at the hotel across the street from where we were while watching TV. We entered the party and mingled. We asked the winning candidates to work for particular concerns within the black community. Of course, we got no promises and a bunch of dull unrelated stories from the newly elected representatives, but that was expected. What I didn't expect was the blatant begging republicans were doing for us to start attending meetings and becoming members of the party. A lady at the gathering expressly stated that we needed to join because they needed more blacks. I guess that's outreach. I was asked if I had any political aspirations and that if I did, the Republicans would make sure I could get as far as I wanted and provide me with all the support needed. I could have been Nincompoop Nelson, and it wouldn't have mattered to them, just as long as they could show America a black face. Hence we get Alan Keyes, Alan West, the late Herman 9-9-9, and Ben Carson.

In the movie Magnum Force, Officer Harry Callahan tells his superior that a man must know his limitations. Some people who know me will probably say this about me writing a book, but that is a very true statement. Ben Carson was a legendary brain surgeon. He made history by being on a team of surgeons who disconnected Siamese twins joined at the head. This was an amazing accomplishment. It showed that Carson was a man with great talent who had done the work necessary to acquire such tremendous skills. However, these things do not make someone a presidential candidate.

These things did not make Carson one either. He became a presidential candidate to some because he stood right next to former President Obama at a breakfast claiming that Obama Care was worse than slavery. Oh, what a prize for the racist subculture. A black man who criticized Obama. "We must put this man on TV." "Certainly, he will say what we need to hear." "He won't be like Sharpton and those other blacks; he will say what we say to blacks, making our racism OK." During his presidential campaign and his time as Secretary of H.U.D, Carson did precisely that. Ben Carson recited the shuffle and jive lawn jockey mambo, ignoring racism and telling blacks how we all need to ignore it and life will be good.

Such accommodation is the problem with black right-wingers who misuse the term conservative. There is a difference between a black conservative and right-wing black sellouts. A black conservative would not deny the racism faced by blacks. A true black conservative should oppose racism because the lack of opportunity created by policies stemming from racism are examples of government overreach into the private lives of its citizens. Let's not be mistaken; black conservatives such as Michael Steele, Shermichael Singleton, Tara Setmayer, and Sophia Nelson are not sellouts. I may disagree with their political ideology, but they are working for the same thing most blacks in America are working for, complete equality. Black right-wingers adopt and ardently defend white racist ideology. It is right-wing blacks who are the sellouts.

Right-wing blacks only help foster division. The only reason the whites they associate with accept them is because each of them validates what the racist subculture has chosen to believe about blacks. These are not independent thinkers. A person of color cannot be thinking independently if what they believe reinforces white racist stereotypes of people who look like them. Blacks who think independently do not believe or repeat what racist whites think of us and challenge that belief. Today, white extremists on the right have tried to insert blacks into our national discourse who believe only a certain way. It is classic divide and conquer.

Indeed, other blacks besides sellouts and Uncle Toms raised themselves out of extreme poverty and made something of themselves. Sellouts are not the ones black people need to emulate. These are the last examples we need to teach our kids to be like. For anyone black to face racism and achieve, then tell other blacks that racism is no big thing is irresponsible. If we are responsible as black people, we reject these individuals because they are not helping us. There are many other blacks with plenty of accomplishments to respect. We are required to teach and empower each other with the necessary tools to defeat racism every time we face it. That will never be done by denying its existence.

Ben Carson is Martin Luther King compared to Thomas Sowell. Sowell is a black man who once claimed that a race war had begun against whites by blacks. Thomas Sowell is responsible for making life more dangerous for black people in America. The racist subculture uses his irresponsible rhetoric as high-level intellectual thought. One can criticize liberals all they want about policies, but when you are black and suggest to whites how blacks are starting a race war with them, you invite problems that no one black should be facing. When you know that your audience consists of white right-wing extremists and you state how they are under attack from blacks and the media hides it, you invite and should be held criminally responsible for the hate crimes you have created.

"More dangerous than these highly publicized episodes over the years are innumerable organized and unprovoked physical attacks on whites by young black gangs in shopping malls, on beaches, and in other public places all across the country today. While some of these attacks make it into the media as isolated incidents, the nationwide pattern of organized black-on-white attacks by thugs remains invisible in the mainstream media, with the notable exception of Bill O'Reilly on the Fox News Channel."
Thomas Sowell, 2013[5]

I remembered those words as I was listening to a stirring rendition of the Old Ship of Zion sung by Rev. Randolph Miller at the funeral for Rev. Clementa Pinckney. As I listened to this old spiritual during the televised funeral, I wondered if Dylan Roof read Sowell's words and did those words validate Roof's feelings of how he needed to do something to end the scourge of black attacks against whites in Sowell's race war.

The elevation of blacks like Sowell into thought leadership has been detrimental to the overall improvement of blacks in America. Furthermore, his opposition to the government solving the problem government made for blacks just doesn't make sense. He ignores almost 200 years of whites exclusively getting government assistance in his analysis. It is essential to show the numeric human cost of what Sowell stated. Sowell made his statement in November of 2013. These are numbers published in the 2015 FBI Uniform Crime Reports.

"According to the 2015 FBI hate crime statistics, there were 613 anti-white-related crimes out of 5,850 total cases. That's around 10.5 percent of all reported hate crimes, and within the yearly average, federal numbers show.

By comparison, the FBI reports there were 1,745 anti-black hate crimes or about 30 percent of all reported incidents. Jews were the most targeted religious group that year and were victims of 11 percent of all hate crimes. It's not clear how many anti-Jewish hate crime victims also may have been attacked because of their race.

The 2015 FBI data showed that of the 734 total reported offenses committed against whites — a single incident could have multiple offenses like assault or theft — 46 percent of those were committed by blacks. In contrast, of the 2,125 reported offenses committed against blacks, 58 percent of those who committed by whites."[6]

Based on this data, how can a black person make such irresponsible and dangerous comments like the ones Sowell made? As stated earlier, more than eighty percent of all crimes committed against whites are by other whites. Whites are five times more likely to be attacked by another white than a person of another race, yet Sowell presents this dangerous and life-threatening opinion to right-wing whites who love him. There is a very long history of violence perpetrated against blacks by whites throughout U.S. history. Most of it came from whites feeling threatened. Sowell is a black man stoking and validating those same fears. I don't know what media Sowell watches, but the local news where I live shows stories on these kinds of crimes every time they happen, complete with pictures of the captured perpetrators. Sowell has half-assed his way into wealth because white right-wing extremists suck up his message only because it validates their racial views.

Then you have Shelby Steele. Here we have another black man who lived through segregation, saying that blacks struggle now because we were "unprepared for freedom." It just gets worse.

"The oppression of black people is over with... We blacks are, today, a free people. It is as if freedom sneaked up and caught us by surprise...

This is what replaced racism as our primary difficulty. Blacks had survived every form of human debasement with ingenuity, self-reliance, a deep and ironic humor, a capacity for self-reinvention and a heroic fortitude. But we had no experience of wide-open freedom...

We can say that past oppression left us unprepared for freedom. This is certainly true. But it is no consolation... Freedom holds us accountable no matter the disadvantages we inherit from the past. The tragedy in Chicago—rightly or wrongly—reflects on black America...

That's why ... We conjure elaborate narratives that give white racism new life in the present: "systemic" and "structural" racism, racist "microaggressions," "white privilege," and so on. All these narratives insist that blacks are still victims of racism, and that freedom's accountability is an injustice..."[7]

His opinion is simply crazy. Steele wrote this madness in response to the NFL player's protests. He claimed that the players had nothing to protest. While Steele was writing those words, police were killing blacks. Steele saw Charlottesville, and he still held this opinion. I understand Steele is in his 70s, but I can't excuse his age for this. He is supposed to be a highly ultra-educated intellectual, but you cannot tell by his opinion. Right-wing whites gladly accept this "alternative" view because it does not hold them accountable. It allows them comfort. I have held many conversations about racism, and whites will cite examples from Steele and Sowell. The views expressed by these two stinks of two old black men who made some money, live comfortably, and now want to pretend everything is OK. It seems that many blacks of his era have pound cake moments.

Steele wrote a book titled *"White Guilt, How Blacks and Whites Together Destroyed the Promise of the Civil Rights Era."* I have generally refused to buy books from people like Steele because I believe that giving them income is counterproductive to race and human relations in this country. The more books they sell, the more crazy stuff they write, enabling members of the racist subculture to believe what they think is true. Consider his opinion in this example.

"Because white guilt is a vacuum of moral authority; it makes the moral authority of whites and

the legitimacy of American institutions contingent upon proving a negative: that they are not racist. The great power of white guilt comes from the fact that it functions by stigma, like racism itself. Whites and American institutions are stigmatized as racist until they prove otherwise."[8]

Maybe it's because I am nowhere as intelligent as Steele is supposed to be, but in my view, his words make no sense. None. Zero. Zilch. Null. Nada. What moral authority did whites lose? Does Steele even consider that a behavior enforced by a series of laws and policies from approximately 1619 until 1965 might be the reason for whatever "stigma" he claims? Would actions done due to racism be a reason to disqualify institutions that maintain a system built on white supremacy? Is holding individuals and institutions accountable to end racism creating a stigma? Does the continuing racism that we see have anything to do with society today?

"I think one of the cruelest things a society can do is to take the best and the brightest young black Americans and basically say to them you simply cannot compete with the best and brightest of other races. We won't allow you to do that. You can't do it. You have to depend on our paternalism."

-Shelby Steele[9]

When a black person makes a comment like this, you must ask if they are participating in the use of crack. Steele is a man who lived his first 19 years of life during legalized Jim Crow. His undergraduate work was done in a small, predominantly white college. Steele did his graduate study at the University of Utah. Today he opposes Affirmative Action. Did it ever cross his mind that maybe, just maybe, he was admitted into any of those schools thanks to Affirmative Action? Was Steele oblivious to everything that was going on around him? Did Steele miss how whites could not compete without rigging the system in their favor?

Let me repeat, I would like those like Steele to explain how it is wrong to ask the government to fix a problem created by the government at every level. Did he miss all the group preferences whites were getting from the government before he decided that blacks were betrayed by so-called group preferences mandated by the government? Whites were getting them all around him, and they didn't seem to have any problems. It has been this type of thinking that has hindered racial progress in this country. If you play football without pads or a helmet and the other team is fully equipped, it is not wrong to demand that you get the same equipment. But Steele would instead have tried tackling the great Earl Campbell while Campbell was fully padded with Steele wearing street clothes, then wonder why he got his collarbone broken after Campbell ran him over.

The late Walter Williams was another favorite black to the white racist subculture. Besides his work as an "educator," William served as a guest host for Rush Limbaugh. That alone rescinded his credibility as a serious speaker about issues in the black community. I am sure there are black right-wingers and white racists who will declare how I refuse to accept anything from blacks outside of some mystical line blacks are supposed to be toeing upon command of white liberals. That is not what I am doing. Toe or line aside, there are some realities that blacks and other non-whites face that cannot be denied. Walter Williams denial of reality is evident in 2 articles he posted at Townhall.com, one dated Jun 13, 2018, the second dated June 27, 2018, titled "Diversity and Inclusion Harm Part 1 and 2." The quote is from part one.

"In conversations with most college officials, many CEOs, many politicians and race hustlers, it's not long before the magical words "diversity" and "inclusiveness" drop from their lips. Racial minorities

are the intended targets of this sociological largesse, but women are included, as well. This obsession with diversity and inclusion is in the process of leading the nation to decline in a number of areas."[10]

Williams was a black man who served as a professor at a private majority-white university. Without a diversity and inclusion program, he probably would not have been hired for that job. My academic record does not come close to what Williams is recorded to have accomplished. A letter grade does not measure common sense, and as you read his writings and look at his situation, the opinion Williams presented in the articles must be critically assessed. Brother Williams is not with us anymore. May he rest in peace, but what he presented while living must be challenged.

The book *"Republicans and The Black Vote"* details the relationship between blacks and the Republican party from the Emancipation Proclamation until the 2008 election. It is an in-depth analysis of what republicans have and have not done for black support. Chapter 4 details a strategy by conservatives to find blacks who could counter civil rights leaders.

"Conservative philanthropy-the network of right-wing foundations- has had a two-sided relationship with black America. On one hand, conservatives have poured millions of dollars into efforts to win over conservative Africa Americans, particularly on issues such as school vouchers, charter schools and gay marriage. On the other hand, conservatives have funded think tanks and have supported black and other scholars who produce research that often takes anti-black positions."[11]

We see that "conservatives" were trying to create a divide in the black community to nullify any additional gains via civil rights. These foundations paid blacks to produce anti-black research. During Walter Williams life, he was paid at least 1.9 million dollars in grants by various conservative organizations.[12] On top of money made by writing books full of nonsense, Thomas Sowell was paid at least 250,000 dollars by the Bradley Foundation.[13] Shelby Steele is another ivory tower black conservative funded by right-wing foundations to research and create silly anti-black positions while claiming everything that helped him rise is somehow bad, demeaning, unfair, and creates a victim mentality in black people. So much for the claim of the liberal college professor. These people have done a disservice to the black community and to America.

> *"To believe Black people need to rescue themselves from the "Democratic plantation" and vote Republican; is a silly myth that conservatives like to push. It's insidious for a number of reasons. Me voting for a Democratic or Republican party is not akin to toiling on a plantation. It's downright idiotic and disrespectful to those who actually did. They were beaten and raped on plantations. Me CHOOSING to vote for a political party is not the same thing. Every time this phrase comes out of their mouth, they should be condemned for this nonsense. I make a choice to vote Democratic. Slaves had no choice about being on a plantation. Stop dishonoring our ancestors."*
> **- black internet forum user, 2020**

Furthermore, some black Republicans today have forgotten the great tradition established by great black Republicans of the past. These people disrespect the memory and honor of those same great black Republicans. This is another reason why they get called Uncle Toms and sellouts. The black Republican tradition was pro-black advancement in the quest for absolute equality, not the garbage you see, read or hear from the people I mentioned earlier and the newest sellout of the moment, Byron Donalds.

More than one decade before blacks were emancipated, Frederick Douglass stood up in front of a crowd of whites one hot 4th of July in Rochester, New York, and gave his legendary speech. Isabella Baumfree, better known as Sojourner Truth, in the 1851 Women's Rights Convention asked a crowd of so-called white Christians, "Ain't I a Woman?" Then there is the legendary Jackie Robinson, who in 1966 told Republicans in Ohio that he was not going to "Uncle Tom."[14] These sellouts and cowards white Republicans put in front of us now who tell us how we should be Republicans would soil their britches in fear if they had to demand such reckonings from whites today. I think the great black Republicans of the past would have some choice words for some of our modern black Republicans.

On April 29, 2021, Senator Tim Scott was given the honor by the Republican Party to give the Republican response to President Bidens State of the Union Address. At this moment, Scott had the opportunity to invoke the spirit of legendary black Republicans. Senator Scott had the chance to address the systemic racism he had admitted on the senate floor that exists, but somehow in prime time, he could not summon up the internal strength necessary for the moment.

Right-wing whites want to deny that racism exists and try bullying anyone who disputes them. I am black, and racism exists in America. Individual and systemic. Senator Scott had the opportunity to stand before the nation and express his experience as a black man; instead, he was the puppet. He had the chance to grab leadership, and he had the opportunity to make blacks look seriously at the Republican party. Senator Scott had the chance to become a legend, but he couldn't do it. This failure to present our case once you have standing and power because it will damage your career is another reason why blacks like Scott are called sellouts.

As I wrote this book, Californians decided to hold a recall election for Governor. One of the Candidates for governor was Larry Elder. On the surface, Elder looked like the perfect candidate to get the support from communities of color and perhaps turn some progressive whites into Republican voters. He was from South Central Los Angeles. He made his way out of the hood, got educated, and made himself relatively wealthy through hard work and resilience. Sometimes the ocean looks nice and calm on the surface, but what goes on underwater is the gruesome survival of the fittest.

> *"George Floyd might be alive had former President Barack Obama not, for eight years, consistently play the anti-cop race card."*[15]

This "gem" is from an opinion piece by Elder after the murder of George Floyd. In standard right-wing fashion, it is full of half-truths and disingenuous statistics. It is a rant that goes in all directions. He blames police killings on blacks instead of looking at the overwhelming evidence that shows racism in law enforcement. His opinion is lazy and simplistic. Elder is a black man who has seen continuing acts of white racism and rallies held by white supremacists but claims white supremacy is fake news. He is proud to claim that his opinions about blacks allow whites to have racists views. He has distorted statistics to help support the racist claim of extra high black crime and violence—almost everything he has done advances the aims and beliefs of white supremacists.

Blacks boycotted his radio show in his hometown. Elder is a man who mentored a white nationalist to help him be more of a racist.[16] He is a 70 something black man who has stated that he would have opposed the Civil Rights Act.[17] Elder has all kinds of criticism for blacks, but what has he done to provide solutions? Friends of mine from South Central Los Angeles tell me Elder has done nothing for the black community. Robert Woodson speaks much of the same crazy, but at least he has created an organization that works to promote black entrepreneurship. But not Elder. Yet Elder is pushed out into the spotlight and empowered by Republican party support to have tried running as a candidate for governor in the largest state in America. This is the type of black person the racist subculture shows to black people and suggests that we emulate. Elder is the epitome of slave mentality.

I wrote about internalized racism in chapter 2, and Elder is the poster boy for the condition. Remember that in chapter 2, Internalized racism was defined as the *"internalization of racial oppression by the racially subordinated."* Furthermore, the mentality described as internalized racism was one that shows a conscious and unconscious acceptance of a racial hierarchy whereby whites are superior. At the beginning of this chapter, I quoted Pam Keith, who defined Uncle Tom as: "a slave who is given prestige & comfort by the master, using his position to tread on the slaves abused by the master." His record is clear. Larry Elder fits the definition. It is not healthy behavior, and quite frankly, Elder is delusional.

Earlier I quoted Booker T. Washington. Whites who are members of the racist subculture love using his words to counter arguments made by blacks today regarding continuing white racism. To reflect our modern reality, I have modified Washington's comments.

"There is another class of white people who make a business of keeping the advantages of whites maintained by gaslighting the public into a belief that white racism is now an illusion and that it is whites who face anti-white racism. ... Some of these people do not want whites to lose preference, because they do not want to lose their jobs ... There is a certain class of white race- "problem solvers" who don't want America to get well."

My best friend, a guy I have known since I was five years old, moved to Texas recently. He worked as a floor manager in shipping and receiving for a large corporation. 2 blacks work in this location. One is in upper management. My friend called me one day, and he was angry. He told me that while at work on that particular day, the other black person on the job mimicked being a slave master with a whip, and my friend was the slave he was whipping to get him to work. This black man who decided to make a joke out of slavery is what the right uses as an example of blacks who think independently, who are sucessful, intelligent, and are the type of black person they push out into our national discourse. This man is another classic example of an Uncle Tom. It is time for the sellouts and Uncle Toms to fall back. Because the house negro does not own the house, and once they think they do, they get evicted.

"If there is no struggle, there is no progress. Those who profess to favor freedom, and yet depreciate agitation, are men who want crops without plowing up the ground. They want rain without thunder and lightning. They want the ocean without the awful roar of its many waters. This struggle may be a moral one; or it may be a physical one; or it may be both moral and physical; but it must be a struggle. Power concedes nothing without a demand. It never did and it never will."

-Frederick Douglass

Blacks Were Republicans for 100 Years

"If you tell a lie big enough and keep repeating it, people will eventually come to believe it. The lie can be maintained only for such time as the State can shield the people from the political, economic and/ or military consequences of the lie. It thus becomes vitally important for the State to use all of its powers to repress dissent, for the truth is the mortal enemy of the lie, and thus by extension, the truth is the greatest enemy of the State."

-Joseph Goebbels

One afternoon a couple of years ago, I was in an online discussion with a member of the white right-wing. Naturally, he disagreed with my opinion. Unveiling typical paternalism, this individual suggested a black person I needed to hear in order "to get a better outlook." I was given a link to a YouTube video. In this video was a young woman named Candace Owens. She was repeating the standard "conservative" lines about how blacks are playing the victim, how we need to be victors, that we need to stop living in the past, etc. Candace Owens is an example of a person who has internalized racism to the extent that she has fallen for a big lie. In her speech, she claimed an ideological battle is going on in black America. In her opinion, there were two sides, blacks looking back to the past; and blacks looking forward to the future. I have never seen or heard anyone black who was not looking to the future in all my years. Not once.

"The past is never dead. It's not even past."
-William Faulkner

When Candace Owens was born, I was 28 years old. I didn't watch old videos of Dr. King; I saw things live and as shown on TV. I watched my father cry while King's funeral was aired on national TV. I did not read about the 1960s civil rights movement. I watched my parents and other older blacks fighting for a future many of them KNEW they would not see. Deacon Alfred Montgomery was an 87-year-old man when he told me in 1970 that there would be a black president one day. Deacon Montgomery died in 1976. He never saw Barack Obama. Deacon Montgomery never saw the day Colin Powell would make it to head the joint chiefs, much less Secretary of State. These are our ancestors. They always have looked to the future.

I was three years old when the Civil Rights Act was signed. I have seen the backlash by whites and how it has modified over time. When the act passed, some whites refused to follow the law. School segregation was supposed to have ended in 1954, but it did not. Millions of people saw the movie "Remember the Titans" We all saw the feel-good story about the white and black players/coaches who inevitably became a team that bought a town together, breaking the chains of race. That was indeed a great thing.

On top of that, it was a true story. However, we should not miss that it took Alexandria, Virginia seventeen years after Brown v Topeka was decided to integrate. Even then, local businesses refused to serve blacks in 1971, long after such discrimination was outlawed. Since the signing of the civil rights act, what I have seen has been a consistent effort to obstruct from following these laws and attempts to erase them. That's happening right now.

People like Owens have fallen for a racist depiction of black people. Adopting the right-wing opinion of the victim limits the greatness from which we came. We are survivors. We descend from people who endured one of the greatest atrocities in human history and have come out so strong that some whites are doing their level best to divide us by filling the heads of blacks who have little common sense full of garbage. We are powerful because of the very past Owens tells us to forget. We are here because of the strength of those before us. They refused to submit and fought until death. We are here on their souls. Whites labeled them too, but they did not stand up declaring, "I'm embarrassed because you are slaves," or "I'm embarrassed because you are complaining about segregation." They destroyed labels instead of validating them. We ARE victors!

For people so dumb as to say slavery was a choice or talk about imaginary political plantations, it's time to wake up. People like this must take an honest look at white America and how they do things. Whites are constantly looking at the past to move forward. Some call this evaluation. The debates held in the halls of congress consistently mention the words and ideas of the so-called founders. It does not get any more looking to the past than that. Laws are changed or modified because of the effects of the past. But according to Owens, blacks should not look back to the past to figure out solutions for today's issues created by past actions. We are not to remember the philosophies of our ancestors.

Poor whites have hollered for years about being oppressed by the elite, and nobody tells them how embarrassed they are because they complain. When they air grievances, no one hears, reads, or sees any other white person lecturing about a victim mentality. Instead, they get listened to, the damages they complain about are given attention, and solutions are implemented. The 2016 election is a prime example. The alleged reason for the defeat of Clinton was that she did not listen to the needs of working-class whites in rust belt states. These were citizens whose median income was higher than blacks, with lower unemployment and poverty rates. No one saw anyone representing these communities running around telling each other they had a victim mentality and needed to be victors. Instead, Republicans said that the Democratic party forgot those people and was only concerned with the "urban" population.

Blacks are not monolithic, but I will repeat that some things are common to blacks regardless of ideology. On issues of racial justice, there are not two competing ideologies in the black community. There is the correct answer and the wrong one. None of it is about staying in the past. It is looking at the past to analyze what is going on now. It is a vital step in forming solutions that meet current issues. Looking at things now, we have a real problem. Today the republican party is led by people who would make George Wallace proud. People like Owens or Kanye West were not alive when Wallace was crusading across America preaching segregation and white victimhood. Wallace did not win. No matter how bad Nixon was, the nation refused to have what Wallace presented. But Wallace would have received approximately 74 million votes in the 2020 election. Today we are looking at Republican led initiatives to suppress nonwhite votes and end policies that allow everyone equal protection. Blacks cannot afford to fall for what the extremist-controlled Republican Party sells. No one can.

"A Wolf found great difficulty in getting at the sheep owing to the vigilance of the shepherd and his dogs. But one day it found the skin of a sheep that had been flayed and thrown aside, so it put it on over its own pelt and strolled down among the sheep. The Lamb that belonged to the sheep, whose skin the Wolf was wearing, began to follow the Wolf in the Sheep's clothing; so, leading the Lamb a little apart, he soon

made a meal off her, and for some time he succeeded
in deceiving the sheep, and enjoying hearty meals."
-Moral of Aesops Fable:
"Appearances are deceptive"

Now that I am officially considered "old," let me say some words to some of our younger folks in the black community. Those of my age are from the generation of the first black president, and perhaps we might have a little wisdom we can pass on for that future Owens thinks we are not looking toward. First, to Owens, I say this: "When you believe that supporting a political view created to exclude us is thinking independently, it is time to think about your mental condition. You want to tell young blacks that the Republican party offers them freedom, and you call that looking to the future? I got news for you kiddo, **BLACKS WERE REPUBLICANS FOR 100 YEARS!** We left the party because the party never wanted us. You're going backward and trying to take others with you."

The racist history of the Democratic party is well documented. The Democratic Party was founded in 1828. Slavery had been in this country since at least 1619. Slavery existed for 209 years before the Democratic party was founded. Republicans today love telling blacks how the Democratic Party was pro-slavery and how it was the Republican Party that freed the slaves. There is a lot modern Republicans choose not to tell young blacks as they try luring blacks into supporting a move back into Jim Crow. First, not all Republicans were for racial equality. The party had several factions in the beginning. One was the Radical Republicans. The Radical Republicans were for the eradication of slavery. They were not conservatives. Frederick Douglass was a Radical Republican. Lincoln was moderate politically. He opposed the expansion of slavery but did not believe in racial equality.

"I am not, nor ever have been in favor of bringing

about in any way the social and political equality of the white and black races, [applause] ... I am not nor ever have been in favor of making voters or jurors of negroes, nor of qualifying them to hold office, nor to intermarry with white people; and I will say in addition to this that there is a physical difference between the white and black races which I believe will forever forbid the two races living together on terms of social and political equality. And in as much as they cannot so live, while they do remain together there must be a position of superior and inferior, and I as much as any other man am in favor of having the superior position assigned to the white race."[1]

Those who have studied Lincoln claim that his views evolved. Did they? The Second Confiscation Act in 1862 had provisions for the colonization of blacks who chose to leave. Both Dr. Henry Louis Gates and the 1619 Project have written about a meeting between blacks and Lincoln whereby he made insulting comments to them, blamed blacks for the Civil War, and demanded they accept his plan to resettle blacks outside of America. According to both sources, on Aug. 14, 1862, Lincoln met with black representatives at the White House to try getting blacks to accept getting shipped out of the country.[2] They refused. The excuses need to stop.

Once Abraham Lincoln was elected, Southern states started leaving. Between Lincoln's victory and his inauguration, seven states seceded.[3] They knew his opposition to slavery could mean the end of the practice. As the country began splitting up, a great panic started consuming the outgoing Buchanan administration and members of congress. They wanted to keep the union together. They did not want the south to leave. They did not want war. President Buchanan declared secession was a constitutional crisis and then asked Congress to develop a plan to keep the south in the union.[4] He wanted Congress to assure the southern states that slavery would be protected once Lincoln took office. Congress offered over 50 different proposals trying to keep the union together. In the end, Congress settled for a proposal by Republican Thomas Corwin. It is called the Corwin Amendment, or more accurately, the slavery amendment.

> *"No amendment shall be made to the Constitution which will authorize or give to Congress the power to abolish or interfere, within any State, with the domestic institutions thereof, including that of persons held to labor or service by the laws of said State."[5]*

The terms *"domestic service"* and *"persons held to service"* meant slaves. Just as the constitution used *"all other persons"* as a substitute for slaves because the so-called founders didn't want people to see they protected slavery, Corwin used the same technique in the wording of his amendment. The Corwin Amendment was proposed in 1861. It passed both houses of Congress and was then signed by President Buchanan on his way out of office. When Lincoln took over, he supported the Amendment.

> *"I understand a proposed amendment to the Constitution—which amendment, however, I have not seen—has passed Congress, to the effect that the Federal Government shall never interfere with the domestic institutions of the States, including that of persons held to service ... holding such a provision to now be implied constitutional law, I have no objection to its being made express and irrevocable."[6]*

Corwin felt that congress did not have the power to interfere with slavery in the states where slavery existed. Lincoln agreed, and that was the actual Republican Party policy. It is probably why Lincoln said, *"My paramount object in this struggle is to save the Union, and is not either to save or to destroy slavery. If I could save the union without freeing any slaves I would do it, and if I could save it by freeing all the slaves I would do it; and if I could save it by freeing some and leaving others alone I would also do that."* During the Civil War, his main goal was to keep the union together. By any means necessary. If that meant keeping slavery, so be it. So the story of Republicans freeing the slaves and the Democratic party being the party of slavery is not really an honest depiction.

As it appeared the south would lose, the attempt to ratify the amendment was withdrawn from consideration by states due to a senate resolution, ending the effort to ratify The Corwin Amendment. Had the south accepted the terms of The Corwin Amendment, it would have become the thirteenth amendment. America came very close to making slavery a constitutionally protected practice that could only have been repealed by passage of a new amendment with votes by 2/3rds of both houses of Congress, then ratified by 3/4ths of the states. That has only happened once in American history-the repeal of prohibition.

Point number 1: **Republicans authored an amendment making slavery a constitutionally protected activity. The Republican Party is the party of The Corwin Amendment that would have made slavery constitutional.**

In 1876, America celebrated its 100th birthday. In that same year, there was an election. If you think the 2020 election was crazy, let's just say that the 1876 election made 2020 look normal except for the insurrection. The 1876 election offered Samuel Tilden from the Democratic party and Rutherford Hayes from the Republican party. Tilden won the popular vote but needed at least 185 electoral votes to become president. He got stuck at 184. Hayes had 166, but 19 unawarded electoral votes remained after the popular vote.[7] The 19 votes belonged to South Carolina, Florida, and Louisiana. To get those 19 votes, Hayes promised to end reconstruction.[8] This promise is known as the 1877 Compromise.

The conditions of the 1877 Compromise are as follows: Hayes would remove federal troops and allow southern states home rule.[9] Rutherford's agreement to withdraw federal troops took away the protection the newly freed blacks had in the south from physical violence and nullified or ended constitutional protections blacks had due to the Union victory. Allowing the south home rule meant the Republican Party would no longer intervene in local issues in the south. At that point, the Republican Party first turned its back on blacks and ended its commitment to black civil rights in the south.

Point number 2: **A Republican president, with the support of the Republican Party, ended reconstruction. The Republican Party is the party of the 1877 Compromise that ended reconstruction and paved the way for Jim Crow.**

During the Civil War period, Radical Republicans had great power and were able to get initiatives passed providing blacks with civil rights. The pressure from Radical Republicans was responsible for creating the 14th Amendment and the implementation of the Reconstruction Acts over President Johnson's veto. These two actions allowed protection to the newly freed blacks. The influence of the Radical Republicans was gone once reconstruction ended, and the Republican Party began to turn away from issues affecting blacks. Southern white Republicans resented that the party had become the "black folks party" to use the kindest description, and felt that they needed to gain support from southern whites to become national.[10] As blacks gained power and started winning elections, white resistance increased, and as a result, there was a backlash against southern black Republicans called the lily-white movement.

"The lily-white movement was an all-white faction of the Republican Party in the Southern United States in the late 19th and early 20th centuries. It battled and usually defeated the biracial element called the Black-and-tan faction.

During Reconstruction, following the U.S. Civil War, black leaders in Texas and around the country gained increasing influence in the Republican Party by organizing blacks as an important voting bloc. Conservative whites attempted to eliminate this influence and recover white voters who had defected to the Democratic Party. The effort was largely successful in eliminating African-American influence in the Republican Party leading to black voters predominantly migrating to the Democratic Party for much of the 20th century.

The term lily-white movement was coined by Texas Republican leader Norris Wright Cuney, who used the term in an 1888 Republican convention to describe efforts by white conservatives to oust blacks from positions of Texas party leadership and incite riots to divide the party.[1] The term came to be used nationally to describe this ongoing movement as it further developed in the early 20th century, including through the administration of Herbert Hoover. Localized movements began immediately after the war but by the beginning of the 20th century the effort had become national." "This movement is largely credited with driving blacks out of the Republican party during the early 20th century, setting the stage for their eventual support of the Democrats."[11]

Point number 3: **Once blacks got a foothold in the Republican Party and gained some semblance of political equality, white republicans took steps to**

purge blacks from leadership positions in the party.

The racism inherent in much of the current Republican base allows a failure to understand that blacks can think critically and make decisions without white input. We know what Republicans have done. Abraham Lincoln signed the Emancipation Proclamation. Rutherford Hayes ended reconstruction with his compromise. The Republican lily-white movement was an effort to purge blacks from the party. From the end of slavery until President Johnson signed the Civil Rights Act, there were 20 presidents, counting Johnson. Twelve Republicans, eight Democrats. Throughout those 100 years, Republican administrations were not friends with blacks.[12] The general opinion on both sides was that blacks had no place. A Republican may have ended slavery on paper, but lynching, convict leasing, and black codes continued in Republican administrations. During this same period, Apartheid became the law of the land. The record of the Republican party is a list of broken promises, most notably during the Great Mississippi Flood.

During the Great Mississippi Flood of 1927, twenty-seven thousand square miles of the United States ended up underwater. This flood is the reason for today's flood prevention systems along the Mississippi River. Because of this flood, more than 200,000 blacks were displaced and forced to live in "relief camps."[13] Calling them relief camps is overly kind. Blacks were treated terribly in those camps. Whites got first dibs on everything while blacks got whatever was left. Blacks could not get needed supplies unless they provided the name of a white employer or had a voucher from someone white. Whites got whatever they needed for evacuation, while blacks were forced to work and could not leave.

Walter White, then the president of the NAACP, left New York to visit Mississippi to see what was going on. Upon his return to New York, he had some very choice words for the conditions he saw that blacks had to endure. "Negroes in hundreds of cases were forced to work at the point of guns on the levees long after it was certain that the levees would break. Conscripted Negro labor did practically all of the hard and dangerous work in fighting the flood. Harrowing as many of these stories are, they are the almost inevitable products of a gigantic catastrophe and are part of the normal picture of the industrial and race situation in certain parts of the South. The greatest and most significant injustice is in the denial to Negroes of the right of free movement and of the privilege of selling their services to the highest bidder. That, if persisted in, would recreate and crystallize a new slavery almost as miserable as the old."[14],[15] White called these facilities concentration camps.

White's report caught the attention of the Secretary of Commerce, who was a guy named Herbert Hoover. Hoover was in charge of flood relief. After the NAACP roasted the government, Hoover started looking for other prominent blacks to evaluate the conditions reported by White to address the criticism from the NAACP. Once he found what he wanted, Hoover created an advisory committee to investigate the NAACP's complaints. It was named The Colored Advisory Commission. The commission consisted of 12 Tuskegee Institute officials, including Chairman Robert Moton, President of Tuskegee Institute.[16] Hoover was using black conservatives in hopes that what came from them would be less critical and could be used to offset the drilling given to Washington by the NAACP. I describe this as using because that is exactly what Hoover did.

Before we go further, I think it's important to understand who Robert Moton was for those who may not know. Moton is a significant figure in black political history. His political story is a cautionary tale for current black accommodationists. Moton was born in 1867. He graduated from the Hampton Institute in 1890. When Booker T. Washington died in 1915,

Moton succeeded Washington as President of Tuskegee. During his time at Tuskegee, Moton expanded the subjects taught at Tuskegee and increased its funding sources. The Tuskegee Experiment began during his time as head of the Institute. Moton supported the study and allowed Tuskegee medical workers to help with the experiment.[17]

Like Washington, Moton believed that the best way to advance the cause was for blacks to prove their worth to whites as if 200 years of dawn to dark seven days a week labor did not already do so. He did not fight segregation or challenge white authority. So in the grand tradition of America's love for the docile, non-confrontational black accommodationist, Moton was popular among the elite of his day. Robert Moton sat on the boards of major philanthropies with people like Andrew Carnegie and John D. Rockefeller Jr.

The Colored Advisory Commission visited Mississippi to investigate the situation. On December 12, 1927, The Colored Advisory Commission sent Hoover a letter with the findings of their investigation. The commission reported what they saw and made 13 recommendations to Hoover.

Conditions as We Observed Them

1. Notwithstanding the fact that the Red Cross memoranda of May 12th, 19th and 25th state specifically that flood relief is to go directly to tenants and share croppers and not to landlords, this condition does not always obtain. Negro tenants must secure their rations either on the recommendation of the landlord or the landlord secures the rations himself and distributes them to his tenants either direct or through his own commissary. Persistent reports have come to us that the land owners, who themselves distribute rations to the returned refugees are charging for these rations.

2. *It came to our notice from sources that we do not question that in numerous instances in the second period relief there appeared to be an understanding between the landowners and the Red Cross officials. Reports to our commission from colored people themselves indicated that in numerous instances they were forced to go back from the camps to the plantations. Some of the colored people who had been on the plantations attempted to leave. Those who were caught, were whipped and at times threatened with death if they left the plantation again.*

3. *The most distressing condition which we observed was the fear on the part of the colored people themselves to talk. They tell you frankly that they are afraid that if they tell the truth, and somehow it is discovered that they have "talked too much," that they would be killed.*

4. *We found numerous instances where the colored people, as a result of years of living under a semi-peonage system, in many communities were afraid to ask for the things to which they were entitled under the Red Cross. In every community we visited we found some colored people of this type and many times their fear caused them a great deal of suffering. We found a number of instances where colored people were in need of medical attention. These cases were reported to local Red Cross officials, and we hope that some steps were taken to assist them.*

5. *The plantation system in the Mississippi Valley led to many peculiar complications in the rehabilitation program. Reference has been made above to the fact that the Negro tenants and share croppers are forced to get their supplies on the recommendation of landlords. This only applies to white landlords. The*

small Negro land owner with tenants are usually not able to secure supplies or rations or repairs for their tenants, while white landlords in the same community secure without difficulty, things that they need for their tenants. The net result being that the Negro land owners suffer the loss of some of their tenants and at the same time are greatly delayed in rehabilitating themselves.

6. We wish to reiterate what we said in our report made to you on June 11th and that is the policy of the national Red Cross is still subject of the interpretation of local white people and the treatment of Negroes is reflected very largely in the personal attitude of local men and women in charge of the Red Cross affairs.[18]

Recommendations

In our report made to you on June 11th at Baton Rouge, the following recommendation was made:

"That at least two colored men in the states of Arkansas, Mississippi or Louisiana with sufficient authority from the Flood Relief Committee to do their work unhampered be delegated to visit the camps for the purpose of giving detailed information and answering questions concerning the reconstruction work. It would greatly expedite the work of such representatives if they could be supplied with placards and circulars containing brief and simple statements of the details of reconstruction of the Red Cross program."

1. We believe that if this recommendation had been carried out that much of the suffering of the colored people would have been prevented. Unless a Negro representative of the Flood Commission has

sufficient authority to inspect the records in local Red Cross offices, it is impossible to get sufficient fact to substantiate the conditions reported by the Negroes themselves. In Louisiana, for example, where our recommendation had a partial trial it furnished the best example of rehabilitation we found.

2. We recommend that at least one tactful colored man with full authority to inspect the records of local Red Cross officials be appointed in the three states of Arkansas, Mississippi and Louisiana, and that he be given a corps of Negro workers of experience to assist him in surveying the conditions in the respective states.

3. We have found upon investigation that a number of Negroes have not received clothing, shoes, bedding and necessary quarters for the winter. We recommend that they receive immediate attention.

4. We recommend that an executive order from the National Red Cross be sent to local communities restating the procedure for distributing rations and supplies as printed in the memoranda of May 12, 19 and 25, 1927.

5. We recommend that the national officers of the Red Cross investigate conditions where the Negroes have made short fall crops and that some provision be made to ration these people through the interim between the short crop of 1927 and the early crops of 1928.

6. We recommend that Agricultural and Home Demonstration Agents; social workers and health nurses be employed at once to go into the three states affected to survey the condition of colored people, and that immediate steps be taken to make these colored people comfortable for the winter.

7. We strongly urge that within the next thirty days that the homes of Negroes be repaired. This phase of the work has been neglected in every section visited.

8. We recommend that a special fund for emergencies be made available for the Negro advisor in every state; such funds to be handled by the chairman of our committee through the Colored State A& M colleges or some other accredited agency for the purpose of giving colored people some means to meet extreme cases of suffering when there is indifference to the colored people's needs on the part of the Red Cross officials.

9. We understand that it is Secretary Hoover's plan to give brood sows to the farmers in the flooded area. We hope that this will be handled in such a way that colored people will be sure to receive their gifts direct; otherwise these hogs in many cases will be given to colored people and charged against them.

10. We recommend that the number of colored workers not only be increased but that they be continued until June 30th 1928 with the understanding that if the emergency continues that some of them may be continued even beyond that date.

11. One of our sub-committees reported to a local Red Cross official that in numerous instances where colored people receive ration orders on some local merchants, that these merchants in turn would cut the order and either keep the difference themselves or charge it against some old account. The local Red Cross official said that she knew this condition was going on but that she could not get any of the colored people themselves to testify. Obviously, the colored people who have for so many years lived in fear of ill treatment as a result of the plantation system will not tell except where they think a friend will help. They are unwilling to give their names in making such reports, for as they say, their lives would be in danger. It seems, therefore, that the responsibility for checking on situations like this should not be left to Negroes when the facts are known and are admitted by Red Cross officials in some of the communities. Confidential investigators from Washington would be able to make some interesting discoveries.

12. *At our meeting in Tuskegee we telegraphed asking the immediate removal of Miss Cordelia Townsend, Red Cross official at Melville. Our investigators were discourteously treated by Miss Townsend and told in a most abrupt manner that they were not needed and were given no consideration. We know of instances where Miss Townsend ordered colored people to give up tents and find some place to live where there was absolutely no place for them to go. We also know that hundreds of homes for white people have been repaired and rebuilt in Melville and these homes furnished with rugs, sewing machines, refrigerators, etc., while only seven Negro homes in Melville have been repaired. Many of the colored people are sleeping on pallets or use mattresses spread upon planks.*

13. *In justice to the Red Cross and this commission that is cooperating with it, we urgently recommend that the Red Cross on its own initiative investigate the conditions which are set forth in these reports, with the definite aim of determining whether or not the colored people have received their proportionate*

share of Red Cross aid.[19]

Moton presented the findings to Hoover and advocated for immediate assistance to those most in need. Hoover then asked Moton not to tell the public about what they saw. In return for doing that, Hoover hinted to Moton that if he got elected president, Moton would be part of the Hoover administration and promised that some of the land from the flood would be turned into African American-owned farms.

Believing Hoover's promises, Moton made sure the Commission did not leak the full story of what they saw and were told by blacks who were suffering mightily due to the flood. Moton then pumped up Hoover's candidacy in the African American community. Hoover had no intentions of putting blacks in his administration. Once he was elected President in 1928, Hoover caught a case of amnesia and forgot about the promises he made to Moton and the black community. Moton got "done with no Vaseline" to paraphrase Ice Cube. In 1932 Moton quit being accommodating, and when he finished, the damage he did to the Republican party continues to this very day. Moton withdrew his support for Hoover and switched to the Democratic Party. His move created a historic shift as African Americans began to abandon the Republican Party, the party of Lincoln, the party of the Emancipation Proclamation, and turned to the Democratic Party.

Despite Hoover's deception, there were still blacks who stayed faithful to the Republican Party after years of the party ignoring blacks and breaking promises. Until 1964. That was when a Democrat signed what amounted to our second Emancipation Proclamation when President Lyndon Johnson signed the Civil Rights Act. Members of today's Republican Party tell a tale about Republican support for the Civil Rights and Voting Rights act. They spin a fabulous story about a Democratic filibuster and will say that by **percentage** more Democrats opposed these bills than Republicans. According to Merriam-Webster the definition of disingenuous is *"lacking in candor: giving a false appearance of simple frankness."* As it pertains to the Civil Rights Act, 153 Democrats and 139 Republicans voted in favor of the legislation in the house.[20] In the senate, 46 Democrats and 27 Republicans voted for the Civil Rights Act.[21] In the house, 221 Democrats voted for the Voting Rights Act, and 112 Republicans did.[22] In the senate, 47 Democrats voted for the Voting Rights Act, and 30 Republicans did.[23]

By 1964 there were blacks whose families had been Republicans since emancipation. They stayed faithful to a party that really did nothing for blacks after Lincoln signed the proclamation. While Republican, blacks endured Jim Crow Apartheid nationwide, redlining, restrictive covenants, acts of terror, white instigated racial violence, and the refusal to respect the constitutional rights of black people. Despite years of loyal black support, in 1964 Republicans nominated Barry Goldwater for president. His nomination was a slap in the face of black people. Goldwater voted against the 1964 Civil Rights Act. When we got civil rights, Republicans decided that extremism in defense of liberty was patriotism, turned their backs on us, and began letting southern white racists become part of the party.

Point number 4: **Republicans consistently broke promises or ignored issues that affected black people. In 1964 the Republican Party turned its back on blacks after nearly 100 years of black support.**

The history of the Republican party is one of broken promises to black people. We are not Republicans because Republicans never respected us. Now they want us to come back so they can implement policies that will return us to the back of the bus. The Republican party is anti-Affirmative Action, anti-civil rights, anti-voting rights, and pro-maintenance of the memory of the confederacy. Still, we are supposed to run to the Republican Party because Abraham Lincoln freed slaves from the same confederacy Republicans defend today.

"The reason African Americans overwhelmingly reject Republicans isn't based on word choices or phrasing. It is based on policy. It isn't how Republicans are talking to black voters that results in 90 percent or more of those voters refusing to vote for Republicans. It's what the Republicans are doing once elected."
-Stuart Stevens[24]

Just who really thinks blacks are stupid? In 2013, it was a 5-4 decision with five conservatives who voted to gut provisions of the Voting Rights Act that has enabled modern voter suppression. Former Republican Attorney General Jeff Sessions ended consent decrees, allowing police departments to continue their racist crusades of murder and harassment of people of color. Under President number 45 and Sessions, white supremacist groups were taken off the terrorist watch list. At the same time, they created a new group of "extremists" called Black Identity Extremists, a nonexistent set of groups according to experts in national security. However, this designation gave law enforcement the right to gangstalk, harass and imprison blacks who protest the continuing racist policies of this nation. We saw Hispanic babies being separated from their parents during this same Republican presidency. William Barr took the baton from Sessions and continued enforcing the racist dictates of President number 45.

On December 6, 2019, The House of Representatives passed H.R. 4, the Voting Rights Advancement Act of 2019, by a vote of 228-186.[25] This bill was proposed to undo the damage caused by the Roberts Supreme Court 2013 decision. There were 187 Republicans in the House of Representatives in 2019. One Republican voted for this bill, Brian Fitzpatrick from Pennsylvania. In 2021, The John Lewis Voting Rights Act was opposed by every Republican in the senate.[26] Senate

Republicans wouldn't even let the bill come to the floor for debate. They filibustered the John Lewis Voting Rights Act like Dixiecrats did the Voting Rights Act in 1965.

Study after study shows America that members who control the modern Republican Party are either virulently racist, highly resentful of anyone not white, willing to accept and tolerate racists as elected leaders or support racist policies. The campaign of eventual President number 45 began with racism. Members of the Republican base flocked to his racist festivals by the thousands when he should have been finished after he came down the escalator. Republican politicians who have ties to white supremacist organizations have held elected office. Republicans have run for office waging campaigns where they openly race baited voters when running against nonwhite candidates. Over the past 30 years, we have heard a steady stream of racist comments from Republican leaders who only apologize after days of public outcry. And then there was Steve King; a man finally voted out after being elected to term after term spewing racism. This is the modern Republican Party.

In 2007, Candace Owens filed a claim of victimhood. Oops, she sued the Stamford Connecticut Board of Education because she got some racist phone calls. I guess racism ended after she was awarded a $37,500 settlement. She was an anti-Trump liberal until she woke up and claimed to have had an epiphany one morning. This type of schizophrenic thinking is what Republicans believe blacks should have for leaders. I'm expecting Owens to send out a press release announcing that she suffers from revitiligo and is setting up a Go Fund Me page for skin bleach. A family friend who is an entrepreneur once said that if you want to get rich quickly, turn into a black right-winger. He was right. Racists will pay top dollar to a black person to hear or read themexpressing anti-black views. Owens is raking in the bucks. She has literally sold out. She's so pathetic that Booker T. Washington is spinning in his grave like he's on a rotisserie.

Owens claimed there is an ideological battle going on in black America. One where blacks are looking back to the past, and the other, blacks are looking forward to the future. What is this future Owens sees? What does Owens offer as a solution? Blexit? She's such an independent thinker that she used a term first made up by Me'Lea Connelly to encourage blacks to exit America. So what is her plan? Leave the Democratic party, and suddenly racism will end? Take a red pill? Does she think this is the Matrix? Wandering aimlessly with no plan, talking a bunch of dumb bull excrement about a Democratic plantation is not a plan. It is not looking into the future either. It's repeating what a bunch of racists say so that person can be the center of attention. We tried the Republican Party. Doing the same thing over and expecting different results is insanity. Quite frankly, when I listened to what Owens had to say, I believe those red pills she talks about are opioids.

So to these so-called independent thinkers, you might take the time to look back to the past to understand what a belief in states' rights meant for blacks. It meant voter suppression, racially gerrymandered voting districts, blacks being purged from voter rolls, racist police killing unarmed blacks, and lying about being threatened. Karens yelling about black men threatening them or other things even worse when the man is just walking by. Does this look familiar? Young blacks like Owens, Kanye, and others who think turning Republican is the road to freedom best take a page from elders and ancestors who walked away from the Republican Party to win the battle against overt racism. Take notes on how to play the game from the generation who have supported a Democratic party that produced the first black president and black vice president. The same Democratic party where blacks are in leadership positions at every level. This "independent thinking" is taking you back to Jim Crow. The Democratic Party has been far, far, far, from perfect but years of hard work and lost lives have gotten us to this point, and now that the most prominent Democrats are a black man and his wife, it is no time to be fooled by extremists lying to you about the 1860s. So let's review:

Point number 1: **Republicans authored an amendment making slavery a constitutionally protected activity. The Republican party is the party of the Corwin Amendment that would have made slavery constitutional.**

Point number 2: **A Republican president, with the support of the Republican Party, ended reconstruction. The Republican Party is the party of the 1877 Compromise that ended reconstruction and paved the way for Jim Crow.**

Point number 3: **Once blacks got a foothold in the Republican party and gained some semblance of political equality, white Republicans took steps to purge blacks from leadership positions. The Republican Party is the party of the Lily White movement, a group of Republicans that worked to purge blacks from the party.**

Point number 4: **Republicans consistently broke promises or ignored issues that affected black people. When blacks got Civil Rights, the Republican Party did not believe that was civil or right and decided that extremism in defense of liberty was no vice. In 1964 the Republican Party turned its back on blacks after nearly 100 years of black support.**

Point number 5: **Today's Republican Party is controlled by a racist Anti-Black base.**

"Republicans have been trying to scoop up African Americans on the merits of their Christian faith for decades. It never works because unlike racist white evangelicals we actually believe what was written, not use it for personal agendas or distort its message to judge and demonize others. This is why we use our votes to support the party that shows compassion for the poor over the one that shows cruelty. Because we do indeed have faith in God."
- black internet forum poster, 2020

Whitelash is Nothing New

"Whites, it must frankly be said, are not putting in a similar mass effort to reeducate themselves out of their racial ignorance. It is an aspect of their sense of superiority that the white people of America believe they have so little to learn. The reality of substantial investment to assist Negroes into the twentieth century, adjusting to Negro neighbors and genuine school integration, is still a nightmare for all too many white Americans...These are the deepest causes for contemporary abrasions between the races. Loose and easy language about equality, resonant resolutions about brotherhood fall pleasantly on the ear, but for the Negro there is a credibility gap he cannot overlook. He remembers that with each modest advance (the Negro makes) -- the white population promptly raises the argument that the Negro has come far enough. Each step forward accents an ever-present tendency to backlash."

-Martin Luther King Jr.

On September 22, 1862, President Abraham Lincoln issued an executive order called Proclamation Number 95, better known as the Emancipation Proclamation. Proclamation Number 95 freed all persons enslaved in the states in rebellion against the United States. On December 6, 1865, the 13th Amendment was ratified, officially ending slavery in the United States, except as punishment for a crime. On July 9, 1866, the 14th Amendment was ratified, granting American citizenship to everyone regardless of race or former condition of servitude. On February 3, 1870, the 15th Amendment was ratified, supposedly giving all men the right to vote irrespective of race or former condition of servitude. On March 1, 1875, President Ulysses S. Grant signed the Civil Rights Act of 1875. This law protected citizens from discrimination in public accommodations, transportation and made it illegal to exclude any citizen from jury duty. I present this legislation because of what these laws were supposed to end. That would be the end of white racism by practice, law, and policy. But that did not happen. Every time a nonwhite group has been allowed more and more of what whites have gotten, there has been a white backlash. Or, to borrow a term from Van Jones- whitelash.

The backlash to these laws was almost immediate. Much has been written about the Black Codes, vagrancy laws, convict leasing, etc. None of these things had to be. But thanks to the supreme court, they were. This was achieved due to supreme court rulings on five cases that were combined to come to one judgment. *United States v. Stanley, United States v. Ryan, United States v. Nichols, United States v. Singleton, and Robinson et ux. v. Memphis & Charleston R.R. Co.* These were the Civil Rights Cases, and they took place in 1883.

In each case, blacks sued because they had been discriminated against in violation of both the 14th Amendment and the Civil Rights Act of 1875. The business owners claimed the 1875 Civil Rights Act was unconstitutional and that Congress, which is constitutionally allowed *"To regulate Commerce with foreign Nations, and among the several States, and with the Indian Tribes;"* should not be able to interfere with their right to property.

Republican Justice Joseph P. Bradley rendered the Supreme Court opinion. In his last paragraph, he states that *"when a man has emerged from slavery ... there must be some stage in the progress of his elevation when he takes the rank of a mere citizen and ceases to be the special favorite of the laws."[2]* That opinion was made two decades after emancipation. I think the supreme court was a little ahead of itself. His view shows us purposeful blindness to reality by some whites that continues today. To ignore the special favorite of the law status whites had perpetually enjoyed is another early example of the history of denial that has existed in parts of white America. The eventual whitelash to the Emancipation Proclamation started with the Civil Rights Cases. The final blow in reestablishing white racial preferences was the decision in Plessy vs. Ferguson, which formally legalized apartheid in America.

Let us fast forward to the 1960s. Both the Voting Rights and Civil Rights Acts became law. Affirmative Action was issued as an executive order. But over time, there has been a slow and steady resistance to these acts that have been fought with policy modifications, the election of more right-wing lawmakers, and coded policies intended to maintain white racial preferences.[3] While laws were passed, they have not been adequately enforced. Affirmative Action was limited, as it only applied to government jobs and businesses getting government contracts. Despite these laws being passed in the mid-1960s, It was not until the 1980s that the last local government agency decided to comply. In the years since companies have still refused to follow the law.

In 1992-93, I was involved in a class-action lawsuit against R.L. Polk and Company for sexual harassment and racial discrimination. Due to information volunteered to us by assistants to the manager, Patrick Ivey, we found that Mr. Ivey would instruct his assistants to stop hiring blacks once enough blacks were hired to meet the EEOC requirements. Mr. Ivey would white out parts of documents and put in numbers showing that either he met EEOC requirements or that not enough minorities were applying and send copies of the doctored paperwork to the EEOC.

I lost the case because I took a temporary job with UPS over the Christmas season, and the Manager took that opportunity to promote another person. But that's not the issue. The issue is that Mr. Ivey was not the only person in corporate management who used that tactic. How many companies are doing the same thing today? How many Patrick Iveys exist right now? The next few lines are from a white poster on an internet discussion forum in 2020.

"I can say for sure that happens because I did it. Before retirement, I was an Engineer. For the last 20 years of my career, I was a Manager and Director and I hired hundreds of people. I reviewed well over a thousand resumes for all kinds of positions. Everything from Secretaries to Engineering Managers. Both Salary and Hourly. I always culled out the resumes with Black Ethnic names. Never shortlisted anybody with a Black Ethnic name. Never hired them."

"Since the Fortune 50 company I worked for had a stupid "affirmative action" hiring policies I never mentioned it to anybody and I always got away with it. A couple of times I was instructed to improve my departmental "diversity" demographics but I always ignored it and never got into any trouble. My stereotype is that anybody with a stupid ghetto Black ethnic name is probably worthless. I could have been wrong a couple of times but I was also probably right 99% of the time.

Glad I did it. I would do it again."

Laws or policies made to create equality are not stringently enforced or followed. Today, it is common knowledge that having a "Black" name can often lead to discarded employment applications and other similar forms of discrimination. Studies have shown that people of all colors with black-sounding names get rejected at the interview stage. Despite the evidence, some people still deny the problem.

"Plausible deniability is the ability to deny any involvement in illegal or unethical activities, because there is no clear evidence to prove involvement. The lack of evidence makes the denial credible, or plausible."
-Teagan Goddards Political dictionary

While Jim Crow apartheid has ended, racism today has morphed into a more subtle form. It is not overt in practice but covert in policy and attitudes. The covert nature of racism allows members of the racist subculture to claim plausible deniability. The problem subculture in the white community has complained since the Civil Rights Act was passed and has consistently claimed fake discrimination they have taken to the supreme court time after time in the hopes of eroding equal protection under the law for non-whites. We now face perhaps an insidious and arrogant type of white backlash— whites who are "tired of hearing" blacks and other nonwhites protesting and complaining about white racism.

"In short, a large number of white Americans have become comfortable with as much racial inequality and segregation as a putatively nondiscriminatory polity and free market economy can produce. Hence, the reproduction and, on some dimensions, the worsening of racial inequalities. These circumstances are rendered culturally palatable by the new ideology of Laissez Faire Racism.
-Lawrence Bobo, James R. Kluegel, Ryan A. Smith - LAISSEZ FAIRE RACISM: The Crystallization of a 'Kinder, Gentler' Anti-Black Ideology

Rising out of the ashes of Jim Crow racism was an attitude of Laissez-Faire racism. Laissez-Faire racism is sometimes described as the "kinder form of racism," as if there is such a thing. It is based on a theory of racial prejudice that Herbert Blumer developed in 1958. Blumer posits that racial prejudice is a result of group position. Blumer's view is at odds with the current claim by the American right of individualism, but that claim is fake news. According to Blumer, *"There are four basic types of feelings that seem to be always present in race prejudice in the dominant group. They are (1) a feeling of superiority, (2) a feeling that the subordinate race is intrinsically different and alien, (3) a feeling of proprietary claim to certain areas of privilege and advantage, and (4) a fear and suspicion that the subordinate race harbors designs on the prerogatives of the dominant race."*[4]

As Jim Crow apartheids hold on America was removed, those feelings remained a vital part of the group belief in a portion of the white population. Instead of looking at the demands blacks made and continue to make as efforts towards true democratic equality, the racist subculture looks upon these efforts as infringements on their rights. *"Laissez-Faire Racism involves persistent negative stereotyping of African Americans, a tendency to blame blacks themselves for the black-white gap in socioeconomic standing, and resistance to meaningful policy efforts to ameliorate America's racist social conditions and institutions."*[5]

"I do not dispute that racism still exists. I dispute that it is the primary cause of all the dysfunction in the black community. When humans must endure drugs, gangs, violence, abortion, teenage childbirth, lack of fathers, poor schools, filthy run-down neighborhoods, lack of good jobs, lack of effective policing, etc, on a daily basis, succeeding life is nearly impossible."
-white internet forum poster, 2020

Modern racism is a belief that reflects an underlying prejudice towards black and non-white people in the United States. The difference in contemporary racism from Jim Crow racism is that the attacks focus on a group's culture instead of claiming genetic superiority. Modern racism is primarily done online on social media. Modern racists will not express openly racist views. They believe racism is over and that racism is a thing of the past. Modern racism happens like this:

1. **Avoiding any meaningful contact with the minority group.**
2. **Practicing racial discrimination when the circumstances allow it.**
3. **Rather than criticizing a minority group, those with racist beliefs will attack a policy or action, and use that as an outlet for their attitudes.**
4. **Making a distinction between groups in terms of their 'values'**[6]

No better example of modern racism exists than what many in America saw during the confirmation hearings of Kitanje Brown-Jackson. Knowing they could not openly object to her based on race or qualifications, Republican senators latched on to decisions by Jackson in a very narrow portion of her cases to use to voice their disapproval of her nomination.

Symbolic racism is a belief that: 1. Blacks no longer face much prejudice or discrimination, 2. Black failure to progress results from their unwillingness to work hard enough, 3. Blacks are demanding too much too fast, 4. Blacks have gotten more than they deserve." [7],[8] This belief exemplifies a culture of amnesia as it comes from people who have received direct economic development assistance from the government on multiple occasions throughout American history.

"We have got this tailspin of culture, in our inner cities in particular, of men not working and just generations

of men not even thinking about working or learning the value and the culture of work, and so there is a real culture problem here that has to be dealt with,"
-Former U.S. Speaker of the House Paul Ryan[9]

These are three examples of how racism has morphed to meet modern society. These are all part of white backlash. Each of these forms is subtle. People who practice these forms of racism claim to be non-racist while expressing negative feelings or beliefs about members of other races. Edward Bonilla-Silva has called it "colorblind racism." Regardless of the subtlety, these forms of racism have resulted in significant and harmful actions that mirror the effects of overt racism. These significant and harmful actions are called entitlement reform, immigration policy, welfare reform, voter fraud/ integrity, stand your ground, stop and frisk and many other policies that target non-whites. "I'm colorblind, and if you talk about racism, you are the racist," This is how racism gets played today.

"This discussion thread points out the difficulty in doing anything about racism in America. Any discussion of the problem provokes a reflexive, violent denial of the responsibilities of its perpetrators and beneficiaries, and the very existence of the problem itself. As long as our society cannot accept this country's sins with the same equanimity as its virtues, no progress can be possible."
-white internet forum poster, 2021

Barack Obama was elected president in 2008 due to what was called the Obama coalition. Obama received 75 percent of the nonwhite vote. He also won 59 percent of all the votes from Americans between the ages of 18-44. He won in 2008 despite John McCain getting 55 percent of the white vote. After this, a deep concern arose in the old boy network based on fear of losing power, and something had to be done.

We started hearing more and more about illegal votes or dead people voting, anything but the realization that a black man ran a successful campaign for President and won on the merits of his ideas.

> *"The Republican Party, like the Democratic Party, is a vastly wealthy, powerful force. Though there is no mention of parties in the Constitution, these conglomerates have come to be the most powerful forces in our democracy. Each party is a multibillion-dollar industry that, like any powerful business will respond when threatened. The greater the threat, the more desperate the reaction."*
>
> **-Stuart Stevens**[10]

Today we are looking at measures explicitly designed to limit or negate nonwhite participation in voting. Voting is democracy, and every legal tactic must be employed to oppose the attempts to stop or reduce our right to vote. This reduction is a lie called voter integrity. It is not funny how a subculture in the white community works to alter laws they don't like or appears not to give them the advantage they want. It is pathetic how this group of people can consistently make up grievances from nothing, and they get turned into law. In contrast, proven legitimate grievances by blacks/nonwhites/women get treated like they don't exist.

> *"Allegations of widespread voter fraud, however, often prove greatly exaggerated. It is easy to grab headlines with a lurid claim ("Tens of thousands may be voting illegally!"); the follow-up — when any exists — is not usually deemed newsworthy. Yet on closer examination, many of the claims of voter fraud amount to a great deal of smoke without much fire. The allegations simply do not pan out."*[11]

Voter suppression is not just about an ID; it is backlash

against a demographically changing country by members of the racist subculture to maintain white preference or privilege. When I have talked to people about voter suppression and how voter fraud is fake news, I get "Why can't black people get an I.D?" I also hear this one coming from members of the American right-wing, "Democrats think blacks are too dumb to get an I.D." Then after saying something like that, the white person making that comment acts amazed because they get angry words spoken or typed to them. How can anyone be so obtuse?

The Brennan Center for Justice published a report called *"The Truth About Voter Fraud."* This paper dispels the many inaccurate claims made about fraud in our elections. The study found that most claims of voter fraud are just not true. Furthermore, it found that many things that are not fraud are called that for political purposes. Here is what the study says about voter I.D:

> *"The most common example of the harm wrought by imprecise and inflated claims of "voter fraud" is the call for in-person photo identification requirements. Such photo ID laws are effective only in preventing individuals from impersonating other voters at the polls — an occurrence more rare than getting struck by lightning.*
>
> *By throwing all sorts of election anomalies under the "voter fraud" umbrella, however, advocates for such laws artificially inflate the apparent need for these restrictions and undermine the urgency of other reforms.*
>
> *Moreover, as with all restrictions on voters, photo identification requirements have a predictable detrimental impact on eligible citizens. Such laws are only potentially worthwhile if they clearly prevent*

more problems than they create. If policymakers distinguished real voter fraud from the more common election irregularities erroneously labeled as voter fraud, it would become apparent that the limited benefits of laws like photo ID requirements are simply not worth the cost."[12]

Professor Justin Levitt of Loyola Marymount Law School did an extensive investigation to find voter fraud. Levitt investigated every type of election in this country, from presidential to local primary elections. He evaluated over 1 billion ballots from 2000 to 2014 and found 31 cases of legitimate voter fraud.[13] On August 6, 2014, Professor Levitt wrote an op-ed in the Washington Post with his findings. I will play with these numbers for a moment.

159,633,396 Americans voted in the 2020 general election. Levitt evaluated every election: county, state, and federal. I am trying to make this easy, so I will use the nationwide 2020 general election to make my point. Levitt found 31 cases of fraud out of 1 billion ballots cast, which is six times more than the number of votes cast in 2020. Since Levitt found 31 cases of fraud, in my hypothetical, we divide that by 6, which means there would be 5 cases of fraud in the 2020 election. The loser in 2020 lost by approximately 7 million votes. Even though such fraud was so negligible that you can say it is nonexistent, states began crafting voter integrity measures. Ironically, these measures targeted areas with high black populations and procedures primarily used by blacks to register or vote. I call it "Make America Stop Blacks from Voting Again." There is no integrity in what's going on. After all, what is the point of denying water to people standing in voting lines?

Elie Mystal laid bare the racism of both the current majority in the supreme court and inherent in so-called voter integrity measures. Mystal wrote an article in The Nation titled, "No Attack on Voting Rights Is Too Racist for This Supreme Court."[14] In this article, Mystal begins by citing Merrill vs. Milligan.[15] Merrill vs. Milligan is a redistricting case taken to the Supreme Court from the state of Alabama. The case was brought before the supreme court because Alabama used racial gerrymandering in its redistricting process. Racial gerrymandering is illegal, and according to Chief Justice Roberts in Shelby vs. Holder, such gerrymandering is a thing of the past.

The black population of Alabama is 25 percent. Due to redistricting done after the 2010 Census, Alabama had a black legislative representation of 14 percent. Alabama diluted black representation by creating one big majority-black district. Two State Senators with four voters filed a lawsuit requesting a change in redistricting to "afford African Americans an opportunity to elect candidates of their choice in at least two districts."[16] I don't think I have to say much more than this is Alabama for you to understand the problem.

> *"In five of the six redistricting cycles since 1960, the U.S. Department of Justice or federal courts have found that Alabama's legislative districts — congressional, state, or both — violate the rights of voters under the U.S. Constitution or the Voting Rights Act."*
> **- NAACP Legal Defense Fund**[17]

Shelby County is in Alabama, but the Supreme Court decided to gut provisions of the Voting Rights Act in 2013 even while Alabama used the 2011 map that diluted black representation. A district court determined that Alabama did employ racial gerrymandering in its 2021 redistricting plan. As a result of that ruling, the map drawn in the process was invalidated.[18] In a 5-4 decision made on February 7, 2022, The Supreme Court of the United States of America decided to let Alabama maintain racially gerrymandered voting districts, thereby continuing the underrepresentation of blacks in state and federal legislatures. The five justices voting to allow racial gerrymandering in Alabama were: Alito, Coney-Barrett, Gorsuch, Kavanaugh, and Thomas. Chief Justice Roberts was a temporary no.

The current Supreme Court poses a danger for all marginalized groups. On June 24, 2022, the Supreme Court made a decision regarding abortion that is a threat to the life and health of American women. This is one result of a right-wing effort over the last five decades to get into a position to undo laws and policies created by the Civil Rights, Roe v. Wade and Voting Rights Acts. Redistricting based on census data in several states has allowed legislatures to split up and combine large minority populated districts into majority-white districts, thereby lessening minority representation. In several states, these so-called voter integrity measures have produced policies restricting voting access to people of color. This was the goal of the American right, and this 6-3 right-wing majority is due to the evil of Mitch McConnell.

McConnell stole at least two democratic judges from the supreme court, beginning with refusing to allow Merrick Garland to get a hearing. Justice Gorsuch is sitting in a seat that should be Garlands. McConnell then rushed two other right-wing judges into seats during successive election years, which was his excuse for not letting Garland stand for a hearing. Like I wrote earlier, there is no integrity involved in what's going on. It is simply a continuance of whitelash.

> *"Affirmation action is a failed policy who's time has long since came & went. It's a liberal failed policy of reverse discrimination."*
> **- Anonymous internet poster**

A prime example of the length and consistency of whitelash is the distortion of Affirmative Action. As written earlier, the policy has benefitted whites the most. The discomfort some whites have in recognizing how they benefit from race-based law and policy is evident in any discussion a person of color has with a person who opposes equal rights legislation. Do they not understand how long whites were hired, promoted, admitted into colleges, and even allowed citizenship rights only because of the color of their skin? What the right has done with this policy may be the most outstanding modern example of both race-baiting and race pimping in the history of the United States of America.

I have not seen such a willful refusal to recognize the completeness of American history by one group of people who blatantly do so to maintain the racial preferences they have always been provided as what is argued in opposition to Affirmative Action. In chapter 5, I presented a series of government policies and judicial decisions that enforced racial preferences for whites based on race from 1618 until 1965. What I showed represented just a few laws and policies providing racial preference for whites. We are looking at a minimum of 189 years and a maximum of 347 years where Affirmative Action was given exclusively to whites, specifically white males. Today, just over sixty years since Kennedy first had the idea, there are whites in America who say that blacks and people of color have had enough time to catch up.

"You do not take a person who, for years, has been hobbled by chains and liberate him, bring him up to the starting line of a race and then say, 'You are free to compete with all the others,' and still justly believe that you have been completely fair. Thus it is not enough just to open the gates of opportunity. All our citizens must have the ability to walk through those gates."
-President Lyndon B. Johnson[19]

A former southern segregationist, President Johnson saw that it was unfair to say, "Hey, you got equal rights now, so everything is settled." Even with the policy in existence, as

I stated earlier in this chapter, there were and continue to be racists who refuse to follow the law. We talk about the need for a conversation. How do you discuss this matter with someone white who ignores America's history to complain about how race-based preferences are unfair? I have read many interesting things over the years; one is a concept I read in a blog by a writer whose online name is Abagond. It is called the "Teflon Theory of American History." It makes a lot of sense if you engage right-wing whites on issues such as Affirmative Action. The Teflon Theory of American history states:

> *"That anything that took place over 30 years ago is Ancient History. It has Absolutely No Effect on the present. Or not much. Unless it was something good like the light bulb or the Declaration of Independence. Therefore those who make a big deal of the bad stuff in the past, like slavery, are Living in the Past and need to Get Over It.*
>
> *Jim Crow laws were overturned by the civil rights movement in the 1950s and 1960s. Therefore according to Teflon Theory the Jim Crow period is now Ancient History. It has Absolutely No Effect on how White Americans alive today think and act. None whatsoever. Or not much. So racism is pretty much dead.*
>
> *Instead of Jim Crow's effect slowly weakening over time like you would expect, Teflon Theory would have you suppose that it just disappeared like magic one afternoon sometime in the late 1960s. Even though many White Americans alive now were alive back in Jim Crow times. Even though many others were brought up and shaped by those who were alive back then: parents, grandparents, aunts, uncles, teachers, writers, film directors, television producers, news editors and so on."*[20]

317

This is what right-wing whites think justifies their opposition to Affirmative Action. The stroke of a pen made racism magically vaporize in the 1960s, and no one today is impacted by the legacy of that racism. It is incredible to hear and read the illogical rants and so-called intellectual arguments of those who oppose Affirmative Action. For some whites to say that it is not suitable for race to be a consideration for anything when race was the only consideration for much of what they have achieved is infuriating. How can anyone make such a claim? America was built by providing opportunities or excluding people based on skin color.

The intransigence from a particular section of the white community to do their share of the work required to create the equality denied has been spectacular. From 1941 until 1965, at least four presidential executive orders were made to stop discrimination based on race. Executive Order 8802 (1941) was issued to stop discrimination in the military.[21] Executive Order 10479 (1953) created the Government Contract Committee to ensure that no qualified person seeking sub-contracted or contracted to work for the government was discriminated against.[22] Executive Order 10925 (1961) required government contractors to take "affirmative action" to make sure people are hired and treated fairly as employees regardless of race, creed, color, or national origin.[23] Executive Order 11246 is President Johnson's executive order generally referred to when discussing Affirmative Action.[24] Each of these actions faced opposition from members of the white community. Affirmative Action is still opposed, and was brought to an end by the Supreme Court session based on a bogus case bought to the court by a racist man named Edward Blum.

Equal protection means that government entities must treat all individuals the same when the circumstances or situations are the same. In some cases, the opposition to Affirmative Action has been based on a perceived lack of equal protection for whites. Again, I am not a lawyer; I am sure my opinion will be opposed by those who are, but I can read and do not see any equivalence in the arguments against Affirmative Action based on lack of equal protection.

Marco DeFunis Jr. v. Odegaard (1974) was the first case heard on affirmative action.[25] Marco DeFunis Jr. was a white University of Washington med school student who took his case to the supreme court claiming that the University violated the equal protection clause of the 14th amendment because the University had admitted, according to him, unqualified minority students. DeFunis was eventually accepted before the supreme court could hear the case.

Undeterred, the opponents of equal rights continued. Enter Alan Bakke. Despite being rejected twice by the University of California-Davis medical school, Bakke went to the supreme court complaining that the 16 out of 100 spots allowed for QUALIFIED minority admissions into the Cal Davis medical school violated his right to equal protection and the 1964 Civil Rights Act.[26] The supreme court ruled against the med school relative to reserving the seats because the court felt that constituted a quota. It did uphold that race could be a consideration. I think it is time to get in the DeLorean and travel back in time to review the equal protection clause of the 14th amendment.

The equal protection clause in the Fourteenth Amendment was made after slavery to protect blacks from discrimination. When the 14th Amendment passed, "quotas" were 100 percent white, blacks need not apply. So I see a problem with using the equal protection clause in a case where 84 seats were available for Bakke, and 16 seats were available for Blacks, Asians, Hispanics, and Native Americans. In both situations, whites were the majority of students admitted to those medical schools. Still, DeFunis and Bakke made claims of racial discrimination. I doubt one court in this country would hear a case of racial discrimination by a black person or any other person of color if they were in a situation where 100 available admissions existed, and 84 were for blacks or any other person of color.

These two cases began the legal attempts to end Affirmative Action. While there have been challenges, the supreme court has upheld Affirmative Action in some cases while rejecting it in others. But not in one case did the white who complained face what blacks did that caused the creation of the 14th Amendment. In each case I have read regarding admission, whites were the majority of admitted students to the university in question, yet white plaintiffs charged that the university in each case denied them based on race. I was listening to the Roland Martin Show the other day and one of his guests was a President from an HBCU. In that conversation, I heard that 20 percent of the students in HBCU's are white. I would like to see a black student who was denied entry into Grambling try taking a case to the Supreme Court claiming racial discrimination because Grambling admitted a white student. I doubt there would be a law firm anywhere in America that would touch this case and if there was, it would die in District Court. But we continue to see white students in predominantly white institutions challenging Affirmative Action claiming they were racially discriminated against because they were not admitted.

Today with a right-wing majority on the supreme court, thanks to the two stolen seats I referred to earlier, Affirmative Action was ended on June 29, 2023. This is due to the tireless racism of one Edward Blum. Blum has tried countless times to end Affirmative Action. He latched on to Asians to use this time in his maniacal quest to return America to white supremacy. Let us look at the particulars in Students for Fair Admissions v. President & Fellows of Harvard College. It is a case first filed in 2014.

In this case, the contention was that Asians were

discriminated against based on the number of Asians turned down for Harvard admission. More than 30,000 students each year apply to Harvard. In 2019, there were 36,000 applicants for 1,600 slots.[27] That meant 34,400 students of all races were not admitted. The claim was Asians got excluded to add black and Hispanic students. Ironically the claim was not made about Asians being passed over for white legacy students. Students for Fair Admissions claimed that Harvard violated Title VI of the Civil Rights Act.[28] Title VI "prohibits discrimination based on race, color, and national origin in federal financial assistance programs and activities."[29] Here is where the claim gets sticky. But before we get to that, we need to understand what courts use as regulations guiding a decision in cases such as this.

When a case such as this goes to court, the court considers many things. As it pertains to this case, the First Circuit Court determined that Harvard's policy satisfied "strict scrutiny" and did not discriminate against Asians relative to admissions.[30] Strict scrutiny comes into play in equal protection cases such as this one because race is considered a suspect category under the law. As a suspect category, if race is used as a classification in situations like this, it must be proven that using race is necessary to further a "compelling interest," and the objective could not be accomplished without doing so.[31] The use of racial classifications in this situation makes sense if a university is trying to create a learning atmosphere that utilizes students, faculty, and staff's diverse life experiences.

It is time to look at Blum's claim. He claimed Asians were discriminated against in admissions. Harvard admission numbers do not support his claim. Asians are 6 percent of the American population,[32] but they were 25.9 percent of the students entering Harvard in 2021.[33] That is a full ten percentage points more than African Americans (15.9%) and more than double the percentage of both Hispanics(12.5%) and Native Americans(11%).[34] In fact, there were more Asians admitted into Harvard than Hispanics and Native Americans combined. Additionally, a study published by the National Bureau of Economic Research and reported on the NBC.com website on September 20, 2019, revealed this:

> *"Using publicly released reports, we examine the preferences Harvard gives for recruited athletes, legacies, those on the dean's interest list, and children of faculty and staff (ALDCs). Among white admits, over 43% are ALDC. Among admits who are African American, Asian American, and Hispanic, the share is less than 16% each.* **Our model of admissions shows that roughly three quarters of white ALDC admits would have been rejected if they had been treated as white non-ALDCs.** *Removing preferences for athletes and legacies would significantly alter the racial distribution of admitted students, with the share of white admits falling and all other groups rising or remaining unchanged."*[35], [36]

Here, we see that whites are provided entry by a plethora of other preferences they would not qualify for if not for connections they have due to their race. The study shows that Asians were not adversely impacted because Harvard must admit blacks and Hispanics that are presumably unqualified. Instead, we see white ALDC students who would not qualify under any other circumstance who got accepted at more than double the percentage of Asians, Blacks, Hispanics, and Native Americans who met the same criteria. Edward Blum and his fake Students for Fair Admissions "organization" whined to the Supreme Court for years, bringing meritless garbage case after case. The Supreme Court ended Affirmative Action even when the facts plainly show that more unqualified white students were admitted into Harvard due to preferences they get that nonwhites would not. Those preferences were the real cause of whatever reduction in admissions Blum claims. This is a true example of white privilege.

Equal protection means that government entities must treat all individuals the same when the circumstances or situations are the same. Students for Fair Admissions claimed that Harvard violated Title VI of the Civil Rights Act. Title VI "prohibits discrimination based on race, color, and national origin in federal financial assistance programs and activities." The numbers show that when the circumstances and situations are the same, meaning ALDC preferences, 2.68 times more whites were admitted due to this preference than Asians, Blacks, Hispanics, and Native Americans. Judging by the Equal Protection clause, those same groups are not receiving equal protection as determined by the 14th Amendment relative to ALDC preferences.

Having complete knowledge of history should be something we all should strive to accomplish before building our opinions or beliefs about issues such as Affirmative Action. Public Policy can not be debated based on inaccurate perceptions or thoughts, and the backlash against Affirmative Action is based on precisely those things. If we accept the American right's claims, we might also believe Paul Bunyan existed with a big blue ox and used his plow to create the Rocky Mountains. The truth is that whites have been the preferred group and have been afforded things others have not been able to get, only because of the color of their skin.

"The second key maneuver, which flowed naturally from the first, was to redefine racism itself. Confronted with civil rights headlines depicting unflattering portrayals of KKK rallies and jackbooted sheriffs, white authority transformed those damning images of white supremacy into the sole definition of racism. This simple but wickedly brilliant conceptual and linguistic shift served multiple purposes. First and foremost, it was conscience soothing. The whittling down of racism to sheet-wearing goons allowed a cloud of racial innocence to cover many whites who,

although 'resentful of black progress' and determined to ensure that racial inequality remained untouched, could see and project themselves as the 'kind of upstanding white citizen(s)' who were 'positively outraged at the tactics of the Ku Klux Klan". The focus on the Klan also helped to designate racism as an individual aberration rather than something systemic, institutional and pervasive."

- Carol Anderson, White Rage:
The Unspoken Truth of Our Racial Divide[37]

Dr. Carol Anderson has called white lash, white rage. She has accurately noted that acts of white racial violence could not just describe white rage. She states that white rage happens in the courts, the legislatures, city councils, and school boards. It's not about a Klan rally. It's about the passing of laws and policies. When we talk about racism today, it is essential for white people to understand what we have seen as nonwhites. This nation was built on slavery and the direct denial of human rights to Blacks, Asians, Pacific Islanders, Hispanics, Women, and Native Americans. Each time any of these groups gained rights supposedly granted according to the constitution, there has been a backlash. This backlash continues today at the local level relative to zoning, law enforcement policies, referendums, bond issues, mill levies for community improvements, economic development projects, various tax incentives such as abatements or TIFFS, and school board policy. It goes on at the state level with the various voter suppression measures and gerrymandering. White backlash can be summed up on the national level by two words: the filibuster.

"The Maser's Tools Will Never Dismantle the Master's House"

-Audre Lorde

Keep Dr. King's Name Out of Your Mouth!

"Whenever any black person utters words that make white people adjust their collars, white people unfailingly respond with a variation of the phrase "but not all white people." If they are bold enough, they might even challenge you with the Super Saiyan Caucasian preamble of all preambles: "What would Martin Luther King say about ..."

-Michael Harriot[1]

D r. Martin Luther King Jr. fought against white racism. When he made his famous speech in 1963, he said that he wanted his kids to live in a world without white racism. Almost every word Dr. King spoke was in opposition to that same racism. Some Americans need to learn that he was asking whites to stop being racists and that whites start looking at blacks not for the color of their skin but that WHITES begin looking at us for the content of our character. He was not asking blacks to ignore white racism while lying to themselves about being colorblind. His dream was about the end of white racism.

Dr. King has been dead for over 50 years now, and just like in almost every other matter of race relations, a specific part of the white community has amnesia about King. The racist subculture has deconstructed King's life to make him a black right-wing accommodationist. When discussing race, there is always somebody who tries telling a black person how what they say would not be approved by King because that person opposes white racism in no uncertain terms or without regard to the feelings of those continuing to practice racism.

I was seven years old when James Earl Ray murdered King. I remember feeling like the world had come to an end. It seemed that all hope was gone. Before his murder, King was organizing a poor people's march on Washington. King felt the United States must begin to provide for the economic damage caused by the years of racism against blacks by the government of this country. He pledged that he was coming to get a check when he went to the White House. It is very plain that King was moving toward demanding economic equality and economic justice. That includes reparations. Those who hijack his words miss this reality. King did not make it to Washington, and the goal of economic equality remains unmet.

King was killed because the content of his character dictated that he was required to stand up and oppose injustice. Not that he sat idly by ignoring the whites practicing it so he would not be considered a racist. Nor was it to sit at home like a fattened calf spouting off elitist BS about pound cakes and how racism has ended because you got a cushy job teaching at a HWCU. If you think Kings views or the views of the civil rights soldiers in the 1960s were accepted as this grand colorblind view that asks blacks not to hold whites accountable, you are sorely mistaken. Ask any of the still-living warriors from the Civil Rights Movement in your town who fought for local change if there are whites that still judge us by the color of our skin. Ask whites who today operate in the spirit of those like James Reeb just exactly how "colorblind" some of their white friends are.

For those whites who have the unmitigated gall to dare lecture us about Dr. King, Ava Duvernay created a solid rebuttal to your racial amnesia and attempts to gaslight. The title is "When They See Us." As you watch this series, the NYPD did not consider the content of those young men's character or their parents. They saw the color of their skin and assumed. George Zimmerman did not consider the content of Trayvon Martins's character as he was walking back home with a bag of skittles and a can of tea. He saw skin color, then called police dispatch while mumbling about some crimes. Millions of whites and TV hosts at Fox News did not consider the content of Martins's character. Instead, they created a false characterization of Martin based on what they believed about young men with his skin color.

The great historian Dr. Henry Louis Gates was harassed by a police officer in his home because a white neighbor did not believe a black man had such great character that he could have the skills necessary to earn the income in order to live in that neighborhood. Some of our finest young minds are harassed on campuses as they strive for so-called "higher education." Someone created a hashtag called #whileblack because there are people who refuse to see the content of our character.

"First, I must confess that over the past few years I have been gravely disappointed with the white moderate. I have almost reached the regrettable conclusion that the Negro's great stumbling block in his stride toward freedom is not the White Citizen's Counciler or the Ku Klux Klanner, but the white moderate, who is more devoted to "order" than to justice; who prefers a negative peace which is the absence of tension to a positive peace which is the presence of justice; who constantly says: "I agree with you in the goal you seek, but I cannot agree with your methods of direct action"; who paternalistically believes he can set the timetable for another man's freedom; who lives by a mythical concept of time and who constantly advises

the Negro to wait for a "more convenient season." Shallow understanding from people of good will is more frustrating than absolute misunderstanding from people of ill will. Lukewarm acceptance is much more bewildering than outright rejection."
-Dr. Martin Luther King Jr.[2]

Like almost everything else in contemporary American racial issues, some realities must be faced. I was alive when King lived and saw how whites hated him. According to right-wing whites, Dr. King was widely loved and accepted in their community. In reality, he was called everything members of the racist subculture call blacks who oppose the continuing white racism of today. I know because I heard them saying it. King was loved so much for his dignity, non-violence, and responsibility that some whites claim to champion that a white man ended his life using ultimate violence. Now some whites try telling us what King stood for. Really?

When Dr. King gave his famous "I Have A Dream" speech, from which every right-wing Republican has memorized one sentence, he was hated by 50 percent of white America, and at the time of his murder, 75 percent of all Americans hated his guts.[3] Some went so far as to say he bought his death on himself. Now the same people or their descendants want to lecture blacks about what King stood for, and it's defined by this: *"I have a dream that my four little children will one day live in a nation where they will not be judged by the color of their skin, but by the content of their character."* But the truth is that King did not stop talking after August 28, 1963.

"We have waited for more than 340 years for our constitutional and God-given rights. The nations of Asia and Africa are moving with jetlike speed toward gaining political independence, but we still creep at horse-and-buggy pace toward gaining a cup of coffee

at a lunch counter. Perhaps it is easy for those who have never felt the stinging darts of segregation to say, "Wait." But when you have seen vicious mobs lynch your mothers and fathers at will and drown your sisters and brothers at whim; when you have seen hate-filled policemen curse, kick and even kill your black brothers and sisters; when you see the vast majority of your twenty million Negro brothers smothering in an airtight cage of poverty in the midst of an affluent society; when you suddenly find your tongue twisted and your speech stammering as you seek to explain to your six-year-old daughter why she can't go to the public amusement park that has just been advertised on television, and see tears welling up in her eyes when she is told that Funtown is closed to colored children, and see ominous clouds of inferiority beginning to form in her little mental sky, and see her beginning to distort her personality by developing an unconscious bitterness toward white people; when you have to concoct an answer for a five-year-old son who is asking: "Daddy, why do white people treat colored people so mean?"; when you take a cross-country drive and find it necessary to sleep night after night in the uncomfortable corners of your automobile because no motel will accept you; when you are humiliated day in and day out by nagging signs reading "white" and "colored"; when your first name becomes "nigger," your middle name becomes "boy" (however old you are) and your last name becomes "John," and your wife and mother are never given the respected title "Mrs."; when you are harried by day and haunted by night by the fact that you are a Negro, living constantly at tiptoe stance, never quite knowing what to expect next, and are plagued with inner fears and outer resentments; when you are forever fighting a degenerating sense of "nobodiness"—then you will understand why we find it difficult to wait. There

comes a time when the cup of endurance runs over, and men are no longer willing to be plunged into the abyss of despair."
**Rev. Martin Luther King Jr.,
"Letter from A Birmingham Jail"**[4]

"We are taking the black young men who had been crippled by our society and sending them 8,000 miles away to guarantee liberties in Southeast Asia which they had not found in Southwest Georgia and East Harlem"
**-Rev.Martin Luther King Jr.,
"Beyond Vietnam: A Time to Break the Silence"**[5]

"One America is beautiful for situation ... millions of young people grow up in the sunlight of opportunity," he says in the speech. "But tragically and unfortunately, there is another America. This other America has a daily ugliness about it that constantly transforms the ebullience of hope into the fatigue of despair ... They find themselves perishing on a lonely island of poverty in the midst of a vast ocean of material prosperity."
**-Rev.Martin Luther King Jr.,
"The Other America"**[6]

"For those who are telling me to keep my mouth shut, I can't do that," he said at the end of his speech. "I'm against segregation at lunch counters, and I'm not going to segregate my moral concerns. And we must know on some positions, cowardice asks the question, 'Is it safe?' Expediency asks the question, 'Is it politic?' Vanity asks the question, 'Is it popular?' But conscience asks the question, 'Is it right?' And there're times when you must take a stand that is neither safe nor politic nor popular, but you must do it because it is right."
**-Rev. Martin Luther King Jr.,
"The Three Evils of Society"**[7]

King informed white society of our responsibility to abide by just laws and to disobey or reject unjust ones. None of that involves being quiet or not talking about race, thinking that will make the problem disappear. Indeed, we are to continue taking direct action against unjust laws and policies. Americans on the right love to bring up his philosophy of nonviolence when blacks start speaking in harsh tones. King did advocate nonviolence, but he did not support shut up and take it. His nonviolence plan was about direct action and confrontation. Dr. King's nonviolence campaign consisted of 6 steps:

STEP ONE: INFORMATION GATHERING. *Identify the issues in your community and/or school in need of positive change. To understand the issue, problem or injustice facing a person, community, or institution, you must increase your understanding of the problem. Your investigation should include all sides of the issue and may include formal research and listening to the experiences of others.*

STEP TWO: EDUCATE OTHERS. *It is essential to inform others, including your opposition, about your issue. In order to cause change, the people in the community must be aware of the issue and understand its impact. By educating others you will minimize misunderstanding and gain support and allies.*

STEP THREE: PERSONAL COMMITMENT. *Check and affirm your faith in the philosophy and methods of nonviolence. Causing change requires dedication and long hours of work. Meet with others regularly to stay focused on your goal. Prepare yourself to accept sacrifices, if necessary, in your work for justice.*

STEP FOUR: NEGOTIATIONS. *Using grace, humor and intelligence, confront the individuals whom need to participate in this change. Discuss a plan for addressing and resolving these injustices. Look for what is positive in every action and statement the opposition makes. Do not seek to humiliate the opponent but call forth the good in the opponent. Look for ways in which the opponent can become an ally.*

STEP FIVE: DIRECT ACTION. *These are actions taken to convince others to work with you in resolving the injustices. Direct action imposes a "creative tension" into the conflict. Direct action is most effective when it illustrates the injustice it seeks to correct. There are hundreds of direct action, including:*
- *Boycotts --- refusal to buy products*
- *Marches and rallies*
- *Letter-writing and petition campaigns*
- *Political action and voting*
- *Public art and performance*

STEP SIX: RECONCILIATION. *Nonviolence seeks friendship and understanding. Nonviolence does not seek to defeat the opponent. Nonviolence is directed against evil systems, oppressive policies, and unjust acts, not against persons.*[8]

It is easy to quote a sentence and conflate it to mean something it doesn't. Dr. King did not say that his dream was for blacks not to call out white racism; it was quite the opposite. He called us to refuse to accept the unjust systemic racism in this society. Because we face an opposition that refuses to acknowledge the existence of systemic racism, it is up to all nonracist Americans to become informed about systemic racism. We must educate ourselves about systemic racism. America must make a sincere national commitment to end it and negotiate with all who represent us to create a plan for federal action to reverse the damage caused by more than 245 years of systemic racism. We saw in 2020 a continuing campaign using various forms of direct action targeting unjust policies designed to maintain the systemic racism that created conditions for unrest. As we do all these things, it is vital to support Representative Barbara Lee's call for a United States Truth and Reconciliation Commission.[9]

Republicans have tried giving themselves credit for everything but the creation of man, and I wouldn't doubt that in a church somewhere in America, a pastor is giving Republicans credit for that. Republicans have taken credit for King even as his children say differently. King's positions were plain, and trying to make him partisan is unwise, but some things he advocated do not match what the current Republican party stands for. For example, King was for a universal income. He supported Affirmative Action. He called for a redistribution of wealth as well as reparations. King was demanding GOVERNMENT undo the damage GOVERNMENT created.

"Few people consider the fact that in addition to being enslaved for two centuries, the Negro was during all those years robbed of the wages of his toil. No amount of gold could provide an adequate compensation for the exploitation and humiliation of the Negro in America down through the centuries. Not all the wealth of this affluent society could meet the bill. Yet, a price can be placed on unpaid wages. The ancient common law has always provided a remedy for the appropriation of the labor of one human being by another. This law should be made to apply for American Negroes. The payment should be in the form of a massive program by the Government of special compensatory measures which could be regarded as a settlement in accordance with the accepted practice of common law. Such measures would certainly be less expensive than any computation based on two

centuries of unpaid wages and accumulated interest."[10]

"It is my great feeling that a massive program must be developed by the federal government to bring new hope into being. Among the many vital jobs to be done, the Nation must not only radically readjust its attitude toward the Negro and the compelling present, but must incorporate in its planning some compensatory consideration for the handicaps he has inherited from the past. It is impossible to create a formula for the future which does not take into account that our society has been doing something special against the Negro for hundreds of years."[11]

"America must seek its own way of atoning for the injustices she has inflicted on her Negro citizens [not for] atonement's sake, . . .[but as a] way to bring the Negro standard to a realistic level. . . .The moral justification for special measures for Negroes is rooted in the robberies inherent in the institution of slavery."[12]

"You mentioned "white racism" over and over in 2 paragraphs while discussing Dr. King. In how many of the good doctors remarkable speeches did he ever utter the words "white racism"? Perhaps he never used those words in his speeches because he was truly, in his heart and mind, against racism. I'll admit I can learn a lot from MLK, so could you if you would read his words, rather than change them."
-white internet forum poster, 2020

For those who want to turn Dr. Martin Luther King Jr. into a right-wing house negro, that's the wrong answer. If anyone today believes that if King were living, he would denounce blacks who hold whites who still practice racism accountable, you are sorely mistaken. If you think King would have sat quietly as young, unarmed blacks are getting murdered by police or that he would not have supported the Black Lives Matter movement, his words speak for themselves:

Where do we go from here? First, we must massively assert our dignity and worth. We must stand up amid a system that still oppresses us and develop an unassailable and majestic sense of values. We must no longer be ashamed of being black. The job of arousing manhood within a people that have been taught for so many centuries that they are nobody is not easy.

Even semantics have conspired to make that which is black seem ugly and degrading. In Roget's Thesaurus there are some 120 synonyms for blackness and at least sixty of them are offensive, such words as blot, soot, grim, devil, and foul. And there are some 134 synonyms for whiteness and all are favorable, expressed in such words as purity, cleanliness, chastity, and innocence. A white lie is better than a black lie. The most degenerate member of a family is the "black sheep." Ossie Davis has suggested that maybe the English language should be reconstructed so that teachers will not be forced to teach the Negro child sixty ways to despise himself, and thereby perpetuate his false sense of inferiority, and the white child 134 ways to adore himself, and thereby perpetuate his false sense of superiority. The tendency to ignore the Negro's contribution to American life and strip him of his personhood is as old as the earliest history books and as contemporary as the morning's newspaper.

To offset this cultural homicide, the Negro must rise up with an affirmation of his own Olympian manhood. Any movement for the Negro's freedom that overlooks this necessity is only waiting to be buried. As long as the mind is enslaved, the body can never be free. Psychological freedom, a firm sense of self-esteem, is the most powerful weapon against the long night of physical slavery. No Lincolnian Emancipation Proclamation, no Johnsonian civil rights bill can totally bring this kind of freedom. The Negro will only be free when he reaches down to the inner depths of his own being and signs with the pen and ink of assertive manhood his own emancipation proclamation. And with a spirit straining toward true self-esteem, the Negro must boldly throw off the manacles of self-abnegation and say to himself and to the world, "I am somebody. I am a person. I am a man with dignity and honor. I have a rich and noble history, however painful and exploited that history has been. Yes, I was a slave through my foreparents, and now I'm not ashamed of that. I'm ashamed of the people who were so sinful to make me a slave." Yes, yes, we must stand up and say, "I'm black, but I'm black and beautiful." This, this self-affirmation is the black man's need, made compelling by the white man's crimes against him.

Now another basic challenge is to discover how to organize our strength in to economic and political power. Now no one can deny that the Negro is in dire need of this kind of legitimate power. Indeed, one of the great problems that the Negro confronts is his lack of power. From the old plantations of the South to the newer ghettos of the North, the Negro has been confined to a life of voicelessness and powerlessness. Stripped of the right to make decisions concerning his life and destiny he has been subject to the authoritarian and sometimes whimsical decisions of the white power structure. The plantation and the ghetto were created by those who had power, both to confine those who had no power and to perpetuate their powerlessness. Now the problem of transforming the ghetto, therefore, is a problem of power, a confrontation between the forces of power demanding change and the forces of power dedicated to the preserving of the status quo. Now, power properly understood is nothing but the ability to achieve purpose. It is the strength required to bring about social, political, and economic change.[13]

As a young black boy, Dr. King let me know that my life mattered. His example told our generation and all others since he left this realm of existence that black lives matter. Yes, he believed all lives mattered, but all lives were not facing the injustice that black lives were then and are today. Those elders who have now graduated to the realm of ancestor taught us an age honored truth that has been in effect here since the first Africans got off the slave ship. That truth is: "Black Lives Matter. No matter what we endure, black lives matter." That truth is timeless and does not dismiss the importance of all humans. So for those who cannot understand this truth: "Keep Dr. King's name out of your mouth!"

"We are now faced with the fact that tomorrow is today. We are confronted with the fierce urgency of now. In this unfolding conundrum of life and history, there 'is' such a thing as being too late. This is no time for apathy or complacency. This is a time for vigorous and positive action."

Dr. Martin Luther King Jr.

The White Rebellion
1-6-2021

*"Self-defined victimhood is a psychological state whereby, regardless of the etiology of the feeling or the **truth** of the matter, one who perceives herself to be a victim is a victim. The perception of being wronged is victimhood. We are not concerned with the **truth** of one's victimhood. As such, concepts like intent to harm or genuine unfairness do not bear on self-defined victimhood. One must merely think of oneself in such terms, or behave in such a way, to **be** a victim."*

- Miles T. Armaly and Adam M. Enders
'Why Me?' The Role of Perceived
Victimhood in American Politics

America is full of right-wing whites who complain about leftist fascism because their views are rejected. This particular group can't be disliked because they want to end healthcare for millions of people, cut school lunch programs, food stamps, any assistance for people in need, or how they want to protect the ultra-rich by any means necessary. Oh no, it's because they are white. People can't be rejecting right-wing speakers because their speeches are hate fests; oh no, it's because the "left" doesn't tolerate opposing views. I can keep going with examples, but I won't. The fact is that white right-wing extremists who hijacked the term conservative have created a grievance industry whereby they claim to be victims of imaginary oppression that no one else sees only because they are white. It led to an insurrection. I call it "The White Rebellion."

On January 6th, 2021, The White Rebellion took place at the United States Capitol in Washington D.C. It is a day that no one will ever forget. Most have described this day as an insurrection incited by then lame-duck President number 45. While it is true about this being an insurrection, the fact is that like most everything in his miserable failure of a presidency, President number 45 stumbled into conditions that were created long before he took office. He just happened to be the straw that broke the proverbial camel's back. I won't rehash the decomposed horse that has been beaten about this day; instead, let us look at things from another angle.

> *"Racism has distorted reality for many whites. Teachings about history, the world, the pursuits of thought, expressions of culture, and personal relationships have for most whites been both limited and false."*
>
> **-Horace Seldon**[1]

As I get older, I seem to be better able to see some things I should have seen years ago. First and foremost, it is not excusing whites for what has happened to say that it must be challenging to be white. Now those in the racist subculture should not claim this as me saying that whites have it just as tough as we do. No, you don't. You aren't hated, denied opportunities, then blamed for not achieving after being denied. So let's cut that one off right there. I say this because it must be tough for those who do so to live in a fake existence believing things that never were. The America you claim never existed. The belief that your skin color makes you better is untrue. The story that whites have what they do only because of hard work and merit is not so. The belief that the only real Americans are white was disproven by the fact that people of color were standing on the shores of this country when European ships first landed here. White racism has had a substantial negative impact on whites outside of the social, political, and economic benefits some have gained.

> *"Racism burdens Whites by silently holding us up as the standard of excellence, leaving few excuses available to the majority of us who don't measure up. It burdens us with a narrow bandwidth of options for how to be – White or otherwise. It burdens us with our own suffering, since no one seems to sympathize when our lives are difficult. Racism coddles Whites by not requiring us to learn what all people of color must do to survive – how to live in multiple worlds, speak multiple languages and quickly navigate complex realities. It coddles us by making us too fragile to fully hear, understand and receive what people of color are saying, much less take responsibility for our part. It makes us too fragile to talk with people of color in any way that doesn't meet our standards of comfort and familiarity, much less tolerate being in groups where we are the racial minority. These are skills people of color utilize almost everyday, and in some respects makes them more resilient, creative and intelligent than us."*

-Susana Rinderle[2]

Members of the racist subculture live in an alternate reality. In this "reality," America belongs to them. Since they are the rightful owners of this land, only they are entitled to the rights and privileges of citizenship. These rights include the right to rule or govern. Such a belief forced us to endure the embarrassing and inept reign of the 45th President of this nation. A black man had just been President, and a woman dared to think she could be President; that was the red line in the sand right-wing white men could not let be crossed. So instead of electing one of the most qualified candidates for President in modern times based on the merits of her achievements, we got an imbecile whose incompetence cost over four hundred thousand Americans their lives.

Racism has damaged every citizen that has ever lived in this nation. It has stunted the growth of this country. America is the wealthiest nation on earth, but we have colossal wealth inequality because that wealth is concentrated at the top. Gandhi once said, *"a nation's greatness is measured by how it treats its weakest members."* Because of racism, valuable human resources do not get used. America is also one of the most violent nations globally and has the most people in prison.[3] Despite these things, members of the racist subculture believe in their individual and collective exceptionalism.

> *"Racism has taught whites that we are entitled to privilege as a right of birth, undercutting the assumption of achieved merit which is one of the cornerstones of democracy."*
>
> **-Horace Seldon**[4]

The arrogance created by a belief in white supremacy was partly responsible for a predominantly white crowd attacking the U.S. capital. For years a portion of the white community believed their nation was getting taken from them. According to these people, far too many "non-Americans" were being afforded rights they thought only belonged to them. After all, "whites built this country," according to them. Not only does racism teach some whites a lie about the accomplishments of others, thereby creating an arrogance in which they refuse to see or accept the reality that others besides whites have contributed to civilization but:

> *"Racism has set whites who are made poor in our society in competition with people of color and has also increased the separation between classes among whites."*
>
> **-Horace Seldon**[5]

For the past 400 years, wealthy whites have used race to pit moderate to low-income whites against people of color. In 2016, working-class whites developed a cult-like following behind a rich inheritance baby who never really had to worry about a job or anything else ever in his life. He was a man born on third base with a gold spoon stuck in his mouth. Yet they believed this man was the one fighting for them. He baited working-class whites by using the politics of fear and racial resentment. But this division was not invented by President number 45. It started with the so-called founders. After all, a declaration was made in the late 1700s that all men were created equal, but those words were just quill pen ink written on parchment.

> "It is certain in theory, that the only moral foundation of government is the [agreement] of the people, but to what an extent shall we carry this principle? Shall we say, that very individual of the community, old and young, male and female, as well as rich and poor, must [agree] to every act of legislation?...

> Is it not equally true, that men in general in every society, who [are poor and do not own property], are also [unfamiliar] with public affairs to form a right judgment, and too dependent upon other men to have a will of their own? ...Few men, who have no property, have any judgment of their own. They talk and vote as they are directed by some man of property, who has attached their minds to his interest.

> Depend upon it, sir, it is dangerous to open [such a] source of controversy and altercation, as would be opened by attempting to [change] the qualifications of voters. There will be no end of it. New claims will arise. Women will demand a vote. Lads from 12 to 21 will think their rights not enough attended to,

and every man, who has not a [dime], will demand an equal voice with any other in all acts of state. It tends to confound and destroy all distinctions, and [surrender] all ranks, to one common level."
-John Adams to James Sullivan, 26 May 1776[6]

Earlier I cited the 1790 Naturalization Act. This act allowed only white citizenship in this country. While whites could be citizens, only property-owning whites could vote. So from the beginning, poor white men did not have equal rights. White women had no rights, yet both played to race. By 1856 poor white men could vote. By 1920 white women could vote. Even after being given the right to vote, both groups were not given actual equal status with wealthy white males. Working-class whites had no work protections and were at the whims of owners. The labor unions were weak, there were no workplace safety regulations, no minimum wage, no maximum on working hours, no child labor laws, nothing.

As blacks moved north after slavery, the wealthy owners told their white laborers how blacks took jobs that white men were entitled to. The rich were getting richer, and all they had to do to keep the poor in line and dependent on the crumbs they were getting was to tell them how much they were better than blacks or others of color. All along, moderate to low-income whites have been race baited by the wealthy who did so to keep them in their place. And throughout American history, those whites have fallen for it.

When blacks got civil rights and Affirmative Action became a policy, once again, wealthy whites started telling poor ones how unqualified blacks were taking their jobs. Owners and CEOs laid off millions of "working-class whites" over the decades while they shipped American jobs overseas to exploit foreign workers in "third world" nations for pennies per hour. As they did so, white workers were told that unqualified blacks or illegal immigrants were taking jobs from them. As usual, "working-class whites" fell for the race-baiting. Like Pavlov's dogs, a subculture in the white community begins to salivate in anger at the mention of other races having the same opportunity as they do.

Since 1980, American businesses have needlessly sent jobs out of this country. Everybody's hero, Reagan, implemented a government business philosophy of laissez-faire economics that has cost the workers of this nation millions of jobs.[7] "Unqualified" blacks, Asians, illegal immigrants from the southern border, or whoever else was blamed had nothing to do with taking jobs from the white working class. CEOS and corporate owners sent those jobs away. Their pockets got fat while race baiting white working-class citizens into a victim mentality.

"Since the beginning of the 1980s, employment relations in U.S. industrial corporations have undergone three major structural changes—which I summarize as rationalization, marketization, and globalization— that have permanently eliminated middle-class jobs. From the early 1980s, rationalization, characterized by plant closings, eliminated the jobs of unionized blue-collar workers. From the early 1990s, marketization, characterized by the end of a career with one company as an employment norm, placed the job security of middle-aged and older white-collar workers in jeopardy. From the early 2000s, globalization, characterized by the movement of employment offshore, left all members of the U.S. labor force, even those with advanced educational credentials and substantial work experience, vulnerable to displacement."[8]

The quote was from a paper titled *"The Financialization of the U.S. Corporation: What Has Been Lost, and How It Can Be Regained,"* by William Lazonick. In this paper, he describes the forces that created the changes in American business that are the causes for the current weakened state of the American worker. Beginning in 1980, he says America went through a phase where factories began closing. These closings started the end of good-paying union jobs that allowed workers to raise families and live in relative middle-class comfort. The appearance of Windows and PCs around 1990 helped begin a phase in American business that ended the one job career for white-collar workers.

As the new century arrived, so did a new business strategy. In 2000, America outsourced even more jobs to lower-wage paying countries eliminating more jobs formerly held by Americans.[9] American business strategy shifted from using profits to create jobs to match the changes caused by progress as was done in the past and focused on increasing the return on shareholder investments. According to Lazonick, this was based on "agency theory," a theory with the premise that only shareholders have a stake in the distribution of corporate profits because they invest the money. The implementation of agency theory into practice appears to have left out one crucial aspect in the corporate equation: the value of the worker's time.

"Once U.S. corporations adopted these structural changes in employment, however, they often pursued these employment strategies purely for financial gain. Some companies closed manufacturing plants, terminated experienced (and generally more expensive) workers, and offshored production to low-wage areas of the world simply to increase profits, often at the expense of the companies' long-term competitive capabilities and without regard for displaced employees' long years of service. Moreover, as these changes became embedded in the structure of U.S. employment, business corporations failed to invest in new, higher value-added job creation on a

343

sufficient scale to provide a foundation for equitable and stable growth in the U.S. economy."[10]

Once the fairness doctrine ended, disinformation and racist rhetoric began to flow irresponsibly on American airwaves. Racist whites started to get radio programs financed by corporate advertising to propagandize to the poor and moderate-income whites that were listening about how they were being left out and that "others" were getting things at their expense. While these chatterboxes race baited the working class, the corporations financing the airtime of talk radio were shipping jobs out of the country.

"On the contrary, with superior corporate performance defined as meeting Wall Street's expectations for quarterly earnings per share, companies turned to massive stock repurchases to "manage" their own corporations' stock prices. Trillions of dollars that could have been spent on innovation and job creation in the U.S. economy over the past three decades have instead been used to buy back stock for the purpose of manipulating the company's stock price. This financialized mode of corporate resource allocation has been legitimized by the ideology, itself a product of the 1980s and 1990s, that a business corporation should be run to "maximize shareholder value." Through their stock-based compensation, corporate executives who make these decisions are themselves prime beneficiaries of this focus on rising stock prices as the measure of corporate performance."[11]

The corporate heads didn't give a damn about the working-class white person. While working-class whites lost jobs, executives and wealthy shareholders made money. While working-class whites were increasingly becoming members of food lines, executives and business owners were increasing their memberships in exclusive private clubs. While white working-class people were losing their homes, rich white men like president number 45 purchased the properties they lost. The white working class was getting played while wealthy CEOs were paid exorbitant incomes from stock options included in their compensation. Corporations were buying back billions of dollars worth of stocks while claiming that blacks, Japanese, illegals from the south, or the Chinese were taking jobs from "real Americans." Like marks manipulated by con men, working-class whites fell for the race-baiting and began electing people who would move more jobs away.

Most of us grew up and were told a fabulous story about an America where if a person did everything right, they would have a decent paying job waiting for them. Some believed that if they had a good idea, only if they scrimped and saved, they could start a business making enough money to live comfortably. As I grew up, my father consistently told me that big money ran this country. Of course, growing up, you listen to such words and go outside and play. But the reality for many of us is that the "America Dream" is just hoping to break even. Some of us believe the officials we elect work for our best interest, but from the very first day of this country, it has always been about extra rights for the rich and well-connected. It remains that way.

"Over the course of the 1980s, the stock market came to react favorably to permanent downsizings of the blue-collar labor force. As secure middle-class jobs for high-school educated blue-collar workers permanently disappeared, there was no commitment on the part of those who managed U.S. industrial corporations, or the Republican administrations that ruled in the 1980s, to invest in the new capabilities and opportunities required to upgrade the quality, and expand the quantity, of well-paid employment opportunities in the United States on a scale sufficient to reestablish conditions of prosperity for displaced

members of the labor force."[12]

These things have occurred with Republicans or Democrats in power. I used the movement of jobs out of this country as an example, but we have suffered through many scams initiated primarily by rich white men who were greedy. Junk bonds, mortgage-backed securities, credit default swaps, and derivatives are all done by legalized gamblers, better known as stockbrokers in the main casino on Wall Street. These people have stolen a lot of money and have killed jobs. Maybe it's time to stop talking about the drug dealer and start looking at the criminal stockbroker who destroys lives by robbing people of their life savings.

"During the post-World War II decades, for both blue-collar and white-collar workers, the norm in large, established U.S. business corporations was career employment with one company. When layoffs occurred, they tended to be temporary and, in unionized workplaces, on a last-hired, first-fired basis. Supported by a highly progressive income tax system, countercyclical government fiscal policy sought to reduce the severity of business fluctuations, while employment generated by ongoing government spending, particularly on higher education, healthcare, advanced technology, and physical infrastructure (for example, the interstate highway system), complemented the employment opportunities provided by the business sector. The result was relatively equitable and stable economic growth from the late 1940s to the beginning of the 1970s."[13]

We heard the slogan, "Make America Great Again," from 2016 to 2020. Millions of working-class whites purchased red baseball caps, proudly sporting them on their heads. M.A.G.A refers to a return to days right-wing whites believed America grew and prospered based on hard work and merit. The leader of this movement was a man born in 1946. This is important because most people in national leadership today were born shortly after World War Two and grew up in the prosperous aftermath. They were children while their parents availed themselves of the massive government assistance primarily given to whites. They grew up in racially segregated suburbs in homes their parents paid for with the help of guaranteed loans backed by the government. Their parents, primarily fathers, were able to take advantage of all the government benefits from the G.I. bill. They watched the government enact a massive infrastructure project that has created permanent jobs in all 50 states called the interstate highway system. As children during that era, they were oblivious to the enormous government assistance whites received. As they grew up during this era and the so-called American work ethic was preached about, they saw only the progress and grew up to believe it was due to rugged individualism and earned by merit.

These are the people telling us today that government cannot help us. I focus on Reagan mainly because that was the first presidential election I voted in. I saw him start his campaign in Mississippi, talking about states' rights. I saw him try telling blacks in a situation like the "What the hell do you have to lose" speech by President 45 that he knew he didn't have much to offer black people but that we should consider him. His famous quote, "The most terrifying words in the English language are: I'm from the government and I'm here to help," is contradicted by history, but Reagan was good at one thing, race pimping low to moderate-income whites. He used welfare as a racial issue whereby he created the lie that "working-class whites" were paying their hard-earned money to support lazy, shiftless blacks who wanted nothing more than a free handout. That was race pimping 101.

"Corporate welfare often subsidizes failing and mismanaged businesses and induces firms to spend more time on lobbying rather than on making better

products. Instead of correcting market failures, federal subsidies misallocate resources and introduce government failures into the marketplace."[14]

The problem with making welfare about nonwhites and poor white people is that wealthy whites get most of the government handouts and always have. In 2006, approximately 59 billion was spent on welfare for poor and moderate-income Americans.[15] About 92 billion was spent on corporate subsidies.[16] In 2012, 98 billion was spent on corporate subsidies.[17] These are handouts to corporations. People yell and scream about welfare to the poor because they have been race-baited to envision a black woman with many little kids looking different following her around like baby ducks. But the major recipients of welfare are white men wearing black and blue suits who get up every morning and drive to work in their Mercedes or Range Rovers. "The American government spends more on corporate welfare than it does on food stamps and financial assistance for needy families with children."[18],[19],[20],[21]

The extent of the bait, pimp, and hustle strategy to divert the attention of working-class whites away from who was taking from them is legendary. Welfare has been used to race-bait low to moderate-income whites into voting against their best interest. For most of the last 30 years, Americans from one party have put people into public office at nearly every level of government with a philosophy of "government is worthless" and "we must cut taxes for the rich." These politicians souped up the white working class with claims of how everybody else is getting benefits on the white man's dime. They preached about reducing government spending while promising that by cutting taxes for the very rich, the benefits would trickle down to everyone, and all would be fine. Predictably, the usual suspects fell for it.

Again, I am not Einstein, but the people we elect work for us. This is my understanding of how the system is supposed to work. Ask yourself this question: If you were hiring a person for a job and you interviewed a candidate who told you that your company is useless, the less your company got in the way, the better, would you hire that person? I wouldn't, but that is what many American voters did from 1995 through 2007 and from 2011 to 2019. They elected a congress where the majority of the elected representatives believed that government has no role and then wondered why Washington wasn't working. But that's where they got it wrong. Washington was working. The federal government was working exactly how the people we hired promised. *"The most terrifying words in the English language are: I'm from the government and I'm here to help."* They didn't want to terrify us, so they didn't help.

In 2020, planet earth was in the midst of a pandemic. In America, millions of citizens lost jobs. Businesses closed. It has been said that 2.9 million American businesses closed, some never reopened again. While millions of Americans were either parked or standing in long lines with masks on waiting for food and 8 million Americans fell into poverty, between March and December of 2020, American billionaires made 3.9 trillion dollars.[22] One of them was the billionaire who took the stage on a day that most certainly will go down in infamy, telling Americans to walk over to the Capital and "Stop the Steal."

So it was with over 40 years of self-inflicted damage, a belief of victimhood whereby working-class whites got filled with "woe is me" due to award-winning culture pimping from the right-wing chattering class, a misunderstanding that allowed people to believe that equality for others is a loss for whites, a President who race baited working-class whites by telling them he would build a wall because illegal immigrants were taking American jobs, that once again working-class whites allowed themselves to be duped. This time they were taken advantage of by a master con man and on 1-6-2021, committed The White Rebellion.

349

The Price of Racism

"When you spend your dollar out of the community in which you live the community in which you spend your dollar becomes richer and richer; the community out of which you take your money becomes poorer and poorer."

- Malcolm X

Malcolm X did not attend the Harvard School of Business, Brandeis, or Penn State. He earned his "undergrad degree" at State Pen U. However, his opinion relative to economic development is spot on. It is one thing to believe we are now all equal. It is another to look at the numbers derived from the policies made to see if what you think is true. America operates a capitalist economic system. Such a system determines equality by the ability to accumulate capital. Blacks and other people of color have not had the same access to capital as whites, specifically white males. The American system excluded equal access to capital based on race for over 300 years. Blacks were capital by colonial and American law from at least 1619 until 1863.

One morning I woke up and turned on CSPAN to watch Washington Journal. On this day, one of the guests was Robert Woodson. Mr. Woodson is a right-wing black individual who founded the Woodson Center, an agency working to address issues in low-income neighborhoods. Mr. Woodson has done some tremendous things. He advocates for increased economic development in black communities, and he is right in looking at such development as the key to reducing inequality. If he had stayed on the topic of black economic growth, he would have been fine. But he didn't.

Mr. Woodson has authored a book called *"Red White and Black."* I have yet to read it. As I said earlier, I generally don't buy or read books by people like Woodson because his opinions dismiss a reality he has faced his entire life. Paying for his books allows him to continue publishing crazy stuff that gets used against blacks by members of the white racist subculture. Sure enough, in the standard black right-wing fashion, he denied the impact of racism upon the black community and started talking about how blacks need to leave race out of a problem caused by race. He claimed that making whites less racist would not stop the issues in black communities. Mr. Woodson is a long-time advocate for entrepreneurship. I agree that we must create and develop more businesses, but we cannot ignore racism in the process. Racism has created the conditions facing blacks in every area of life, and it is even more apparent in how it impacts black entrepreneurs trying to develop and grow businesses. Let's look now at the price of racism.

> *"The persistent racial wealth gap in the United States is a burden on black Americans as well as the overall economy."*
> **- The economic impact of closing the racialwealth gap, McKinsey and Company**[1]

First, let's look at individual poverty. In 1959 poverty for blacks was 55.1 percent. For whites, it was 18.1.[2] Black poverty was 3.04 times that of whites. This was five years before the Civil Rights Act and during legalized segregation. In 1966, poverty for Blacks was 41.8 percent. For whites, it was 11.3 percent.[3] Black poverty was 3.69 times that of whites.

This was two years after the Civil Rights Act, and the country was trying to figure out how to get to equality. In 1974, poverty for Blacks was 30.3 percent. For Whites, 8.6 percent.[4] Black poverty was 3.52 times that of whites ten years after the Civil Rights Act was passed. In 1984, poverty for Blacks was 33.8 percent. For Whites, 11.5 percent.[5] Black poverty was still 2.94 times that of whites 20 years after the Civil Rights Act. One would think that if a real concerted effort had been made relative to hiring and equal pay, this would not be the case.

In 2004, the poverty rate for Blacks was 24.7 percent. For Whites, 10.8 percent.[6] Black poverty was 2.28 times that of whites 40 years after the Civil Rights Act. In 40 years, black poverty was still twice that of whites. The difference between blacks and whites had decreased by less than 1 point. Either programs and policies designed to lower poverty in the black community did not work, or the necessary emphasis was not placed on trying to do what it takes to reduce poverty in the black community so that it was at least comparable to that of whites.

In 2014, the Black poverty rate was 26.2 percent. For Whites, 12.7 percent.[7] Fifty years after the Civil Rights Act was passed and members of the American right determined that racism was a thing of the past, black poverty was still two times that of whites., In 2020 we heard all the bragging from President number 45 and his followers about all the great things he did for black people. When he left office, poverty for Blacks was 19.3 percent. For Whites, it was 8.2 percent.[8] Despite the claims of President number 45, Black poverty was two times that of whites. Since 1959 no matter how low or high poverty has been, blacks have continued living at double the white and overall American poverty rate. Increased high school and college graduation rates have not changed this inequality.

In 1959 the poverty rate for all American families was 20.8 percent.[9] For white families, it was 16.5 percent. For black families, 54.9 percent.[10] During the time people declare that black families were "intact," black family poverty was 3.33 times that of white ones. In 1966, the American poverty rate was 13.1 percent.[11] For white families, the poverty rate was 9.7 percent, and for black families, 40.9 percent.[12] In 1966, black family poverty was 4.2 times that of white families. In 1974 the poverty rate for all American families was 9.9 percent.[13] Poverty for Black families was 29.3 percent. For Whites 7.3 percent.[14] Black family poverty was four times that of whites ten years after Civil Rights was passed. In 1984, the poverty rate for all American families was 13.1 percent. 15 For Black families, it was 33.3 percent, Whites 10.1 percent.[16] Black family poverty was 3.29 times that of whites 20 years after Civil Rights was signed into law.

In 2004 the poverty rate for all American families was 11 percent.[16] For white families, it was 9 percent. Black families, 23.8 percent.[17] We are now 40 years past Johnson's signing of the Civil Rights Act. These numbers are well within our lifetimes. In 2004 black family poverty was 2.64 times that of a white family. In 2014, the American poverty rate was 12.7 percent.[18] For white families, the poverty rate was 10.7 percent, and for black families, 24.6 percent.[19] 50 years had passed since the Civil Rights Act, and black families still had at least double the white family poverty rate. In 2014 black family poverty was 2.3 times that of white families. In 2020 the poverty rate for all American families was 9.5 percent.[20] Poverty for black families was 17.4 percent, white families 8.2 percent.[21] Despite increases in educational attainment and breakthroughs at every level of American society, in 2020, black family poverty remained two times that of white families. No matter how it is measured, poverty for whites is lower than the national average, and black poverty is consistently double the national average.

In 2011, DEMOS did a study named "The Racial Wealth Gap, Why Policy Matters," which discussed the racial wealth gap, its problems, and solutions and outcomes if the gap did not exist. DEMOS determined that policy decisions primarily drove the racial wealth gap in this study.

*"**The U.S. racial wealth gap is substantial and is driven by public policy decisions**. According to our analysis of the SIPP data, in 2011 the median white household had $111,146 in wealth holdings, compared to just $7,113 for the median Black household and $8,348 for the median Latino household. From the continuing impact of redlining on American homeownership to the retreat from desegregation in public education, public policy has shaped these disparities, leaving them impossible to overcome without racially-aware policy change."*

-DEMOS[22]

On October 24, 2013, the Kellogg Foundation and Altarum Institute sent out a press release about a report they had done titled, *"The Business Case for Racial Equity."* This was a study done by both organizations, using information studied and assessed from the Center for American Progress, National Urban League Policy Institute, Joint Center for Political and Economic Studies and the U.S. Department of Justice.

"Striving for racial equity – a world where race is no longer a factor in the distribution of opportunity – is a matter of social justice. But moving toward racial equity can generate significant economic returns as well. When people face barriers to achieving their full potential, the loss of talent, creativity, energy, and productivity is a burden not only for those disadvantaged, but for communities, businesses, governments, and the economy as a whole. Initial

research on the magnitude of this burden in the United States (U.S.), as highlighted in this brief, reveals impacts in the trillions of dollars in lost earnings, avoidable public expenditures, and lost economic output."

**-The Kellogg Foundation
and Altarum Institute**[23]

On September 3, 2019, Brentin Mock, wrote an article on the Bloomberg.com CityLab website titled, *"White Americans' Hold on Wealth Is Old, Deep, and Nearly Unshakeable"* based on a study done by McKinsey and Company called "The economic impact of closing the racial wealth gap." In this study McKinsey and Company predicted a bleak future if current race based wealth inequality continues.

"It will end up costing the U.S. economy as much as $1 trillion between now and 2028 for the nation to maintain its longstanding black-white racial wealth gap, according to a report released this month from the global consultancy firm McKinsey & Company. That will be roughly 4 percent of the United States GDP in 2028—just the conservative view, assuming that the wealth growth rates of African Americans will outpace white wealth growth at its current clip of 3 percent to .8 percent annually, said McKinsey.

If the gap widens, however, with white wealth growing at a faster rate than black wealth instead, it could end up costing the U.S. $1.5 trillion or 6 percent of GDP according to the firm."[24]

Groups like DEMOS, the Kellogg Foundation, Altarum Institute, Pew Research and others have done extensive research on the public policies that created these disparities. As we look at the numbers, we see what has caused our economic problem, and it's not the loss of jobs by the white working class. The numbers show us that many of our national difficulties do not have to exist. Study after study shows that racism is costing America trillions of dollars. We hear all the rhetoric about debts and deficits by our elected officials. The federal government has basically spent more than what it's taken in for most of the past 50 years. While we have been continually told over time that our deficit comes from entitlements or programs subsidizing people who don't want to work, multiple studies show that the damage is self-inflicted. If the deficit is a matter of spending vs. revenue, the fact that racism exists in this country robs the government of the income necessary to stay away from deficits and debt. America has a debt of over 30 trillion dollars. Our debt is due to lost taxable income denied because of racism.

Citygroup did a study focusing on U.S. GDP from 2000 until 2020. The study revealed huge losses in GDP due to continuing discrimination against blacks in business revenue, education, housing credit, and income. The study determined that since the year 2000, continuing discriminatory practices in the four areas mentioned in the prior sentence resulted in a loss of 16 trillion dollars in GDP.[25] The breakdown is as follows:

"Closing the Black racial wage gap 20 years ago might have provided an additional $2.7 trillion in income available for consumption and investment.

Improving access to housing credit might have added an additional 770,000 Black homeowners over the last 20 years, with combined sales and expenditures adding another $218 billion to GDP over that time.

Facilitating increased access to higher education (college, graduate, and vocational schools) for Black students might have bolstered lifetime incomes that in aggregate sums to $90 to $113 billion.

Providing fair and equitable lending to Black entrepreneurs might have resulted in the creation of an additional $13 trillion in business revenue over the last 20 years. This could have been used for investments in labor, technology, capital equipment, and structures and 6.1 million jobs might have been created per year."[26]

That 16 trillion dollars lost from 2000 until the publication of the study amounted to 800 billion dollars in lost GDP per year. The 13 trillion dollars in lost business revenue averages 650 billion dollars annually. That money could have created approximately 6.1 million jobs PER YEAR. That is more than 120 million jobs lost over 20 years. Jobs that would have reduced expenditures for public assistance because fewer people would have needed such help. The 2.7 trillion dollars of lost income averages 135 billion dollars of potential lost taxable revenue annually. This money would circulate through the economy, with part of it returning to the government as revenue. This money would have helped reduce the deficit between what the government takes in and what it spends. We're talking about losing billions of dollars annually and it was lost because of racism.

Payscale did a two-year study from 2017 to 2019, and this is their conclusion: *"we find equal pay for equal work is still not a reality."*[27] They studied the earnings of white men and men of color using data from 1.8 million employees. They found that no matter how far they advanced, black men made less than white men with the same qualifications.[28] According to the study, *"black men were the only racial/ethnic group not achieving pay parity with white men at some level."*[29] The study showed that black men had the most significant pay gap relative to white men and that on average, black men earned 87 cents for every dollar a white man earned.[30] The Payscale study showed that black men are paid less compared to all other men. Even when black and white men had the same job, experience, education, and worked at the same geographic location, the study shows that black men earned less. Executive-level black men still earn less than white men at that same level. At that level, black men are paid 97 cents for every dollar a white man is paid but face the same executive responsibilities and are expected to produce the same or superior results.[31]

The National Women's Law Center also showed that black women are paid less than other women. Black women are paid 63 cents for every dollar paid to white men based on calculations used in the study.[32] Where this impacts black single mothers is this study shows a pay difference of over 20,000 dollars per year.[33] *"Black women have to work more than 19 months—until the very last day of July—to make as much as white, non-Hispanic men did in the previous 12-month calendar year."*[34] Black women in high-wage occupations earn 64 cents for every dollar a white man earns.[35] On average, that is 40,000 dollars per year less than white men in those same occupations.[36] This renders the unwed mother, fatherless home opinion meritless relative to income and poverty because a black couple can get married, daddy lives at home, and the family still makes less than whites. This is not about lack of education. Nor is it about the field of study.

> *"Even after completing undergraduate and graduate degrees, black and Hispanic workers earned less than non-Hispanic white workers with the same, or often less, education."*
> **- Roy Eduardo Kokoyachuk, ThinkNow Research**[37]

Kokoyachuk found that blacks and Hispanics with college degrees were paid less than whites and Asians with comparable education. His study showed that blacks and Hispanics who graduated in S.T.E.M majors earned less than whites and Asians with degrees in those same majors.

"Even when Blacks and Hispanics go the extra mile and earn professional degrees, their incomes still don't break six figures. Whites and Asians, however, double their incomes by earning professional degrees, allowing them to make well over $100,000 a year."[38]

So let's review. In low-wage paying occupations, Black men are paid 87 cents for every dollar a white man makes and black women 63 cents. In high-paying occupations, black men earn 97 cents for every dollar a white man makes, and black women 64 cents. A black married couple will earn less than a white couple even when all other factors are the same. Throughout a 40 year work career, a black married couple in low-paying occupations will lose well over 1 million dollars of income compared to white married couples in the same jobs. A black married couple in a high-paying profession will earn approximately 2 million dollars less than a white couple at the same level during the same 40 year period.

"In 1965, Senator Daniel Patrick Moynihan's report, The Negro Family: The Case for National Action, attributed racial inequality as well as poverty and crime in the black community to family structure, particularly the prevalence of families headed by single mothers. Not only did research at the time cast doubt on this causality, but evidence over the last the 50 years demonstrates that rates of child poverty, educational attainment, and crime do not track rates of single parenthood. Thus, even though the share of children living with a single mother rose for all racial and ethnic groups through the mid-1990s and has remained high since then, school completion and youth arrests for violent crimes have declined significantly, while poverty rates have fluctuated according to economic conditions. Family structure does not drive racial inequity, and racial inequity persists regardless of family structure."

**-Amy Traub, Laura Sullivan,
Tatjana Meschede and Thomas Shapiro,
DEMOS, "The Asset Value of Whiteness:
Understanding the Racial Wealth Gap."**

The median income for black households compared to non-Hispanic whites for the last 50 years show a history of earnings inequality. The numbers used here are from the U.S. Census Bureau, Current Population Survey Annual Social and Economic Supplements (CPS ASEC), Table H-5 Race and Hispanic Origin of Householder--Households by Median and Mean Income: 1967 to 2020. Again, this will reflect that the unwed mother and fatherless home are not the sole cause of economic hardship. It is caused by a problem most want to deny.

In 1972, the American household median income was $9,697 per year.[39] The median income for non-Hispanic white households was $10,318 per year; for Black households, it was $5,938.[40] Black household median income was 58 percent of white households. In 1974, the American household median income was $11,197 per year.[41] The median income for non-Hispanic white households was $11,810 per year; for black households, $6,964.[42] Black household median income was 59 percent of what whites made.

Twenty years after the Civil Rights Act was passed (1984), the American household median income was $22,415 per year.[43] The median income for non-Hispanic white households was $24,138 per year; for Blacks, $13,471.[44] Black household median income was 55.8 percent of non-Hispanic white households. In 2004, the annual American household median income was $44,334.[45] The median yearly income for non-Hispanic white households was $48,910; for blacks it was $30,095.[46] Black household median income was 61.5 percent of non-Hispanic whites.

In 2014, the annual American median income was $53,657 per year.[47] The median yearly income for non-Hispanic White households was $60.256; for Black households, $35,398.[48] Black household income was 58.7 percent of what Whites made. In 2020, the American household median income was $67,521 per year.[49] The median income for non-Hispanic White households was $74.912; for Blacks households, $45,870.[50] Black household median income was 61 percent of white households in 2020.

At no time from 1959 through 2020 have whites and blacks come close to having equal income. It has not mattered whether America was practicing segregation. It has not mattered that blacks have become better educated. It has not mattered if black households were traditional two parent, two cars, a dog, two children having, good church-going members of American society. We have had two terms of a black president, and still, the median income for blacks has been less than whites. Most certainly, if a black man can manage a nation, he can run a corporation. If a black woman can run the second-largest Department of Justice in America and serve as Vice President, she can manage your local Wal-Mart. Seventy years ago, Brown v. Topeka ended segregation in schools. Sixty years ago, Civil Rights for everyone became law. This situation is not about the failure of "black culture" or so-called liberal handout policies. The root cause of the problems blacks face today is continuing white racism. But people like Robert Woodson get put on TV to tell us that making whites less racist will not stop the issues in black communities.

In 2017, Demos published a study titled, *"The Asset Value of Whiteness: Understanding the Racial Wealth Gap."* On page 10 this statement is written: *"The median white single parent has 2.2 times more wealth than the median black two-parent household and 1.9 times more wealth than the median Latino two-parent household."*[51] Certainly, as a black man, I support men being in the lives of their children, but it is time to stop denying the real problem. Black economic difficulties have nothing to do with a man sitting in a house with his wife and children. The media must quit pushing blacks like Woodson out into the debate because he says what they want to hear. Reducing white racism to the point of irrelevance is the key to solving many issues in black communities, all other communities of color, and white communities.

Citigroup determined that discrimination against blacks has cost America 13 trillion in taxable earnings since the beginning of this century. That does not include the lost revenues from discrimination against other people of color or women. I am no economist, but I can guess with the best, and I am willing to estimate that America has lost at least 50 trillion dollars in taxable earnings since the 16th Amendment was ratified in 1913. The national debt is 30 trillion.[52] Fair pay and fair employment instead of racism may have made it so no national debt exists with budget surpluses for most of the 109 years the income tax has been in place. These surpluses could have funded free college, a nationalized health care system, safeguarded Medicare and social security, kept our infrastructure modern, provided a world-class public education for all Americans, top-notch law enforcement, and a strong military.

True equality in the American capitalist system means all races must have control of capital equal to their proportion of the population. Racism in America has and continues to deprive blacks of capital. Blacks are 13 percent of the American people but have 4 percent of the wealth.[53] This did not happen because of laziness. In discussion with some whites about this, you get told about Oprah, Tiger Woods, Michael Jordan, or Floyd Mayweather. At the time if this writing, out of nearly 20 million black families, less than 400,000 have a net worth of 1 million dollars.[54] There are only ten black billionaires in America.[55] Their collective worth is just over 31 billion dollars. Contrast that to Elon Musk who is worth over 200 billion dollars by himself.

This did not happen because blacks are not interested or had not tried. I know personally from my experience in the insurance field that it is tough to sustain a career in that industry unless you have venture capital or have saved enough money to support yourself as you build your client base. Without adequate venture capital, all it takes is one downturn in sales, and a person could be completely wiped out or accumulate debt while trying to do the things necessary to build the business. It isn't easy to earn the venture capital required to start if you're paid less than everyone else while you're saving to start a business.

"When you spend your dollar out of the community in which you live the community in which you spend your dollar becomes richer and richer; the community out of which you take your money becomes poorer and poorer."

-Malcolm X

Let's apply the Malcolm X doctrine to the American economy. In the last chapter, I presented a paper written by William Lazonick that detailed 40 years of American companies moving jobs out of the country while not investing in creating new American jobs. American companies took dollars from American citizens to pay foreign workers. By doing this, corporations, with the blessing of our government, stimulated foreign economies and increased wealth in those countries while making most Americans poorer. This shift hit black and other non-white communities the hardest.

A trade deficit occurs when a country's imports exceed its exports. This is also called a negative trade balance. While much is made about foreign trade deficits, and we heard many rants about that during the reign of President number 45, Americans face internal trade deficits or a negative trade balance of our own making. People of all races spend their money in businesses owned by whites, but such trade/business is not reciprocal. In 2020, there were 5.9 million employer businesses in America, 134,567, or 2 percent, were owned by blacks.[56] According to the U.S. Department of Commerce Minority Business Development Agency, there are just over 3.1 million non-employer Black-owned businesses in the United States.[57] Blacks/African Americans, who, as is so astutely stated in reference to crime, make up 13% of the U.S. population, own less than 10 percent of all the businesses in the country, and generate less than one-half of 1 percent of the total business receipts. There are 3,671 public companies in the United States, and blacks own eight.[58] That number equals less than 1⁄4 of 1 percent of all publicly traded companies in America. While blacks who can, invest in white-owned businesses, whites who can invest don't appear to be investing in black companies.

Historically, according to Shawn Rochester in his book *"The Black Tax, The Cost of Being Black in America"* blacks have lived with the 2 percent rule. The 2 percent rule holds that blacks have been restricted to 2 percent or less of all things that are important to wealth accumulation in America.[59] Right now Rochester's 2 percent rule for blacks is in effect in these fields: Investment and Business Financing, Corporate Leadership, Education, Media, Medicine, Law, Financial Services, Agriculture, Residential Real Estate, and businesses such as Information Technology, Finance and Insurance, Manufacturing, Agriculture, Oil, Gas and Mining, Utilities and Wholesale Trade.[60]

Equality in a capitalist system means changing the 2 percent rule to the 13 percent rule. Blacks must have 13 percent of the wealth in America. Blacks must be represented by 13 percent of the businesses owned and workers in every field. Blacks have approximately one-third the wealth we should have in proportion to our population and in most cases are represented by less than 1/6th of what we should be in most categories of American business. These are numbers the per capita people seem to miss. I don't think demanding that we have the wealth, business ownership and business participation equal to our representation in the population is asking too much. These numbers are not the result of blacks not wanting to work hard enough or are because we are raised not to recognize the value of work.

So how do we get to that 13 percent? For years we have heard the sermons telling us to shop black. I watch TV and see ads from major corporations who use black employees to advertise a product or have black actors playing roles. This is fantastic and certainly an improvement from the past, but what I do not see in national prime-time broadcasts are commercials from black-owned businesses. To help support black-owned businesses, we must increase the use of every tool available to increase the visibility of black-owned businesses. Because black businesses lack visibility, a nationwide saturation advertising campaign may be one solution. The infrastructure is in place to do so. I humbly suggest that our needs relative to marketing and advertising can be met by increasing our support of the United States Black Chamber of Commerce and its affiliates. Black Chamber affiliates are uniquely positioned to create advertising campaigns for businesses in their areas.

In addition, it is of the UTMOST importance to support the modern revolutionaries who are in black owned media, such as Roland Martin and the Black Star Network.. These are individuals who can completely change the game.

"The United States is the largest advertising market in the world, with ad spending amounting to 240 billion U.S. dollars in 2020. Looking at breakdowns of expenditures by medium, in 2021 and 2025, approximately 153 billion U.S. dollars were directed towards internet ads in 2021, which is estimated to

increase even further in 2025. This was followed by over 72 billion U.S. dollars spent on ads on TV in 2021 and is expected to increase by roughly 10 billion in 2025."[61]

Blacks are competing in business with companies that use every advertising/marketing technique possible, and black businesses must have the ability to do the same. We must not only solicit black dollars, but to get 13 percent of the sales receipts, we must put the names of black-owned businesses in the minds of other races as an option when they go shopping or need professional services.

"It is projected that digital advertising expenditures in the United States will increase by more than a 100 percent between 2019 and 2024. In that five years period U.S. digital ad spend will grow from 132.46 to 278.53 billion dollars. These figures will represent roughly 53 percent of global digital ad spending, which is expected to surpass 526 billion U.S. dollars in 2024, up from the 283 billion recorded in 2018."[62]
"In 2021, radio advertising spending in the United States is predicted to grow by nearly 19 percent year-on-year, reaching 11 billion U.S. dollars. In 2022 the growth is set to slow down to three percent."[63]

In 2020, Advertising was a 240 billion dollar industry. For years television was the most used medium for advertising. Now more money is invested in digital ads. Projected American businesses spending in the digital ad market in 2022 was over 200 million dollars.[64] As shown by the quote, digital advertising ad spending was predicted to double between 2019 and 2024. The majority of that spending will be for ads located on search engines. The average ad spend in the digital market today is $286.60.[65] It is anticipated that by 2026, 75 percent of all digital ad spending will be on mobile.[66]

"Mobile device technology is the main driver of next years' developments in Video Advertising. High mobile processing power together with new 5G internet connection speeds will allow more complex mobile video ad strategies. Formats such as live broadcasting, 360° panoramas, or virtual reality videos will transfer the concept of immersion to the advertising field and make the Video Advertising environment increasingly attractive. This development promises highly positive effects on the global mobile market growth. However, as there are no such disruptive technological innovations on the rise in the desktop market, it will struggle keeping up with its mobile pendant and will likely stagnate."[67]

By 2026 more than 69 million dollars is expected to be spent on digital video ads. At the time of this writing, the average ad spend for digital videos was 151 dollars. However, as mobile device technology increases, it may allow small businesses to create and upload their own commercials or show live events on various social media platforms.

"One of the main trends within Social Media Advertising is the further monetization of social networks and messenger apps. The integration of shopping and payment solutions into social networks combined with exact localization will increase user engagement, conversions, and performance of advanced targeting. Besides the growth potential in the field of social networks, an integration or proliferation of advertising spaces within messenger apps such as WhatsApp or Instagram will rapidly increase the revenue potential of current market key players like Facebook."[68]

Projected spending for social media advertising in 2022 was nearly 63 million dollars, with an average growth rate of 8.8 percent. By 2026 it is anticipated that ad spending for social media will increase to just over 88 million dollars. 88.6 percent of all projected social media spending in 2026 will be for mobile ads.[69] More than 220 million Americans used various social media platforms in 2020. By 2025 it is anticipated that 243 million Americans will use social media.[70]

Even with the company's problems, Facebook/Meta is the most popular social media platform in America. As of January 2022, Facebook/Meta had 179.65 million accounts and a 71.8 market share as of February 2022.[71] [72] Other platforms such as Instagram are on the rise, especially among the Millenials and Gen Z populations.

"The vast majority of Americans – 97% – now own a cellphone of some kind. The share of Americans that own a smartphone is now 85%. About three-quarters of U.S. adults now own a desktop or laptop computer, while roughly half own a tablet computer. 15% of American adults are "smartphone-only" internet users – meaning they own a smartphone, but do not have traditional home broadband service. Reliance on smartphones for online access is especially common among younger adults, lower-income Americans and those with a high school education or less."
-Pew Research, Mobile Fact Sheet, April 10, 2021[73]

"93% of American adults use the internet."
-Pew Research, Internet/Broadband Fact Sheet, April 7, 2021[74]

"Today, 72% of the public uses some type of social media. YouTube and Facebook are the most-widely used online platforms, and its user base is most broadly representative of the population as a whole. Smaller shares of Americans use sites such as Twitter,

Pinterest, Instagram and LinkedIn. Seven-in-ten Facebook users – and around six-in-ten Instagram and Snapchat users – visit these sites at least once a day."

-Pew Research, Social Media Fact Sheet, April 7, 2021[75]

Malcolm X spoke about the importance of keeping our money in the black community. Blacks must expand that community to include every neighborhood of the cities and towns we live in. Cooperative economics has never really applied to American business. Blacks drive to the suburbs to buy products or for services provided. In the 21st Century, people from the suburbs must drive into black communities and do business. Blacks and other non-whites have made white business owners very wealthy. Money from blacks helped grow what are now giant multinational corporations. For America to become great, the concept of Ujamaa must be part of not only black culture but American culture.

The earliest blacks in America recognized that white racism was a problem that stood in the way of progress in the black community. As I have stated before, far too many blacks who get in leadership positions go too far to accommodate the wishes of whites who care nothing about them. Some do so to maintain funding. Others do so to stay employed. Either way, this must stop. We can no longer continue holding things inside us to the detriment of our health to curry favor. There can be no solution to the problems created by white racism without reducing or eradicating the racist subculture in America.

"A recent study conducted by a team of researchers from the National Community Reinvestment Coalition, Utah State University, Brigham Young University, Rutgers University, and Lubin Research found that banks were three times more likely to

request follow-up appointments with white business owners than better-qualified Black business owners, and the Black business owners were subjected to far greater personal and financial scrutiny compared to their equal or less creditworthy white counterparts."[76]

This is an example of the error in Woodson's thinking. Racism is a huge obstacle for potential black entrepreneurs before they open, and it affects the bottom line when we consider the total receipts. It impacts the number of businesses blacks start, and the type of business started. It impacts the potential of receiving a business loan, the amount loaned, and the terms of payment of those loans. Unfortunately for Mr. Woodson, white racism is an issue in the black community. It is just plain wrong to say we won't solve problems in the black community by making whites less racist.

"Racial inequality in the United States today may, ultimately, be based on slavery, but it is also based on the failure of the country to take effective steps since slavery to undermine the structural racial inequality that slavery put in place. From the latter part of the nineteenth century through the first half of the twentieth century, the Jim Crow system continued to keep Blacks "in their place," and even during and after the civil rights era no policies were adopted to dismantle the racial hierarchy that already existed."
Jonathan Kaplan and Andrew Valls[77]

If I have not made you unhappy yet, here is the part that will make some people very angry. So before you read further, if you are opposed to reparations, return this book and get your money back because this is the part where the topic will be presented. When discussing racial issues with many white Americans, learned forgetfulness is on display when the subject turns to reparations. The opposition to black reparations today is based on the "I'm not to be blamed for the sins of my ancestors" excuse. The problem with the lack of merit in that argument is obvious, but the call for reparations has been distorted to discredit the cause.

The late honorable John Conyers, D-Michigan, first introduced a bill to congress in 1989, H.R.3745 - Commission to Study Reparation Proposals for African Americans Act. Conyers said this about his proposed legislation: *"My bill does four things: It acknowledges the fundamental injustice and inhumanity of slavery; It establishes a commission to study slavery, its subsequent racial and economic discrimination against freed slaves; It studies the impact of those forces on today's living African Americans; and the commission would then make recommendations to Congress on appropriate remedies to redress the harm inflicted on living African Americans."*[78]

Conyers introduced this bill in every Congress until he left the body in 2017. For 28 years, American lawmakers refused to pass this legislation. Instead, the American right dishonestly distorted the issue. At every level, the American government owes reparations to not only descendants of slaves, but due to continuing acts of racism, all black citizens of this country. We hear the excuses of how we weren't slaves and whites today didn't own slaves. Well, the argument or demand has nothing to do with what or who individual whites owned. The demand is for reparations from the government(s) that made the laws and policies.

Many who argue against reparations start and end their opposition based only on slavery. That is a mistake. In "The Black Tax, The Cost of Being Black in America" Shawn Rochester categorizes the financial damage to blacks as a result of America's history of racism. Rochester's summary of the losses are as follows:

Slavery from 1619-1865 = $50 trillion. Present value of

Black labor in 1860 = $22 trillion. Homestead Act from 1862-1935 = $16 trillion. Jim Crow Apartheid from 1870-1935 = $15 trillion. Great Economic Expansion from 1935-1965 = $8.15 trillion. Post Civil Rights era from 1960 to right now = 7.5 trillion.[79] Add to that $615 billion annually in continuing costs based on *"lost equity value, missing black teachers, income lost due to over incarceration, the consistent racial gap in employment, money lost due to subprime lending, and discrimination in the workplace."*[80]

"The Congress shall have power to lay and collect taxes on incomes, from whatever source derived, without apportionment among the several States, and without regard to any census or enumeration."[81]

On February 25th, 1913, the 16th Amendment of the United States Constitution was ratified. This amendment created the income tax. Today, every working American must pay income tax unless their income is below a certain level. Since 1913 blacks have paid federal income taxes to help finance programs and policies that have excluded us. Most states began income taxes during Jim Crow Apartheid, and working blacks paid income taxes that helped states implement policies enforcing apartheid.[82]

More than 50 billion dollars (based on 1930's value) was spent on The New Deal and Servicemen's Readjustment Act.[83][84] That is the equivalent of 1 trillion dollars today. Both programs are credited with providing a significant boost to wealth accumulation in America. Both policies excluded vast numbers of black who worked and paid taxes. According to the study, "Black Reparations for Twentieth Century Federal Housing Discrimination: the Construction of White Wealth and the Effects of Denied Black homeownership" written by Jane Kim," Federal housing policies that excluded blacks from funding provided the equivalent of 1.239 quintillion dollars to create white wealth in the 20th century.[85] Education, paid for by tax dollars blacks pay into the system, continues underfunding schools in black neighborhoods. Blacks pay taxes to fund law enforcement who kill blacks at three times our population, even as whites are more than double the arrests. Tax money working blacks pay into the system allocated for social services or community development are not equally invested in organizations, services, or policies that would increase positive outcomes in black communities. I have seen this personally.

Professor William Darity has done an extensive study on the issue of reparations and his book, *From Here to Equality* provides a plan. When the discussion is reparations, we can leave slavery out of the debate and still demand trillions of dollars from city, county, state, and federal governments for policies that have denied or continues to deny equal protection as defined by American law.

For years I have listened to the "I'm not responsible" or "I didn't own anybody" and "I was not alive then" membership sections of the United States of America. Citigroup determined money lost due to racial discrimination against blacks since 2000. At a minimum, reparations can be requested for money lost from 2000 until right now. If we only take lost income from racism starting in 2000, it equals more than $57,000 per black person in America based on the 2020 U.S. Census. Including all losses due to racial discrimination equals more than 277,000 per black person in America. This is money owed NOW for things done in OUR LIFETIMES. For those who want to play this off as "black money," think again. This is money the United States of America has lost.

I am quite sure no one living in 1980 was alive when the U.S. government made the Fort Laramie treaty with the Sioux Nation or were participants in Custers violation of that treaty. Nor were they alive when President Grant decided it was OK to let settlers and people prospecting for gold trespass into land promised to the Sioux thereby violating the treaty. No one in 1980 was alive when the U.S. government decided to take the land from the Sioux by military force. No one in 1980 was alive when the U.S. government decided to cut off supplies they promised the Sioux as condition for their surrender after whipping the U.S. Army at The Battle of Little Bighorn. But in 1980, the government of the United States decided reparations were due to the Sioux Nation for what was done to them in the 1800's. They awarded the Sioux nation 105 million dollars.[86]

Fixing the damage caused by centuries of racism cannot be done on the cheap. If you do one hundred dollars' worth of damage, it will not be fixed by handing somebody a twenty. Yet it has been "finger in the dike" thinking that has created the racial wealth and equality gap. Folks, this is the minimum cost of racism. I have not even included the cost of discrimination against other communities of color. There are members in all communities of color who can better articulate their American experience than I. I speak about what blacks have experienced because it is my experience. This goes beyond my words because far more outstanding men and women than me have said these same things for the nearly two and one-half centuries that America has officially been a nation. Those responsible for the wrongs always refuse to listen. Instead of listening, people lied to themselves, creating a false reality that tells them this nation was great at one time. This false reality is no more than a delusion of grandeur that has ignored the long-term damage created by an economic system that started with unpaid forced labor.

> *"Where justice is denied, where poverty is enforced, where ignorance prevails, and where any one class is made to feel that society is an organized conspiracy to oppress, rob and degrade them, neither persons nor property will be safe."*
> **-Frederick Douglass**

It's Time to Get in Trouble!

"Get in good trouble, necessary trouble, and help redeem the soul of America."

-John Lewis

I f you have not thrown away or burned this book yet, then here is where I say that the "conversation" we are having is coming to an end. I have been very critical throughout this book, but I stated from the beginning that I would be. During the time I have written this book, I have seen some things that simultaneously give me hope and dread. I will continue with the dread for a little while longer, but it would not be right to end this book with dread.

I am 63 years old as of this writing. Whites of my age tell me not to blame them for what their grandparents did, yet we all were born when Jim Crow was the written law of the land, and because of what some of you were taught as children, we ended up getting into fights on streets, playgrounds, and schoolyards. While many of you stopped having racist beliefs, many did not. While you tell me not to blame you for what your grandparents did, whites who are my age grew up in suburban developments like Levittown because of government-guaranteed loans blacks could not get. Being that I am from the Midwest, I know some whites live on family-owned land passed down due to homesteading. Yet today, many of them stand up declaring they have never benefitted because of race. I believe it is time for some of us to understand that living in the past is not possible, but things that occur in the past impact us now. We are all here because of acts performed in the past that ended up with us being born. We do not forget those who made our lives possible. As Americans, we should face all of our history, not just the part that makes some of us feel superior.

> *"Memory and justice are intricately linked. To adequately address historical wrongs, contemporary liberal democracies must engage the past. Historical memory provides a connective tissue between past wrongs and present injustices. Without the agony of historical memory, liberal societies slide into a politics of national forgetting, where the innocence of the present is affirmed through a disavowal of the past."*
> **-David Myer Temin and Adam Dahl**[1]

Collective amnesia has swept across the land. After whites were given land as part of the Homestead Act, I am sure they worked very hard to farm that land. After whites were given loans guaranteed by the government to buy homes, I am pretty sure they worked hard to make the payments. I'm sure that white person who got a business loan blacks were denied only because of race, worked hard to make sure that business was successful. While blacks could not get certain jobs because of their race, I'm sure whites who were hired worked hard to remain employed. I'm sure that the whites who got admitted into colleges that did not allow blacks worked hard to get those degrees.

The issue is not how hard whites worked after they got the opportunity. It is the fact they got the chance while others didn't because of skin color. This reality has been ignored. Maybe now that we are into the 21st century, it is time to face this reality. There are some additional things much of white America needs to understand. Blacks are owed reparations. Some have tried making this an argument about payment for slavery, but as Ta Nehisi Coates so eloquently expresses in *"The Case For Reparations,"* the argument goes far past slavery. The damage caused by atrocities committed against blacks after slavery are numerous and are the reason many blacks suffer right now. Whether it's done by writing individual checks or massive funding for community and economic development, the governments of the United States of America owe black people back pay and then some.

Blacks and whites have had different experiences in America. Whites tell a story of a group of people who came over on the Mayflower. Blacks tell stories about being stuck in the bowels of ships like the Amistad. We did not see the Beaver Cleaver nation many whites talk about. During the 50s, we were protesting having to sit on the back of the bus and segregated schools. We didn't have time to worry about Lumpy Rutherford. Let me add this, and maybe the whites who are the problem can understand better how things are now. Today no freedom riders are going into towns to teach children how to read and then finding whole communities of adult blacks who also can't read. Those days are over. Blacks are educated now, and more blacks than ever before are entering colleges or post-secondary training. We know what you mean when you say certain things. Dogs don't whistle, and "Make America Great Again," means that "we want white dominion." We know how the system works and how it should work according to the words written in the constitution. It is not working right now, specifically for people of color no matter how many loudmouths are put in front of microphones.

At the 2017 Pro Football Hall of Fame induction ceremony, LaDainian Tomlinson spoke for me and millions of others in this nation by asking that we in America begin working as a team. A team works together to reach goals. When a team member faces difficulty their mates back them. They don't tell their mate, "Oh well, move beyond it. Everyone has it tough." A team respects the experiences of every member of that team. No teammate's experience is more significant than another's. This is what we must become. It is how America finally becomes great.

> *"There is very little truth in the old refrain that one cannot legislate equality. Laws not only provide concrete benefits, they can even change the hearts of men—some men, anyhow—for good or evil."*
> **-Thurgood Marshall**

During my life so far, I have known many people who just settle for the world the way it is and do not question it. When a person declares how things are not supposed to be this way, they are looked at by others as if they are crazy. The world DOES NOT have to be like this. Racism can be eliminated. WE CAN change hearts and minds. WE CAN legislate equality. A few years ago, a man stood up and told us "Yes We Can!" And then he proved it by making history.

> *"Someday, we are going to have to have that oft spoke of Conversation about Race....but not until people like the Original Poster realize that such a conversation WILL NOT be merely: Sit down and shut up White Boy---while we tell you about our grievances."*
> **- white internet forum poster, 2021**

What the conversation will not be is a place for racist whites to fire off on us based on fact less perceptions of "black culture" that deny the impact of white racism. It is time that we stop believing what we want and start believing what is real. The word construct used as a noun means: *"an idea or theory containing various conceptual elements, typically one considered to be subjective and not based on empirical evidence."* As written in the first chapter, the definition of empirical is: *"originating in or based on observation or experience. 2: relying on experience or observation alone often without due regard for system and theory. 3: capable of being verified or disproved by observation or experiment. 4: of or relating to empiricism."*

Race is not biological, nor are there any differences in human beings other than genitalia, skin color, and hair texture. Cultural differences may exist relating to mores, spirituality, or norms but there is zero empirical evidence of different species of humans based on skin color. The idea of race is a construct. In America, this construct led to the creation of a system where initially, nonwhite people could neither be legal citizens nor protected by the laws of this country. Laws and policies were made that protected the interests of whites, specifically white males. *The 1790 Naturalization Act, Fugitive Slave Act, Dred Scott v. Sandford, Chinese Exclusion Act, Ozawa v. United States, Korematsu v. United States, Plessy vs. Ferguson, The Indian Removal Policy, The Donation Land Act, The Dawes Act, Black Codes, and Manifest Destiny* are just a small number of legal or policy decisions made to maintain white preference or further white interests. As the system is currently maintained, racism is an inherent structural flaw.

> *"Racism is a fact of life that minorities have to live with and manage to the best of their ability."*
> **-white internet forum poster, 2022**

Racism is a genuine national security threat that must be seriously addressed. As written earlier, at least 31 percent of white Americans held racist views according to a IPSOS Poll that was conducted online from Aug. 21 to Sept. 5, 2017.[2] Extrapolating this using the entire white population hopefully will allow you to see just how much of a potential threat racism is. According to United States Census projections there were 248,503,000 whites in America in 2017.[3] If 31 percent of the white population held racist views, there were potentially 77,035,930 whites with racist views living in America at that time. According to the same census projection, 43,001,000 blacks were living in America in 2017.[4] This shows that there were 34 million more whites who held racist views than the total number of blacks in the American population. Contrast this to the projected 2017 American population (323,128,000)[5], and potentially 23.8 percent of the American people held racist views. That is basically 1 in 4 Americans.

We spare no expense to reduce crime, but society is hesitant when it comes to racism. In 2020 there were 7 million people who committed crimes. If the same 31 percent polled in the 2017 IPSOS poll hold racist views now, over 80 million whites are potentially holding racist views in America. That is potentially 11 whites who are racists to every criminal offender in America as categorized in the FBI Uniform Crime Report. Over 19,000 people were murdered in 2020. There are approximately 400 racists to every murder committed in the United States. On the bright side, these numbers show that about 170 million whites are not racists.

The racist subculture tries dismissing things that do not validate their view of race relations in America. They want to force people to see history only from their perspective. But what they present is often false and incomplete. The part I have tried offering is the part they refuse to admit. If someone white presents this, they are called anti-white racists, self-hating whites who pander to black people out of fear of being called racists or worse. If a black person or anybody of color presents this information, they are called whiners, losers who blame whites for their failures, victims, or racists by members of the racist subculture who want to keep part of history hidden or canceled altogether.

The summer of the Floyd protests showed me that perhaps America might be able to move the boulder of racism a little bit closer to the end of the cliff with a little harder work. But the time has come for white Americans. Nobody wants to keep hearing how ending racism is going to take time. If whites had preached such patience while being under the thumb of Britain, America would still be a British colony. Why should nonwhites in this country continue waiting for whites to end racist behavior and seriously enforce the laws written to stop it?

The Gosar family is a prime example of whites taking the lead to disavow or disown a family member for holding racist views. If the Gosar family can each make a commercial to state their disapproval of a sibling who they opened Christmas presents with as children, shared the ups and downs of puberty, as well as most of the best and worst of adulthood, then other whites with family members and friends who are racists can step up to the plate and begin providing the necessary shame and disapproval this behavior deserves. If we are to reduce racism to irrelevance, there can be no more excuses made. The we can't change hearts and minds attitude must go.

I know such racism can end because I have known many non-racist whites in my personal life. The businessman in my hometown who started a wrestling club that provided some of us who were no good at basketball with another sport to compete in that was good for the body and mind. Various ladies I have shared parts of my life with, teammates I have had in sports, people who became friends as a result of employment, classmates, and many others. In writing this book, I have used at least 249 citations. I estimate that 200 of these citations are from studies or research done by whites looking for a way to address or end racism in America. The fact is that many whites are tired of the racist subculture and it is wrong not to recognize their existence. More are needed.

From his 20s until his very last day of life, John Lewis fought white racism. I know some people probably tried telling Lewis how he should stop and how he was a racist, or how he was obsessed with an issue that did not apply now. There is no doubt that he heard how he hated white people and did not speak for all black people. Lewis was born during the overt era of American apartheid. He was 24 before he could vote. He saw it all, and up until his transition, he did not declare that he was happy with the improvements he had seen so it is time to be quiet.

John Lewis saw the worst of segregation, a man who got his skull busted so that I can do the things I can today. Lewis will go down in history as one of the greatest Americans of all time. His sacrifice made it so blacks can vote, enter more colleges, and have an improved quality of life. By every measure, this was a successful man. But until his last breath, Lewis told us that there is still work to do regardless of the improvements we have seen. If John Lewis, a man who saw the harsh reality of the past can say that, today's black sell-outs have NOTHING to say. Lewis was a legendary freedom fighter. A warrior for justice every second he breathed. He set the example.

Another American hero, Colin Powell, a black republican, was a pioneer in the military. He reached the top of his profession and ascended to one of the highest offices in our land. Powell, who also suffered the indignities of Jim Crow as a young serviceman, went to his final days telling America that we still have much to do regarding the issues surrounding race. If both these men who saw the worst of American Apartheid can say that in the 21st century, we have come a long way relative to race, but we still have a long way to go, that's the undisputed truth no one can deny. It also means that we all together still need to work instead of congratulating ourselves for a half-done job.

The claim that everybody has had it tough, while accurate, should not be used to dismiss legislative and public policy hurdles put in front of people of color. These same hurdles should not be dismissed for women either. This book was written about racism, yet I understand that there is no such thing as the "struggle competition." Our history tells us that a faction in this country has consistently worked to keep us divided and at each other's throats so they can prosper.

I've spent over two hundred pages writing about white racism, but blacks and people of color are also part of the story.

People have claimed and presented evidence of how Africa is where humanity began. I have been told how blacks are the first created. As blacks, if we are what some have claimed us to be, then it is certainly our responsibility to live up to the standards set by the creator. We are required as human beings to provide the same grace and forgiveness that we are given from whoever the higher power is that we recognize in our spiritual journey. If extremism in defense of liberty is not a virtue, neither is extremism in opposition to oppression. So as blacks, we too must strive to live by the timeless teachings that recognize love's power. But love sometimes includes direct confrontation. Racism in America must end.

When does it end? This is the question that I now ask. As I have said, I am nobody great, just an average guy. I don't pretend to speak for every black American; others far greater have done that and still are doing so. But it seems to me by everything I continue to see, is that millions of Americans, black, white, and all people of color, are asking the same question hoping that one day we can get an answer. Now is the time. Get your knee off our necks. Thank you for reading this book.

I've often heard that white is right
You better believe black is alright too
So is blue and green and yellow
What difference should it make to you
These ties we got on us just ain't to hip
I know you got your thing and I've got mine
We've been judging people by colors
Maybe we should all be color blind
There's a saying you can't judge a book by it's cover
What are we doing but just that
We've been judging people by color
Love ain't got no color that's a fact
From the song, "Color Blind"
by Maze featuring Frankie Beverly (1977)
https://theconversation.freeforums.net/

Notes

Chapter 1: The Root Cause of The Problems Blacks Face Is White Racism

1 John A. McCone, Warren M. Christopher, Asa V. Call, the Very Rev. Charles Cassasa, the Rev. James Edward Jones, Earl C. Broady, Dr. Sherman M. Mellinkoff, Marlen E. Neumann, Violence in the City, Governors Commission On The Los Angeles Riots, December 2, 1965, pp.7, https:// archive.org/ details/ViolenceInCity/mode/2up

2 Ibid., pp.10

3 Natasha Frost, The story of segregation in Los Angeles was only preserved by its black-owned papers, September 18, 2018, https://qz.com/1394245/city-of-segregation-housing-discrimination-in-los-angeles/

4 John A. McCone, Warren M. Christopher, Asa V. Call, the Very Rev. Charles Cassasa, the Rev. James Edward Jones, Earl C. Broady, Dr. Sherman M. Mellinkoff, Marlen E. Neumann, Violence in the City, Governors Commission On The Los Angeles Riots, December 2, 1965, pp.20, https://archive.org/ details/ViolenceInCity/mode/2up

5 Dr. Anthony Asadullah Samad, The New William H. Parker Center Controversy: Revisionist History Cannnot Override Long Racial Legacy, LA Progressive, https:// www.laprogressive.com/the-racist-legacy-of-the-lapd/

6 Darrell Dawsey, 25 Years After the Watts Riots : McCone Commission's Recommendations Have Gone Unheeded, Los Angeles Times, JULY 8, 1990, https://www.latimes. com/archives/la-xpm-1990-07-08-me-455-story.html

7 Ibid.,

8 Los Angeles County Commission on Human Relations, McCone Revisited: A Focus On Solutions To Continuing Problems In South Central Los Angeles, January 1985

9 Janelle Jones, John Schmitt, Valerie Wilson, "50 years after the Kerner Commission," Economic Policy Institute, February 26, 2018, https://www. epi.org/publication/50-years-after-the-kerner-commission/

10 Richard Rothstein, "50 years after the Kerner Commission, minimal racial progress.", New York Daily News, February 28, 2018

11 Report of the National Advisory Commission on Civil Disorders (New York: Bantam Books, 1968), pg.2. http://www.eisenhowerfoundation.org/docs/ kerner.pdf

12 ibid.

13 ibid., pg.7.

14 ibid.

15 ibid., pg.9.

16 Lester Graham, The Kerner Commission, and why its recommendations were ignored, Detroit Journalism Cooperative, https://www.detroitjournalism. org/2016/02/25/the-kerner-commission-and-why-its-recommendations-were-ignored/

17 ibid.

Chapter 2: Racism Is Abuse

1 Ryan C.T. DeLapp, MA, and Monnica T. Williams, Ph.D., "Proactively Coping With Racism, Getting back to our lives in the aftermath of racial violence in the media.", July 18, 2016, www.psychologytoday,com

2 Natasha Tracy, Types of Abuse: What are the Different Forms of Abuse?https://www.healthyplace.com/abuse/abuse-information/types-of-abuse-what-are-the-different-forms-of-abuse/

3 Ryan C.T. DeLapp, MA, and Monnica T. Williams, Ph.D., "Proactively Coping With Racism, Getting back to our lives

in the aftermath of racial violence in the media.", July 18, 2016, www.psychologytoday,com

4 Emily Friedman, Va. Tech Shooter Seung-Hui Cho's Mental Health Records Released, August 7, 2009, https://abcnews.go.com/us/seung-hui-chos-mental-health-records-released/story?id=8278195

5 Pike, Karen D, "What is Internalized Racial Oppression and Why Don't We Study It? Acknowledging Racism's Hidden Injuries", December 1, 2010, Sociological Perspectives, Vol. 53, Issue 4, pp. 551–572 Internalized Racism Among Asians https://medium.com/a-m-awaken-your-inner-asian/internalized-racism-among-asians-49980f984401

6 Ibid.,

7 Jason Riley, "50 Years of Blaming Everything on Racism", The Wall Street Journal, March 6, 2018, https://www.wsj.com/articles/50-years-of-blaming-everything-on-racism-1520381047

8 Ibid.,

9 National Center for Education Statistics, Table 181. College enrollment and enrollment rates of recent high school completers, by race/ethnicity: 1960 through 2004, https://nces.ed.gov/programs/digest/d05/tables/dt05_181.asp

10 Ross, C., Danziger, S. & Smolensky, E. The level and trend of poverty in the United States, 1939–1979. Demography 24, 587–600 (1987). https://doi.org/10.2307/2061394

11 Table 2. Poverty Status of People by Family Relationship, Race, and Hispanic Origin: 1959 to 2014, US Department of the Census, http://www.census.gov/hhes/www/poverty/data/historical/people.html

12 Jason Riley, "50 Years of Blaming Everything on Racism", The Wall Street Journal, March 6, 2018, https://www.wsj.com/articles/50-years-of-blaming-everything-on-racism-1520381047

13 Dennis R. Upkins, Denying Racism And Other Forms Of Gaslighting, Aug 24, 2016, Mental Health Matters, derived from: https://mental-health-matters.com/denying-racism-and-other-forms-of-gaslighting/

14 Mayo Clinic-Post-Traumatic Stress Disorder, https://www.mayoclinic.org/diseases-conditions/post-traumatic-stress-disorder/symptoms-causes/syc-20355967

15 Angelique M. Davis & Rose Ernst (2019) Racial gaslighting, Politics, Groups, and Identities, 7:4, 761-774, DOI: 10.1080/21565503.2017.1403934

16 World Health OrganizationDefinition of Health, https://www.publichealth.com.ng/world-health-organizationwho-definition-of-health/

17 Cheyna Roth, Racism Declared A Public Health Crisis In New Whitmer Executive Directive, Aug 05, 2020, https://www.mlive.com/public-interest/2020/08/racism-declared-a-public-health-crisis-in-new-whitmer-executive-directive.html

18 Is Racism a Public Health Issue? Center for the Study of Racism, Social Justice & Health, October 9, 2017, https://www.racialhealthequity.org/blog/racism-is-a-public-health-issue

19 Camara Jules P. Harrell, Tanisha I. Burford, Brandi N. Cage, Travette McNair Nelson, Sheronda Shearon, Adrian Thompson, and Steven Green, Multiple Pathways Linking Racism to Health Outcomes, US National Library of Medicine National Institutes of Health

20 Trauma, Racism, Chronic Stress and the Health of Black Americans, Compilation by the SAMHSA Office of Behavioral Health Equity, June 3, 2020, https://www.mhanational.org/sites/default/files/AfricanAmericansRaceViolenceandHealth%20SAMHSA%20OBHE%20%206.3.20.pdf

21 Geronimus, A. T., Hicken, M., Keene, D., & Bound, J. (2006). "Weathering" and age patterns of allostatic load scores among blacks and whites in the United States. American journal of public health, 96(5), 826–833. https://doi.org/10.2105/AJPH.2004.060749

22 B.S. McEwen, J.C. Wingfield, Allostasis and Allostatic Load, Encyclopedia of Stress (Second Edition), 2007,

https://www.sciencedirect.com/science/article/pii/B9780123739476000258

23 B.S. McEwen, Stress: Homeostasis, Rheostasis, Allostasis and Allostatic Load, Encyclopedia of Neuroscience, 2009, https://www.sciencedirect.com/science/article/pii/B9780128093245028674

24 Ibid.,

25 Lukachko, Alicia & Hatzenbuehler, Mark & Keyes, Katherine. (2014). Structural racism and myocardial infarction in the United States. Social science & medicine (1982). 103. 42-50. 10.1016/j.socscimed.2013.07.021.

Chapter 3: Racism Is NOT A Thing of The Past

1 McLeod, S. A. (2018, Febuary 05). Cognitive dissonance. Simply Psychology. https://www.simplypsychology.org/cognitive-dissonance.html

2 Matthew 23: 37 – 39, NIV Bible, https://www.biblegateway.com/passage/?search=Matthew%2023:37-39&version=NIV

3 Zechariah 2:12, NIV Bible, https://www.biblegateway.com/passage/?search=Zechariah+2%3A12&version=NIV

4 Halimah Abdullah, Justice Scalia Under Fire For Comments About Black Students, NBC News, Dec. 11, 2015, https://www.nbcnews.com/news/nbcblk/justice-scalia-under-fire-comments-about-black-students-n478681

5 Paul Magnarella, Explaining Rwanda's 1994 Genocide, Human Rights and Human Welfare, Volume 2:1 – Winter 2002, https://www.du.edu/korbel/hrhw/volumes/2002/2-1/magnarella2-1.pdf

6 History Of Rwanda, http://www.historyworld.net/wrldhis/PlainTextHistories.asp?historyid=ad24

7 Troy Riemer, How Colonialism Affected the Rwandan Genocide, August 16, 2011, https://umuvugizi.wordpress.com/2011/08/16/how-colonialism-affected-the-rwandan-genocide/

8 Ibid,.

9 Ibid,.

10 Ibid,.

11 Ibid,.

12 Ibid,.

13 Ibid.,

14 Ed Lavandera and Jason Hanna,, El Paso suspect told police he was targeting Mexicans, affidavit says, CNN, August 9, 2019, https://www.cnn.com/2019/08/09/us/el-paso-shooting-friday/index.html

15 Kimmy Yam, There were 3,800 anti-Asian racist incidents, mostly against women, in past year, NBC News, March 16, 2021, https://www.nbcnews.com/news/asian-america/there-were-3-800-anti-asian-racist-incidents-mostly-against-n1261257

16 Emma Ockerman, Homeless Black Man Fatally Shot by Sheriff's Deputy After Jaywalking, Vice.com, February 19, 2021, https://www.vice.com/en/article/akd93a/homeless-black-man-fatally-shot-by-sheriffs-deputy-after-jaywalking

17 Maya Oppenheim, 22 million Americans support neo-Nazis, new poll indicates, Tuesday 22 August 2017, https://www.independent.co.uk/news/world/americas/us-neo-nazi-support-american-public-charlottesville-white-supremacists-kkk-far-right-poll-a7907091.html

18 Sarah Ruiz-Grossman, Most Americans Oppose White Supremacists, But Many Share Their Views: Poll, Sep. 15, 2017/ Updated Sep 16, 2017, https://www.huffpost.com/entry/reuters-poll-white-supremacist-views_n_59bc155fe4b02da0e141b3c8

19 Thomson Reuters and the University of Virginia Center for Politics, Reuters/Ipsos/UVA Center for Politics Race Poll, September 11, 2017, https://centerforpolitics.org/crystalball/wp-content/uploads/2017/09/2017-Reuters-UVA-Ipsos-Race-Poll-9-11-2017.pdf

Chapter 4: Entitlement Mentality

1 Hume, David, "Of Natural Characters," Part I Essay XXI of Essays, Moral, Political, and Literary

2 Ryan Very, Kant's Racism, https://www.academia.edu/1802951/Kants_Racism

3 A'ndrea Elyse Messer, Scientific racism's long history mandates caution, Penn State News, February 14, 2014

4 Kenan Malik, On The Enlightenment's 'Race Problem', https://kenanmalik.com/2013/02/13/on-the-enlightenments-race-problem/

5 Bernasconi, R. (2001) 'Who Invented the Concept of Race? Kant's Role in the Enlightenment Construction of Race' in Bernasconi, R. (Ed.) Race, Oxford: Blackwell Publishers

6 Voltaire, Les Lettres d'Amabed, Volume 21 (p. 462-463)., https://fr.m.wikisource.org/wiki/Les_Lettres_d%E2%80%99Amabed/Lettre_7b_d%E2%80%99Amabed

7 Benjamin Rush, Race, Slavery, And Abolitionism, https://www.dickinson.edu/info/20043/about/3480/benjamin_rush

8 Samuel Cartwright, "Report On The Diseases And Physical Peculiarities Of The Negro Race". The New Orleans Medical and Surgeon Journal, pg. 691, May 1851

9 ibid., pg.692

10 ibid., pg. 694,

11 ibid., pg. 715

12 Madison Grant, "The Passing of the Great Race: Or, The Racial Basis of European History, pg.xxviii, https://archive.org/details/passingofgreatra00granuoft

13 Walter Rodney, How Europe Underdeveloped Africa, London, Bogle-L'Ouverture Publications, 1972, pg 246

14 Ibid., pg 247

15 Headrights, https://www.lva.virginia.gov/public/guides/va4_headrights.htm

16 Ibid.,

17 What was the Headright System? https://study.com/learn/lesson/headright-system-history-significance.html

18 Thomas Jefferson, "Notes on the State of Virginia."(1785),pg.240

19 Shawn D Rochester, The Black Tax: The Cost of Being Black in America, pp, 49, Good Steward Publishing, Southbury CT., 2018

20 Ibid.,

21 Ibid.,

22 Williams, T. (2000). The Homestead Act: A major asset-building policy in American history (CSD Working Paper No. 00-9). St. Louis, MO: Washington University, Center for Social Development. Pg.11 https://openscholarship.wustl.edu/csd_research/46/

23 Freedmen's Bureau Act, http://freedmensbureau.com/freedmens-bureau-act-march-3-1865

24 Williams, T. (2000). The Homestead Act: A major asset-building policy in American history (CSD Working Paper No. 00-9). St. Louis, MO: Washington University, Center for Social Development. Pg.12 https://openscholarship.wustl.edu/csd_research/46/

25 John Soos, The Freedmen's Bureau: Success or failure? https://www.umbc.edu/che/tahlessons/pdf/The_Freedmens_Bureau_Success_or_Failure(PrinterFriendly).pdf

26 How Do You Define Free Labor Ideology? https://www.reference.com/world-view/define-labor-ideology-2d9260efebb9f55

27 Morrill Act, 1862, https://soh.omeka.chass.ncsu.edu/items/show/343

28 The Morrill Land Grant Act Of 1890, http://www.blackbottomarchives.com/blackhistory/2015/2/18/morrill-act-of-1890#:~:text=THE%20MORRILL%20LAND%20GR ANT%20ACT%20OF%201890%20The,the%20existing%20land%20grant%20colleges%20in%20the%20state.

29 James Chen, National Housing Act, Updated Sep 3, 2019, https://www.investopedia.com/terms/n/national-housing-act.asp

30 Alexis C. Madrigal, The Racist Housing Policy That Made Your Neighborhood, The Atlantic, May 22, 2014, https://www.theatlantic.com/business/archive/2014/05/the-racist-housing-policy-that-made-your-neighborhood/371439/

31 PBS, Race-The Power of An Illusion, Uncle Sam Lends A Hand, Did the Government Racialize Housing and Wealth? http://www.pbs.org/race/000_About/002_06_a-godeeper.htm

32 The Social Security Act of 1935, https://www.ssa.gov/history/35act.html

33 Larry DeWitt, The Decision to Exclude Agricultural and Domestic Workers from the 1935 Social Security Act, Social Security Bulletin, Vol. 70, No. 4, 2010

34 Brad Plumer, A second look at Social Security's racist origins, Washington Post, June 3, 2013, https://www.washingtonpost.com/news/wonk/wp/2013/06/03/a-second-look-at-social-securitys-racist-origins/

35 Linda Gordon and Felice Batlan, The Legal History of the Aid to Dependent Children Program, https://socialwelfare.library.vcu.edu/public-welfare/aid-to-dependent-children-the-legal-history/

36 Johnathan Grossman, Fair Labor Standards Act of 1938: Maximum Struggle for a Minimum Wage, U.S. Department of Labor, https://www.dol.gov/general/aboutdol/history/flsa1938

37 Richard Rothstein, Color of Law, New York: Liveright Publishing, 2017, pg. 4

38 Servicemen's Readjustment Act (G.I. Bill), http://totallyhistory.com/servicemens-readjustment-act-g-i-bill

39 Erin Blakemore, How the GI Bill's Promise Was Denied to a Million Black WWII Veterans, https://www.history.com/news/gi-bill-black-wwii-veterans-benefits, June 21, 2019

40 Brandon Weber, How African American WWII Veterans Were Scorned By the G.I. Bill, The Progressive, November 10, 2017, https://progressive.org/dispatches/how-african-american-wwii-veterans-were-scorned-by-the-g-i-b/

41 Ibid.,

42 Jone Johnson Lewis, Law of Coverture, Women Losing Their Legal Existence With Marriage, Thoughtco.com, February 24, 2019, https://www.thoughtco.com/coverture-in-english-american-law3529483#:~:text=updated%20february%2025%2c%202019%20in%20english%20and%20american,property%20rights%20and%20cert-ain%20other%20rights%20were%20concerned.

43 What Was Coverture? Understanding The Rights Of Women In Early America, https://www.americanhistoryusa.com/what-was-coverture-understanding-rights-of-women-in-early-america/

44 Married Women's Property Acts United States [1839], https://www.britannica.com/event/Married-Womens-Property-Acts-United-States-1839

45 Ibid.,

46 Sally Kohn, Affirmative Action Has Helped White Women More Than Anyone, Time, JUNE 17, 2013, https://time.com/4884132/affirmative-action-civil-rights-white-women/#:~:text=But%20study%20after%20study%20shows%20that%20affirmative%20action,affirmative%20action%20helps%20the%20most%20in%20America%20today.

47 Fact Sheet: Affirmative Action and What It Means for Women, July 1, 2000, The National Womens Law Center, https://nwlc.org/resources/affirmative-action-and-what-it-means-women/

48 Tim Wise, Is Sisterhood Conditional?: White Women and the Rollback of Affirmative Action, September 23, 1998, http://www.timwise.org/1998/09/is-sisterhood-conditional-white-women-and-the-rollback-of-affirmative-action/

49 Victoria M. Massie, White women benefit most from affirmative action — and are among its fiercest opponents, https://www.vox.com/2016/5/25/11682950/fisher-supreme-court-white-women-affirmative-action

50 Emily Walton, Flashback: All college students should take a mandatory course on black history and white privilege, USA TODAY, September 23, 2019, https://www.usatoday.com/story/opinion/2019/09/23/black-history-white-privilege-course-graduation-requirement-column/2389375001/

Chapter 5: Africans Sold Other Africans

1 Rukewve Ochuko, What Is Africa's Original Name?, 08 MARCH 2020, https://guardian.ng/life/what-is-africas-original-name/

2 REVEALED: The Ancient Name For Africa Was "Alkebulan" Meaning "Mother Of Mankind", https://afropolitain.com/index.php/2020/08/27/revealed-the-ancient-name-for-africa-was-alkebulan-meaning-mother-of-mankind/#:~:text=In%20Kemetic%20History%20of%20Afrika%2C%20Dr%20cheikh%20Anah,the%20Mtaloors%2C%20Nubians%2C%20Numidians%2C%20Khart-

3 Cheikh Anta Diop and the African Origin of Civilization, January 25, 2012, https://afrolegends.com/2012/01/25/cheikh-anta-diop-and-the-african-origin-of-civilization/

4 Africans did NOT sell their own people into slavery, https://www.africaw.com/africans-did-not-sell-their-own-people-into-slavery

5 Schomburg Center for the Research of Black Culture "The Abolition of the Slave Trade-African Resistance." http://abolition.nypl.org/essays/african_resistance

6 Ibid.,

7 Ibid.,

8 Lerone Bennett, The Shaping of Black America. Chicago: Johnson Publishing Co., 1975, pp. 61-82. Originally

published in Ebony, vol. 25 (August, 1970), pp. 71-77). https://msuweb.montclair.edu/~furrg/essays/bennettroad.html

9 Ned & Constance Sublette, The American Slave Coast: A History of the Slave-Breeding Industry, Chicago, Lawrence Hill Books, 2016, pp.1

10 William W. Henning, The Statutes at Large; Being a Collection of all the Laws of Virginia, v.2 (1823). http://www.hackettlatinacademy.weebly.com/uploads/2/2/5/1/22510182/virginiaslavecodes.pdf#:~:text=Document%20E%3A%20October%2C%201669.%20Act%20I%3A%20An%20act,means%20suppressed%2C%20Be%20it%20enacted%20and%20declared%20by

11 Dr. Martin Luther King Jr., Where Do We Go from Here: Chaos or Community? Beacon Press, Boston Massachusetts, 1967, pp. 39-40

12 Ben Davis, What is the seasoning process for slaves? April 10, 2021, https://www.mvorganizing.org/what-is-the-seasoning-process-for-slaves/

13 Paulette Brown-Hinds, "Seasoning" The Slaves, Black Voice News, February 19, 2009, https://blackvoicenews.com/2009/02/19/qseasoningq-the-slaves/

14 Ibid.

15 Ned & Constance Sublette, The American Slave Coast: A History of the Slave-Breeding Industry, Chicago, Lawrence Hill Books, 2016, pp.1

16 Malcolm Harris, A Future History Of The United States, Jan 26, 2016, https://psmag.com/social-justice/a-future-history-of-the-united-states

17 William Spivey, The Truth About American Slave Breeding Farms, June 9,2019, https://medium.com/the-aambc-journal/the-truth-about-american-slave-breeding-farms-ee631e863e2c

18 William J. Anderson, Life and Narrative of William J. Anderson, Twenty-FourYears a Slave, Chicago: Daily Tribune Book and Job Printing Office, 1857. https://

docsouth.unc.edu/neh/andersonw/andersonw.html

19 Solomon Northrup, Twelve Years a Slave, Narrative of Solomon Northup, a Citizen of New-York, Kidnapped in Washington City in 1841, and Rescued in 1853, from a Cotton Plantation near the Red River in Louisiana, Project Gutenberg E-book, May 11, 2014 [EBook #45631], pg.189

20 Elizabeth Keckley, Behind the Scenes: Or, Thirty Years a Slave, and Four Years in the White House, 1868, New York: G. W. Carleton & Co., Publishers, 1868., pp. 38-39, https://docsouth.unc.edu/neh/keckley/keckley.html

21 Robert E. Lee, Letter To His Wife On Slavery, (selections; December 27, 1856), http://fair-use.org/robert-e-lee/letter-to-his-wife-on-slavery

22 Elizabeth Ofosuah Johnson, 5 horrifying ways enslaved African men were sexually exploited and abused by their white masters, https://blackmediagroupgermany.com/2019/06/19/5-horrifying-ways-enslaved-african-men-were-sexually-exploited-and-abused-by-their-white-masters/

23 Ibid.,

24 Ibid.,

25 Ibid.,

26 Isaac Somto, Buck Breaking, How African Male Slaves Were Raped, July 27, 2020, https://vocalafrica.com/buck-breaking-afrcan-male-slaves/

27 Jason Kottke, A History of the Slave-Breeding Industry in the United States, Feb 02, 2016, https://kottke.org/16/02/a-history-of-the-slave-breeding-industry-in-the-united-states

28 Edward E. Baptist and Louis Hyman, American Finance Grew on the Back of Slaves, Chicago Sun-Times.com March 7, 2014, derived from: https://norbertobarreto.blog/2014/03/14/american-finance-grew-on-the-back-of-slaves/

29 Ned & Constance Sublette, The American Slave Coast: A History of the Slave-Breeding Industry, Chicago, Lawrence Hill Books, 2016, pp.11-12

30 Ibid.,

31 Liam Hogan, All of my work on the "Irish slaves" meme (2015–'19), https://medium.com/@Limerick1914/all-of-my-work-on-the-irish-slaves-meme-2015-16-4965e445802a

32 Liam Hogan, Irish slaves': the convenient myth, https://www.opendemocracy.net/en/beyond-trafficking-and-slavery/irish-slaves-convenient-myth/

33 Sarah Kendzior, How do you become "white" in America?https://thecorrespondent.com/5185/how-do-you-become-white-in-america/1466577856645-8260d4a7

34 Art McDonald, Ph.D., How the Irish Became White, http://www.pitt.edu/~hirtle/uujec/white.html

35 Sarah Kendzior, How do you become "white" in America?https://thecorrespondent.com/5185/how-do-you-become-white-in-america/1466577856645-8260d4a7

36 Mari J. Matsuda, Where Is Your Body? And Other Essays On Race Gender And The Law, Boston, Beacon Press, pp.150, 1996, http://www.dariaroithmayr.com/pdfs/assignments/Matsuda,%20We%20Will%20Not%20Be%20Used.pdf

37 ibid., pp.151-152

38 ibid., pp. 152-153

39 ibid., pp.153-154

40 ibid., pp. 155-156

41 ibid., pp. 156-157

42 Carol Anderson, White Rage, New York, Bloomsbury Publishing, pp.39-66, 2016

43 Sherman's Special Field Orders No. 15," in The War of the Rebellion: a Compilation of the Official Records of the Union and Confederate Armies, Series I, Vol. 47, Part II (Washington: GPO, 1895), pp.60-62 http://ldhi.library.cofc.edu/exhibits/show/after_slavery_educator/unit_three_documents/document_five

44 Circular #13 War Department Bureau of Refugees, Freedmen, and Abandoned Lands. Washington July 28, 1865," Source: National Archives and Records Administration, Record Group 105, Entry 24, No. 139 Asst Adjutant General Circulars 1865-1869, Bureau of Refugees, Freedmen, and Abandoned Lands, pp. 14-15. (Transcribed from the original by John Soos, August, 2003)

45 Freedmen's Bank Fails, Devastating Black Community, https://calendar.eji.org/ racial-injustice/jun/28

46 Constantine Yannelis, A 150-Year-Old Bank Failure May Still Be Haunting Black Communities, Video Transcript, July 07, 2020, https://www.chicagobooth.edu/ review/150-year-old-bank-failure-may-still-be-haunting-black-communities

47 John Steele Gordon, The Mismanagement of the Freedman's Bank, ABA Banking Journal, May 2, 2019, https://bankingjournal.aba.com/2019/05/the-mismanagement-of-the-freedmans-bank/

48 Ibid.,

49 Ibid.,

50 Freedman's Bank Demise, https://home.treasury.gov/ about/history/freedmans-bank-building/freedmans-bank-demise

51 Angie Chatman, Black Americans' rocky relationship with banks can be traced back to an institution that promised wealth but collapsed after just 9 years, Business Insider, Sep 23, 2020, https://www.businessinsider. com/personal-finance/freedmans-bank-collapse-black-americans-wealth-2020-9

52 Constantine Yannelis, A 150-Year-Old Bank Failure May Still Be Haunting Black Communities, Video Transcript, July 07, 2020, https://www.chicagobooth.edu/ review/150-year-old-bank-failure-may-still-be-haunting-black-communities

53 July 19, 1919: White Mobs in Uniform Attack African Americans — Who Fight Back — in Washington, D.C.,

https://www.zinnedproject.org/news/tdih/red-summer-dc/

54 Anthony Dittmar, Omaha Race Riot, https://njdigitalhistory.org/1919/omaha-race-riot/

55 B.C Franklin, The Tulsa Race Riots and Three of It's Victims, https://www.smithsonianmag.com/smithsonian-institution/long-lost-manuscript-contains-searing-eyewitness-account-tulsa-race-massacre-1921-180959251/

56 Survivors of 1921 Tulsa Race Massacre share eyewitness accounts, https://thecincinnatiherald.com/2021/05/survivors-of-1921-tulsa-race-massacre-share-eyewitness-accounts/

57 William L. Patterson, We Charge Genocide, 4th edition, International Publishers Co., Inc., New York, 2017 pp.60-61

58 ibid

59 Peter Salwen, A "Northern Lynching," Remembering the Trenton Six Case, August 6, 1998, http://www.salwen.com/trenton6.html

60 Ibid.

61 Ibid.

62 Sharon Schlegel, Harrowing case of the "Trenton Six", The Times of Trenton, Jan 28, 2012, Updated Mar 30, 2019, https://www.nj.com/times opinion/2012/01/harrowing_case_of_the_trenton.html

63 Ibid.

64 Ibid.,

65 Richard Rothstein, Color of Law, Liverright Publishing, pp.144, 2018

66 Ibid, pp.145

67 Ibid.

68 Ibid, pp.147

69 Jae Jones, Cicero Race Riot: Mob of 4,000 Destroys Apartment Building with One Black Family Tenants, November 14, 2018, https://blackthen.com/cicero-race-riot-mob-of-4000-destroys-apartment-building-with-

one-black-family-tenants/

70 Charles Abrams, The Time Bomb That Exploded in Cicero: Segregated Housing's Inevitable Dividend, https://www. commentarymagazine.com/articles/charles-abrams/the-time-bomb-that-exploded-in-cicerosegregated-housings-inevitable-dividend/

71 Christy Clark-Pujara and Anna-Lisa Cox, How the Myth of a Liberal North Erases a Long History of White Violence, smithsonianmag.com, August 27, 2020, https://www.smithsonianmag.com/smithsonian-institution/how-myth-liberal-north-erases-long-history-white-violence-180975661/

Chapter 6: The Thirteen Percent Excuse

1 Heather Mac Donald, The Lies told by the Black Lives Matter Movement, New Yok Post, September 6, 2016, https://nypost.com/2016/09/06/the-lies-told-by-the-black-lives-matter-movement/

2 Charles Blow, "Black Dads Are Doing Best of All," New York Times June 8, 2015, https://www.nytimes.com/2015/06/08/opinion/charles-blow-black-dads-are-doing-the-best-of-all.html

3 Jo Jones, Ph.D., and William D. Mosher, Ph.D., Fathers' Involvement with Their Children: United States, 2006–2010, National Health Statistics Report, Number 71, December 20, 2013, Division of Vital Statistics

4 Gretchen Livingston And Kim Parker, Pew Research, A Tale of Two Fathers, pg.2, https://www.pewresearch.org/social-trends/2011/06/15/a-tale-of-two-fathers/

5 Tara Culp-Ressler, The Myth of the Absent Black Father, Think Progress, January 16, 2014, https://archive.thinkprogress.org/the-myth-of-the-absent-black-father-ecc4e961c2e8/

6 Walter Williams, How Important Is Today's Racial Discrimination?, Aug 14, 2019, https://townhall.com/columnists/walterewilliams/2019/08/14/how-

important-is-todays-racial-discrimination-n2551543

7 Ross, C., Danziger, S. & Smolensky, E. The level and trend of poverty in the United States, 1939–1979. Demography 24, pg.596 (1987)

8 US Department of the Census, Table 2. Poverty Status of People by Family Relationship, Race, and Hispanic Origin: 1959 to 2014, https://www.census. gov/data/tables/time-series/demo/income-poverty/historical-poverty-people. html

9 Debra J. Dickerson, Know Your Enemy: Heather Mac Donald, Mother Jones, May 6, 2008

10 Rachel E. Morgan, U.S. Department of Justice, Office of Justice Programs Bureau of Justice Statistics, Race and Hispanic Origin of Victims and Offenders, 2012-15, https://bjs.ojp.gov/content/pub/pdf/rhovo1215.pdf

11 Ibid.,

12 Mike Males, "Why the Gigantic, Decades-Long Drop in Black Youth Crime Threatens Major Interests," The Center on Juvenile and Criminal Justice,
August 15, 2013, http://www.cjcj.org/news/6523

13 Ibid.,

14 Juvenile Delinquency Report of the Committee on the Judiciary, United States Senate Subcommittee on Juvenile Delinquency, (85th cong., 2d ~ss.), March 27, 1958, pg. 1, United States Government Printing Office, Washington, D.C. https://digitalcommons.usf.edu/cgi/viewcontent. cgi?article=1006&context=dozier_school

15 Ibid., pg.2

16 Ibid.,

17 Ibid., pg.6

18 Mike Males, "Why the Gigantic, Decades-Long Drop in Black Youth Crime Threatens Major Interests," The Center on Juvenile and Criminal Justice, August 15, 2013, http:// www.cjcj.org/news/6523

19 Frederick Hoffman, "The Race Traits and Tendencies of the American Negro" pg. 228, https://archive.org/ details/racetraitstenden00hoff 20 W.E.B. Du Bois,

"Race Traits and Tendencies of the American Negro. By Frederick L. Hoffman, F.S.S." [Review]. Annals of the American Academy of Political and Social Science, v. 9 (January 1897): pp.127-133., http://www.webdubois.org/dbReviewOfHoffman.html

21 Ibid..

22 Kelly Miller, A Review Of Hoffman's Race Traits And Tendencies Of The American Negro, The American Negro Academy. Occasional Papers, No. 1, 1897, pp. 35. https://www.gutenberg.org/cache/epub/31279/pg31279-images.html

23 Mike Males, "Why the Gigantic, Decades-Long Drop in Black Youth Crime Threatens Major Interests," The Center on Juvenile and Criminal Justice, August 15, 2013, http://www.cjcj.org/news/6523

24 Ibid.,

25 Heather Mac Donald, The Lies told by the Black Lives Matter Movement, New Yok Post, September 6, 2016, https://nypost.com/2016/09/06/the-lies-told-by-the-black-lives-matter-movement/

26 Federal Bureau of Investigation, Crime in the United States, Offenders by Race and Ethnicity, 2020, https://www.fbi.gov/news/pressrel/press-releases/fbi-releases-2020-incident-based-data

27 Ibid.,

28 Ibid.,

29 Christopher Tremoglie, Most of the people killed by the police are white, Washington Examiner, October 05, 2021, https://www.washingtonexaminer.com/opinion/most-of-the-people-killed-by-police-are-white

30 Federal Bureau of Investigation, Crime in the United States, Offenders by Race and Ethnicity, 2020, https://www.fbi.gov/news/pressrel/press-releases/fbi-releases-2020-incident-based-data

31 U.S. Department of the Census, U.S. and World Population Clock, April 1, 2020, https://www.census.gov/popclock/

32 Federal Bureau of Investigation, Crime in the United

States, Arrests by Race and Ethnicity, 2020 Table 43

33 Erika Harrell, Lynn Langton, Marcus Berzofsky, Lance Couzens, Hope Smiley-McDonald, Bureau of Justice Statistics, Poverty and Nonfatal Violent Victimization, 2008-2012, NCJ Number 248384, November 2014, https://bjs.ojp.gov/library/publications/household-poverty-and-nonfatal-violent-victimization-2008-2012

34 Ibid.,

35 Rav Arora, These black lives didn't seem to matter in 2020, NY Post, February 6, 2020, https://nypost.com/2021/02/06/these-black-lives-didnt-seem-to-matter-in-2020/

36 Mary Dunklin, High blood pressure increasingly deadly for Black people, American Heart Association News, July 13, 2020, https://www.heart.org/en/news/2020/07/13/high-blood-pressure-increasingly-deadly-for-black-people

37 Federal Bureau of Investigation, Crime in the United States, Offenders by Race and Ethnicity, 2020, https://www.fbi.gov/news/pressrel/press-releases/fbi-releases-2020-incident-based-data

38 Ibid.,

Chapter 7: Where Are The Good Cops?

1 Action Legal Group, The Alarming Statistics of Police Misconduct and Brutality, https://www.policebrutality.com/the-alarming-statistics-of-police-misconduct-and-brutality/

2 The JAMA Network Journals. (2017, April 19). Study examines emergency department visits for patients injured by law enforcement in the US. ScienceDaily. Retrieved January 3, 2022 from www.sciencedaily.com/releases/2017/04/170419131729.htm

3 German Lopez, Police officers are prosecuted for murder in less than 2 percent of fatal shootings, Apr 2, 2021, https://www.vox.com/21497089/derek-chauvin-george-

floyd-trial-police-prosecutions-black-lives-matter

4   Nathan S. Chapman and Kenji Yoshino, The Fourteenth Amendment Due Process Clause, https://constitutioncenter.org/interactive-constitution/interpretation/amendment-xiv/clauses/701

5 Ibid.,

6 Janell Ross, How police justify shootings: The 1974 killing of an unarmed teen set a standard, Jan. 23, 2020, https://www.nbcnews.com/news/nbcblk/officer-killed-unarmed-teen-1974-it-changed-how-police-justify-n1120611

7   Tennessee vs. Garner, https://www.oyez.org/cases/1984/83-1035

8 Ibid,.

9 Matt DeLong, Dave Braunger and Brandon Stahl, Breaking down the dashcam: The Philando Castile shooting timeline, Minneapolis Start Tribune, June 21, 2017, https://www.startribune.com/breaking-down-the-dashcam-the-philando-castile-shooting-timeline/429678313/

10 Ibid.,

11 Trymaine Lee, The 911 call that led to Jonathan Ferrell's death, Sept. 17, 2013, https://www.msnbc.com/msnbc/the-911-call-led-jonathan-ferrells-msna157916

12 Ibid

13   Harvard Law Review, The Shooting of Samuel DuBose, 29 Harv. L. Rev. 1168, FEB 10, 2016, pp.1, https://harvardlawreview.org/wp-content/uploads/2016/02/1168-1177-Online.pdf

14 Kevin Grasha, and Sharon Coolidge, Video expert: Ray Tensing was not dragged, Cincinnati.com,, November 3, 2016, https://www.cincinnati.com/story/news/tensing/2016/11/03/what-expect-thursday-ray-tensing-murder-trial/93199114/

15 Elizabeth Chuck, 'He Can't Hear You!': Deaf Man Shot Dead by Oklahoma City Police as Neighbors Scream in Horror, Sept. 20, 2017, 1:01 PM CDT / Updated Sept. 20, 2017, 1:01 PM CDT / Source: Associated Press https://www.nbcnews.com/news/us-news/deaf-man-shot-dead-

oklahoma-city-police-neighbors-scream-horror-n803031

16 Eliott C. McLaughlin, Sara Sidner and Michael Martinez, Oklahoma City cop convicted of rape sentenced to 263 years in prison, January 22, 2016, CNN, https://www.cnn.com/2016/01/21/us/oklahoma-city-officer-daniel-holtzclaw-rape-sentencing/index.html

17 Abdel Jibri Omar, Timothy Loehmann biography: 13 things about Tamir Rice's killer from Parma, Ohio, Conan Daily, December 30, 2020, https://conandaily.com/2020/12/30/timothy-loehmann-biography-13-things-about-tamir-rices-killer-from-parma-ohio/

18 Independence PD Timothy Loehmann Records, pp.56, https://www.scribd.com/doc/252024886/Independence-PD-Timothy-Loehmann-Records

19 Viswa Vanapalli, Where is Timothy Loehmann Now? https://thecinemaholic.com/where-is-timothy-loehmann-now/

20 Ibid.,

21 Peggy Gallek, Police officer who shot Tamir Rice hired as part-time officer in southeastern Ohio, Oct 5, 2018, https://fox8.com/news/police-officer-who-shot-tamir-rice-hired-as-part-time-officer-in-southeastern-ohio/

22 Edgar Sandoval, Joel Landau and Bill Hutchinson, Ferguson Officer Darren Wilson Once A Member Of Police Force Disbanded Over Racial Tension: Report, NOV 24, 2014, https://www.nydailynews.com/news/national/darren-wilson-part-force-disbanded-racial-tension-report-article-1.1914982

23 Change In Law Allows Closer Look At Complaints Against Of Daniel Pantaleo, NYPD Officer Fired For Eric Garner Chokehold Death, https://newyork.cbslocal.com/2020/06/23/daniel-pantaleo-complaints-eric-garner-death/

24 National Conference of Black Lawyers, the International Association of Democratic Lawyers, and the National Lawyers Guild, Report of the International Commission of Inquiry on Systemic Racist Police Violence against

People of African Descent in the U.S. pg. 155, https://inquirycommission.org/website/wp-content/uploads/2021/04/Commission-Report-15-April.pdf

25 Ibid., pg.156

26 Ibid., pg.155

27 Jacob Sullum, Will the Cops Who Killed Kenneth Chamberlain After Illegally Breaking Into His Apartment Ever Be Held Accountable?, June 11,2020, https://reason.com/2020/06/11/will-the-cops-who-killed-kenneth-chamberlain-after-illegally-breaking-into-his-apartment-ever-be-held-accountable/

28 Meg Wagner, Kansas cop fired for Facebook threat against stranger's 5-year-old daughter after Dallas police attack: 'We'll see how much her life matters soon", New York Daily News, July 9, 2016, https://www.nydailynews.com/news/national/kansas-fired-facebook-threat-dallas-woman-child-article-1.2705351

29 Marina Trahan Martinez, Nicholas Bogel-Burroughs and Dave Montgomery, Woman Was Playing Video Game With Her Nephew When Shot by Fort Worth Police, New York Times, Published Oct. 13, 2019, Updated Oct. 24, 2019, https://www.nytimes.com/2019/10/13/us/fort-worth-texas-shooting-jefferson.html

30 Eliott C. McLaughlin, 'I thought it was my apartment,' Dallas officer says 19 times in tearful 911 call after shooting Botham Jean, April 30, 2019, https://www.cnn.com/2019/04/30/us/dallas-botham-jean-911-police-officer-amber-guyger/index.html

31 National Conference of Black Lawyers, the International Association of Democratic Lawyers, and the National Lawyers Guild, Report of the International Commission of Inquiry on Systemic Racist Police Violence against People of African Descent in the U.S. pg. 55, https://inquirycommission.org/website/wp-content/uploads/2021/04/Commission-Report-15-April.pdf

32 Ibid.,

33 Jordan B. Woods, Policing, Danger Narratives, and

Routine Traffic Stops, 117 MICH. L. REV. 635 (2019). https://repository.law.umich.edu/mlr/vol117/ iss4/2

34 Congressional Research Service, Policing the Police: Qualified Immunity and Considerations for Congress, pg.1, https://crsreports.congress.gov/product/pdf/ LSB/LSB10492?__cf_chl_jschl_tk__=kB7IgeoTjNhL v4is8ITaQNOYIN7UxnmzNlkY8j6jkDc-1641354559-0- gaNycGzNC70

35 Ibid., pg.2

36 Ibid., pg. 4

37 National Conference of Black Lawyers, the International Association of Democratic Lawyers, and the National Lawyers Guild, Report of the International Commission of Inquiry on Systemic Racist Police Violence against People of African Descent in the U.S. pp 23, https:// inquirycommission.org/website/wp-content/ uploads/2021/04/Commission-Report-15-April.pdf

38 Ibid.,

39 Ibid., pg. 14

40 Ibid.,

41 Ibid.,

42 National Conference of Black Lawyers, the International Association of Democratic Lawyers, and the National Lawyers Guild, Report of the International Commission of Inquiry on Systemic Racist Police Violence against People of African Descent in the U.S., pp 15, https:// inquirycommission.org/website/wp-content/ uploads/2021/04/Commission-Report-15-April.pdf

43 JOHN ELDER, Investigative Update on Critical Incident, https://web.archive.org/web/20210331182901/https:// www.insidempd.com/2020/05/26/man-dies-after- medical-incident-during-police-interaction/

44 GBD 2019 Police Violence US Subnational Collaborators, Fatal police violence by race and state in the USA, 1980– 2019: a network meta-regression, The Lancet, VOLUME 398, ISSUE 10307, P1239-1255, OCTOBER 02, 2021, https://www.thelancet.com/journals/lancet/article/

PIIS0140-6736(21)01609-3/fulltext

45 Ibid.,

46 Ibid.,

47 Ibid.,

48 Alice Speri, The FBI Has Quietly Investigated White Supremacist Infiltration Of Law Enforcement, The Intercept, January 31 2017, https://theintercept. com/2017/01/31/the-f bi-has-quietly-investigated-white-supremacist-infiltration-of-law-enforcement/

49 Michael German, Hidden in Plain Sight: Racism, White Supremacy, and Far-Right Militancy in Law Enforcement, August 27, 2020, Brennan Center for Justice, https:// www.brennancenter.org/our-work/research-reports/ hidden-plain-sight-racism-white-supremacy-and-far-right-militancy-law

50 Vanessa Romo, Ghost Skins' And Masculinity: Alt-Right Terms, Defined, NPR, September 6, 2017, https://www. npr.org/2017/09/06/548858850/-ghost-skins-and-masculinity-alt-right-terms-defined

51 Federal Bureau of Investigation, "White Supremacist Infiltration of Law Enforcement," October 17, 2006, pg.3, https://oversight.house.gov/sites/democrats.oversight. house.gov/files/White_Supremacist_Infiltration_of_ Law_Enforcement.pdf

52 Annalisa Merelli, More black people were killed by US police in 2015 than were lynched in the worst year of Jim Crow, July 7, 2016, https://qz.com/726245/more-black-people-were-killed-by-us-police-in-2015-than-were-lynched-in-the-worst-year-of-jim-crow/

53 Rev. Martin Luther King Jr., "The Other America," March 14, 1968, https://www.crmvet.org/docs/otheram.htm

54 Sanya Mansour, 93% of Black Lives Matter Protests Have Been Peaceful, New Report Finds, September 5, 2020, https://time.com/5886348/report-peaceful-protests/

55 The Armed Conflict Location & Event Data Project, Demonstrations & Political Violence In America: New Data for Summer 2020, https://acleddata.com/2020/09/03/

demonstrations-political-violence-in-america-new-data-for-summer-2020/

56 Ibid.,

57 Ibid.,

58 Ibid.,

59 Erica Chenoweth and Jeremy Pressman, Black Lives Matter Protesters Were Overwhelmingly Peaceful, Our Research Finds, Harvard Radcliffe Institute, October 20, 2020 https://www.radcliffe.harvard.edu/news-and-ideas/black-lives-matter-protesters-were-overwhelmingly-peaceful-our-research-finds

60 Ibid.,

61 Ibid.,

62 Ibid.,

63 Ibid.,

64 Daniel Byman, Riots, White Supremacy and Accelerationism, https://www.lawfareblog.com/riots-white-supremacy-and-accelerationism

65 Report of the National Advisory Commission on Civil Disorders (New York: Bantam Books, 1968), pg.14. http://www.eisenhowerfoundation.org/docs/kerner.pdf

66 Ibid., pg.16

67 National Conference of Black Lawyers, the International Association of Democratic Lawyers, and the National Lawyers Guild, Report of the International Commission of Inquiry on Systemic Racist Police Violence against People of African Descent in the U.S. pg. 16, https://inquirycommission.org/website/wp-content/uploads/2021/04/Commission-Report-15-April.pdf

Chapter 8: America Has Taken A Knee on Us!

1 David Barton, The Founding Fathers and Slavery, https://www.patriotacademy.com/founding-fathers-slavery/

2 Ibid.,

3 Ibid.,

4 Ibid.

5 Ibid.,

6 Ibid.,

7 List of the Founding Fathers who Owned Slaves, https://slaveryadvocate.com/list-of-founding-fathers-who-owned-slaves/

8 Ibid.,

9 Slavery in the President's Neighborhood FAQ, https://www.whitehousehistory.org/slavery-in-the-presidents-neighborhood-faq

10 Ibid.,

11 WEST VIRGINIA STATE BOARD OF EDUCATION et al. v. BARNETTE et al., 319 U.S. 624 (1943), https://caselaw.findlaw.com/us-supreme-court/319/624.html

12 Ibid.,

13 David Dorado Romo, Excerpts: 'Ringside Seat to a Revolution', The Bath Riots,https://www.npr.org/templates/story/story.php?storyId=5176177

Chapter 9: He Hate White People

1 Rebecca Beatrice Brooks, The Boston Tea Party, History of Massachusetts Blog, September 27, 2011, https://historyofmassachusetts.org/the-boston-tea-party/

2 The Boston Smallpox Epidemic, 1721, https://curiosity.lib.harvard.edu/contagion/feature/the-boston-smallpox-epidemic-1721

3 Bernadette Giacomazzo, The Story Of Onesimus, The Enslaved Man Who Helped Save Boston From Smallpox, August 30, 2021, https://allthatsinteresting.com/onesimus

4 Lashyra Nolen, The Slave Who Helped Boston Battle Smallpox, https://undark.org/2020/04/02/slave-smallpox-onesimus/

5 George Bryjak, Black Americans in the Revolutionary War, March 20, 2014, https://www.newyorkalmanack.com/2014/03/black-americans-in-the-revolutionary-war/#:~:text=Although%20military%20

rosters%20from%20that%20period%20have%20 been,5%2C000%20African-American%20soldiers%20 served%20in%20the%20Revolutionary%20War.

6 Kathy Weiser-Alexander, Salem Poor – From Slave to Hero, https://www.legendsofamerica.com/salem-poor/

7 Ibid.,

8 John Anderson, Christiana Riot Of 1851, November 19, 2013, https://www.blackpast.org/african-american-history/christiana-riot-1851/

9 Ibid.,

10 Don Gonyea, Majority Of White Americans Say They Believe Whites Face Discrimination, NPR, October 24, 2017, https://www.npr.org/2017/10/24/559604836/majority-of-white-americans-think-theyre-discriminated-against

11 Ibid.,

12 Samuel Sommers and Michael Norton, White people think racism is getting worse. Against white people, Washington Post, July 21, 2016, https://www.washingtonpost.com/posteverything/wp/2016/07/21/white-people-think-racism-is-getting-worse-against-white-people/

13 Bob Whitaker, "The Mantra," http://www.robertwwhitaker.com/mantra/

14 David Marcus, How Anti-White Rhetoric Is Fueling White Nationalism, The Federalist May 23, 2016,

15 https://bittergertrude.com/2014/12/12/the-white-guy-problem/

16 Mike King, Aggrieved Whiteness: White Identity Politics and Modern American Racial Formation, May 4, 2017, https://abolitionjournal.org/aggrieved-whiteness-white-identity-politics-and-modern-american-racial-formation/

17 Roland Merullo, In Defense of the White Male, Boston Globe, July 3,2017, https://www.bostonglobe.com/opinion/2017/07/02/defense-white-male/Me9UoUrcPbcljxRkPFlXAP/story.html

18 The 1900 Buganda Agreement In Summary, https://www.studocu.com/row/document/uganda-christian-

university/bachelor-of-law/the-1900-buganda-agreement-in-summary/10691716

19 Lwanga-Luwyiigo, Sanwiri (25 September 1987). "The Colonial Roots of Internal Conflict in Uganda" (Makerere University),History of Uganda, Historyworld.net.

20 Roland Merullo, In Defense of the White Male, Boston Globe, July 3,2017, https://www.bostonglobe.com/opinion/2017/07/02/defense-white-male/Me9UoUrcPbcljxRkPFlXAP/story.html

21 Plessy v. Ferguson, 163 U.S. 537 (1896), https://supreme.justia.com/cases/federal/us/163/537/

22 Irwin Katz, (1991). Gordon Allport's "The Nature of Prejudice." Political Psychology, 12(1), 125–157. https://doi.org/10.2307/3791349

23 Alex Blasdel, Is white America ready to confront its racism? Philosopher George Yancy says we need a 'crisis" The Guardian, April 24, 2018,

24 Dr. Robin DiAngelo, White Fragility: International Journal of Critical Pedagogy, Vol 3 (2011) pp. 54, http://libjournal.uncg.edu/ijcp/article/view/249/116#

25 Dr. Robin DiAngelo, Why Can't We All Just Be Individuals? Countering the Discourse of Individualism in Anti-racist Education, pg. 16 https://projects.iq.harvard.edu/files/deibexplorer/files/why_cant_we_all_just_be_individuals.pdf

26 Ibid.pg. 5

27 Francis E. Kendall, (2002) Understanding White Privilege, pg.1 https://www.american.edu/ocl/counseling/upload/understanding-white-privilege.pdf

28 Norton, Michael I., and Samuel R. Sommers. "Whites See Racism as a Zero-Sum Game That They Are Now Losing." Perspectives on Psychological Science 6, no. 3 (May 2011): 215–218, https://www.hbs.edu/ris/Publication%20Files/norton%20sommers%20whites%20see%20racism_ca92b4be-cab9-491d-8a87-cf1c6ff244ad.pdf

Chapter 10: Playing The Victim

1 DiAngelo, R. J. (2010). Why Can't We All Just Be Individuals?: Countering the Discourse of Individualism in Anti-racist Education. InterActions: UCLA Journal of Education and Information Studies, 6(1). https://escholarship.org/ uc/item/5fm4h8wm
2 Zaid Jilani, John McWhorter Argues That Antiracism Has Become a Religion of the Left, New York Times, Oct. 26, 2021, https://www.nytimes.com/2021/10/26/books/review/john-mcwhorter-woke-racism.html

Chapter 11: Sellouts and Uncle Toms

1 Booker T. Washington, My Larger Education, Garden CITY New York, Doubleday, Page & Company, 1911, pg. 118, https://docsouth.unc.edu/fpn/washeducation/washing.html
2 Ta-Nehisi Coates, The Tragedy And Betrayal Of Booker T. Washington, The Atlantic, March 31, 2009
3 W.E.B DuBois, Black reconstruction: An Essay Toward a History of the Part Which Black Folk Played in the Attempt to Reconstruct Democracy in America, 1860-1880, 700-701 (NY: Harcourt Brace & Company, 1935)
4 Joseph P. Williams, A Different take on Race, President Obama and Ben Carson have a drastically different approach to race on the campaign trail. US News and World Report, October 2, 2015
5 E Thomas Sowell, Early Skirmishes in a Race War, National Review, October 24, 2013
6 Chicago Tribune news services, Crimes against whites equals small percentage of hate crimes, FBI statistics show, Januay 6, 2017
7 Shelby Steele, Black Protest Has Lost Its Power, Wall Street Journal, Jan. 12, 2018, https://www.wsj.com/articles/black-protest-has-lost-its-power-1515800438?shareToken=st686fa34b9a09403cbd2b86f0474e3e42&reflink=arti

cle_email_share

8 Shelby Steele, "White Guilt, How Blacks and Whites Together Destroyed the Promise of the Civil Rights Era, (2006) Harper Collins Publishers, pg. 27

9 Shelby Steele, Is White Guilt Destroying the Promise of Civil Rights?, Independent Policy Forum lecture, May 9, 2006, https://www.independent.org/events/transcript.asp?id=116

10 Walter E. Williams, Diversity and Inclusion Harm, Jun 13, 2018, https://townhall.com/columnists/walterewilliams/2018/06/13/diversity-and-inclusion-harm-n2489469

11 Michael K. Fauntroy, Republicans and the Black Vote, (2007) Lynne Rienner Publishers, pg. 72

12 Ibid., pg. 73

13 Ibid.,

14 Leah Wright Rigueur, Jackie Robinson: Militant Black Republican, April 13,2016, https://www.theroot.com/jackie-robinson-militant-black-republican-1790854938

15 Larry Elder, Had Obama not played the race card, George Floyd might be alive, April 8, 2021, https://www.bizpacreview.com/2021/04/08/larry-elder-had-obama-not-played-the-race-card-george-floyd-might-be-alive-1056950/

16 Ian Spiegelman, Larry Elder Once Said He'd Like to See a Stephen Miller Presidency, Los Angeles Magazine, August 30, 2021, https://www.lamag.com/citythinkblog/larry-elder-stephen-miller/

17 Ryan Bort, A Guide to Larry Elder, the Right-Wing Extremist Who Could Be the Next Governor of California, Rolling Stone, Sep 14, 2021, https://www.msn.com/en-us/news/politics/a-guide-to-larry-elder-the-right-wing-extremist-who-could-be-the-next-governor-of-california/ar-AAOqCJs

Chapter 12: Blacks Were Republicans for 100 Years!

1 Arthur Zilversmit, Lincoln and the Problem of Race: A Decade of Interpretations, Journal of the Abraham Lincoln Association, Volume 2, Issue 1, 1980, pp. 22-45, https://quod.lib.umich.edu/j/jala/2629860.0002.104?view=text;rgn=main

2 Henry Louis Gates Jr., Did Lincoln Want to Ship Black People Back to Africa? https://www.theroot.com/did-lincoln-want-to-ship-black people-back-to-africa-1790858389

3 The Corwin Amendment, https://heritagepost.org/article/the-corwin-amendment/

4 Ibid.,

5 Robert Longley, The Corwin Amendment, Enslavement, and Abraham Lincoln, Updated July 24, 2019, https://www.thoughtco.com/corwin-amendment-slavery-and-lincoln-4160928

6 Ibid.,

7 The Reconstruction Act, https://www.american-historama.org/1866-1881-reconstruction-era/reconstruction-acts-1867.htm

8 Louis Kleber, The Presidential Election of 1876, History Today Volume 20 Issue 11 November 1970, https://www.historytoday.com/archive/feature/presidential-election-1876

9 The Compromise of 1877, https://www.khanacademy.org/humanities/us-history/civil-war-era/reconstruction/a/compromise-of-1877

10 Jeff Charles, Lily-White Movement: Why Black Americans Left The GOP, Liberty Nation News, April 02, 2021, https://www.libertynation.com/lily-white-movement-why-black-americans-left-the-gop/

11 Lily-white movement, https://www.americanhistoryusa.com/topic/lily-white-movement/

12 Tsahai Tafari, The Rise and Fall of Jim Crow, https://www.thirteen.org/wnet/jimcrow/print/p_struggle_

president.html

13 Laura Coyle, The Great Mississippi Flood of 1927-Ain't Got No Place to Go, Published Sept. 7, 2016; updated Jan. 11, 2019, https://nmaahc.si.edu/explore/stories/collection/great-mississippi-river-flood-1927

14 Malik Simba, The Mississippi River Great Flood of 1927, https://www.blackpast.org/african-american-history/mississippi-river-great-flood-1927/

15 Walter White, The Negro and the Flood, The Nation, Vol. 124, No. 3233, April 15,1927, https://www.scribd.com/document/261892691/April-15-1927

16 Robert Moton and the Colored Advisory Commission, https://www.pbs.org/wgbh/americanexperience/features/flood-moton-cac/

17 Robert Russa Moton - Legacy - Tuskegee Syphilis Experiment, https://www.primidi.com/robert_russa_moton/legacy/tuskegee_syphilis_experiment

18 Robert Moton's Second Report, https://www.pbs.org/wgbh/americanexperience/features/flood-moton-second-report/

19 Ibid.,

20 HR. 7152, Senate vote on the Civil Rights Act of 1964, Jun 19, 1964 https://www.govtrack.us/congress/votes/88-1964/s409

21 H.R. 7152. Civil Rights Act of 1964. Adoption of a resolution (h. Res. 789) providing for house approval of the bill as amended by the Senate, Jul 2, 1964 https://www.govtrack.us/congress/votes/88-1964/h182.

22 TO PASS S. 1564, The Voting Rights Act Of 1965, May 26, 1965, https://www.govtrack.us/congress/votes/89-1965/s78 .23 TO PASS H.R. 6400, The 1965 Voting Rights Act, Jul 9, 1965, https://www.govtrack.us/congress/votes/89-1965/h87 .24 Stuart Stevens, It was All A Lie, How the Republican Party Became Donald Trump, New York, Random House, pp. 16-17, 2020 25 116TH CONGRESS, 1ST SESSION, Roll Call 654, Bill Number: H. R. 4, Voting Rights Advancement Act, DEC 06, 2019,

https://clerk.house.gov/Votes/2019654

26 Josh Israel, Every Senate Republican just voted against voting rights — again, American Independent, January 20, 2022, https://americanindependent.com/senate-republicans-voting-rights-filibuster-mitch-mcconnell-john-lewis-voting-rights-advancement-act-freedom-to-vote-act/

Chapter 13: Whitelash Is Nothing New

1 Randy E. Barnett, Andrew Koppelman, The Commerce Clause, https://constitutioncenter.org/interactive-constitution/interpretation/article-i/clauses/752

2 United States Supreme Court, CIVIL RIGHTS CASES(1883), Decided:October 15, 1883, https://caselaw.findlaw.com/us-supreme-court/109/3.html

3 Eoin Higgins, The White Backlash to the Civil Rights Movement, May 22, 2014,https://eoinhiggins.com/the-white-backlash-to-the-civil-rights-movement-1817ff0a9fc·

4 Herbert Blumer, Race Prejudice as a Sense of Group Position, The Pacific Sociological Review, Vol. 1, No. 1 (Spring, 1958), pp. 3-7, University of California Press, http://www.jstor.org/stable/1388607

5 Lawrence Bobo, James R. Kluegel, and Ryan A, Smith, "Laissez-Faire Racism: The Crystallization of a 'Kindler, Genter' Anti-black Ideology" (Russell Sage Foundation: June 1996, Copyright 1996. http://epn.org/sage/rsbobo1.html

6 N., Sam M.S., Modern Racism, https://psychologydictionary.org/modern-racism/

7 Binna Kandola and Pearn Kandola, What is modern racism and how and why has racism mutated?, https://www.thehrdirector.com/features/diversity-and-equality/modern-racism-racism-mutated/

8 Sears, D. O., & Henry, P. J. (2003). The origins of symbolic racism. Journal of Personality and Social Psychology, 85(2),

259–275. https://doi.org/10.1037/0022-3514.85.2.259

9 Paul Ryan: There's An Inner City 'Culture Problem' Of Men Not Working, March 12, 2014, https://talkingpointsmemo.com/livewire/paul-ryan-inner-city-men-poverty

10 Stuart Stevens, It was All A Lie, How the Republican Party Became Donald Trump, New York, Random House, pg. 260, 2020

11 Justin Levitt, The Truth About Voter Fraud, pg.5, Brennan Center for Justice at New York University School of Law, copyright 2007, https://www.brennancenter.org/sites/default/files/2019-08/Report_Truth-About-Voter-Fraud.pdf,

12 Ibid., pp.8

13 Justin Levitt, A comprehensive investigation of voter impersonation finds 31 credible incidents out of one billion ballots cast, Washington Post, August 6, 2014, https://www.washingtonpost.com/news/wonk/wp/2014/08/06/a-comprehensive-investigation-of-voter-impersonation-finds-31-credible-incidents-out-of-one-billion-ballots-cast/

14 Elie Mystal, No Attack on Voting Rights Is Too Racist for This Supreme Court, February 8, 2022, https://www.thenation.com/article/society/supreme-court-alabama-voting/15 MERRILL v. MILLIGAN, https://www.law.cornell.edu/supremecourt/text/21A375

16 Kim Chandler, Lawsuit: Alabama congressional map 'racially gerrymandered', APNews, September 28, 2021, https://apnews.com/article/alabama-lawsuits-race-and-ethnicity-redistricting-montgomery-38e76cb85abe91e9007db0f278764c4d

17 NAACP Legal Defense Fund, Case: Alabama Racial Gerrymandering Lawsuit, https://www.naacpldf.org/case-issue/alabama-racial-gerrymandering-lawsuit/

18 Elie Mystal, No Attack on Voting Rights Is Too Racist for This Supreme Court, FEBRUARY 8, 2022, https://www.thenation.com/article/society/supreme-court-alabama-voting/19 President Lyndon B. Johnson, "To Fulfill These

Rights," Commencement Address at Howard University, June 4, 1965, https://www.brown.edu/Departments/Economics/Faculty/Glenn_Loury/louryhomepage/teaching/Ec%20137/Ec%20137%20spring07/President%20Lyndon%20B%20Johnson%27s%20Howard%20University%20Speech.pdf

20 Abagon, "Teflon Theory of American History." www.abagon.com

21 Executive Order 8802—Reaffirming Policy Of Full Participation In The Defense Program By All Persons, Regardless Of Race, Creed, Color, Or National Origin, And Directing Certain Action In Furtherance Of Said Policy, https://www.presidency.ucsb.edu/documents/executive-order-8802-reaffirming-policy-full-participation-the-defense-program-all-persons

22 Executive Order 10479—Establishing the Government Contract Committee, https://www.presidency.ucsb.edu/documents/executive-order-10479-establishing-the-government-contract-committee

23 Executive Order 10925—Establishing the President's Committee on Equal Employment Opportunity, https://www.presidency.ucsb.edu/documents/executive-order-10925-establishing-the-presidents-committee-equal-employment-opportunity

24 Executive Order 11246, https://www.justice.gov/sites/default/files/crt/legacy/2010/12/15/Exec_Order11246.pdf

25 Marco DeFUNIS et al., Petitioners, v. Charles ODEGAARD, President of the University of Washington. https://www.law.cornell.edu/supremecourt/text/416/312

26 REGENTS OF the UNIVERSITY OF CALIFORNIA, Petitioner, v. Allan BAKKE, https://www.law.cornell.edu/supremecourt/text/438/265

27 Ian Millhiser, The Supreme Court case that could end affirmative action,explained, Mar 2, 2021, https://www.vox.com/22301135/supreme-court-affirmative-action-harvard-college-race-students-for-fair-admission-ed-

blum

28 Students for Fair Admissions, Inc. v. President & Fellows of Harvard College, First Circuit Holds that Harvard's Admissions Program Does Not Violate the Civil Rights Act., https://harvardlawreview.org/2021/05/ students-for-fair-admissions-inc-v-president-and-fellows-of-harvard-college

29 TITLE VI OF THE CIVIL RIGHTS ACT OF 1964 42 U.S.C. § 2000D ET SEQ., https://www.justice.gov/crt/fcs/TitleVI-Overview

30 Students for Fair Admissions, Inc. v. President & Fellows of Harvard College, First Circuit Holds that Harvard's Admissions Program Does Not Violate the Civil Rights Act., https://harvardlawreview.org/2021/05/ students-for-fair-admissions-inc-v-president-and-fellows-of-harvard-college

31 Russell W. Galloway Jr., Basic Equal Protection Analysis, 29 Santa Clara L. Rev. 121 (1989). http://digitalcommons.law.scu.edu/lawreview/vol29/iss1/432 The diverse demographics of Asian Americans, https://usafacts.org/articles/the-diverse-demographics-of-asian-americans/

33 Admissions Statistics, A Brief Profile of the Admitted Class of 2025, Harvard welcomes students from across the country and all over, https://college.harvard.edu/admissions/admissions-statistics

34 Ibid.,

35 Daniella Silva, Study on Harvard finds 43 percent of white students are legacy, athletes, related to donors or staff, https://www.nbcnews.com/news/us-news/study-harvard-finds-43-percent-white-students-are-legacy-athletes-n1060361

36 Peter Arcidiacono, Josh Kinsler, Tyler Ransom, National Bureau Of Economic Research, Legacy And Athlete Preferences At Harvard, Working Paper 26316, http://www.nber.org/papers/w26316

37 Carol Anderson, White Rage, New York, Bloomsbury Publishing, pg. 100, 2016

Chapter 14: Keep Dr. King's Name Out of Your Mouth

1 Michael Harriot, What Martin Luther King Jr. Would Say About White People and Their 'Shithole' Silence, Jan. 12, 2018, https://www.theroot.com/ what-martin-luther-king-jr-would-say-about-white-peop-1822030959

2 Rev. Martin Luther King Jr., "Letter From A Birmingham Jail" "https://www.theatlantic.com/magazine/archive/2018/02/letter-from-a-birmingham-jail/552461/

3 James C. Cobb, Even Though He Is Revered Today, MLK Was Widely Disliked by the American Public When He Was Killed, SMITHSONIANMAG.COM, APRIL 4, 2018, https://www.smithsonianmag.com/history/why-martin-luther-king-had-75-percent-disapproval-rating-year-he-died-180968664/

4 Rev. Martin Luther King Jr., "Letter From A Birmingham Jail" "https://www.theatlantic.com/magazine/archive/2018/02/letter-from-a-birmingham-jail/552461/

5 Frank Olito, 8 powerful speeches from Martin Luther King Jr. that aren't 'I Have a Dream', https://news.yahoo.com/8-inspirational-speeches-martin-luther-153700835.html?soc_src=social-sh&soc_trk=tw&tsrc=twtr#:~:text=1%20Martin%20Luther%20King%20Jr.%20delivered%20his%20%22I,Mountaintop%2C%22%20is%20also%20famous%20for%20being%20strangely%20prophetic.

6 Ibid.,

7 Ibid.,

8 Martin Luther King Jr,, Six Steps for Nonviolent Direct Action, https://kinginstitute.stanford.edu/sites/mlk/files/lesson-activities/six_steps_for_nonviolent_direct_action_2.pdf

9 "H.Con.Res. 100 — 116th Congress: Urging the establishment of a United States Commission on Truth, Racial Healing, and Transformation." www.GovTrack. us. 2020. February 26, 2022 https://www.govtrack.us/congress/bills/116/hconres100

10 David B. Oppenheimer, Dr. King's Dream Of Affirmative Action, pg. 32, https://harvardlalr.com/wp-content/uploads/sites/16/2019/11/Oppenheimer_Vol21.pdf

11 Ibid., pg.33

12 Ibid.,

13 Rev. Martin Luther King Jr., "Where Do We Go From Here," Annual Report Delivered in August of 1967 at the 11th Convention of the Southern Christian Leadership Conference in Atlanta Georgia. https://www.mlkcelebration.com/mlk-the-man/famous-speeches/where-do-we-go-from-here/

Chapter 15: The White Rebellion

1 Horace Seldon, Racism: Negative Effects on Whites, Convictions About Racism In the United States of America, November, 1991, http://horaceseldon.com/racism-negative-effects-on-whites/

2 Susana Rinderle, MA, ACC, How Racism Hurts White People Too, May, 10,2017, Huffington Post, https://www.huffpost.com/entry/the-dirty-secret-of-racism-it-hurts-white-people-too_b_59133f53e4b0e3bb894d5c93

3 Emily Widra and Tiana Herring, States of Incarceration: The Global Context 2021, https://www.prisonpolicy.org/global/2021.html

4 Horace Seldon, Racism: Negative Effects on Whites, Convictions About Racism In the United States of America, November, 1991, http://horaceseldon.com/racism-negative-effects-on-whites/

5 John Adams to James Sullivan, 26 May 1776; from Charles Francis Adams, ed., The Works of John Adams, Second President of the United States (Boston: Little, Brown, and Company, 1854). https://shec.ashp.cuny.edu/items/show/1645

6 Linette Lopez, The White House is only telling you half of the sad story of what happened to American jobs, Business Insider, Jul 25, 2017, https://www.businessinsider.com/

what-happened-to-american-jobs-in-the-80s-2017-

7 William Lazonick, The Financialization of the U.S. Corporation: What Has Been Lost, and How It Can Be Regained, 36 SEATTLE U. L. REV. 857 (2013). pp.858 https://digitalcommons.law.seattleu.edu/cgi/viewcontent. cgi?article=2158&context=sulr

8 Ibid., pp.859,868

9 Ibid., pp. 859

10 Ibid.,

11 Ibid., pp. 863

12 Ibid., pp. 860

13 Tad DeHaven, Corporate Welfare in the Federal Budget, Policy Analysis, No. 703, July 25, 2012, https://www.cato.org/sites/cato.org/files/pubs/pdf/PA703.pdf

14 Government Spends More on Corporate Welfare Subsidies than Social Welfare Programs, https://thinkbynumbers.org/uncategorized/corporate-vs-social-welfare/, original source, Time Magazine, Vol. 152 No. 19

15 Donald L. Barlett and James B. Steele, Corporate Welfare: Corporate Welfare, Time Magazine, Vol. 152 No. 19, Nov. 09, 1998, http://content.time.com/time/subscriber/article/0,33009,989508,00.html

16 Stephen Slivinski, The Corporate Welfare State:How the Federal Government Subsidizes U.S. Businesses, Policy Analysis, No. 592, May 14, 2007, https://www.cato.org/sites/cato.org/files/pubs/pdf/pa592.pdf

17 Rob Borrow, Welfare Inequality: The Rise of Corporate Welfare, October 9, 2020, https://soapboxie.com/government/welfareinequality

18 Robert Reich, How Corporate Welfare Hurts You, The American Prospect, July 23, 2019, https://prospect.org/economy/corporate-welfare-hurts/

19 Scott Lincicome, Calculating the Real Cost of Corporate Welfare, The Federalist, September 30, 2013, https://thefederalist.com/2013/09/30/calculating-the-real-cost-of-corporate-welfare/

20 Robert Reich, The Corporate Welfare During Covid-19 Pandemic Is Morally Repugnant, Wednesday, April 22, 2020, https://www.commondreams.org/views/2020/04/22/corporate-welfare-during-covid-19-pandemic-morally-repugnant

21 Juliana Kaplan, Billionaires made $3.9 trillion during the pandemic — enough to pay for everyone's vaccine, Business Insider, Jan 26, 2021, https://www.businessinsider.com/billionaires-made-39-trillion-during-the-pandemic-coronavirus-vaccines-2021-1

Chapter 16: The Price of Racism

1 Nick Noel, Duwain Pinder, Shelley Stewart III and Jason Wright, The economic impact of closing the racial wealth gap, https://www.mckinsey.com/~/media/mckinsey/industries/public%20and%20social%20sector/our%20insights/the%20economic%20impact%20of%20closing%20the%20racial%20wealth%20gap/the-economic-impact-of-closing-the-racial-wealth-gap-final.pdf

2 U.S. Census Bureau, Current Population Survey, 1960 to 2021 Annual Social and Economic Supplements (CPS ASEC). Table 2. Poverty Status of People by Family Relationship, Race, and Hispanic Origin: 1959 to 2020, http://www.census.gov/hhes/www/poverty/data/historical/people.html

3 Ibid.,
4 Ibid.,
5 Ibid.,
6 Ibid,.
7 Ibid.,
8 Ibid.,
9 Ibid.,
10 Ibid.,
11 Ibid.,
12 Ibid,.

13 Ibid.,

14 Ibid.,

15 Ibid.,

16 Ibid.,

17 Ibid.,

18 Ibid,.

19 Ibid.,

20 Ibid.,

21 Ibid.,

22 Laura Sullivan, Tatjana Meschede, Lars Dietrich, & Thomas Shapiro, Amy Traub, Catherine Ruetschlin, Tamara Draut, The Racial Wealth Gap, Why Policy Matters, pg.4 https://www.demos.org/sites/default/files/publications/RacialWealthGap_2.pdf

23 Ani Turner, The Business Case for Racial Equity, https://altarum.org/sites/default/files/uploaded-publication-files/WKKellogg_Business-Case-Racial-Equity_National-Report_2018.pdf

24 Brentin Mock, "White Americans' Hold on Wealth Is Old, Deep, and Nearly Unshakeable," CITILAB, September 3, 2019, https://www.citylab.com/equity/2019/09/racial-wealth-gap-history-slavery-black-white-family-income/597100/?utm_source=pocket-newtab

25 Dana M Peterson, Catherine L Mann, Closing the Racial Inequality Gaps, The Economic Cost of Black Inequality in the U.S., pg. 4, https://www.citivelocity.com/citigps/closing-the-racial-inequality-gaps/

26 Ibid., pg.7

27 Stephen Miller, Black Workers Still Earn Less than Their White Counterparts, www.shrm.org/resourcesandtools/hr-topics/compensation/pages/racial-wage-gaps-persistence-poses-challenge.aspx

28 Ibid.,

29 ibid.,

30 Ibid.,

31 Ibid.,

32 Brandie Temple and Jasmine Tucker, Equal Pay for Black

Women, https://nwlc.org/resource/equal-pay-for-black-women/,

33 Ibid.,

34 Ibid.,

35 Ibid.,

36 Ibid.,

37 Roy Eduardo Kokoyachuk, Education Alone Can't Close The Racial Wage Gap, https://www.mediapost.com/publications/article/348809/education-alone-cant-close-the-racial-wage-gap.html

38 Ibid.,

39 U.S. Census Bureau, Current Population Survey, 1968 to 2021 Annual Social and Economic Supplements (CPS ASEC)., Table H-5. Race and Hispanic Origin of Householder--Households by Median and Mean Income: 1967 to 2020, https://www.census.gov/data/tables/time-series/demo/income-poverty/historical-income-households.html

40 Ibid.,

41 Ibid.,

42 Ibid.,

43 Ibid.,

44 Ibid.,

45 Ibid.,

46 Ibid.,

47 Ibid.,

48 Ibid.,

49 Ibid.,

50 Ibid.,

51 Amy Traub, Laura Sullivan, Tatjana Meschede and Thomas Shapiro, DEMOS, The Asset Value of Whiteness: Understanding the Racial Wealth Gap, pg. 10 https://www.demos.org/sites/default/files/publications/Asset%20Value%20of%20Whiteness_0.pdf

52 https://usdebtclock.org/

53 Emily Moss, Kriston McIntosh, Wendy Edelberg, and Kristen Broady, The Black-white wealth gap

left Black households more vulnerable, December 8, 2020, https://www.brookings.edu/articles/the-black-white-wealth-gap-left-black-households-more-vulnerable/#:~:text=Furthermore%3A%201%20In%20the%20second%20quarter%20of%202020%2C,4%20per-cent%20%28%244.6%20trillion%29%20of%20total%20household%20wealth.

54 Antonio Moore and Matt Bruenig, Without the Family Car Black Wealth Barely Exists, https://www.peoplespolicyproject.org/2017/09/30/without-the-family-car-black-wealth-barely-exists/

55 Chisom Michael, Meet America's richest black billionaires of 2024, January 22, 2024, https://businessday.ng/life-arts/article/meet-americas-richest-black-billionaires-of-2024/

56 Ward Williams, Black-owned Public Companies, https://www.investopedia.com/black-owned-public-companies-5076818

57 https://www.census.gov/newsroom/press-releases/2021/nonemployer-statistics-by-demographics.html

58 Ward Williams, Black-owned Public Companies, https://www.investopedia.com/black-owned-public-companies-5076818

59 Shawn D Rochester, The Black Tax: The Cost of Being Black in America, pg, 89, Good Steward Publishing, Southbury CT., 2018

60 Ibid., pg. 91-94

61 Advertising spending in North America from 2000 to 2024, https://www.statista.com/statistics/429036/advertising-expenditure-in-north-america/#:~:text=The%20United%20States%20is%20the%20largest%20advertising%20market,is%20estimated%20to%20increas-e%20even%20further%20in%202025.

62 A. Guttmann, Advertising spending in the U.S. 2021-2025, by medium, https://www.statista.com/statistics/191926/

us-ad-spending-by-medium-in-2009/, Oct 11, 2021

63 A. Guttmann, Radio ad revenue in the U.S. 2021-2022, https://www.statista.com/statistics/272412/radio-advertising-expenditure-in-the-us/, Feb 25, 2022

64　　　https://www.statista.com/outlook/dmo/digital-advertising/united-states

65 ibid.,

66 ibid.,

67　　　https://www.statista.com/outlook/dmo/digital-advertising/video-advertising/united-states#analyst-opinion

68　　　https://www.statista.com/outlook/dmo/digital-advertising/social-media-advertising/united-states#analyst-opinion

69　　　https://www.statista.com/outlook/dmo/digital-advertising/social-media-advertising/united-states#analyst-opinion

70 Statista Research Department, Social media usage in the United States - Statistics & Facts, https://www.statista.com/topics/3196/social-media-usage-in-the-united-states/#dossierKeyfigures

71 Statista Research Department, Countries with the most Facebook users 2022 https://www.statista.com/statistics/268136/top-15-countries-based-on-number-of-facebook-users/ Mar 8, 2022

72 Statista Research Department, U.S. market share of leading social media websites 2022, https://www.statista.com/statistics/265773/market-share-of-the-most-popular-social-media-websites-in-the-us/ Mar 8, 2022

73 Pew Research, Mobile Fact Sheet, https://www.pewresearch.org/internet/fact-sheet/mobile/

74 Pew Research, Internet/Broadband Fact Sheet, https://www.pewresearch.org/internet/fact-sheet/internet-broadband/

75 Pew Research, Social Media Fact Sheet, https://www.pewresearch.org/internet/fact-sheet/social-media/#:~:text=Today%20around%20seven-in-ten%20

Americans%20use%20social%20media%20to,below.%20 How%20often%20Americans%20use%20social%20media-ia%20sites

76 Study: Black Entrepreneurship in the United States, https://www.unlv.edu/news/release/study-black-entrepreneurship-united-states

77 Jonathan Kaplan and Andrew Valls, Housing Discrimination As A Basis For Black Reparations, Public Affairs Quarterly, Volume 21, Number 3, July 2007

78 H.R.3745 - Commission to Study Reparation Proposals for African Americans Act, https://www.congress.gov/bill/101st-congress/house-bill/3745

79 Shawn D Rochester, The Black Tax: The Cost of Being Black in America, pg,82, Good Steward Publishing, Southbury CT., 2018

80 Ibid.,

81 https://constitution.congress.gov/constitution/amendment-16/

82 https://taxfoundation.org/when-did-your-state-adopt-its-income-tax

83 Jim Powell, The 'Old' New Deal Still Isn't Paid For, https://www.forbes.com/2009/02/11/new-deal-stimulus-opinions-contributors_0211_jim_powell.html?sh=6def214745b3

84 https://www.archives.gov/milestone-documents/servicemens-readjustment-act

85 Jane Kim, Black Reparations For Twentieth Century Federal Housing Discrimination: The Construction Of White Wealth And The Effects Of Denied Black Homeownership, Boston University Public Interest Law Journal, Volume 29, Issue 135, Winter 2019 pg. 5

86 United States v. Sioux Nation of Indians: 448 U.S. 371 (1980) :: Justia US Supreme Court Center, https://supreme.justia.com/cases/federal/us/448/371/

Chapter 17: It's Time To Get In Trouble

1 Temin, D. M., & Dahl, A. (2017). Narrating Historical Injustice: Political Responsibility and the Politics of Memory. Political Research Quarterly, 70(4), 905–917. https://doi.org/10.1177/1065912917718636

2 Thomson Reuters and the University of Virginia Center for Politics,Reuters/Ipsos/UVA Center for Politics Race Poll, September 11, 2017, https://centerforpolitics.org/crystalball/wp-content/uploads/2017/09/2017-Reuters-UVA-Ipsos-Race-Poll-9-11-2017.pdf

3 United States Census Bureau, 2017 National Population Projections Tables, https://www.census.gov/data/tables/2017/demo/popproj/2017-summary-tables.html

4 Ibid.,

5 Ibid.,

6 https://theconversation.freeforums.net/

The Chronicle Journal

T H E   N E W S P A P E R   O F   T H E   N O R T H W E S T

2024 Readers' Choice

VOTING HAS ENDED.
RESULTS JULY 27

Confronting the Truth: Isaac Madison's "Get Your Knee Off Our Necks" on Race and Justice

By: AB Newswire

MANHATTAN, Kan. — Isaac Madison's book "Get Your Knee Off Our Necks: Essays On Race In America" explores racial injustice while sharing sobering realities on race and criminal justice. His book educates readers about these long-standing issues.

"It is considered by critics as one of the most influential and poignant collections of honest prose. It confronts uncomfortable truths, ongoing disparities, and complexities of race relations in recent years. It is important for understanding how incarceration rates impact the community and the efforts to bridge equality gaps."

He writes: "People of color keep getting told how much better things are today, yet we see the same things happening that occurred 50-60 years ago. While we have seen improvements, we have not seen complete equality."

"Get Your Knee Off Our Necks" is a powerful book that helps readers feel heard, find healing, and make sense of their experiences. It also reminds us of the progress being made toward creating a more equal future. The author's words cultivate empathy for those who experience racism and help us better understand the systems that perpetuate racial inequality and the importance of fighting against it. The author emphasizes how individual biases can impact society as a whole and offers practical strategies for reducing prejudice in our daily lives.

"Get Your Knee Off Our Necks" is a powerful 400-page testament to the experiences of Black men and women. It serves as a brutal reminder of a haunting past that continues to echo in today's society.

"Get Your Knee Off Our Necks: Essays On Race In America" By Isaac Madison
Kindle | $4.99
Paperback | $15.99
Available at Amazon, Barnes & Noble and other online book retailers

ABOUT THE AUTHOR

Isaac Madison is a lifelong activist who has been involved in a wide variety of issues affecting low to moderate-income communities to include: at at-risk youth, court-mandated adults, adults on public assistance, the homeless, and individuals with HIV/AIDS. This is his first book, and it has been written after decades of discussions with whites on the issue of race in almost every social setting where people interact. I keep getting told how much better things are for blacks today, yet I saw the same things happening to blacks fifty years ago. When does it end? I have asked myself that question for a long time. As a younger man, I fooled myself into believing things had dramatically changed after watching the civil rights battles as a child growing up in the 1960s. While we have seen improvements, we have not seen complete equality. This book is a series of essays that takes an unapologetic look at race in America.

https://www.tiktok.com/@imadison1961
https://www.facebook.com/isaac.madison.9/
https://www.instagram.com/im21961/
https://x.com/isaacmadison50
https://www.linkedin.com/in/isaac-madison-317860245/
https://www.threads.com/@im21961
@isaacmadison50.bsky.social□
https://theconversation.freeforums.net/